THE LEGACY OF THE TÜBINGEN SCHOOL

THE LEGACY OF THE TÜBINGEN SCHOOL

*The Relevance of Nineteenth-Century
Theology for the Twenty-First Century*

Edited by
Donald J. Dietrich and Michael J. Himes

A Crossroad Herder Book
The Crossroad Publishing Company
New York

1997

The Crossroad Publishing Company
370 Lexington Avenue, New York, NY 10017

Printed in the United States of America

Library of Congress Cataloging-in-Publication Data

The legacy of the Tübingen school   :   the relevance of nineteenth
-century theology for the twenty-first century / edited by Donald J.
Dietrich and Michael J. Himes
        p.   cm.
Includes bibliographical references.
ISBN 0-8245-1700-8 (pbk.)
    1. Tübingen School (Catholic theology)   I. Dietrich, Donald J.,
1941– . II. Himes, Michael J.
BX1747.L44   1997   97-30950
230'.2--dc21   CIP

Don would like to dedicate this book to his wife, Linda,
and Michael to his sister, Eileen Mary Himes

CONTENTS

THE LEGACY OF THE
TÜBINGEN SCHOOL

Introduction

I

Late in the eighteenth century a distinctive movement known as German idealism emerged and subsequently dominated German cultural life from 1770–1840 and, in many respects, continued to influence German thought into the twentieth century. German idealism itself can be characterized as a search for a new religious orientation as well as a reaction to the rationalism and natural theology of the Enlightenment. For Catholic theologians idealism and its later union with a romanticism and historicism represented a challenge as well as an opportunity for cultural adaptation, which could scarcely be ignored. While Catholics, they were also Germans, and, as such, they sought inclusion into the mainstream of German thought. They were compelled, therefore, either to reject German idealism-romanticism or to find some way to harmonize its principal tenets with the Catholic faith.

Catholic theologians, of course, realized that philosophical principles and methodologies could not be used to determine positive, i.e., historical, Christianity, but that philosophy could help in analyzing tradition and revelation in a way that would allow faith significantly to engage culture. German Catholic theologians hoped to steer a middle course between extremes by seeking ways to utilize philosophy in their systematic and apologetical formulations. This effort to fuse potentially irreconcilable viewpoints was not without value to German Catholicism. In dissecting the theological and philosophical systems of their contemporaries, Catholic scholars developed new perspectives with which to analyze the church. This revitalized theological consciousness, grounded in the developmental methodologies that characterized the Tübingen School of Theology in the first half of the nineteenth century, helped evolve theological perspectives that have been fruitful up to the present.

This Catholic Tübingen School, which included Johann Sebastian Drey, Johann Adam Möhler, Johann Baptist Hirscher, Franz Anton Staudenmaier, and Johannes Evangelist Kuhn analyzed and to a degree imitated the philosophical insights and historical-critical methodologies of the German idealists with their emphases on the maturation of consciousness within organic communities. They hoped to infuse new life into a Catholic theology made moribund by Baroque Scholasticism and distorted by the rationalistic thrust of the Aufklärung. In diverse and yet complementary ways these scholars succeeded in promoting innovative perspectives and showed a courage under attack as well as a capacity for theological rigor, which can amply testify to the resurgence of German Catholic intellectual life in the first half of the nineteenth century.

II

The theological founder of the Tübingen School was Johann Sebastian von Drey (1777–1853). Drey had mastered the philosophical systems of Kant, Fichte, and Schelling. The speculative methodologies, which he nurtured during his formative years, appear clearly in his own scholarly works on eschatology, revelation and tradition. As early as his first work, *Entwurf zu meinen Vorlesungen aus der Physik* (1806–1813), Drey showed an affinity for romantic idealism which would pervade all his written works. The maturation of the early Drey's scholarly abilities is reflected in his *Mein Tagebuch über philosophische, theologische und historische Gegenstände* (1812–1817), in which he revealed his commitment to an organic conception of history and tradition as well as to the use of the philosophical dialectic in his analysis of religious thought and faith. He also depended heavily on Schelling's stress upon the life of consciousness. In his "Revision des gegenwärtigen Zustandes der Theologie" (1812), influenced by contemporary romantic perspectives, he attacked both religious and philosophical rationalism.

For Drey, the Catholic tradition of each era was supposed to express past historical realities, which were being transmitted by the faith community whose spirit they were to express. Tradition and the church are still living. This concept of a mutable, historical, religious tradition was not compatible with the rationalistic individualism that matured during the Aufklärung. Drey viewed the development of dogma as a process analogous to the growth of a seed. In his "Vom Geist und Wesen des Katholizismus" (1819), Drey perceptively insisted that the concept of tradition was the organic and vibrant unfolding of historically transmitted revelation. Like Scheiermacher, only perhaps more concretely, he insisted that the *kerygma* was present during each era of the church's history. The basis for Drey's interpretation was an organic and historical frame of reference, which made possible the uninterrupted persistence and development of primitive revelation, which appeared anew and more fully explicated in each generation.

Drey utilized contemporary viewpoints on organicism, history, consciousness, and development in order to reappropriate an enlivened Catholicism in language relevant to his time. His contributions did not end, however, in just "modernizing" theological "formulae," crucial though that might have been. He helped develop a new ecclesiology to meet the challenges of the era as well as grappled with the perennial problem of how reason and revelation could be related to one another, which appeared most explicitly analyzed in his *Kurze Einleitung in das Studium der Theologie mit Rücksicht auf den Wissenschaftlichen Standpunkt und das katholische System* (1819). In "Über den Statz der allein seligmachenden Kirche" (1822), Drey theologically adopted a dialectical methodology, which he hoped would help preclude interdenominational indifferentism as well as non-productive polemics. Drey's most extensive theological analysis was his *Die Apologetik als wissenschaftliche Nachweisung der Göttlichkeit des Christentums* (1838–1847). Whereas he had initially concurred with Schleiermacher in assigning to apologetics the relatively narrow task of crystallizing the generic essence of Christianity, in this work he came to the conclusion that the true task of apologetics was to create, on the basis of the concrete model of revelation within the Catholic Church, the foundation for all disciplines devoted to the expanding knowledge of God. Substituting a scholarly response to polemical religious issues, he opposed both the apriorism of rationalism as well as the limited insights of pure traditionalism.

Through his baptized romanticism combined with the force of his personality, Drey profoundly influenced the theological orientations of his pupils, Möhler, Staudenmaier, and Kuhn. The historico-developmental frame of reference, which he provided for the study of dogma, along with his enthusiastic reception of Johann Michael Sailer's experiential theology helped shape the responses that marked the major efforts of the Tübingen Catholic scholars as they sought to incorporate the idealistic reflection on consciousness into a theological comprehension of God. His ecclesiology emphasizing tradition would not be complete without his unique viewpoint on reason and revelation as both historically developed in the ever-deepening human consciousness. For many of Drey's contemporaries, dogma was considered an immutable system born in the patristic church and thereafter protec-tively swaddled by a network of restrictive bonds. Drey uncovered within this ossified system of concepts a living organism. Historical progress had infatuated the Aufklärer and now within the historical framework of romantic idealism it ap-peared in Catholic theology. Progress in religious consciousness and the develop-ment of the understanding of dogma need not be risky, thought Drey, but could evolve within the security of spontaneous, natural organic growth under the watchful care of properly informed and creative theologians, many of whom found a conviv-ial home in the Tübingen tradition that Drey established.

III

Johann Adam Möhler (1796–1838) began his study of theology in 1815 at Ellwangen. In 1817, the faculty and students were transferred to Tübingen and attached to the already existent Protestant theological faculty. In 1821 he was appointed tutor in the Wilhelmsstift where he concentrated on ecclesial literature and philosophy. The Tübingen theological faculty offered him a position as tutor in church history, and, to prepare for this, he visited German centers of theology in 1822–23. In Berlin he was particularly impressed by the scientific treatment of theology popular among Protestant scholars.

Under the influence of Schleiermacher's experiential affirmation of God, for example, both Möhler and Drey focused on an internalization of faith. This faith was for the Möhler of *Einheit* not merely an *actus intellectus*, not merely a concep-tual and cognitive exercise, but rather an immediate interiorization of the divine life in the mind, coupled with an intuition of God through grace. *Einheit* was Möhler's initial step toward a confrontation with the rationalistic as well as with the romantic and idealist schools of thought. Fascinated with the Protestant intellectual climate at Tübingen, he was responsive to the *Glaubenslehre* of Scheiermacher. *Einheit* was a significant product of Möhler's own maturation as he worked to make Ca-tholicism responsive to the religious issues of his era. Möhler's genius lay in his ability to synthesize the insights of others into an imaginative and sensitive analy-sis of religion and a delineation of the roles of revelation and tradition within a framework of historicism.

With the publication of *Symbolik* (1832), Möhler challenged the idealism that had impregnated the Protestant theological faculty at Tübingen. For Ferdinand Christian Baur the Hegelian dialectic was the best tool for achieving an understanding of original sin and its resultant human anthropology. The Fall appeared in idealist systems as the antithesis (rational development of humanity) opposed to the thesis (humanity's original condition). The synthesis would be the realization of original innocence, only then fully and completely present after a total development of reason as the spiritual force shaping human culture. While for Möhler the original condition of humanity was that of a partaker in the divine life, it was for the Hegelian Baur only the idea which originated and determined the dialectical development of the rational concept in humankind. Baur's system was ruled by the dialecticism of Hegel. Here original sin as a philosophical good was still not overcome through Christianity, and human nature was necessarily still in a constrained stage of spiritual development.

Opposition to subjective German Idealism along with his own intellectual evolution ultimately led Möhler to a more traditional Catholic position. Between *Einheit*, which dealt with the Holy Spirit, consciousness, and community, and *Symbolik*, in which humanity and Christ offered the dual anthropological basis for objective theological truth, there was a clear metamorphosis. The former work can be described as subjective and almost lyrical in places; the latter work was objective in tone as well as in content. After *Einheit* Möhler modified his anthropology and made his theology more objective by limiting subjective, experiential components.

From his earliest work Möhler stressed the organic connection of church, Scripture, and Tradition. In the course of his own intellectual development, he approached these elements differentially to help clarify their meanings. For example, in the pneumatologically based *Einheit* the organic living unity of the church unfolding itself has its original image in the mystery of the divinity of Christ. In the more anthropologically oriented *Symbolik*, the Incarnation God serves as the initial sacramental grounding for the authoritative objectivity of the church.

The unique contribution of Drey and Möhler was that these theologians saw in the historicism of the era a new technique that could be applied to understanding revelation. These Tübingers utilized the romantic-idealistic *Weltanschauung* and elaborated a theology of historical and hence objective tradition opposed not just to post-Tridentine neoscholasticism, but to the limiting mysticism of the earlier Sailer as well. Möhler himself pointed to the seminal role of historical tradition by asserting that if it were to be ignored, the church and Christianity itself would cease to have any spiritual meaning. Inspired by the imaginative analyses and syntheses that Drey and Möhler offered, the next generation of Tübingers, i.e., Staudenmaier, Hirscher and Kuhn, embraced romantic idealism as a viable perspective, albeit with serious pitfalls, and focused on Catholic dogma with an eye to adapt it to at least the forms of their contemporary culture.

IV

In the course of his own career, Staudenmaier (1800–1856) evolved from a subjective viewpoint, modeled on the early Möhler, to an objective theologico-philosophical orientation based on the powers of human reason and the God-man acting in history. Imitating Drey and Möhler, he dissociated himself, only more decisively, from romantic perspectives. Then, after 1840 his final works reflected the more mature Tübingen approach grounded on an objective and historical revelation, in which humans were to play a vital role. Staudenmaier began from a commitment to Catholic doctrine, which essentially repudiated German idealism as a pantheistic and rationalistic outlook hostile to Catholic teaching. In the idealistic approach, he vigorously rejected subjective pantheism and rationalism. Such a position was not surprising , since Christianity is based on the fact that God has intervened historically. The subsequent unfolding of this primitive revelation was designed to make manifest more fully the divine message. Staudenmaier's voluminous output focused on studying the role of revelation, reason and tradition as these unfolded through the human use of free will and philosophical reflection. In Hegel's view, God surged through history as He unfolded himself. Staudenmaier rejected this notion in favor of a revelation that unfolded in the developing consciousness of historical humanity. He also felt that idealism invariably produced a God merely fit for philosophical speculation, and did not reflect the historical reality. To "modernize" theology without any significant awareness of the God of revelation had to be rejected as essentially anti-Christian. Staudenmaier preferred to utilize philosophical innovations so that theological speculation would conform to the constantly changing culture, but in the process he insisted that the essence of dogma was the expression of truth communicated in revelation. His contemporary, Kuhn, showed a similar sensitivity to the philosophical-theological issues as well as to the terminology and methodology then in vogue.

V

In 1832, Kuhn (1806–1887) became professor of New Testament exegesis on the Catholic theological faculty attached to the University of Giessen and in 1837 joined the faculty of Tübingen, where from 1839 until 1882 he held the Chair of Dogmatic Theology. Devoted to rigorous philosophical and theological speculation, Kuhn continued the Tübingen tradition focused on the objective explication of dogma and the meaning of historical religion for humanity. Kuhn was probably the most accomplished systematic theologian that the Tübingen school produced in the 19th century.

The role of Scripture and tradition had earlier been philosophically treated by Drey and then by Möhler, who had been trained as an historian. Now the issue drew the attention of Kuhn whose initial competence was in exegesis. Kuhn's work at Giessen included *Das Leben Jesu wissenschaftlich bearbeitet* (1838), in which he opposed the revolutionary implications of Strauss's *Leben Jesu Kritisch bearbeitet* (1835). In Strauss' work the historical reliability of the gospels was challenged. He interpreted them as myth and legend created by historical communities, which embodied the eternal truths that powered the Hegelian order. Myth, Strauss claimed, was a natural and intelligible way of thinking, since it was a parade of expressions, which religious enthusiasm spontaneously created and adopted.

In the view of Strauss, Jesus Christ was fundamentally an *Idee*, not the individual historical person who has affected humanity. In refuting Strauss' view, Kuhn reaffirmed that the gospels were credible as historical events and as reflections written to communicate the reactions of the witnesses of the primal faith. Kuhn devoted his first major work to the growing issue of the historicity of Jesus. Kuhn asserted that the written gospels were not just historical records, but were dependent on the apostolic salvific preaching that aimed to support faith with the proof that Jesus is the incarnated God historically experienced by living men and women.

Kuhn concentrated ultimately, however, on systematic theology and published three volumes of his *Katholische Dogmatik* (1845–68), an extensive undertaking, although never completed. During his lengthy career he analyzed the relation of revelation to reason, of philosophy to theology, and in the process opposed, because of their rationalistic proclivities, the Hermesians and Güntherians. In response to such neoscholastics as Clemens and Schäzler, Kuhn remarked that reverting to the philosophical outlook of Aquinas was a step backward in theological development. Thomas, after all, had himself adapted the unchangeable truth to his own contemporary philosophical forms, which the Tübingen theologians were also attempting to do. Although biblical and patristic theology continued to fascinate Kuhn, he was both naturally disposed and inwardly driven to philosophical reflection. He incorporated the accomplishments of the earlier Tübingen theologians as well as those of his own contemporaries into a comprehensive synthesis that was delicately balanced in all its details. Essentially, Kuhn completed the process of dissociation from the romantic movement begun by Drey and Möhler and now relied increasingly on Hegel's philosophy of the objective spirit. He never totally discarded the revitalized concepts of religious consciousness, which his predecessors had devised, however, but only refined them more objectively.

Revelation, Kuhn felt, should be understandable to persons in every age. He hoped to depict the unfolding of dogma by concentrating, however, on the historical character of revelation, which he sought to analyze speculatively by using an Hegelian dialectical methodology. In discussing heresies, for example, he felt that faith develops in a dialectical process that is not only logical, but also real and historical, ultimately mediating opposites into a real unity meaningful for the specific historical culture. The rigorous dialectic operant in his dogmatic theology was rooted in a knowledge of historical facts, which was designed to yield an orthodox theology sensitive to historical facticity and contemporary idealistic methodology. On the one hand, he wanted to utilize the innovations in methodology and terminology so useful for expressing old truths in new forms. On the other, he had to avoid the pitfalls of the agnosticism and pantheism inherent in the systems of Schelling and Hegel. Kuhn's insistence on the ongoing dialogue between God and humanity, both free, could negate pantheism. Scripture and tradition were to proclaim the Word that was both divine and human. God ultimately determined all human acts, but did not infringe on humanity's free, spontaneous self-determination. The Bible related God's will but was the literary responsibility of the human authors. Hence, there was certainly a positive utility in the historical criticism that probed Scripture from human perspectives. In most of his work the chief focal point was this *gott-menschlich* relation, in which both God and humanity helped shape the human religious dimension.

Adhering to the Tübingen spirit of Catholic renewal and impressed by such philosophers as Jacobi and Hegel, Kuhn synthesized divergent viewpoints as he analyzed the relation between faith and reason. He modified the subjective orientations of Drey and Möhler, while simultaneously integrating their creative perspectives into a unified system. Kuhn focused the meaning of faith on the relationship between reason and revelation, on the development or unfolding of dogma in history, and on the contemporary philosophical methods with their applicability to theology, tradition, and the church. In Kuhn's systematic theology, faith was to confront contemporary philosophy in a living, open dialogue. Reform and change in the church and theology should, therefore, be understood as the harmonious connection of the absolutely essential elements of Scriptural revelation and tradition with the historical and epistemological reflections present in the ever-changing human culture. Faith was to engage culture philosophically and, as Hirscher would point out, politically as well.

VI

Johann Baptist Hirscher (1788–1865) in 1817 occupied the Chair of Moral and Pastoral Theology at Tübingen and in 1837 became Professor of Moral Theology and Catechetics at Freiburg University. Hirscher's anthropology, ecclesiology, and political theory were derived from "the Kingdom of God" (*Das Reich Gottes*) as a theological referent. Hirscher's works reflect his desire to analyze morality and religion within the context of the historically changing and organic body of the *Reich Gottes* as a necessary prelude to reform. In his mind, for example, justice and love were relevant not only to the individual but also to the structures of human interaction. The kingdom of God is pointedly political as well as moral in his work.

Hirscher's principle of organization, the "kingdom of God", appeared as the theme of his three-volume *Die Christliche Moral als Lehre von der Verwirklungen des göttlichen Reiches in der Menschheit*. Five editions were printed between 1836 and 1851, each changing as he matured and had to reconcile personal, spiritual, and political experiences within his theological framework. From his perspective, Christian morality was the realization of the kingdom of God ultimately in humankind, but initially in the individual person. Christian moral theology, therefore, had to be the scholarly and practical explication of how persons through the merits of Jesus Christ could establish a proper relationship to God. During his lifetime conservative neoscholastics were already questioning Hirscher's orthodoxy, since he seemed to rely to such an extent on the romantic-idealistic philosophical models so popular in the German academic disciplines. Hirscher's work as a whole offered a very orthodox reaction against the Kantian morality of the Enlightenment, against rationalism in theology, and against the long, abstract moral disquisitions, irrelevant to all but a few, and so popular in the eighteenth and nineteenth centuries. Always eager to promote religious faith, Hirscher carefully traced the moral act to a religious end.

The union of the individual person with God initially was on the level of faith, from which matured the love for God. The people of God in the community of faith existed as a reflection of the infinite power and love of the creator. To concentrate, therefore, just on morality without faith, which some during the Enlightenment tried to do, would be fruitless. The final objective of the kingdom of God, therefore, should correspond to the moral foundation guiding the individual Christian who presumably was trying to conduct a spiritual and temporal life in consonance with God's command. Hirscher emphasized the intimate connection between the individual and society in the practice of morality. A person's obligation was to proclaim God publicly through word and deed, and the moral theologian was to proceed in light of that theme. Human moral obligations were to be derived after perceiving the kingdom of God as the human community united through faith and love.

Hirscher's anthropology and ecclesiology have a direct bearing on the moralizing role that he envisioned for the church in society. For Hirscher, the church was a community concerned with religion and, as a temporal institution as well, was designated to influence human affairs. He maintained that the church and state were independent, although they did have analogous responsibilities and so should cooperate with one another. The state was to promote justice through a legal framework, so that the life of the church could be nurtured and developed more freely. For its part, the church was obligated to support justice through its spiritual contributions and so make compulsion increasingly unnecessary. Conscious of its mandate and responsibility, the church was to live through the faithful, while cooperating with the state. The laity, for example, would be acting responsibly in the world when they made moral decisions on the basis of the faith and love, which were nourished by an active participation in the spiritual *Reich Gottes*.

In Hirscher's view, the kingdom of God was revealed in Scripture as well as in tradition, was nurtured by a church that was a community of the people of God, and was communicated to the state through the church. Organic community, love, and respect for personal dignity were to characterize the operant framework, in which the church, state, and society as a whole were to function. He emphasized the personal God living with humanity in opposition to the German idealism that concentrated on the idea of God developing through the self-consciousness of men and women. As a moral theologian active in politics, Hirscher was not as interested in organizing a political party as he was in seeking to encourage an attitude among Catholics that would stimulate a renewal in the church, facilitating a positive, rather than just a defensive, Catholic participation in politics.

VII

In essence, then, the Tübingen perspective maintained that tradition and the Scriptures were sources of revelation that conveyed Christ's Word, which was guaranteed by the Spirit. In line with the Incarnation, the Christian faith was founded on a divine-human foundation—in content, in expression, and in the dynamics of growth. God did not just speak to humans; he still lived with men and women, gradually disclosing his nature and our condition. The church's continuous meditation on this record of grace should yield a faith always on the move, a consistent and yet organically growing and unfolding doctrinal development, for which Scripture would serve as the anchor by being the earliest—and hence the most primitive—expression. The Tübingen theologians stressed that God's intercession as well as human responsibility were concurrent, not antagonistic. With great foresight these theologians succeeded in developing systematic and moral theological models as well as a very creative ecclesiological framework, which inspired their successors right up to the present to re-examine the fundamental structure of theology and the social implications of the gospels for civic and ecclesial life. The Tübingen theologians made the church and its theology historical and helped surface engaging responses to modernity. They helped delineate the meaning of faith and the church, which could help support thoughtful Catholics, who were and still are seeking realistic responses to nineteenth and twentieth century modernization phenomena, resting on an urban culture based on industrialism, mass political movements, and the intensifying secularization that has fed postmodernism.

The Tübingen theologians helped develop a theological response to culture that has been modeled in the papers that follow, which were originally presented at a symposium at Boston College, September 18–20, 1996. Both editors would like to thank Patricia Fleming, who helped organize the symposium as well as prepared the copy for this book.

DONALD J. DIETRICH
MICHAEL J. HIMES

1

Perspectives toward the Future in the Dogmatics of the Tübingen Theologians

— PETER HÜNERMANN —

The fact is that in tradition there is always an
element of freedom and of history itself.
Hans-Georg Gadamer[1]

This quotation from Hans-Georg Gadamer states the goal of this essay. My attempt is to uncover certain theological points developed by the first and second generation of Tübingen theologians, (Johann Sebastian Drey, Johann Baptist von Hirscher, Johannes Evangelist von Kuhn, Johann Adam Möhler and Anton Staudenmaier.)[2] So to be historically precise, my concern is not historical interpretation, but rather the present value of these historical points. Their significance and the richness of their perspective for the development of contemporary theology will be sketched here; anything beyond that is impossible given the scope of this article. The point, according to Gadamer is that freedom and truth emerge in the past-consciousness of tradition. These examples[3] are two basic points that appear in the domain of dogmatic principles. We will also examine a central theme from the doctrine of God, Christology, the doctrine of grace, and ecclesiology. We will follow the same method throughout: the point at hand will be outlined with respect to a particular Tübingen theologian; then, it will be shown how the particular point arises today as we consider contemporary questions.

Fundamental Theology

"Philosophy of Revelation" in Johann Sebastian Drey
From the time of his first publications, Drey's thought and research dealt with the idea of theology as such.[4] In the introduction to his "Apologetik,"[5] Drey states that theology presupposes a "comprehensive theory of revelation," but this theory is missing. Drey also called this theory of revelation the "philosophy of revelation." The tenets of revelation comprise the confession of "the divine origin...of the manifestation of Christianity" as well as the "salvation of humankind" by God.[6] The basic character of Christianity should be defined in this philosophy of revelation. According to Drey, the philosophy of revelation has to raise the *intellectus fidei* as a whole and then not only to show the connection of the Old Testament economy of salvation to that of the New Testament, but also to illuminate the relationship of other religions in the history of humanity to Christianity.[7] Drey strongly insists that the Christian religion is both positive and historical. There is

an encompassing universality in the Christian religion that is worth elaborating and stating explicitly. This new theological starting point, which is significantly different from the apologetics of an earlier time, has exerted a series of effects on modern theology precisely because it displays the inner trustworthiness and reasonable plausibility of Christianity as well as its relationship to other religions, which are positive from the standpoint of the ideas of salvation, however uncritical they may be. This perspective is richly suggestive because it views the difference and connection between revelation and reason from a new standpoint. In this sense Rahner's transcendental-theological reflection on the mystery of Christian faith and Balthasar's "aesthetic-dramatic view of the form of Christian faith" both serve the same purpose.

What are the perspectives that result from Drey's starting point, especially if we have in mind an historical chain resulting in Balthasar and Rahner? Drey stresses the positive and historical *point de départ* as the fundamental ground of every conceptual or even transcendental reflection. Drey labels this positive quality resulting from revelation as "the basic truth of Christianity."[8] Logically he connects this positive nature with a concept of human reason relating human subjectivity and the capacity for self-consciousness to this positive nature that constitutes the other as other historically. Drey and Staudenmaier, who closely associates himself with his teacher in this regard,[9] rebel sharply against the Hegelian understanding of spirit which begins with the concept of the self in itself. Thus, Drey and Staudenmaier insist on both the historical and the positive on the conceptual level. By contrast, Drey, like Staudenmaier, develops a general understanding of reason, but of course does not refine this into a fully self-reflective transcendental philosophy. Thus Drey established that:

> External manifestations and contemplation reflecting on the divine in an objective manner are the necessary condition for the development of religious consciousness. Such manifestations must truly exist; they must take place in the external world. Humans must be able to find them there, if the human is truly marked by traits which are in the image of God. It is by means of these divine traits that the human being is to obtain individual differentiation, illumination and life, and objective reality and truth in accord with the sensual-spiritual nature of the human being.[10]

This descriptive representation is important to Drey because he uncovers the fictitious opposition of revelation and reason as it appears in a misunderstood supernaturalism and in a too narrow rationalism. Precisely in the synthesis of these two is "the system of true theology" presented.[11]

This theology

> ...is suprarational insofar as it proceeds from a principle that stands above reason and which is the origin of reason itself and of the origin of all knowledge of God within the self. This theology deals not only with the beginning of

religion and the beginning of the idea of God in the individual human being but with the advance of religion in the development of the idea of God in the recognition of God's relation to us.[12]

But Drey locates the truth of rationalism in the fact that revelation is given for the sake of reason:

> The common empirical senses do not discern the divine nature, and the finite understanding is itself incapable of elevation to the infinite just as the imagination limited by finite images is incapable of constructing a picture of the infinite. Divine nature reigns and moves only in the soul. It rises thence to higher conceptualization as an idea and embraces the will in an eager and determined way. What we call reason is encapsulated in these three basic capabilities of our spirit.[13]

The soul is the place where the divine nature reigns. Here it rises to a "higher conceptualization" and becomes a defining impetus that integrates the three basic powers of a human being into reason. This description undoubtedly echoes Schelling's and Schleiermacher's conceptual framework, but at the same time it lacks their development. The basic insight is central because it emphasizes the dialogical character for reason. The most important difference in Drey from such idealistic starting points as Schleiermacher's lies in the historical and linguistic transmission of reason as reason.

The aspects of Drey's thought have something in common with the phenomenological analysis of Gadamer when he stresses the indissoluble connection between thinking and speaking in *Truth and Method*.[14] The form of thinking, the creation of concepts, is not to be separated from its linguistic contents; on the contrary, all the creation of concepts is based upon experience that is always composed linguistically. But the experience of reality, which is made accessible linguistically, at the same time is the fundamental form of the creation of concepts, which enables all other developments, including the conceptual work of transcendental philosophy.[15]

The resolution of the abstract conflict between nature and reason and the neo-scholastic formulation of revelation was definitively advanced by Rahner and de Lubac. The conversion of this insight into an historical-hermeneutic theological epistemology that is transmitted linguistically cannot be ruled out given the perspectives Drey sketches in his Apologetics.[16] There are considerable differences from Balthasar's starting point. Drey does indeed contend, like Balthasar, that reason is in itself of a moral-practical nature by means of its historical constitution at its highest point in revelation since reason always contains a kind of self-relationship. At the same time, Drey's starting point differs from Balthasar's "Theodramatik." Drey speaks of how the spirit "in its action must be led back to itself as a limit by a force found outside itself. This limit becomes the Not-Self for the Self in that it presents the Self to the Spirit's view."[17] This basic structure is universally valid, even for people blessed with the revelation of God through Jesus

Christ. This means, for example, that the development of a theory of revelation, which encompasses the conditions of the relationship of the Christian faith to other religions is an ongoing task that must deal with the differences of other religions under continually new circumstances. This development must be recognized as valid and even though foreign and offensive must have a definite place in the comprehensive view of the *intellectus fidei*. Such a view is foreign to Balthasar. Theology is actually conveyed by means of historical differences and estrangement. It is in this sense *theologia negativa*, for it can articulate limits and objections to its own excess of meaning by means of differences and estrangement. From such a starting point arise new possibilities for incorporating such philosophical reflections as Emanuel Levinas' portrayal of the otherness of the others. There are even possibilities for including the basically hopeful structure of reason and the dynamic of its practical moral character. Here, before theology lie broad, uninvestigated fields for a modern theory of Christianity.

"Tradition" in Johann Evangelist von Kuhn

We now turn to a second element of fundamental theology, the idea of tradition in the thought of Johann Evangalist von Kuhn. In 1959 Joseph Rupert Geiselmann published a book entitled *Die lebendige Überlieferung als Norm des christlichen Glaubens: Die apostolische Tradition in der Form der kirchlichen Verkündigung: Das Formalprinzip des Katholizismus dargestellt im Geiste der Traditionslehre Johann Evangelist Kuhn* (*Living Tradition as the Norm of the Christian Faith: Apostolic Tradition in the Form of Proclamation: The Formal Principle of Catholicism Expressed in the Spirit of the Doctrine of Tradition of Kuhn.*)[18] Geiselmann demonstrates that living tradition with all of its elements is to be understood as a process begun by the *kerygma* of Jesus Christ and carried on by the proclamation of the apostles and the scriptures, which is Kuhn's idea of the church's proclamation. Most important is the insight that the one event of the communication of the faith is expressed in these various forms "and not some sort of logical outgrowth of its expression."[19] It is well known that Geiselmann's work spurred a lively discussion at the first German-speaking congress on dogmatics after World War II in Königstein and had great influence on the conceptualization of revelation in *Dei Verbum*, Vatican II's document on revelation.[20] We will now pay special attention to a strand of Kuhn's notion of tradition and by tracing its effects indicate what of his theology can actually be found in Vatican II.

Kuhn's understanding of tradition[21] is largely determined by his idea of tradition as a linguistic event, indeed an eschatological event: the message of Jesus Christ and the testimony of the Apostles are the event of God's self-revelation for the sake of the salvation of humanity. Divine truth in linguistic form necessarily initiates an ongoing chain of events.[22] This chain of events does not lead "beyond Christian truth to a different content, to a more perfect or purer truth, but rather to a more and more complete development of that truth, which is unchangeable in itself and communicated by the apostles."[23]

The key issue for Kuhn is that in this process of explication and application the truth of the Christian faith is developed. This development is not an increase in truth but rather a preservation of it. Faith is preserved in every new situation and all human interaction because new insights result from such interaction. The truth of faith and its progress in various situations, i.e., the pragmatics of faith, are not to be divided. Important conclusions result from this for Kuhn: *Dogma*, what is held *de fide*, "is Christian truth as it addresses the church at the appropriate time."[24] This Christian truth, *Dogma*, Kuhn differentiates from individual dogmas which he describes as abstract expressions of this one Dogma. These dogmas are formulae for preaching, each specially designed to meet the demands of the situation at hand in order to protect Christian truth in itself. These formulae only make sense in that they give expression to Christian truth. Thus, they can be discarded for the sake of this same Christian truth, which they express—in different times and so in different terms—in distinct church documents and credal statements. So the task of dogmatics as a theological discipline is to give expression to the one Christian truth in its individual aspects: the doctrines on Christian sin, etc.[25]

The individual formulae of faith, whether they are proposed by a council or by a theologian, require prescinding from their varying degrees of authority and usefulness as well as careful analysis and testing. They are always in danger of taking on "official status beyond the limits of truth,"[26] that in striving to protect against heretical tendencies and movements, they end up being exaggerated by their very zeal for the faith. In this way Kuhn takes the topical dialectic a step further than Melchior Cano who originated the method of systematic theology.[27] Kuhn recognizes the various *loci* characterized by Cano and underscores the necessity that faith take concrete form in the particular instantiation of truth, while at the same time stressing the hierarchy of these formulations of faith, which preserve these particular instantiations of truth in the language of faith. Thus, as Kuhn explicitly teaches, hermeneutical rules are required for the explication of faith. In contrast to the neoscholastic use of the *loci* that refers back to the individual instantiation of truth and the isolated definition, new perspectives can result. The loci, like the particular dogmas, manifest the truth of faith in their interplay. Thus the truth of faith is the "thing" which is reported in the historically formed language of faith.

Anyone who has followed the turmoil surrounding the questions of fundamental theology in recent times, especially as it develops from the viewpoint of philosophy of language, and anyone who has studied the meaning and bearing of the official formulae of faith in particular dogmas, will recognize the inspiring and provocative power of Kuhn's position. Truth belongs to the linguistic event with its semantic, grammatical, and pragmatic dimensions. In this event a corrective possibility arises which can uncover prejudice and ideology. In my opinion Kuhn's starting position avoids some of the controversial aspects of positions like those of Lindbeck or Tracy.

Major Dogmatic Themes

The Concept of God in Kuhn and Staudenmaier as a Factor in
Contemporary Theology

Philosophical reflections on the fundamental plurality, historicity, and linguistic character of all reality as well as the dialogue with other religions, especially
Judaism, pose a question to present day theology in a new way: how plausible are
its assertions concerning God? This is especially important with regard to the
profession of faith in the Trinity.

The writings of Kuhn and Staudenmaier provide a real perspective into contemporary efforts to resolve this problem.[28] Staudenmaier, like Kuhn, begins with
the fundamental incapacity of human thought to grasp the mystery of God fully.
Human awareness of and reflection about God are always confined to the realm of
analogy. At the same time, however, the human spirit possesses an immediate
relationship to God, because the idea of God which makes the human spirit truly
spirit is an originative revelation from God to the human race. Thus, in any analogical understanding of God, no matter how limited, God is the one experienced and
understood. God reveals Self continually to human understanding without becoming either a simply or hospitably welcomed guest or a humanly constructed intellectual concept. Knowledge of God is constructed "dialogically' and fully perfects
itself within human beings by a series of gradual steps. God has become a neighbor
to humanity so that knowledge of God is always historically mediated and results in
a dialogical relationship to God, i.e., in the historical revelation of God.[29] The divine
initiative in this process has been treated above in the discussion of the concept of
revelation.

The significance of this starting point in theology can hardly be overesti-
mated, especially in view of the fact that many modern philosophical treatments,
which handle God as a "foreign term," do not deal with this subject at all.[30] Kuhn's
and Staudenmaier's treatment of the idea of God as the force of the divine, active
self-gift may still offer a bridge to an insight into the phenomenology of religion
which characterizes religious experiences as a "reversal" of thought, which can
offer an adequate way of treating religion.[31]

But almost more important in present-day theological dialogue with other religions, especially with Judaism, may be the teaching of the Tübingen theologians
concerning the Trinity as *concrete monotheism.* They contrast this concrete monotheism with an abstract monotheism which does not allow God to be thought of as
living sovereign or free. Kuhn tersely states, "Christian Trinitarianism is nothing
other than concrete monotheism."[32] Kuhn gives positive proof of this by going
through the Old and New Testament designations for God as well as more recent
designations from the tradition and tries to demonstrate the conceptual unity of all
these faith statements. The many Old and New Testament assertions of mediation
through creation and the characterization of God as free, sovereign creator, ruler of
history, and redeemer of humankind imply the necessity of thinking of the one God
as self-differentiating and self-mediating. God defines Self as creator, redeemer, and

perfecter of humankind. The notion of identity is no more suitable to divine life than the notions of otherness and mediation. But the designations for God that are obtained, which indicate that Spirit is both understanding and will, i.e., self conscious and freely self-determining person,[33] must be strictly defined because they are analogical. Kuhn demonstrates the fact that neither an abstract monotheism nor a polytheism which entails limitation are sufficient. This demonstration is strengthened by a detailed critique of the positions of Hegel, Schelling, Anton Günther, Schleiermacher and other contemporaries.

From this starting point Kuhn favorably evaluates the great attempts within the tradition to gain an *intellectus* of the trinitarian mystery of God. He examines Augustine's *De trinitate*, Anselm's *Monologion*, and both *Summae* of Thomas in order to show how they develop an understanding of the hypostatic character of Word and Spirit from the logical structure of *"id quo manius cogitari nequit."* At the same time he dares to move beyond the great theologians of the patristic era and of the middle ages. He characterizes these important treatments as given within a "propositional and reflective mode of thought,"[34] because they do not take into consideration the spiritual unity of the different hypostases in accord with the reflection on self-determination. "In order completely to do justice to the unity of God, we must recognize Father, Son, and Spirit as absolutely consubstantial. We must recognize not just the Father but the divine Trinity as the one true God."[35] Father, Son and Spirit are of absolutely one and the same nature and are to be recognized as one nature, as God who knows Self and exercises Self in the Trinity of hypostases, as "personal Spirit who acts as such in a self-conscious and free fashion, who in thinking and willing is the creator of the world, which God is or can be by God's very nature in that God is by nature the self-sufficient ground of all things which have their possibility only in God."[36]

But the reduction of the three hypostases to unity is necessary. For this reason, according to Kuhn, every attempt at such reduction is valuable in order to prevent this language from becoming approximate or indeterminate. To think the *unity* of the divine Trinity is undoubtedly one of the great tasks for contemporary theology.[37] The work of Indian theologians in dialogue with the Hindu tradition and the debate surrounding the position of J. Hick are just two examples of this.

Jesus Christ—Norm, Paradigm, and Redeemer of Humanity

In his two volume *Apologetik*, Johann Sebastian Drey develops a view of Jesus Christ, which corresponds to his concept of the philosophy of revelation. He differentiates between the form and the content of revelation and shows how certain aspects of God are made accessible through *Nature* as a form of revelation, in which God even makes sinful human beings within their historical situation an organ of his self-revelation. Finally, Drey characterizes Jesus Christ as a form of the revelation of God in that he, as the perfect image of the Father, carries within himself the fullness of divinity, wisdom, holiness, and power and so is capable of "presenting God in his being and in his person."[38]

> This revelation of God in the Son, this being, dwelling, and acting of the Father in the Son thus had a profound threefold effect for humankind and at the same time worthy fashion. It presented the being and characteristics of the content of the true doctrine of God for us to see. And finally it established the standard and model for the morally perfected human in mind and deed in the life and workings of the Son of Man.[39]

The idea that Drey sketches out here has profound significance for Christology.

Franz Anton Staudenmaier follows the path blazed by his teacher Drey in his Christology, when he names and establishes Jesus Christ as the paradigm (*Urbild*) and norm for human beings: "his teaching is consequently a self-presentation."[40] In this sense, Jesus Christ is not simply religious for Staudenmaier. He is religion.[41] This perspective is only meaningful if humanity ultimately is fulfilled in the revelation of God. The most basic human action is to be in relation with God.

The gradation in Drey's forms of revelation are reminiscent of traditional medieval distinctions: a) God is present in every being as a vestige (*in vestigiis*). Because of his power as creator, he is present in every creaturely being, (*in alio*), in the way that a cause is an effect. b) God is present in humans as in a mirror (*in speculo*). The human being, who is by nature an image of God in a formal abstract way, can become a messenger of God, although on account of his sinful nature, he can only reflect God as a broken mirror would. In this context Thomas speaks of the human as *imago imperfecta*.[42] c) Jesus Christ is the perfect image of the Father, the one who reflects God's being not only in a formal abstract way according to his nature. He is the real and perfect image of God, because He fulfills communion with God in every respect. Jesus Christ is for Thomas the *imago Dei perfecta*.[43]

But Drey decisively advances this traditional starting point by interpreting the gradation linguistically. The human being is that being capable, when perfected, of being the disclosure of God, or God coming to expression. Just as one makes verbal distinctions, so one must distinguish between the word in its immutable uniqueness and the word as uttered at this moment. Because the being of a human in its fullness is characterized by speech, God is able to address his Word to human beings so they become fully human.

Gadamer pondered these relationships in his analysis of truth and the reality of speech.[44] Christology serves to prepare the way for a new anthropology that reconciles the human spirit in its finitude with the divine infinitude in a new way. This is where the so-called hermeneutical experience can find its grounding.[45] Karl Rahner has introduced these basic ideas into his Christology without referring specifically to the issues of theological language.

It is apparent that both Drey and especially Staudenmaier do not carry these ideas through in the development of their Christological discussions. Both rely on the Chalcedonian formula and speak of a divine and human consciousness in Christ. Thus Staudenmaier introduces his treatment of salvation with the statement:

> In Christ the divine and the human nature were hypostatically united in one person. By means of this union of the two natures, Christ had a divine and a human consciousness, one just as truly as the other. This means that he knew that he was God and human at the same time. ...His divine consciousness is no mere rational awareness but rather the purest recognition of his divine being; he and the Father are one.[46]

Drey thought it necessary to supply a certain correction to his earlier reflections on the form of revelation. In the context of a more careful reflection on the relationship of Christianity to Judaism, he writes,

> The Christian revelation is as much above the Mosaic-prophetic revelation as an immediate divine organ is above a merely human one or as the Son of God is above a human being. This is the reason that Christian revelation cannot be called the fulfillment or perfection of the Judaic revelation any more than it is the fulfillment of the original revelation (in nature). For human beings are no more fulfilled or perfected nature than God or the Son is fulfilled or perfected humanity. Rather, each of these categories is its own complete level of being which, because it is complete, is also fulfilled or perfected in itself.[47]

Clearly there is an unresolved problem here. We are trying to think an appearance of the divine in human form while at the same time God maintains God's own divine form. At this point the original way of thinking about the doctrine can no longer be regarded as a linguistic event. But it is precisely in this unresolved problem that we can see how we must think about Christology today. The present author has tried to follow this position through in his Christology which has been substantively influenced by Welte and Rahner.[48]

Grace and Charism in Kuhn and Staudenmaier

Kuhn composed his work "The Christian Doctrine of Divine Grace"[49] to defend his doctrine of grace in response to denunciation in Rome. Consequently it should not be interpreted outside the context of the controversy with Constantine von Schäzler.[50] The following is not directly concerned with any of the peculiarities of Kuhn's doctrine of grace resulting from this situation but rather with the constant fundamental direction of his understanding of grace which is also found in Staudenmaier's doctrine of charism,[51] although only in a peculiar fashion.

Kuhn emphasized that the core of his disagreement with Schäzler is that every grace is to be understood as substantially "physical."[52] By the infusion of grace, "a physical change comes about in the human soul, and the resulting 'supernature' is the physical basis of the supernatural virtuous actions of a human being."[53] "By means of sanctifying grace,...rational nature...participates in the divine nature in an actual physical way."[54] Thus Kuhn stresses that grace is to be understood as a supernatural *perfectio personae*.

> Since he is truly born again of the divine Spirit, he is a child of the divine Spirit. He is ordered toward God and filled with his Spirit, with the Spirit of justice and holiness, with the Spirit of faith and love. But this divine Spirit of the born again human is not a physical quality of his soul; rather it is something supernatural. It is not a sharing in divine nature, but rather a way in sharing in the divine Spirit and will.[55]

Essentially Kuhn's understanding is that the human being is personal in his mode of being, but precisely as a person he has to possess himself as a "content" in order to attain "personality."[56] This development toward personality, a task which the human being as a person cannot disregard, proceeds by means of freedom. So the sinner needs grace as the "principle of personality" that strengthens his wounded capacity for freedom and will.

Kuhn interprets Thomas' doctrine of grace as *"in essentia animae sicut in subjecto"* in the following way:

> By being born again or anew, he (the human being) becomes a completely different, new human being; in its depths, at the intersection of intellect and will, the human spirit is new, different, and in the divine likeness. It is a newly created spirit. Its supernatural perfection is the principle of the perfection of the intellect and the will, both of which are rooted in it and proceed from and are the principles of the corresponding thinking, reflecting, willing, and acting.[57]

Starting from his first publication,[58] Staudenmaier characterizes human life through the moment of being in oneself and the moment of interaction. First, in and by interaction with another, the human being unites self and becomes a real self. This interaction occurs substantially through the Spirit of God who is also the Spirit of Jesus Christ. Guided by the Spirit, the human being comes to communion with God in the concrete historical dimension of his life, to the true identity of self, and to communion with others. The person thus establishes an individuality and recognizes this individuality as a charism, a gift of the Spirit.

> Individuality is that special form in which a life comprises itself with all of its strength, ability, and activity according to a special principle, the work of the Holy Spirit, and thus fashions itself into personhood through which a human being gains a true view of the self, feels, knows, and lives in accord with his own will and which is nothing other than the constant realization of the inner idea of his life.[59]

Thus, grace, salvation, and charism are concerned with the successful, authentic existence of a person and with the free development of his personhood.

What perspectives for the future have we gained from this brief outline of points drawn from Kuhn and Staudenmaier? In his book *Erlösungsglaube und Freiheitsgeschichte: Eine Skizze zur Soteriolgie*,[60] Thomas Pröpper noted difficulties and questions which are connected today with the term "soteriology." With reference to the proclamation of redemption he speaks of a "supply without a demand?"[61]

Basing himself on Karl Rahner's theology Pröpper seeks to set forth a concept of redemption largely based on a modern analysis of freedom. This starting point seems essential to me, although it requires a broadening of its base because its point of reference is similar to Pannenberg's theological anthropology.[62] The structure of humanity, the *nature* of freedom is to be defined in a transcendental philosophical or transcendental theological way. Both theological anthropology and the doctrine of grace largely leave out of consideration the various forms of human spirituality and of human existence, ways of perfecting human individuality and concrete meditations of grace. But only in this way can the modern experience of life, questions of spirituality, spiritual direction, and systematic theology be once again linked. Such a new orientation of the doctrine of grace corresponds to the basic stance of modern philosophy. Thus, Dieter Henrich has shown how the human being as self-conscious is essentially oriented to self-interpretation. In this he sees the starting point for religion and faith in human existence.[63]

The Question of the Form of Primacy

It is the task of ecclesiology to deal with the question of primacy. For quite some time the ecclesiology of the Tübingen systematicians has not been thoroughly studied. Besides Kuhn's work there were creative contributions from other Tübingen scholars before Vatican I. The question of the relationship of their writings to the Council's statement on faith has been investigated. But the same attention has not been paid to their foundational and theological interpretation of the papacy. This is an area ripe for study, for the question of the development of the papacy can in no way be seen as a closed subject.

The theological and canonical debates before and after Vatican I show that its teaching on the primacy and infallible teaching authority of the pope in 1870 did not sufficiently take into account modern theological and canonical understanding. While the concordats of the German Empire with Eugene IV and Nicholas V explicitly referred to the decisions of Constance and Basel,[64] the subordination of the pope to the council was of less import than the independence of the bishops. The schism of the Old Catholics, the silence of the Catholic faculty at Tübingen on the decrees of Vatican I, the reactions of the Protestant and Orthodox churches, and the impassioned debate surrounding Hans Küng's "Infallible?—An Inquiry"[65] are all symptoms of an enormous festering problem. For this reason I regard the initiative of the present pope suggesting a dialogue on the future shape of the papacy in his 1995 encyclical *Ut unum sint* as extraordinarily important.[66] The results may be of great consequence.[67] Theology confronts the question of how to ground the papacy within this dialogue and how to transform the papacy in such a way that various strands within the tradition and the current needs of the contemporary church are both given due weight. The issues must be formed so that the divided churches and all Christians can recognize the chair of Peter.

In this context the work of the Tübingen theologians on the papacy is of the greatest interest. Beginning with Drey's *Apologetik* and Mohler's *Symbolik*[68]— major works of the two authors—several important lines of convergence emerge. The office endowed with the power to teach, sanctify, and govern is grounded in the body of the church and is inseparable from it according to both these theologians. While Drey refers at this point to divine revelation which includes the church as a constitutive element,[69] Möhler roots the church and the papal office in the Incarnation of the divine Word.[70] Necessarily both see the primacy as an important issue for the unity of the church. The primatial office exercises a balancing tension to the bishops to maintain good governance of the individual churches. To be sure, Möhler describes this tension in *Symbolik* very differently from the way he did in his famous earlier work *Einheit in der Kirche*.[71] But even in *Symbolik* he speaks of the "beneficial complementarity" of the episcopal papal system.[72]

In a way similar to Möhler's lectures in church history,[73] Drey treats the changing nature of this relationship.[74] Both Drey and Möhler stress that the individual structure of leadership in the church cannot be understood as monarchical or aristocratic or democratic. Although Drey ascribes the authority to the pope to depose bishops for good and sufficient reasons, there is no monarchical sovereign authority in the church, "because the bishops as direct successors of the apostles rule their dioceses independently and both bishops and pope are bound by common laws."[75]

Möhler states in his lectures on church history of 1826/27: "It can certainly be said that the pope did not exercise any monarchical power over the church in this [post-Constantinian] period."[76] Like Drey, Möhler holds that by divine ordinance the pope is entrusted with the unity of the church just as the bishops are devoted to the care of the individual churches. "When each recognized the existence of the other as divine, they formed very beneficial complements in ecclesiastical life, so that through their tension the proper free development of the parts was maintained just as the connection of these parts was united in an inseparable vital whole."[77] These statements clearly show that both Drey and Möhler regard both the universal church and the local church as *iuris divini*. This holds true as well for both the spiritual office of the bishop of Rome and the episcopacy. Although Vatican II teaches that the church is constituted by local churches,[78] the 1983 Code of Canon Law contains no corresponding affirmation of the divine right of the constitutive local churches or of their bishops.

But there is a further important conclusion from the ideas of Drey and Möhler concerning the form of church unity. Neither of them attempted to suggest the thesis that the universal church is produced by an amalgamation of the constitutive local churches. Both held that, from its human side, the unity of the church is marked by a free reciprocal recognition. From the divine side, the unity of the church is grounded in its foundation by Jesus Christ and the gift of the Holy Spirit. These fundamental relationships in the church can yield us useful perspectives on the contemporary question about the role of the papacy both for conversation among Catholics and in ecumenical dialogue.[79]

Final Comments

The themes presented from fundamental theology and the four doctrinal areas—God, Christology, Grace, and ecclesiology—are given as examples. They are intended to illustrate the rich array of insights in the early Tübingen theology. Examples can often be juxtaposed, used to demonstrate any number of things, and be replaced by other examples. Certainly it is true that one who knows the Tübingen theology well could have selected other examples than the ones I have given. But this does not mean that the examples, different as their contexts may be, do not show certain basic common trends. It is worthwhile considering these common trends.

All these examples show that the Tübingen theologians exercise rigorous inquiry into the *intellectus fidei*. This inquiry is both rigorous and basic because it works from the ground of both reason and revelation. This common theme is historically composed and characterized by dialogical reason that is structured linguistically through and through. The listener interacts with the word. Therefore the *intellectus fidei*—mediated by many signs—can be elevated only in a view of the entire tradition. Kant originally established that concepts without intuition are empty.[80] For the Tübingen theologians it is necessary that one possess a living intuition of the historically existing organism of the revelation-event to be able to present the truth of theological claims at any given time. But this understanding of these claims, this grasp of their truth at any particular time implies a specific conceptual framework apart from which the truth cannot be grasped. This conceptuality is not simply at hand in either thought or objects. It is also not available simply from the tradition. It is located at a specific moment in time and thus makes possible communication both with history and with others. Such creative conceptual work presupposes an open mind and is furthered by a wide-ranging education. Surely the Tübingen theologians possessed such an education in an extraordinary degree. Through their constant recourse to "Petavius," they became familiar with the patristic and medieval tradition. Their attempts to enter into dialogue with the work of Jacobi, Schleiermacher, Kant, Schelling, and Hegel gave them assured facility in dealing with conceptually complex issues. But this open, critical spirit that they gained from a deep reverence for thought may well be their decisive contribution.

They developed their theology after the fall of the *ancien regime* and the end of the "Reichskirche." At the same time they carried out—with luminous ability—the first great development of modern scientific inquiry and research and anticipated new dimensions of the task. Thus, their theology has achieved paradigmatic status. We find perspectives here that can still function as guides for contemporary theological reflection.

NOTES

1. Hans Georg Gadamer, *Wahrheit und Methode: Grundzüge einer philosophische Hermeneutik, Hans Georg Gadamers Gesammelte Schriften* 1, 6th ed. (Tübingen: Mohr, 1990), English trans., *Truth and Method*. 2nd ed. rev., trans. Joel Weinsheimer and Donald G. Marshall (New York: Crossroad, 1989), p. 281.

2. The scope of this article does not permit consideration of the differences among the various Tübingen theologians. This essay takes material from one or another author as that material furthers its discussion. Usually parallel passages are mentioned in the notes.

3. This prescinds from the debate about whether and in what sense the theologians mentioned here are to be accorded the status of classics. (See Anton van Harskamp, " 'Revision'!—Welche Revision? Ideologie kritisches zum theologischen Projekt Dreys," in *Revision der Theologie—Reform der Kirche: Die Bedeutung des Tübinger Theologen Johann Sebastian Drey (1777–1853) in Geschichte und Gegenwart*, ed. Abraham Peter Kustermann [Würzburg: Echter, 1994], pp. 60–91, esp. 89f.) This interpretation is that the Tübingen theologians grasped and identified the essential elements of the responsible contemporary affirmation of faith with great astuteness, but did not conceptually develop them far enough. Careful examination of the history of theology shows that fundamental conceptual elaboration is often a long-term effort. For this reason our examples have been selected, which carry implications for the contemporary work on theological concepts.

4. See Johann Sebastian von Drey, "Revision des gegenwärtigen Zustandes der Theologie," in Johann Sebastian von Drey, *Revision der Kirche und Theologie*, ed. Franz Schupp (Darmstadt: Wissenschaftliche Buchgesellschaft, 1971), pp. 1–24; English trans., "Toward the Revision of the Present State of Theology," in Joseph Fitzer, ed., *Romance and the Rock: Nineteenth-Century Catholics on Faith and Reason* (Minneapolis: Fortress Press, 1989), pp. 62–73. Also, Johann Sebastian Drey, *Kurze Einleitung in das Studium der Theologie mit Rücksicht auf den wissenschaftlichen Standpunct und das katholische System* (Tübingen 1819; repr., Minerva: Frankfurt, 1966); English trans., *Brief Introduction to the Study of Theology with Reference to the Scientific Standpoint and the Catholic System*, trans. Michael J. Himes (Notre Dame: University of Notre Dame Press, 1994).

5. Johann Sebastian von Drey, *Die Apologetik als wissenschaftliche Nachweisung der Göttlichkeit des Christentums in seiner Erscheinung*, 3 vols. (Mainz, 1838–1847; repr., Frankfurt: Minerva 1967).

6. See Drey, *Apologetik*, 1:vi. Also, Eberhard Tiefensee, *Die religiöse Anlage und ihre Entwicklung. Der religionsphilosophische Ansatz Johann Sebastian Dreys (1777–1853)*, Erfurter Theologischen Studien 56 (Leipzig: St. Benno-Verlag, 1988).

7. Max Seckler has correctly described the idea of the Kingdom of God as the core of Drey's earlier theology and has pointed out both the philosophical and theological character of this idea; see most recently Max Seckler, "Das Reich Gottes als 'höchste Idee des Christentums' in der Theologie Johann Sebastian Dreys. Ein Anstoß zur Revision in der Drey-Forschung," in Kustermann, ed., *Revision der Theologie—Reform der Kirche*, pp. 292–308. Anton van Harskamp suggests that Drey subsequently abandoned this idea and with it the character of his earlier theology; see Harskamp, p. 90. In my opinion substantial structural elements of the idea of the Kingdom of God are retained and developed within Drey's later "philosophy of revelation."

8. Drey, *Apologetik* 1:2.

9. See Franz Anton Staudenmaier, *Geist der göttlichen Offenbarung, oder Wissenschaft der Geschichtsprinzipien des Christentums* (Gießen, 1837; repr., Frankfurt: Minerva 1967).

10. Ibid, p. 131.

11. Drey, *Apologetik*, 1:289.

12. Ibid.

13. Ibid.

14. Gadamer, p. 432.

15. For the conceptual development of this framework by Johann Evangelist von Kuhn, see Hans Günther Türk, "Philosophie—Spekulative Theologie—Unmittelbare Gottesidee," *Zeitschrift für Katholische Theologie* 104 (1982): 147–171, esp. 155–158.

16. See Tiefensee, p. 239 and the refences cited there.

17. Ibid., p. 128.

18. See Josef Rupert Geiselmann, *Die lebendige Überlieferung als Norm des christlichen Glaubens. Die apostolische Tradition in der form der kirchlichen Verkündigung—das Formalprinzip des Katholizismus dargestellt im Geiste der Traditionslehre Johannes Ev. Kuhn* (Freiburg: Herder, 1959).

19. Ibid., p. 293.

20. See Peter Hünermann, "Deutsche Theologie auf dem zweiten Vaticanum," in *Kirche sein: Nachkonziliare Theologie im Dienst der Kirchenreform*, ed. Wilhelm Geerlings and Max Seckler (Freiburg, Basel, Vienna: Herder, 1994), pp. 141–162.

21. See Adrian Brants, *Erkenntnis und Freiheit Rekonstruktion der philosophisch-theologischen Erkenntnislehre J.E. Kuhns* (Berne, New York, Paris: Lang, 1989), pp. 288–378.

22. Johannes Evangelist Kuhn, *Einleitung in die katholische Dogmatik*, 2nd ed. (Tübingen 1859; repr., Frankfurt: Minerva, 1968). p. 150: "All higher truths and especially divinely revealed truths set into action the human spirit, which is understanding and will, so that on the one hand they become the object of faith, thought and recognition and on the other hand they become the norm and guiding principle for behavior and life.... This divine truth is maintained in its pure objectivity and the danger of subjective opinion and error are eliminated. Consequently, the divine fount from which this truth flows must always be kept open and preserved and protected from the torrent of floodwaters. The development which it initiates in which it is related to the religious opinion of the multitude and the philosophical systems of intellectuals, to the ordinary as well as the educated reason of people must constantly be kept in living connection with principle and source from which it takes its being."

23. Ibid., p. 152.

24. Ibid., p. 195.

25. See ibid., p. 208: "What church doctrine wants to say finally and definitively, for example, in the case of original sin, cannot necessarily be derived from what the church stated on the subject at the Council of Trent against the Reformers. How then do we achieve clarity as to what the secure path is to discover concerning the fundamental thinking of the church on a dogma and to demonstrate it as such? ... The only sure path, fully faithful to the church's principles, is to trace the objective development of the dogma from its beginning in the church. To do this the proof of tradition has to be laid out and the groundwork prepared for the speculative task of dogmatics in which it fulfills the conditions for resolving the problem." This text clearly shows how Kuhn connects the individual dogmas to the actual dogmatic context.

26. Ibid., p. 196.

27. Peter Hünermann, "Dogmatik—Topische Dialektik des Glaubens," in *Fides quaerens intellectum. Beiträge zur Fundamental Theologie*, ed. Michael Kessler, Wolfhart Pannenberg, and Hermann Josef Pottmeyer (Tübingen: Francke, 1992), pp. 577–592.

28. In their doctrine of God Staudenmaier and Kuhn have many points in common. Kuhn is nevertheless the theologian who argues his case with greater conceptual acuity. For this reason the subsequent text tends to cite Kuhn more often. There are fewer than half as many citations to Staudenmaier, largely confined to bibliographic notes.

29. See Brants, pp. 227–244.

30. See Richard Schaeffler, *Das Gebet und das Argument: Zwei Weise des Sprechens von Gott. Eine Einführung in die Theorie der religiösen Sprache*, Beiträge zur Theologie - und Religionswissenschaft (Düsseldorf: Patmos, 1989), p. 290: "The word of 'God' is not native to the language of philosophy."

31. Important among the works on this topic is Richard Schaeffler, *Erfahrung als Dialog mit der Wirklichkeit. Eine Untersuchung zur Logik der Erfahrung* (Freiburg and Munich: Alber, 1995). See esp. the chapter "Der Aufbau einer religiöse Erfahrung," pp. 414–474, as well as the chapter "Die sittliche und religiöse Erfahrung—Ihre Sondergestalt und ihre allgemein-transzendentale Bedeutung," pp. 732–750.

32. Johannes Evangelist Kuhn, *Katholische Dogmatik*, Bd. 2: *Die christliche Lehre von der göttliche Dreieinigkeit* (Tübingen, 1857; repr. Frankfurt: Minerva, 1968), p. 498.

33. Ibid., p. 500.

34. Ibid., p. 617.

35. Ibid., p. 618.

36. Ibid., p. 620.

37. On Kuhn's doctrine of God, see Franz Kreuter, *Person und Gnade* (Frankfurt: Lang, 1984), pp. 123–214.

38. Drey, *Apologetik*, 2:203.

39. Ibid.

40. Franz Anton Staudenmaier, *Johannes Skotus Erigena und die Wissenschaft seiner Zeit* (Frankfurt, 1834), p. 215.

41. See Franz Anton Staudenmaier, *Enzyklopädie der theologischen Wissenschaften als System der gesammten Theologie* (Mainz, 1834; repr., Frankfurt: Minerva, 1968), p. 302: "Thus he was not only religious but religion in its own living reality; he was not merely connected with some great idea, he was the idea itself."

42. For this idea in Saint Thomas, see *Summa Theologiae* I, q. 93, a. 1 c.

43. Ibid., a. 1, ad 2.

44. See Gadamer, pp. 409–442.

45. Ibid., p. 432.

46. Staudenmaier, *Enzyklopädie*, pp. 387ff.

47. Drey, *Apologetik*, 2:211.

48. See Peter Hünermann, *Jesus Christus—Gottes Wort in der Zeit* (Münster: Aschendorff, 1994).

49. Johannes Evangelist Kuhn, *Die christliche Lehre von der göttlichen Gnade* (Tübingen, 1868: repr., Frankfurt: Minerva, 1968).

50. Hubert Wolf, *Ketzer oder Kirchenlehrer? Der Tübingen Theologe Johannes von Kuhn (1806–1887) in den kirchenpolitischen Auseinandersetzungen seiner Zeit*, Veröffentlichungen der Kommission für Zeitgeschichte, Reihe B, Bd. 58 (Mainz: Matthias Grünewald Verlag, 1992), pp. 309–311.

51. Franz Anton Staudenmaier, *Der Pragmatismus der Geistesgaben oder das Wirken des göttlichen Geistes im Menschen und der Menschheit* (Tübingen, 1835; repr., Frankfurt: Minerva, 1975); see also Franz Anton Staudenmaier, *Die christliche Dogmatik*, vol. 3 (Freiburg: Herder, 1852).

52. See Kreuter, pp. 233–418.

53. Kuhn, *Die christliche Lehre von der göttlichen Gnade*, p. viii.

54. Ibid.

55. Ibid., p. 381.

56. See ibid., pp. 22ff.

57. See ibid., p. 420.

58. See Franz Anton Staudenmaier, "Der Pragmatismus der Geistesgaben," *Theologische Quartalschrift* (1828): 389–432, 608–640.

59. Ibid., p. 406.

60. 2nd ed. (Munich: Kösel, 1988).

61. See Wolfhart Pannenberg, *Anthropologie in theologischer Perspektive* (Göttingen:

Vandenhoeck und Ruprecht, 1983); English trans., *Anthropology in Theological Perspective*, trans. Matthew J. O'Connell (Philadelphia: Westminster Press, 1985).

62. 2nd expanded ed. (Munich: Kösel, 1988).

63. See Dieter Henrich, *Fluchtlinien* (Frankfurt: Suhrkamp, 1982), pp. 99–124.

64. See Johann Stephan Püttner, *Institutiones Iuris Publici Germanici* (5th ed.; Göttingen, 1792). For the consequences of this imperial law and the discussion resulting from it in Württemberg at the time of the council, see Hubert Wolf, "Ist es möglich, bis zum 18. Juli etwas für unwahr von da an für wahr zu halten?," *Zeitschrift für neuere Theologiegeschichte* 3 (1996): 88–115.

65. (Zürich: Einsiedeln, 1970).

66. See *Ut unum sint*, 96.

67. See Peter Hünermann, "Amt und Evangelium. Die Gestalt des Petrusdienstes am Ende des zweiten Jahrtausends," *Herder Korrespondenz* 50 (1996): 298–302.

68. It is impossible to give in particular detail the differences which are found in the various works of Drey and Möhler. For Möhler, see the comprehensive treatment by Josef Rupert Geiselmann in Johann Adam Möhler, *Symbolik oder Darstellung der dogmatischen Gegensätze der Katholiken und Protestanten nach ihren öffentlichen Bekenntnisschriften*, 2 vols. ed. by Josef Rupert Geiselmann (Cologne: Jakob Hegner, 1960), 2:666–698; English trans. of Möhler's text, *Symbolism: Exposition of the Doctrinal Differences Between Catholics and Protestants as Evidenced by Their Symbolical Writings*, trans. James Burton Robertson, introduction by Michael J. Himes (New York: Crossroad Herder, 1997).

69. See Drey, *Apologetik*, 3:1–7.

70. See Möhler, *Symbolik*, 1:387.

71. See Johann Adam Möhler, *Die Einheit in der Kirche oder das Prinzip des Katholizismus. Dargestellt im Geiste der Kirchenväter der drei ersten Jahrhunderte*, ed. by Josef Rupert Geiselmann (Cologne: Jakob Hegner, 1956); English trans. *Unity in the Church or the Principle of Catholicism Presented in the Spirit of the Church Fathers of the First Three Centuries*, ed. and trans. Peter C. Erb (Washington, DC: Catholic University of America Press, 1996). Stemming from his romantic understanding of life, the concept of flourishing life necessarily implies for him a wide-ranging restriction of any institutionalizing impetus. Thus, for Möhler it is an indication that the church is in "a very sad and confused state," when the primacy is most emphasized; ibid., p. 239.

72. Möhler, *Symbolik*, 1:453ff.

73. See Geiselmann in Möhler, *Symbolik*, 2:691–699.

74. See Drey, *Apologetik*, 3:210–276.

75. Ibid., p. 275.

76. Quoted by Geiselmann in Möhler, *Symbolik*, 2:691.

77. Möhler, *Symbolik*, 1:454.

78. See *Lumen gentium*, 23.

79. See Peter Hünermann, "Der Römische Bischof und der Weltepiskopat," in Peter Hünermann, *Ekklesiologie im Präsenz* (Münster: Aschendorff, 1995), pp. 248–265.

80. Immanuel Kant, *Kritik der reinen Vernunft*, B 75; English trans., *Critique of Pure Reason*, trans. Norman Kemp Smith (New York; St. Martin's Press, 1965), p. 93: "Thoughts without content are empty, institutions without concepts are blind. It is, therefore, just as necessary to make our concepts sensible, that is, to add the object to them in intuition, as to make our intuitions intelligible, that is, to bring them under concepts."

2

Observations Concerning the Tübingen "Axiom" Then and Now

"That there must exist within the church an analogy to what within the state is called public opinion"

— ABRAHAM PETER KUSTERMANN —

There must have been a mild sensation when Pius XII (of all people), nearing the end of one of his many addresses in February, 1950, spoke of "public opinion." For all practical purposes he reintroduced the notion into the life of the church: "She [i.e. the church] would be lacking something in her life if public opinion were absent within her, an absence for which the clergy as well as the faithful are to blame."[1] The perceptive mind of Karl Rahner quickly seized on this papal exhortation for careful examination for the sake of "free speech in the church" within the realm of Catholic Action.[2] Of course, Rahner knew perfectly well that this postulate or rather this postulated situation was nothing new in itself but that it was certainly new coming from the papal lips, a fact which seemed to break a long-standing ban on any such idea. But in his sorting through the evidence for the claim that "there has always been something like public opinion in the church,"[3] one misses any reference to the first and, in some respects, classic call for this in modern theology. This is found in 1819 in the *Kurze Einleitung in das Studium der Theologie*[4] by the then forty-two-year-old theologian at Tübingen, Johann Sebastian Drey (1777–1853).[5] Until evidence to the contrary is uncovered by further research on this theme in the history of theology, Drey may rightly be considered as the first person to advance this claim clearly and publicly. Many who know virtually nothing else about Drey and his work connect this "discovery" with his name.

This essay attempts (1) to describe the historical meaning, i.e. the intention and limits, of the position Drey takes, (2) to determine the intellectual and historical impetus at work in it, (3) to cast some light on its concrete critical effects, at least within the Tübingen theology, and (4) in light of the present to indicate the epochal changes of its range of application as well as, by way of example, some actual considerations which should be taken into account in explaining or, better, in "applying" the Drey maxim today.

I

The passage in which Drey formulates his claim in the text must be read with particular care because it holds several surprises and because the strands of his argument lead back to it as the literal center of his case even though they may not actually have begun there.

As mention has repeatedly been made, especially in #259, that there must exist within the church an analogy to what within the state is called public opinion, and as within the church this can only be the position taken by officially recognized teachers and writers, so finally an introduction to church government must provide guidelines as to how the church can support this channel of opinion and what the correct attitude ought to be toward it.

This is followed by the explanatory note:

> Church history demonstrates that such a channel of opinion has always existed in the church. Explanation and inquiry by private scholars and authors always preceded the definitions of church doctrines, and most recommendations for improvements in the liturgy and in the church's discipline came not from the church's prelates but from zealous and wise private persons.[6]

(1) Drey introduces his position in this passage as the repetition of a claim which he has made several times before. But the phrase "public opinion" is not to be found in the preceding 229 pages of his book, not even in #259 to which he refers.

(2) Thus, at the point of its explicit statement, Drey's position remains somewhat axiomatic, propositional, even a bit terse. So the strands of his argument must first be accepted independently of the concrete assertion in #342.

(3) What is lacking—rather surprisingly in view of the emphatic tone—is any appeal to a theological reason why there must be within the church something like public opinion.

(4) And finally one ought to note what is here explicitly claimed: not for the actual and precise public opinion within the church, but rather for an *Analogon*, an analogy to what is elsewhere, in the state, called public opinion.

Our subsequent comments will not deal with these observations with equal weight or in this order. But they are *prima facie* important for us so that we do not impose exaggerated expectations from today's perspective on Drey's position in #342.

1. Since Drey does not actually use the phrase "public opinion" at any point prior to #342, speculation about what passages he could have had in mind in his statement there ("as mention has repeatedly been made") is fairly futile. All the more significant therefore is his own reference to #259 which is augmented in the context of #258 and #260.

> And in this we see the connection of science to Christian doctrine and to the church. Science gives ever-new stimulus to the development of Christian

doctrine and leads its mutable elements toward their final forms. Hence it labors on the church's behalf, since the impetus toward further developments and more precise conceptual formulation can only come from individuals, and before the final form of an idea can be reached, science must prepare the way. This is the role of science in the formation of the church's doctrine.[7]

In order to treat this passage systematically we must briefly recall that in the encyclopedic style[8] of *KE* Drey divides theology into three branches:[9] (1) historical theology (or historical propaedeutic) with subdivisions of biblical study, exegesis, and historical theology (the history of Christianity or church history); (2) scientific theology (or systematic theology) subdivided into foundational studies and special science; and (3) practical theology. Each of these three branches is structured and characterized by the methodological perspective with fundamental consequences for their function in and relation to the whole of theology. Historical theology (or historical propaedeutic)—the general historical construction of the data of Christianity (#218)—follows the pragmatic historical method typical in a historical discipline (#218, 312); it deals *more historico* with attested historical data, events, and texts (#109). Only scientific theology[10]—the scientific presentation of the essence of Christianity (#229), the internal construction of Christianity as a necessary phenomenon (#312)—employs the scientific method in the fullest sense (#312), and only its study is "the scientific study of theology in its proper and most rigorous sense" (#309). And finally, practical theology—limited to "how to apply what is already known (from other disciplines)" (#380)—deals merely with guidelines or skills or suggestions (#353, 365, 380, 388) with no pretense to scientific rigor.

With #259 Drey turns his attention to the levels of argument in scientific theology and in the statements of this paragraph and—to put it in a nutshell—gives the germ of his notion of the development of theological doctrines or the development of ecclesial dogmas (#255–263). It is apparent that at this point in very large part he is in agreement with Schleiermacher.[11]

This notion will not be further discussed here.[12] We will simply accept it so that we can describe the various interactions which Drey subsumes under the term "public opinion" (or phrases analogous to it):

The fluid (not yet "defined") element in Christian doctrine is called "opinion."

> And when disagreement on it still reigns among scholars within the church, it is called an *opinion of a school* or a *theological opinion.* ... For this reason and because it is characteristic of Christian doctrine to unfold itself ever more clearly and the theologian as a teacher of his church is called to participate in this, opinions are not merely accidental but necessary subjects of investigation and study in dogmatics and moral theology.[13]

This means that interaction has to do with some disagreement with reference to doctrine. The interacting subjects are "the church" on the one hand and on the other theological researchers and teachers, i.e. professional theological scholars both as individuals and as an institutional body ("science"). The objective motivation for the interaction is the vocation of theologians to collaborate toward ever-greater clarity in the elucidation of doctrine (from mere opinion to dogma), at least by way of preparation (#260). Controlling the process, if one can so describe it, is beyond strategic and deliberate management; it lies in the straight-forward confrontation of opinions which are in conflict or are moving toward clarity; this is, in that sense, "necessary," a demand placed on the actors, as it were, "a must."

So in the first place what Drey includes in his insistence on public opinion in the church turns out to be much narrower than his "axiom" seems to mean at first glance. Its intended theological meaning has to do primarily with dogmatic development in the strict sense and secondarily with further growth in theological knowledge in the broad sense (between the extremes of the heterodoxy of free-wheeling speculation and the hyperorthodoxy of traditionalism (#260)). The designated subjects in the interaction are on the one side exclusively the members of the "republic of letters," i.e. individual and corporate participants in the community of scientific conversation (*ordo theologorum in universitate litterarum*). The purely "analogical" character of the case is further underscored by the fact that Drey offers no apparent way of making it work at this point, i.e. he suggests no effective or even preliminary rules for this conversation.[14] Even though he ascribes to theologians a strikingly strong role, in fact, a really creative role, the delineation of "public opinion" remains somewhat vague: it is described as a particular sphere of activity for theological experts—but in this general sense, of course, this has always been a "given" in the church (#342).

2. In #342 we find ourselves on a quite different plane of discussion. We are actually working in the methodologically and functionally quite differently organized context of *practical theology*. To be able to grasp the way Drey formulates his case and its fundamental direction, we must turn to the note to #342:

> Church history demonstrates that such a channel of opinion has always existed in the church. Explanation and inquiry by private scholars and authors always preceded the definitions of church doctrines, and most recommendations for improvements in the liturgy and in the church's discipline private persons.[15]

The striking points about #342, taking the text and note together, may be briefly summarized:

(1) The sphere of public opinion (or an "analogy" to it) has always been a fact in the church. So decidedly is it part of the church's life that it actually must exist ("*geben müsse*"). Thus far the *quaestio facti*.

(2) The discussion is not concerned with a new "discovery" which it tries to secure within the church; rather, it is clearly aimed in a totally different direction: as part of a practical-theological "introduction" to the subject of "church govern-

ment," it has as its goal the establishment of "guidelines as to how the church can support this channel of opinion and what the correct attitude toward it ought to be." And so the *quaestio iuris* is raised both in regard to a guaranteeing of a sphere of public opinion within the church by church government[16] as well as in regard to the *institutional self-organization* of church government (its self-restraint and self-limitation) in relation to this sphere. This means that Drey here does not in fact call for public opinion within the church—it can be taken as an already-existing fact —but for an unequivocally regulated guarantee and respect for it from church leadership.

(3) While "definitions of church doctrines" are certainly included as *quaestiones disputatae* within the domain of public opinion or developing opinion, concentration on them is broadened to include "recommendations for improvements in the liturgy and in the church's discipline." Discussion in the domain of public opinion thus include questions *de fide, de cultu,* and *de disciplina*—whereby, especially under the last heading, a wide range of issues is opened.

(4) Specifically mentioned as bearers of public opinion are: official teachers (of theology), authors, private scholars (see #342 and 344). This means that necessarily we are dealing with the class of professional theologians who can be corporately described as "science." Its membership remains somewhat vaguely defined, however, thanks to the fact that the scientific status of "authors" and "private scholars" who do not possess the status of a *professor ordinarius publicus* must be determined *ad hoc* from case to case. Participation in forming public opinion determines one's qualifications to do so.

The question of the theological issues involved in Drey's position which has still been open until now is answered in the following paragraph of *KE* (#343)—in connection with the fundamental principle which Drey formulates on the subject of church government:

> ... church government neither can nor ought to suppress the activity and influence of individuals which are addressed to the church at large through the spoken or written word, because it would at the same time deprive itself of the devotion and insight inherent in the mass of its members. But neither can a church government acknowledge or admit an influence acting in this way which is not directed toward preserving and edifying the church.... Thus there ought to be maxims for church governance such that free expression of religious zeal and insight can exist and yet the church can restrain through appropriate means the dangers which might possibly be incurred by this.[17]

Thus, the theological reason for the necessity of something like public opinion in the church according to Drey is the priority of *productive* creative elements in "devotion" (religious living, "practical religious life" [#344]) and "insight" (*intellectus fidei*) to any *regulative* control by ecclesiastical administration. It is more important to allow these productive creative forces to find expression; what is at stake is their ability to become effective, to be able to advance ideas "which are actually introduced" (#342*). And even if Drey thinks he knows how properly to safeguard church government's agencies for "preserving and edifying the church" (#343),[18] these agencies must never trespass beyond their self-limitations to the detriment of public opinion which requires "that free expression of religious zeal and insight can exist" (ibid.).

Of course there are also guidelines for the other side, as can be readily seen from Drey's closing comment about the way the participants are to deal with one another—with something like a presumption of friendship: "In all the instances mentioned, the more clearly those charged with the supervision of the church and the channels of public opinion are aware of their roles and the limits of their work, the more harmoniously and peacefully will developments proceed in the church" (#344).[19]

In summary we can say: Drey's famous position in #342 does not really require, as is generally thought, the institutional realization of a long overdue option, public opinion within the church. Rather, it is an appeal with reference to church government (a) to take seriously the existence in fact and the legitimacy in principle of this domain (instead of treating it off-handedly or even ignoring it), (b) to acknowledge it openly as an essential theological and ecclesiological reality (instead of letting it remain indefinite), and (c) voluntarily to adopt a clearly defined relationship to it (instead of maintaining an imaginary absolute supremacy).

II

This next section is largely a series of observations. It does not pretend to offer any new perspectives but rather deals with the general "common sense" within which the slogan "public opinion" is to be understood against the background of spiritual and social movement of that time. It is simply a reminder that Drey's position on the issue of "public opinion within the church" does not advocate a system of suffrage on matters theological or ecclesial but is rather the outcome of his involvement in a particular culture and mind-set[20] which was to become characteristic of modernity viewed as a whole but about which many in theology and the church of Drey's day harbored reservations which encountered definite opposition in still wider circles after 1830.

— 1 —

Only after the *Aufklärung* can one really speak of a "public" in Germany,[21] that is of a self-reflective group- or class-consciousness which is publicly articulated in cultural, social, political and literary expressions and through which the formative process of a public in the customary sense was initiated. The first instances and likewise the most powerful bearers and propagators of this style of thought were the various "learned" associations, societies, academies, lodges, etc. As the first representatives of a "public" in the sociological and intellectual sense they created a situation in which the ideas which developed in their midst had public importance and in this way provided a model "public forum" in its modern form. Their developing expertise and enhanced professionalism brought them into fruitful competition with the old universities which were in turn forced into field specialization and specialized professionalization (the institution of academic chairs within particular fields); they also became the driving force behind the founding of new universities.

A parallel movement developed within the relatively public forum of the literary world with its manageable circle of individual writers and pundits. (Remnants of these lived on in the famous "salons.") The more individuals this movement in literature and life encompassed, the more rapidly and broadly it spread, the greater its growth and momentum became, and the more communal power and intellectual and social influence it gained, the more it produced new forms: precisely those vast new realities, "the public" and "the society," within which ideas, needs, criticisms, etc., were publicly articulated and propagated. "Publicly" here means literarily. Publication of particular ideas sought "publicity" within the "public." Publicly expressed opinion aimed by means of the increasingly present public at the formation of "public opinion." Each step in this direction was an attempted act of emancipation from dictatorial authority, mere custom and external interference. Not unjustly has the *Aufklärung* been regraded as the heyday of "thinking for oneself."

This process had liberating effects on still other planes. It showed how state and society are to be distinguished as two different realities, distinct in both form and goal. To the measure in which critical self-consciousness developed, the concrete dissociation of state and society was carried through. The absolutist feudal state was gradually transformed into the enlightened absolute state—until finally the point came at which "enlightened" society would no longer brook any absolute regime and instead raised constitution questions with democratic insistence.

Thus "public opinion" (first translated into German from the French *opinion publique* in 1790[22]) was not an "innocent," or neutral concept but a politically shaped one: "as a measure of progress whose direction is itself determined by public opinion, it [i.e. public opinion] asserts the autonomy of the mind of the time."[23] In 1819 it was still a concept which carried connotations of the *Aufklärung*, especially connotations critical of authority. It was derived from civil society and was then taken over into the church or theological discussion; it stood for open and uncensored speech and insisted especially on the authority of concrete reality. Did Johann Sebastian Drey employ it in spite of or precisely because of this double-edged quality? That Drey was somehow unaware of it is simply unimaginable. Does this perhaps explain his speaking of it as an "analogy," which carries something of a saving conditional quality about it? But then what could it mean— *mutatis analogaliter mutandis*—that would actually be so different from it?

— 2 —

As is well known, the concept of the "public" gained precise specificity both philosophically and politically thanks to Immanuel Kant; one could even say he made it immediately familiar intellectually. His provocative transformation of the prevailing terminology was significant both for the further understanding of the issue itself and for the self-understanding of intellectuals:

> The public use of one's reason must always be free, and it alone can bring about enlightenment among men.... By the public use of one's reason I understand the use which a person makes of it as a scholar before the reading public. Private use I call that which one may make of it in a particular civil post or office which is entrusted to him.[24]

> The possession of reason morally entails the responsibility of its public use. For only public use can make reason universally binding. Thus public opinion, publicity, becomes a social and political force.[25]

Kant specifically goes out of his way repeatedly (and ironically) to refer to theology's situation in this regard, especially its institutionalized form in a university, the theology faculty.[26] Drey's position can be seen as a late but responsive echo of this. Its concentration on the professional elite particularly suggests its unbroken descent from the spirit of Kant.

— 3 —

And finally we recall in a general way the whole movement of the "Catholic *Aufklärung*,"[27] with whose directions and maxims (contrary to all the denials and mystifications of so many interpreters) Drey demonstrates that he is in full and deliberate continuity, at least in his early period—not, to be sure, with its radical elements, but with the "mainstream" of its activity in southwest Germany where its symbolic figure is the last vicar general of Constance, Ignaz Heinrich Freiherr von Wessenberg (1774–1860). Nevertheless, one cannot simply ascribe to Drey indiscriminately or by presumption or *per analogiam* every trait of this movement in its contrasting homogeneity. Yet it is legitimate to say that Drey is to be understood *a limine* within the intentions and aspirations of this thought-world rather than within that of its opposition (the "anti-*Aufklärung*").

This connection does not contradict the fact that, on questions of the form of the state or of society, Drey decisively rejected any thoughts of constitutionalism, democracy and popular sovereignty.[28] The pre-democratic form of society was presumed by him basically without question. In this model the only ones invited to collaborate in the realm of public opinion were those "who had something to say"— Drey presumed basically those with professional scientific credentials achieved by education. So too in the church. Even if (but there is no unambiguous evidence for this) in his early days Drey should have had considered the possibility of admitting the laity into the ecclesiastical synods which he wanted—opportunities for the formation of ecclesial public opinion *par excellence*—he subsequently rejected it as an instance of "popular rule."[29] Neither in 1819 nor at any time thereafter did it ever enter Drey's horizon that public opinion might be determined statistically or demographically and that it would become a stage in the democratic formation of opinion. The position which he put forward had a totally different point in a totally different kind of world. These socio-historical limits to his "axiom" must be fully appreciated; otherwise in other contexts we may end up separating mental attitudes from the objective dynamism of historical change.

III

Were we now to give a more general sketch of how publicness and a total openness to the realm of the public came to be seen as characteristic of the theological work of Johann Sebastian Drey or that of the early Tübingen theologians as a group, or what their contribution was to the public character, public weight, and public standing of theology in the scholarly world and in the church, we would have to try to summarize a great deal of what has been accomplished in the scholarship of the last twenty-five years, most of which has been a stirring corrective to the picture which had previously been prevalent.[30] But that would be merely an expanded illustration added to the explanation of Drey's position in its actual sense, which is that Drey demanded from the government of the church a legitimately guaranteed space for public opinion within the church and respect for those factors outside the church which are connected under the rubric of public opinion. So we will finally turn to an instance of conflict in this regard, which we are grateful to Rudolf Reinhardt for bringing to our attention.

To understand this, we should first note that if Drey viewed scientific theologians (i.e. *professores ordinarii publici* of theology) and "authors" as the bearers of public opinion within the church, the point of founding the *Theologische Quartalschrift* in 1819, two years after the inauguration of the Catholic theological faculty at Tübingen, becomes perfectly obvious.[31] For without ever making the *Theologische Quartalschrift* the faculty's formal organ, the Tübingen theologians created for themselves a forum in which they could actively publish undisturbed in their field. Thus, according to Drey's criteria, they were bearers of public opinion in a double capacity: not only did their opinion have public weight within the church thanks to their scholarly competence, but it could "publicly" be made public at any time—inside and outside the church.

From this arose conflict, when in the fourth issue of the second volume of the *Theologische Quartalschrift* a review of two books on celibacy appeared, in which the reviewer[32] did not disguise his own criticism of mandatory celibacy for Catholic priests.[33] The response by the local vicar general to this publication, described as a "pastoral letter," was a critique of the "whole direction which various articles of this periodical especially take," i.e. a general critique of the *Theologische Quartalschrift* and its editors. On the particular issue at hand the superior of the Rottenburg church at the time remarked:

> It must seem very strange to us to find even attacks ... on church superiors in it and to find this defended by the claim that ..., as it is put, they 'do not enter into a serious discussion on this topic.'... Since provocative statements of this sort seem especially detrimental to good relations with church superiors and ecclesiastical authority, we scarcely know how to reconcile them with the attention and respect owed to these, lack of which can only have very harmful effects on the lower clergy.[34]

This means that church authority protested against the "presumption" of questioning it "from below" in a published forum on its handling of a particular issue (in this case, measures for the abolition of mandatory celibacy) and regarded this a serious insubordination.

As the acting dean of the faculty in 1821 Drey was charged with answering this. I do not cite from his drafts his explicit position on the celibacy question but only his lucid explanation of the issue of public opinion:

> We thought that now and then a free statement about specific issues, even in opposition to the authorized positions of church authority, ... need not be anxiously suppressed because, always so long as it is well founded, this has been permitted to ecclesiastical authors from time immemorial and must remain so. Rather than offer many instances, ... let us recall only the courageous rebuke which Saint Bernard unhesitatingly hurled at all the abuses in the church and even at the behavior of popes.... Yet they did not regard the one who rebuked them as their enemy, nor did they think that their authority was undermined by him (but rather pondered and made good use of what he said and wrote). We are certainly far from claiming any parallel to this. But we might ask the freedom to ground on this example the right of theologians and writers on ecclesiastical matters to express their opinions on every issue of church discipline and, when something strikes them as unsatisfactory, to do so (freely and) openly.... What means would remain to alert individual church authorities to defects and abuses, what external prod to amend them, if there were not the courageous voice of the writer on church matters, if public opinion did not find utterance within the church through him! His obligations keep the priest engaged in pastoral work; he has little time and often little gift for thinking about more general church affairs and certainly no vocation to express his criticism of matters once decided for it is precisely his responsibility to put them into practice. But because of the nature of his vocation the theologian has to investigate everything which is done in the church, to examine and probe it. He must thus also possess the right to express the result of his examination, and in this especially his position as a teacher and not merely a subordinate minister in the church serves him well. His free criticism cannot infringe on the respect due to church authority when everything he has to regard as good and proper he acknowledges that he has received from it and can effect only through it. He respects them to the point that he submits to them [!] even when they show no respect for his efforts. But even in this case he will still regard it as his obligation to let his voice be heard.[35]

Drey's response exactly reflects the considerations and guidelines which he had laid out in *KE* #342–344: there is (and always has been) public opinion in the church; it is free to deal with questions of church discipline (certainly in the case in question, i.e. celibacy); its motives are constructive, not destructive; church authority *per se* has an obligation to pay attention to it, especially in pressing questions, for many times it first opens authorities' eyes (particularly in the absence of other official or institutionally regulated opportunities for consultation such as, for example, synods); its bearers are (professional) theologians and writers, and they alone have the "vocation" for it; knowledge of grave problems justifies and obliges their public stance vis-a-vis authority for the sake of remedy; in this role they are in no way subordinated to church authority, not simply "ministers in the church,"[36] there is to be no trespassing between these competencies and responsibilities ("friendly relations"). So far, so good. But with its remarkable new perspective the final sentence of the quotation from Drey's response demands further attention; if church authority gives no respect to carefully expressed public opinion, there is cause for dissent. Expression of public opinion is accordingly not prohibited; the burden of responsibility for its decision to dissent rests on church authority then.

There is no known counter-reply from the Rottenburg church authorities in this case. But with it the lines were clearly—but also fundamentally—drawn on both sides in the microcosm of Rottenburg-Tübingen relations. This meant that one had to await further clarification from both sides in subsequent history. In this particular case, which seems to exemplify the general conflict on the question, the great competency of theology—conceded, or perhaps better, confessed even by church authority—demonstrated itself, clearly and definitely establishing "the theologian as organic leader"[37] or a new "paradigm of theological responsibility."[38]

IV

It would be tempting to make this conflict the hermeneutic and procedural key to the 180-year history of the Tübingen faculty, which really is to some degree a story of conflict, or to list what the faculty has contributed since 1817 to the expression or cultivation of public opinion within the church. One might quickly move to Johann Adam Möhler's plea for civil support of theologically qualified education on the Tübingen model, which, although it was not induced by the faculty, did express its consensus at the time,[39] and perhaps conclude for the moment with Peter Hünermann's initiative in founding the Europäische Gesellschaft für Katholische Theologie (1989) "as a forum for meeting and scholarly discourse."[40] This would be an important work which should perhaps be done at length. But we do not intend to lose sight of the fact of Johann Sebastian Drey's position and his actual point, while following out a long historical tale. Rather, we will point out the issue's systematic and ecclesiological *nervus rerum* in brief theses by way of five notes with a contemporary bearing.

—1—

Drey requires from the government of the church—today we would say from the various levels of church authority and ecclesiastical magisterium—the unequivocal guarantee governed by clear rules for public opinion in the church as expressed in theology and the institutionalized self-commitment of church government to give it hearing.

While far from imputing simple repression to ecclesiastical magisterium (either in practice or in intention), the *unequivocal character* of this guarantee still remains open to question with good reason. On the one hand, for example, it seems emphatic in the generally positive evaluation given theology and its role in Pope John Paul II's two addresses of November 15 and 18, 1980, in Cologne and Altötting,[41] while on the other it certainly seemed, at least to a broad spectrum of observers, to be marginalized once again in the "Instruction on the Ecclesial Calling of the Theologian" from the Congregation for the Doctrine of the Faith (May 24/ June 26, 1990). One voice seems to drown out the other, one document to undercut another document. Rather than an unequivocal character, equivocalness holds sway—consciously and calculatedly? Such equivocalness serves to prolong the old painful history between ecclesial teaching-office and theological scholarship *ad Kalendas Graecas*, as even the unending discussion of the aforementioned Instruction demonstrates.[42] Rather than this "carrot-and-stick" approach, serious people would much prefer a clearly defined and honest procedure.

—2—

Second, Drey implicitly requires self-restraint on the part of church authority with respect to public opinion responsibly expressed in theology. As far as clearly documented and procedurally achieved rules of process are concerned, we are still only in the beginning stages. There is no lack of clearly defined limits to the competency of theology in its relation to the teaching office as given by the teaching office; what is missing is reliable and verifiable self-limitation of the competence of the ecclesiastical teaching office in its relation to theological scholarship. That there are limits which are *de facto* respected seems due more to the concrete institutional situation of theology (whether existing under civilly guaranteed scholarly freedom, or whether functioning in independent or church-controlled universities) than to the magisterium's self-understanding. Attempts in this direction *a parte theologiae* are still treated today as presumptuous violations of the limits of competency. But is not an initiative in this regard *a parte regiminis ecclesiae* long overdue in order to avoid the danger of such violations of competency by providing reliable self-restraint?

—3—

In a situation in which public opinion becomes ineffective, i.e. in situations of dissent, Drey accepted the *rebus-sic-stantibus* rule to the effect that theology's possible courses of action have been exhausted. But in his view even in this case further expression is not forbidden to public opinion. It will steadfastly continue to make its voice heard.

But precisely this right is contested at present and even denied to dissent by "church governance."[43] It is falsely described as propagandizing and agitation. This may be so in particular instances, all the more concrete dissent is an individual matter. But this description scarcely holds as a general rule.

To clarify the situation by an example, two questions arise concerning this process of convincing the ecclesiastical teaching office "not by 'pressure' but by argument":[44] (a) why, in a one-sided explanation of the question of dissent entirely controlled by one party (church authority), should the maintenance of a particular opinion by the other party (theology) be publicly labelled as little or nothing more than illegitimate "pressure"? (b) why must it be taken for granted *a priori* that in a case when a position rooted in public opinion is rejected by the governance of the church that this position had inadequate arguments (or even none at all) on its side? One might test one's responses to these questions—only by way of an example—in the current debate about the ordination of women.

Living with Drey's seemingly rather "tentative" principle is, of course, more difficult for the party which has to reply to dissent, although public opinion can see perfectly well that it does not have the better arguments (or any arguments) on its side. But why should church authority be absolved from that responsibility *a priori* (or even be able to wrap itself in silence)?

—4—

The notion of "public opinion" has a more manifold different cultural, functional, social, and political meaning in the age of democracy, mass-media, the information superhighway, the internet, etc., than it did in Drey's time. His confinement of the notion to a narrowly defined functional or educational elite is irreversibly gone. But now as then the reality itself has its actuality, its right and its weight. No one "escapes public opinion." Drey's sharp division of theological competencies, however understandable in his time, now seems foreign from the perspective both of society and the sociology of knowledge. Even if one maintains with him a normative concept of scientific theology in the strict sense, today many fiery tongues—of scientific understanding of faith—flicker over the members of the church. Today many participate as a matter of course in the varied debates among the many theologians. This is one aspect of the situation.

Another aspect is that classically the theology of faith has always had within its armory its own—*sit venia verbo*, "analogical"—doctrine of "the sense of faith among the faithful" (*sensus fidelium*) which for many different reasons has currently taken deep root within our culture and may possibly grow into a strong tree.[45]

The much-bemoaned divorce between the church and secular culture should provide the stimulus to grasp both strands at their points of compatibility and develop these into an effective culture of participation within the church. The social forms of the church have always been "of this world" and are always taken from it *realiter*. When it tries to render the standards of another world appealing, they should at least not be less appealing than those drawn from this world.

—5—

What Drey actually wrote about was "an analogy to what within the state is called public opinion." He did not offer a new notion by way of analogy; nevertheless it is clear what he meant. He only partially sketched it out; to understand it fully we must draw out the further connotations of this notion introduced by him and taken over from the realm of public discourse.

It is a tried and true gambit, even in the church, to dismiss some plea on the basis of the inadequacy of the conceptual language in which it is couched. This was the case - to take one last example - of the so-called *Kirchenvolksbegehren* ("Desiderata of the People of the Church") in Austria, Germany, and other countries (1995). As a matter of fact, the term "Volksbegehren" was drawn from Austrian and German constitutional law. The objection raised to this usually runs that the church is not the state, nor is it a democracy, and so one cannot apply concepts drawn from those realms to this one (i.e., in the church); this conceptual transference (= conceptual confusion) undercuts the whole issue from the start, etc.

Prescinding from the fact that the church would be pretty well speechless had it always prohibited such borrowing of ideas and language, was not an *analogous* concept introduced both stylistically and intentionally with the phrase *Kirchenvolksbegehren*, Desiderata of the People *of the Church*, in contrast to Johann Sebastian Drey, so careful about his words and sensitive to nuances, who could not manage to do in his day?

As long as the Christian is a citizen of two worlds, and as long as the representative of one of these two worlds acts so that he must experience this even in trivial matters, often needlessly and without just cause, purely out of unthinking habit, it is no surprise that the Christian turns with greater understanding and assurance to ordinary public discourse than to the sacrosanct and veiled formulae and rhetoric of hierarchically fixed linguistic norms. No more criticism should be levelled at such a person than would have been levelled at Johann Sebastian Drey.

NOTES

1. Pius XII, Address (in French) of February 17, 1950, to participants in the international congress of Catholic journalists, *Acta Apostolicae Sedis* 42 (1950): 251–257 at 256.

2. Karl Rahner, "Das freie Wort in der Kirche," in *Das freie Wort in der Kirche: Die Chancen des Christentums: zwei Essays* (Einsiedeln: Johannes Verlag, 1953), pp. 5–36, esp. pp. 5–9. See also Herbert Vorgrimler, "Öffentliche Meinung," in *Lexikon für Theologie und Kirche* 7, 2nd. ed. (Freiburg: Herder, 1962): 1118; also, Werner Post, "Offentliche Meinung, Öffentlichkeit," in *Sacramentum Mundi* 3 (Freiburg: Herder, 1969): 843–849.

3. Rahner, p. 15.

4. Johann Sebastian Drey, *Kurze Einleitung in das Studium der Theologie mit Rücksicht auf den wissenschaftlichen Standpunct und das katholische System* (Tübingen, 1819); reprint, ed. Franz Schupp (Darmstadt: Wissenschaftliche Buchgesellschaft, 1971). English translation: *Brief Introduction to the Study of Theology with Reference to the Scientific Standpoint and the Catholic System*, Notre Dame Studies in Theology 1, trans. Michael J. Himes (Notre Dame: University of Notre Dame Press, 1994). Hereafter in text and notes this is referred to as *KE*. All quotations are from the English translation.

5. For recent discussion, bibliography and literature, see *Revision der Theologie— Reform der Kirche: Die Bedeutung des Tübinger Theologen Johann Sebastian Drey (1777– 1853) in Geschichte und Gegenwart*, ed. Abraham Peter Kustermann, (Würzburg: Echter, 1994). Also, see Abraham Peter Kustermann, "Drey," in *Dictionary of Fundamental Theology*, ed. René Latourelle, (New York: Crossroad, 1994): 247–251, and by the same author, "Drey," in *Lexikon für Theologie und Kirche 3*, 3rd. ed. (Freiburg: Herder, 1995): 373f.

6. Drey, *KE* #342; Eng. trans, p. 157.

7. *KE* #259; Eng. trans., pp. 117f.

8. On this notion, see Wolfgang Ruf, *Johann Sebastian Dreys System der Theologie als Begründung der Moraltheologie*, Studien zur Theologie und Geistesgeschichte des Neunzehnten Jahrhunderts 7 (Göttingen: Vandenhoeck und Ruprecht, 1974); also, John E. Thiel, "J. S. Drey on Doctrinal Development: The Context of Theological Encyclopedia," *Heythrop Journal* 27 (1986): 290–305. Here we have not widely to deal with the intellectual roots of this notion as with the parallel idea in Schleiermacher or the later (significant) modifications which Drey introduced into it.

9. See especially Ruf, pp. 79–89.

10. See Franz Schupp, *Die Evidenz der Geschichte: Theologie als Wissenschaft bei J. S. Drey*, Veröffentlichungen der Universität Innsbruck 59 (Innsbruck: Österreichische Kommissionbuchhandlung, 1970); Wayne L. Fehr, *The Birth of the Catholic Tübingen School: The Dogmatics of Johann Sebastian Drey*, American Academy of Religion Academy Series 37 (Chico, California: Scholars Press, 1981), pp. 117–176; Bradford E. Hinze, *Narrating History, Developing Doctrine: Friedrich Schleiermacher and Johann Sebastian Drey*, American Academy of Religion, Academy Series 82 (Atlanta, Georgia: Scholars Press, 1993), pp. 162–177.

11. Karl-Heinz Menke agrees with this, "Definition und spekulative Grundlegung des Begriffs 'Dogma' im Werke Johann Sebastian Dreys (1777–1853)," *Theologie und Philosophie* 52 (1977): 182–214 at 188f.; so too do all other writers on this issue to the present time. In this connection see also Nico Schreurs, "J. S. Drey en F. Schleiermacher aan het beginn van de fundamentele theologie," *Bijdragen* 43 (1982): 251–288, and Bradford E. Hinze, "Johann Sebastian Drey's Critique of Friedrich Schleiermacher's Theology," *Heythrop Journal* 37 (1996): 1–23.

12. See Schupp, pp. 26ff.; also, John E. Thiel, *Imagination and Authority: Theological Authorship in the Modern Tradition* (Minneapolis: Fortress Press, 1991), pp. 79–85; idem, "Naming the Heterodox: Interconfessional Polemics as a Context for Drey's Theology," in Kustermann, ed., *Revision der Theologie—Reform der Kirche*, pp. 114–139, esp. pp. 128–135; and Hinze, *Narrating History, Developing Doctrine*, pp. 185–203, esp. pp. 199–203.

13. *KE* #258; Eng. trans., p. 117.

14. Of course Drey's statements here have as their *Sitz im Leben* and from other perspectives their theological context the discussion in his time of the question of an (infallible) *iudex controversiarum* in matters of faith or doctrinal conflicts, as Drey learned from the Dogmatics of Engelbert Klüpfel (1733–1811); on this see Franz Xaver Bantle, *Unfehlbarkeit der Kirche in Aufklärung und Romantik: Eine dogmengeschichtliche Untersuchung für die Zeit der Wende vom 18. zum 19. Jahrhundert*, Freiburger Theologische Studien 103 (Freiburg, Basel, Vienna: Herder, 1976), pp. 544–546, 565f., and 568.

15. *KE* #342*; Eng. trans., p. 157.

16. According to *KE* #332–349 "church government" simply means what today we call the (hierarchical) leadership of the church. It may seem surprising (today) that pastoral theology in Drey's sense is also to teach an "introduction to church government" (#332), i.e. the theory of church leadership. On this point he is in agreement with Schleiermacher whose way of connecting these themes has been more closely studied; see Christoph Dinkel, *Kirche gestalten—Schleiermachers Theorie des Kirchenregiments*, Schleiermacher-Archiv, Bd. 17 (Berlin and New York: de Gruyter, 1996).

17. *KE* #343; Eng. trans., pp. 157f.

18. (1) "In its wisdom it must find means to prevent religious life from being stifled for lack of scientific clarity but in such a way that the scientific element does not undermine the religious element and that science does not adopt a profane orientation but remains directed to what is of practical import." (2) Because "its attention is fixed first and foremost on the fact and the importance of what is currently the case," "the new must appear as simply another form of the old and even error as an imperfect grasp of the truth which it must accompany." (3) "Finally, as instruction and discussion always go on within definite limits beyond which they become unintelligible and so must prove unproductive, an introduction to church governance has to designate ways by which ecclesiastical government can prevent the discussion's overstepping those limits in some manner into areas where it would be inappropriate and destructive" (*KE* #344; Eng trans., pp 158f.). It should be sufficiently clear that these guidelines of Drey's do not warrant any magisterial or jurisdictional absolutism and so are not to be cast in opposition to his basic line of argument. It will subsequently become still clearer that they must be hermeneutically examined in terms of their situation and (historical) context.

19. Eng. trans., p. 159.

20. Socio-historical and biographical information may be found in Abraham Peter Kustermann, "Vereine der Spätaufklärung und Johann Sebastian Drey: Ein Beitrag zum sozial- und ideengeschichtlichen Standort des Tübinger Theologen," *Ellwanger Jahrbuch* 28 (1979/80): 23–81; the following section in part draws upon this.

21. As a summary and selective background on this, see Jürgen Habermas, *Strukturwandel der Öffentlichkeit: Untersuchung zu einer Kategorie der bürgerlichen Gesellschaft*, 5th ed. (Neuwied and Berlin: Luchterhand, 1971); Manfred Riedel, "Gesellschaft, Gemeinschaft," in *Geschichtliche Grundbegriffe: Historisches Lexikon zur politisch-sozialen Sprache in Deutschland*, ed. Otto Brunner, Werner Conze, and Reinhart Koselleck (Stuttgart: Klett-Cotta, 1972 and subsequently), vol. 2 (1975): 801–862; idem, "Gesellschaft, bürgerliche," in ibid., 2:719–800; Lucian Hölscher, "Öffentlichkeit," in ibid., vol. 4 (1978): 413–467; Rudolf Vierhaus, "Zur historischen Deutung der Aufklärung: Probleme und Perspektiven," *Wolfenbütteler Studien zur Aufklärung* 4 (1977): 39–54; *Aufklärung und literarische Öffentlichkeit*, Edition Suhrkamp, ed. Christa Bürger et al. (Frankfurt am Main: Suhrkamp, 1980).

22. Hölscher, "Öffentlichkeit," pp. 448–450.

23. Ibid., p. 453.

24. Immanuel Kant, "Beantwortung der Frage: Was ist Aufklärung" (1783), in Immanuel Kant, *Werke in zehn Bänden*, ed. Wilhelm Weischedel (Darmstadt: Wissenschaftliche Buchgesellschaft, 1975), 5:53–61 at 55; Eng. trans. by Lewis White Beck, "What Is Enlightenment?" in Immanuel Kant, *On History*, ed. Lewis White Beck (Indianapolis and New York: The Library of Liberal Arts, Bobbs-Merrill, 1963), pp. 3–10 at 5.

25. Martin Honecker, "Öffentlichkeit," *Theologische Realenzyklopädie* 25 (1995): 18–26 at 19.

26. On this see esp. Karl-Heinz Crumbach, *Theologie in kritischer Öffentlichkeit: Die Frage Kants an das kirchliche Christentum*, Gesellschaft und Theologie: Systematische Beiträge 21 (Munich and Mainz: Kaiser Verlag/Matthias Grünewald Verlag, 1977). Very important for an interpretation of Drey specifically within the horizon of Kant's positions and placement of the questions is still the unpublished dissertation by Hermann Lohmann, *Die Philosophie der Offenbarung bei Johann Sebastian Drey* (Freiburg: Ph.D. dissertation, 1953).

27. See the multi-directional collection *Katholische Aufklärung—Aufklärung im katholischen Deutschland*, Studien zum 18. Jahrhundert 15, ed. Harm Klueting (Hamburg: Felix Meiner Verlag, 1993), as well as the excellent overview, rich in material, by Philipp Schäfer, "Literaturbericht zu 'Katholische Aufklärung,'" *Theologische Revue* 92 (1996): 89–106. As a general principle it is important to remember that in the beginning of the Tübingen faculty both from its inception in 1817 and in its earlier stage at Ellwangen (1812–1817) the theological *Aufklärung* was dominant; see Rudolf Reinhardt, "Die Friedrichs-Universität Ellwangen, 1812–1817: Vorgeschichte—Aufstieg—Ende," *Ellwanger Jahrbuch* 27 (1977/78): 93–115 at 94 and passim; idem, "Die Katholisch-Theologische Fakultät Tübingen im ersten Jahrhundert ihres Bestehens: Faktoren und Phasen der Entwicklung," in *Tübinger Theologen und ihre Theologie: Quellen und Forschungen zur Geschichte der Katholisch-Theologischen Fakultät Tübingen*, Contubernium 16, ed. Rudolf Reinhardt (Tübingen: J. C. B. Mohr (Paul Siebeck), 1977), pp. 1–42 at 19 and passim.

28. See the material in Kustermann, "Vereine der Spätaufklärung und Johann Sebastian Drey," p. 78, n. 269. For detailed discussion of Drey's ideas on the state and society see

Josef Rief, *Reich Gottes und Gesellschaft nach Johann Sebastian Drey und Johann Baptist Hirscher*, Abhandlungen zur Moraltheologie 7 (Paderborn: Ferdinand Schöningh, 1965), pp. 4f., 214–244, 314–321; see also Peter Hünermann, "Soziale und politische Orientierung des Katholizismus im Werk der älteren Tübinger Systematiker," in *Theologie und Sozialethik im Spannungsfeld der Gesellschaft: Untersuchungen zur Ideengeschichte des deutschen Katholizismus im 19. Jahrhundert*, Beiträge zur Katholizismusforschung, Reihe B: Abhandlungen, ed. Albrecht Langner (Munich: Ferdinand Schöningh, 1974), pp. 33–59 at 35–37.

29. For example in *Theologische Quartalschrift* 31 (1849): 684f. In general, for the ecclesiological views especially of the later Drey, see Raimund Lachner, *Das ekklesiologische Denken Johann Sebastian Dreys: Ein Beitrag zur Theologiegeschichte des 19. Jahrhunderts*, Europäische Hochschulschriften XXIII/280 (Frankfurt am Main, Berne, New York: Peter Lang, 1986).

30. On this, consult the summary listing of relevant theological-historical works by Anton van Harskamp, Abraham Peter Kustermann, Rudolf Reinhardt, Josef Rief, Max Seckler and Hubert Wolf which is appended to Kustermann, ed., *Revision der Theologie—Reform der Kirche*, pp. 340–344.

31. See Rudolf Reinhardt, "175 Jahre Theologische Quartalschrift—ein Spiegel Tübinger Theologie," *Theologische Quartalschrift* 176 (1996): 101–124.

32. *Theologische Quartalschrift* 2 (1820): 637–670. The customary anonymous reviewer was the pastoral theologian Johann Baptist Hirscher (1788–1865).

33. Rudolf Reinhardt, "Neue Quellen zu Leben und Werk von Johann Sebastian Drey: Dreys Antwort auf das 'Pastoralschreiben" des Rottenburger Generalvikars vom Jahre 1821," in Reinhardt, ed., *Tübinger Theologen und ihre Theologie*, pp. 117–166 esp. at 117–139 and 152–161. (pp. 152–161 present the text in its various forms; in what follows I cite from this [using Drey's second draft] without individual references.)

34. "Es mußte uns außerdem befremden, sogar Vorwürfe ... gegen die Vorsteher der Kirche darin zu finden und es diesen selbst zur Verantwortung auferlegt zu sehen, daß sie, wie es ... heißt 'auf eine ernstliche Berathung dieses Gegenstandes nicht eingehen'.... Wenn nun Anregungen dieser Art schon an sich den zarteren Verhältnissen zu den Kirchenvorstehern und kirchlichen Oberbehörden überhaupt zuwider scheinen, so wissen wir nur um so weniger dieselben mit der den Vorgesetzten schuldigen Achtung und Rücksicht zu vereinbaren, deren Ermangelung auch auf die übrige untergeordnete Geistlichkeit nicht anders als sehr nachteilig zurückwirken kann."

35. "Ein freyes Wort hier und da im einzelnen, selbst auch gegen Verwaltungsmaximen kirchlicher Behörden glaubten wir ... nicht ängstlich unterdrücken zu müssen; indem ein solches, wenn es nur gegründet ist, dem kirchlichen Schriftsteller von jeher erlaubt war und erlaubt bleiben muß. Statt vieler Beispiele ... wollen wir nur an den freymütigen Tadel erinnern, den der heilige Bernhard rücksichtslos gegen alle Mißbräuche in der Kirche und gegen das Betragen der Päpste selbst aussprach...; und dennoch hielten sie den Mann, der sie tadelte, nicht für ihren Feind, glaubten auch ihr Ansehen nicht durch ihn gekränkt (sondern erwogen und benützten, was er sagte oder schrieb). Wir sind weit entfernt damit eine Parallele ziehen zu wollen; aber die Freiheit möchten wir uns erbitten, auf das angeführte Beyspiel das Recht des Theologen und des kirchlichen Schriftstellers zu gründen, über alle Gegenstände der Kirchenzucht seine Meinung und, wo etwas in dieser sein Mißfallen erregt, auch dieses (frey und) unverhohlen ausdrücken zu dürfen.... Welches Mittel bliebe also den vereinzelten kirchlichen Oberbehörden, auf Mängel und Mißbräuche aufmerksam zu werden, welche äußere Veranlassung, dem abzuhelfen, wenn es nicht die freymütige Stimme des kirchlichen Schriftstellers, wenn es nicht die durch sie! ausgesprochene öffentliche Meinung in der Kirche wäre! Den Geistlichen in der Seelsorge beschäftigt sein Dienst; er hat wenig Zeit, oft auch wenig Geschick, über die allgemeineren kirchlichen Angelegenheiten nachzudenken, auf keinen Fall aber den Beruf, über das nun einmal Bestehende seine Kritik auszusprechen, denn seine Pflicht ist es, gerade dies zu üben. Der Theolog aber hat von Berufs wegen die Natur, alles dessen, was in der Kirche besteht, zu untersuchen, alles zu beweisen, und daher auch zu prüfen; es muß ihm also auch das Recht zustehen, das Resultat seiner Prüfung auszusprechen, worin ihm außerdem seine Stellung, daß er Lehrer und nicht bloß ausführender Kirchendiener ist, zugute kommt. Gegen die der kirchlichen Autorität schuldige Ehrfurcht kann auch seine freie Kritik nicht verstoßen, wenn er alles, was er als gut und zweckmässig vorschlagen zu müssen glaubt, durch sie genehmigt, nur durch sie ausgeführt wissen will. Er ehrt sie dadurch, daß er sich ihnen [!] unterwirft, wenn sie auf seine Vorschläge auch keine Rücksicht nehmen. Aber auch in diesem Falle wird er es noch immer für seine Pflicht erachten, seine Stimme abzugeben."

36. The term "minister of the church" ("Kirchendiener") occurs frequently in *KE* (e.g. #325, 351, 354ff.). It has nothing pejorative about it but rather refers in Drey's work to one occupying a practical church role such as pastor, parish priest, etc., a pastoral worker who as such is a kind of "subordinate officer in the church" (*KE* #364) and precisely by this dependence is to be distinguished from the "theologian," the scientific worker.

37. Hinze, *Narrating History, Developing Doctrine*, pp. 177ff.

38. Thiel, *Imagination and Authority*, p. 90 *inter alia*.

39. [Johann Adam Möhler,] "Ein Wort in der Sache des philosophischen Collegiums zu Löwen," *Theologische Quartalschrift* 8 (1826): 77–110 at 82, 84 and 110. See also Joachim Köhler, "Priesterbild und Priesterbildung bei Johann Adam Möhler (1796–1838): Ein Kommentar zu Möhlers kirchengeschichtlicher Antrittsvorlesung 'De seminariorum theologicorum origine et progressu' aus dem Jahre 1829," in Reinhardt, ed., *Tübinger Theologen und ihre Theologie*, pp. 167–196, esp. pp. 174–181.

40. See the *ET-Bulletin* 1 (1990) and subsequent issues.

41. See the texts in *Theologie und Kirche. Dokumentation*, ed. Sekretariat der Deutschen Bischofskonferenz, March 31, 1991, pp. 57–65 and 66–71.

42. See Peter Hünermann, ed., *Streitgespräch um Theologie und Lehramt. Die Instruktion über die kirchliche Berufung des Theologen in der Diskussion* (Frankfurt am Main: Knecht, 1991).

43. Max Seckler has recently contributed a piece which touches on this theme in a number of ways: "'Lehrer des Christentums im Namen der Kirche' (J.S. Drey): Über das Wesen, die Aufgabe und die Stellung der Theologie in der Kirche sowie über einige Aspekte des Dissensproblems," *Theologische Quartalschrift* 174 (1994): 1–16. In it the problem of dissent is addressed especially in response to Elmar Klinger ("Der Dissens—ein Prinzip der Evangelisierung," in *Fides quaerens intellectum: Beiträge zur Fundamentaltheologie*, ed. Michael Kessler, Wolfhart Pannenberg, and Hermann Josef Pottmeyer (Tübingen: Francke, 1992), pp. 210–221), although without reference to Drey's reply to his vicar general. It is critical to note that in the phrase cited in the title (which appears in *KE* #354) Drey is clearly and expressly referring to the "minister of the church" and precisely not to the "scientific" theologian whom Seckler discusses (see note 36).

44. Thus the Prefect of the Congregation for the Doctrine of the Faith, Joseph Cardinal Ratzinger, cited in Seckler, p. 13.

45. See, for example, Daniel J. Finucane, *Sensus Fidelium: The Use of a Concept in the Post-Vatican II Era*, Ph.D. dissertation, St. Louis University, 1993; Dietrich Wiederkehr, ed., *Der Glaubensinn des Gottesvolkes—Konkurrent oder Partner des Lehramts?*, Quaestiones Disputatae 151 (Freiburg, Basel, Vienna: Herder, 1994).

3

The Universal in the Particular

Johann Sebastian Drey on the Hermeneutics of Tradition

— JOHN E. THIEL —

Commentators on the theology of Johann Sebastian Drey long have recognized his ground-breaking understanding of tradition as a distinctive and important contribution to modern Catholic theology. Although he was much more interested in Johann Adam Möhler's account of a "living tradition," Josef Rupert Geiselmann readily acknowledged the influence of Drey on Möhler, and regarded Drey's theology of tradition as one of his rightful claims to the title of founder of the "Catholic Tübingen School."[1] More recently, Bradford E. Hinze has considered Drey's theology of tradition as an interpretive narrative that offered, and continues to offer, a significant resource to nineteenth- and twentieth-century theology.[2] Geiselmann and Hinze, though, are but earlier and later examples of the critical and constructive attention that has been paid consistently in the secondary literature to Drey's theology of tradition. Indeed, one would be hard pressed to find an interpreter of Drey's theology who does not consider tradition to be a central motif in his thought.

This paper will make a small contribution to a more nuanced understanding of Drey's theology of Catholic tradition by considering how it was informed by his hermeneutics and, more importantly, the hermeneutical theories of his contemporaries. Drey's earliest major work, *Kurze Einleitung in das Studium der Theologie* (1819),[3] presented a view of tradition, in which the ancient Vincentian, and to Drey the more recent Tridentine, stress on the universality of tradition was complemented by a stress on the particularity of tradition's truth that in turn rested on a theological anthropology especially visible in Drey's hermeneutics.

The Self in Tradition

Johann Sebastian Drey's place in the history of theology has been secured by his conception of ecclesial tradition as an organic reality, developing in time and culture. As a faithful Catholic thinker, Drey found it important to portray the tradition of the church as universal, as a tradition in which the unity of Catholic truth manifests itself in the faith of the church, and in its doctrines, practice, and worship. And in keeping with Catholic belief, Drey understands this historical unity to be an expression of the oneness of God and of the unity of the workings of the Spirit of God in history. Yet, Drey's conception of the universality of tradition embraces and fosters the view that its universality is consistent with its development, and that this development takes place in and through the particular, especially in the creative thoughts, words, and deeds of individuals.[4] This judgment suggests that an anthropology lies at the basis of Drey's theology of tradition, and that an understanding of it is a necessary first step toward a full appreciation of that theology.

The reader who searches Drey's *Kurze Einleitung* for an explicit treatment of theological anthropology completes the task empty-handed. None of the 388 paragraphs of the 1819 work is devoted specifically to the elaboration of a theological doctrine of the human person. The most obvious explanation for this absence of a developed anthropology in the *Kurze Einleitung* is that its encyclopedic presentation of method offers a formal perspective on the tasks of theology in which the delineation of particular theological *loci* is not the principal order of business. Yet, Drey's theological encyclopedia does manage to yield substantive discussion of several doctrines such as revelation, the church, authority, and tradition. Since anthropology is such a basic theme in any theological presentation, a closer investigation of any of these explicitly treated doctrines might reveal its underlying anthropological assumptions and so bring to thematic clarity what otherwise would only be suggested unthematically between the lines. As suggested above, Drey's general portrayal of the development of Christian tradition offers a promising vein to be mined for his anthropology, which, once set in relief, clarifies in turn his understanding of tradition.

If our search for Drey's theological anthropology in the encyclopedia must move from the general to the particular, then we would do well to begin with his understanding of the idea of the Kingdom of God, which he describes as "the highest idea of Christianity."[5] In Drey's judgment, the idea of the Kingdom of God derives its theological importance from its comprehensive character. "No concept, no doctrine, and indeed no other idea of Christianity may be named," he insists, "that would not be ranked under that idea, be subordinated to it, or derived from it."[6] The idea of the Kingdom of God as the universal manifestation of divine truth begins in Israel's expectation of the earthly reconciliation of nations and is refined in Christ's preaching of a heavenly kingdom whose moral dominion extends throughout the created universe. Drawing on Lessing's notion of revelation as the education of the human race, Drey portrays the incarnation as an epochal unfolding of the idea of the Kingdom of God in which "the mystery of the past has been disclosed, and [in which] now too the clarity of the present allows for a wider perspective into the future." For Drey, the idea of the Kingdom of God in its Christian form regards

> the decrees of God regarding humanity and the world that have been thought in the divine mind from all eternity [as] revealed and realizing themselves in sacred history, but only gradually and thus yet hidden from human meaning until the fullness of time, until the appearance of Christ who now enlightens those decrees, expresses them in determined concepts, and joins these concepts again to his own history.[7]

There is no sense in which Drey compromises the uniqueness of the Christ

event as God's definitive revelation in history. The eternal decrees of the divine
Spirit appear in the life and teaching of Christ with unprecedented clarity and
conviction, and in a manner that is normative for all times. And yet, Drey maintains,
the "gradually revealed and realized" decrees extraordinarily manifested in the person and work of Jesus Christ continue to be apprehended gradually and more fully
in the ongoing tradition of the church. In Drey's Catholic perspective, which he
defines in opposition to the Protestant Scripture principle, the authentic tradition of
the church is conceived as "a living objective appearance as the continuation of an
original fact."[8] Just as the history of Christianity for believer and unbeliever alike
has "a beginning, and a development as the continuation of the beginning,"[9] so
too does ecclesial tradition, though now only for those who see with the eyes of
faith, have a beginning and a development as the continuation of its beginning in
the eternal decrees of God. While he refuses to reduce the idea of the Kingdom of
God to its temporal dimensions, as though the *Reich-Gottes-Idee* could be conflated
with the tradition of the church, Drey makes every effort to appreciate the historical
richness of the idea as a concrete, revelatory, and progressive manifestation of the
divine will.

Were we to take Drey at his word that all Christian doctrines are latent in the
idea of the Kingdom of God, then we could expect to find an anthropology in the
grand sweep of this vision of an eternal providence utterly enmeshed in the temporal, a conception of God's relationship to the world that represents Drey's Catholic
response to the mechanistic worldview of Enlightenment Deism. In some respects,
the understanding of the self before God suggested by the *Reich-Gottes-Idee* is
rather traditional. The created self finds its meaning not primarily in relation to
nature, its own or the world's, but in relation to the divine nature that is the source
of all things, a view expressed in striking fashion in the encyclopedia's opening
passage: "All faith and all knowledge rests on the dimly felt or clearly known
assumption that everything finite that exists not only only has issued forth from an
eternal and absolute cause but also has its temporal being and life rooted in that
primal cause and is supported by it."[10] Yet Drey expounds this traditional claim for
the self's created dependence on the divine in an untraditional way by drawing on
the categories of transcendental philosophy and portraying, like Schleiermacher
before him, the experience of dependence as religion itself, and religion as an experience definitive of original consciousness.

The religious experience of dependence on God, Drey asserts, is "the original
revelation of God in the human spirit...."[11] This constitutive experience, no different in Drey's estimation from human nature itself, places the self so utterly in
relation to God that even personal freedom must be understood in the context of
this created dependence. The providential order of God's Kingdom may be an
objective reality, the way things truly are. But that Kingdom yet needs to be
brought to fruition in "the religious striving in the inner life of the human person" in
which the misuse of freedom is always a possibility and often an actuality. The self
encounters true freedom only in its own created dependence on God, a state present
to consciousness "as an impulse and a claim to a freely-willed submission." This
submission of the human will to the eternal decrees of God that themselves set the

boundaries of the Kingdom, shape its landscape, and proclaim its providential laws represents the faithfulness of the religious life attuned to the divine order. "The same boundedness to a complete ordering and reciprocity of all individuals in the eternal intelligence," Drey states, "proclaims itself in the human person as an impulse to a harmonious entry into that ordered whole."[12] Through this obedient freedom, "the human person becomes a master of the ego and egoism,"[13] and by doing so subjectively wills the objective necessity of God's love.

This understanding of the authentic self freely choosing the divine inevitability is the closest one comes in the pages of the *Kurze Einleitung* to an explicit theological anthropology. Drey's constructive reliance on the transcendental philosophy of his day leads him to conceive of the self's relation to God as a correspondence in mental acts in which human consciousness aligns itself with the divine consciousness. Had Drey culled his transcendental orientation from the work of Kant or Fichte, this conceptualization of how the idea of the Kingdom of God is realized in experience might very well have been described in a purely formal manner in which a timeless transcendental ego statically fathoms the eternal Transcendental Ego in and perhaps even as itself. But Drey's transcendental perspective was molded not by Kant or Fichte but by Schelling, for whom the ideality of the divine ideas is woven into the reality of time and the events of history. Due to the influence of Schelling, Drey can speak of the necessity of transcendental experience as yet in process and development, and of the idea of the Kingdom of God (and indeed all theological *Wissenschaft*) as both an eternal truth and a temporal *Verlauf*.

Drey's conception of development, and so his understanding of ecclesial tradition, is shaped by this Romantic anthropology of the created self mastering its propensity toward egoism and both freely and obediently choosing its actions in accord with the eternal decrees of God. Living tradition, for Drey, develops in both the belief and practice of the Church, as divine truth unfolds from moment to moment in and through the events, experiences, and actions that bring the eternal decrees of God to historical reality. Tradition presents the idea of the Kingdom of God in renewed, and yet renewable, clarity, as the developing faith and practice of the Church express and re-express the common life of believers in the course of its historical progress. At first glance, this attention to belief and moral action as the sphere of development might seem inordinately anthropocentric, as though human subjectivity, in its most recent act of faith or intention, offers the norm for the authenticity of developing tradition. To the contrary, Drey ascribes the vitality of tradition primarily to the Spirit of God whose love animates the universal religious life of the church, and thus its tradition. The Holy Spirit, in other words, is the very objectivity of tradition, though an objectivity developing in and through the common life of the faithful. For Drey, then, the life of the believer lived meaningfully in tradition is one that freely and obediently wills the life of the Spirit as it flourishes in the whole church. The self-centered ego vitiates that objective and Spirit-filled truth either "by deviation from it or by lagging behind it," the latter a "consequence of the expiring activity of the (religious) principle in its progressive development."[14]

And yet, this subjugation of the self to the living tradition does indeed presuppose and depend on the free belief and action of each member of the Church, which contribute to the unfolding truth of the Spirit. From the perspective of the eternal decrees of God, tradition moves with inexorable necessity, the gradual manifestation of the Kingdom in the life of the church meeting every divine expectation. But from the perspective of historical faith, the twists and turns in the development of tradition often present themselves as causes for wonder, and the moment yet to appear remains shrouded in a mystery whose hiddenness is only slowly revealed in the unfolding life of the Christian community.

Reconstructing the Author's Meaning: Intellectual and Textual Influences on Drey's Hermeneutical Principle

For Drey, then, the truth of the tradition is eventful, and happens as each believer cooperates with the divine Spirit to realize the common life that tradition is, a stance Drey articulates most clearly in the *Kurze Einleitung* in his discussion of the hermeneutical work and responsibility of the theologian. In some respects, Drey's discussion of the vocation of the theologian offers a more developed, albeit indirect, treatment of theological anthropology and its relationship to tradition.

While all members of the church contribute to the development of tradition, and thus to the concrete realization of the *Reich-Gottes-Idee*, theologians have a special role to play in this process. Drey assumes that theologians will possess all the formal skills necessary for the exercise of their vocational responsibility, such as intelligence, good scholarly judgment, a capable memory, and expressive ability.[15] Yet, the most indispensable talent for the theologian lies in what Drey calls "the sense for the holy, the religious sense."[16] This personal predisposition, which Drey understands in analogy to genius, so orients the theologian to the divine that all other capacities, understandings, and imaginative acts are drawn into the ambit of its utterly religious concern. This talent flourishes in every theological endeavor, but especially in the contributions the theologian makes to the development of doctrine. As the divine ideas unfold in the life of the church, it is the power of the religious sense that recognizes the holy amidst the profane, and brings the animated continuity of tradition to what otherwise would be only a lifeless chronicle of past beliefs. This act of recognition is the discernment Drey expects the theologian to be able to make of the present faith of the church considered as "a movement" (*ein Bewegliches*),[17] as a development through which the seeds of truth planted in the soil of contemporary ecclesial experience may one day blossom as time-honored orthodoxy. And this act of bringing the life of tradition to the lifeless reception of the past is the imaginative interpretation Drey believes the theologian particularly qualified to make and without which the vitality of tradition, and so tradition itself, would cease to exist.

Drey understands this act of transforming the dead past into the living present as a process of *Nachconstruiren*, a hermeneutical reconstruction in which the theological discernment of the present movement of the tradition is followed by the theologian's creative efforts to show the present's continuity with the tradition's fixed orthodoxy and to animate the meaningfulness of the past for the present life of the church. The religious sense governs the theological work of *Nachconstruiren*, an activity that Drey understands in analogy to biblical interpretation and which he delineates in the *Kurze Einleitung* under the heading of *"Biblische Hermeneutik."* "The interpreter," he suggests,

> must place himself entirely in the position of his author, transform himself (sich...verwandeln), so to speak (so zu sagen), into the author, and then construct anew what the author originally produced. This is called reconstruction (nachconstruiren). Thus, the calling of the interpreter to his task lies in the ability to transform himself into a foreign writer....[18]

Just as the exegete imaginatively draws the spirit from the letter of the biblical text, so too does the theologian imaginatively draw the spirit from the letter of tradition.[19] Indeed, one might go so far as to say that this hermeneutical application of the religious sense explains in greater detail not only how the theologian interprets past dogmas but also how the theologian discerns the experiential "letter" of contemporary ecclesial experience and fashions it into a particular representation of the tradition as *"ein bewegliches."*

Anyone familiar with Schleiermacher's writings cannot help but be struck by the similarities between Drey's account of the interpretive act and Schleiermacher's. In his 1819 Berlin lectures on *Hermeneutik* Schleiermacher spoke of a technical or psychological side to understanding that filled out interpretation's grammatical, rule-oriented concern with language in the setting of time and culture. The psychological dimension of hermeneutics itself involves what Schleiermacher calls a "divinatory" moment in which "one transforms oneself (sich selbst...verwandelt), as it were (gleichsam), into the other [the author] in order to try to comprehend the [author's] individuality immediately," and a "comparative" moment that "first posits the object of understanding as a universal and then finds the [author's] particularity within it while comparing the particular with other distinctive traits conceived under the same universal."[20] For Schleiermacher, each moment rightly complements the other in any authentic act of understanding and together they constitute "the divinatory objective and subjective reconstruction (Nachconstruieren) of the given speech," a conceptualization of the interpretive act provocatively expressed in Schleiermacher's well-known definition of the hermeneutical task as "understanding the subject matter first as well as and then better than its author."[21]

Is this consistency in conceptualization and language evidence that Drey relied on Schleiermacher's 1819 Berlin lectures on hermeneutics for his discussion of hermeneutics in the *Kurze Einleitung*? This seems a very unlikely possibility. Schleiermacher's 1819 lectures on *"Hermeneutik"* in which the above-cited passages appear were only edited and published posthumously by Schleiermacher's colleague Friedrich Lücke in 1838 for inclusion in his collected works. Drey had no occasion to hear Schleiermacher lecture, nor did he ever meet him.[22] While it is possible that Drey learned of Schleiermacher's 1819 conception of interpretive divination by word of mouth from one of Schleiermacher's colleagues or students, one should not overlook the facts that Schleiermacher began to deliver the 1819 lectures on April 19 and that the preface to Drey's *Kurze Einleitung* is dated July 4, an extraordinarily short period of time for any influence to have transpired and by which time Drey almost certainly already had written his encyclopedia's section on biblical hermeneutics.[23] Schleiermacher's own theological encyclopedia, *Kurze Darstellung des theologischen Studiums* (1811), was the only published work by its author which in 1819 could have provided a resource for Drey's hermeneutical theory, and students of Drey's thought know that the influence of Schleiermacher's theological encyclopedia on Drey is considerable.[24] Yet here again a comparison of the texts fails to offer a satisfactory account of influence. The 1811 edition of Schleiermacher's *Kurze Darstellung* describes the goal of interpretation as "correctly conceiving each individual thought at the same time in its relation to the idea of the whole, and thus reconstructing the act of writing...."[25] This formulation suggests the idea of interpretive reconstruction Drey presents in the *Kurze Einleitung*. And yet absent is any mention of the interpretive moment preceding reconstruction that entails the interpreter's self-transformation into the author, an analogical act that is described in a surprisingly similar manner in the 1819 passages cited above.

How can we account for Schleiermacher's and Drey's shared conception of the hermeneutical act as what we shall call a "two-moment schema" involving an empathetic identification with and subsequent reconstruction of the author's mind and meaning? Answering this question satisfactorily will contribute to our knowledge of the history of ideas. But more importantly, an answer will enable us to appreciate more fully the value of Drey's theology of tradition for his time and ours. Let us consider two previous, and incomplete, answers before proposing our own.

In *Truth and Method* Hans-Georg Gadamer considers the intellectual and textual backgrounds for Schleiermacher's famous axiom that the interpreter can and should understand the author better than the author understands himself. Now Gadamer seems not to know of Drey's 1819 description of the hermeneutical task. And even though Drey does not express his understanding of that task in the short formula of Schleiermacher's axiom, one could rightly judge Schleiermacher's axiom, understood in its 1819 formulation, also to convey the substance of Drey's 1819 conception of the hermeneutical act as empathetic identification with the author and the reconstruction of his mind and meaning.[26] Consequently, one could reasonably expect that Gadamer's account of Schleiermacher's axiom would apply as well to Drey's hermeneutics.

Gadamer observes that precursors of Schleiermacher's axiom appear in the work of Kant, Fichte, Schlegel, and Schelling and rejects Otto Bollnow's explanation that these Enlightenment and Romantic writers were the first to articulate an oral tradition of criticism that eventually came to be identified with Schleiermacher's famous expression of it.[27] Gadamer is inclined to understand the pre-Schleiermacherian variations on the formula as "objective philosophical criticism in the spirit of rationalism" that only seek a higher level of clarity in understanding the author and for which the author remains the target of the interpreter's critical understanding. Schleiermacher, Gadamer concludes, "re-interpreted this principle of philosophical criticism and made it a principle of the literary art of interpretation."[28] In this hermeneutical act, the meaning of the author is raised to a contemporary meaning that flourishes in the interpreter's understanding and that now as a creative reconstruction would no longer be recognized by the author simply as his own. Gadamer, then, considers Schleiermacher's axiom to be a significantly original moment in what was then the short history of this interpretive idea. Even if Gadamer is unaware of Drey's version of the hermeneutical formula, it would be reasonable to assume that its closeness in conceptualization and expression to Schleiermacher's would lead Gadamer to extend his judgment on Schleiermacher's originality to Drey. And since Schleiermacher's distinction is thoroughly dubious for Gadamer, his judgment on Schleiermacher as the archetype of an ahistorical "Romantic" hermeneutics would likely extend to Drey to whom *Truth and Method's* corrective account of the proper workings of understanding in a shared effective-history or tradition equally would apply.

Unfortunately, Gadamer's judgments on Schleiermacher's hermeneutics were not informed by Schleiermacher's discussion of the tasks of historical theology in the *Kurze Darstellung* where interpretation is not presented as the work of ahistorical imagination but as a task that elucidates and serves the developing tradition of the Church. In this regard, Gadamer's charge of hermeneutical psychologism would apply even less to Drey who took greater pains than Schleiermacher to speak of *Nachconstruiren* as a theological judgment measured by faithfulness to the defined dogmas of a living ecclesial tradition. And if it is the case that both Schleiermacher and Drey expounded their hermeneutical theories in full appreciation for tradition as a meaningful context for interpretation and indeed as the ongoing product of creative interpretive reconstruction, then we can judge, (though for a different reason from Gadamer's) that the Enlightenment precursors for Schleiermacher's and Drey's formula noted by Gadamer—Kant and Fichte—can hardly account for Schleiermacher's (and Drey's) tradition-based hermeneutics. Only in an expository note does Gadamer consider the possibility that a tradition-oriented thinker like Schelling might have served as a determinative influence on Schleiermacher's axiom. And Gadamer's concern to preserve Schleiermacher's originality (and ahistorical sensibilities!) leads him to conclude that Schelling's own statements on grasping the meaning of an author represent at most a "point of transition" between Enlightenment rationalism and the "new Romantic interpretation" which he only can understand as Schleiermacherian psychologism.[29]

Our second, and still incomplete, answer to the question of how we can account for Schleiermacher's and Drey's shared 1819 conception of the hermeneutical act is willing to take Schelling more seriously than Gadamer did. In his important book *The Eclipse of Biblical Narrative* (1975), Hans Frei tries to identify the source for Schleiermacher's axiom. Like Gadamer, Frei does not know of Drey's 1819 hermeneutics and yet his analysis, like Gadamer's, can be read as applicable to Drey. Proposing only a "possible parallel" between Schelling and Schleiermacher on the workings of interpretive sensibility, Frei directs his reader particularly to Schelling's discussion of art in the closing section of his *System des transscendentalen Idealismus* (1800). Schelling, Frei points out, portrays artistic intuition in this work as "the one instance where the spontaneously active subject creatively penetrates the material he receives." The artist is "the organ of a creative process that comes to consciousness through him...," but which achieves full consciousness only in the "philosopher who understands what is happening."[30] This able description of Schelling's position is enhanced by considering the words of Schelling himself, which Frei does not specifically quote. According to Schelling,

> as purposeful as he is, the artist, yet, in consideration of the specifically objective element in his production, seems to stand under the influence of a power that distinguishes him from all other persons and compels him to express or represent things that even he himself does not completely perceive, and whose meaning is infinite.[31]

This infinity of meaning accompanies every work of art, which in turn "is capable of infinite interpretation." While the artistic reproduction merely feigns the character of the true work of art, limiting itself to the superficial and standing as no more than "the faithful impression of the conscious activity of the artist and from beginning to end only an object for reflection," the true work of art, Schelling insists, opens itself to intuition (*Anschauung*), "which loves to immerse itself in the intuited (im Angeschauten sich zu vertiefen liebt), and only is able to rest in the infinite."[32]

Frei points out that in his works published immediately after the *System* of 1800 Schelling increasingly portrayed the apprehension of truth as a conscious, reflective, and philosophical act, rather than as the unconscious, intuitive fathoming of aesthetic experience and expression.[33] Yet, however it portrays the role of the subjective faculties, Schelling's account of the dynamics of interpretation evinces the formal traits that Schleiermacher and Drey would highlight in their similar accounts of the hermeneutical act: the importance of empathetic identification, the denial of the primacy of the author's self-understanding, and the inexhaustability of a higher, interpretive meaning. This homology, of course, does not constitute a proof that Schleiermacher and Drey modeled their descriptions of the interpretive act on Schelling's. But Frei's tentative proposal regarding Schelling's influence on Schleiermacher is perhaps strengthened somewhat by our adding Drey's formula to Frei's picture and by our knowing that Schelling's influence on Drey was as great as, if not greater than, his influence on Schleiermacher.[34]

Nevertheless, even if Frei's proposal of Schelling as a likely source of influence on Schleiermacher's axiom is strengthened by the addition of Drey to this influential mix, the Schelling texts cited above do little to explain the striking similarity we find in Schleiermacher's and Drey's 1819 expressions of the interpretive act. While Schelling might very well provide the hermeneutical idea, he does not offer the language and, through the language, the more particular notion that the theologians shared nineteen years after the publication of the *System*. This similarity in language and in specificity of notion seems to point to another author who antedates them and who himself served at least as a textual influence upon them. A very likely candidate, I believe, is Schleiermacher's one-time colleague at the University of Berlin, Friedrich Lücke.

As Lücke assumed the post of *Privatdocent* at the University of Berlin at the end of 1816, his senior colleague Schleiermacher noted his arrival to his friend Johann Christian Gass in a letter dated January 2, 1817: "We have made a very good acquisition to our faculty in one Dr. Lücke, who has arrived from Göttingen. He has been named to the position of Licentiate here and delivers lectures. Indeed, his book on New Testament hermeneutics has recently appeared and it seems to be very thorough and excellently developed. In addition, he is a pious and amiable person."[35] The book that Schleiermacher acknowledges and praises is Lücke's recently published *Grundriss der neutestamentlichen Hermeneutik und ihrer Geschichte* (1817).[36] The body of Lücke's book addresses the expected array of topics suggested by its title—the nature of a New Testament hermeneutics, its exegetical principles and problems, its doctrinal implications, and more—all of which are expounded in 323 paragraphs presented in 219 pages. As a preface to this subject matter Lücke included an expository writing of 80 pages entitled "Akademische Einleitungsrede über das Studium der Hermeneutik des neuen Testaments und ihrer Geschichte zu unserer Zeit," a lecture he delivered on November 2, 1815. It is in the first part of Lücke's hermeneutics proper, which discusses the "principles" of interpretation, that we meet our pertinent text.

Lücke considers the presuppositions of interpretation by noting that "the unity of the human spirit" provides a basis not only for the possibility of understanding a writing in general but also for the necessity "of investigating each individual thought in its relation to the idea of the whole of a writing through the same power of spirit and form of knowledge from which the idea has proceeded."[37] The most perfect understanding of a writing can only occur, Lücke continues, if "one is knowledgable in the most exact way of a writing's language, of all of its national, temporal, local, and personal relations, and if one can possess agility of mind and spiritual kinship in order to reconstruct (nachconstruiren) the act of writing in each moment of the exposition."[38] These same principles apply to the possibility of understanding the New Testament, as Lücke explains in a long sentence that we must quote in full:

> But the most perfect understanding of the New Testament canon can only be open to someone who has come to know the New Testament language and times in the most intimate way, so that he might recognize most clearly the external and internal forms and their relations to each other. The most perfect understanding of the New Testament canon can only be open to someone who can be thought to dwell in the steady completion and sanctification of his Christian inner life through the ecclesial community, so that he might sift out the religious element always more purely and perfectly; to someone who possesses enough agility of mind to transpose himself (sich zu versetzen) with facility and certainty into the individuality of every New Testament writer, who is aware of his spiritual kinship with at least one of the New Testament authors so that he might complete most perfectly the act of reconstruction (Act des Nachconstruirens) in at least that author, and who, finally, through historical study has acquired enough universal-historical meaning and insight to conceive perfectly the idea of the whole, i.e., of *Christian* revelation, in opposition as such to every other.[39]

Here we find a possible textual basis for the similarities in language and specificity in notion of Schleiermacher's and Drey's 1819 accounts of the interpretive act. There are several reasons for positing Lücke's actual influence. First, Lücke, like Schleiermacher and Drey after him, distinguishes two consecutive moments in the interpretive act: an empathetic identification with the author in his particularity and a reconstruction of the author's mind and meaning into a universal understanding that transcends its previous limitations. No text prior to Schleiermacher's and Drey's 1819 formulations articulates these two consecutive moments as pointedly as Lücke's. Second, Lücke, like Schleiermacher and Drey after him, portrays the moment of empathetic identification as the interpreter's "changing into" the author. Schleiermacher's and Drey's language to express this transformation does differ from Lücke's. Lücke uses the verb "versetzen sich," while Schleiermacher and Drey use the verbs "verwandelt (sich selbst)" and "verwandeln sich" respectively. Yet both Schleiermacher's and Drey's use of analogical indicators (S = "gleichsam," D = "so zu sagen") in their formulas might suggest their own efforts to explain a given idea in their own ways while yet remaining close to the given idea, expressions of their own individualities as authors that could very well extend to their choice of words. Third, Schleiermacher's January 2, 1817, letter to Gass refers to his reading Lücke's *Grundriss der neutestamentlichen Hermeneutik*. And none of Schleiermacher's previous writings, published (*Kurze Darstellung*) or unpublished (the aphorisms on hermeneutics from 1805, 1809/10 and the previous lecture plans on hermeneutics from 1809/10, 1810/11), presents the interpretive act in the two-moment schema of empathetic identification with the author and the reconstruction of the author's meaning as found in Lücke's pages. It seems reasonable, then, to conclude that Lücke's words and conceptualization aided Schleiermacher in framing more precisely ideas on which he had reflected seriously since at least 1805. We do not possess hard evidence that Drey read Lücke's book.[40] But if we note the similarities in language and notional specificity between Lücke's and Drey's accounts of the interpretive act, consider the similarities between Schleiermacher's and Drey's 1819 formulas, remember that there could have been no textual influence of one on the other, and that there is hard evidence that Schleiermacher read Lücke, it seems reasonable to conclude that Friedrich Lücke was among those to whom Drey was willing to credit "the modern definition of hermeneutics."[41]

Lücke's influence on Schleiermacher and Drey makes for more than an interesting footnote in the history of ideas. His influence on Schleiermacher and Drey actually shifts the landscape of that history to some degree. Gadamer's claims for the originality of his hermeneutics depend on his portrayal of Schleiermacher's hermeneutics as a prototype for the subjectivist orientation of "Romantic" hermeneutics. In Lücke, Schleiermacher, and Drey we have not only three thinkers who articulated the two-moment hermeneutical schema but also three theologians who understood its workings to be thoroughly informed by the ecclesial tradition it served. Gadamer's configuration of early nineteenth-century hermeneutics in Germany thus shows itself to be less nuanced than it should be, and overdetermined by the interests of his own constructive position. As we have seen, a consequence of Gadamer's interests is his elevation of Schleiermacher's originality in his axiom on understanding the author at the expense of Schelling's influence, a view that Frei calls us to reconsider. Lücke's influence on the language and notional specificity of Schleiermacher's and Drey's 1819 formulations lends further support to Frei's proposal.

In his "Akademische Einleitungsrede," Lücke cites Schelling's *Vorlesungen über die Methode des akademischen Studiums* (1803) to justify his claim that all modern sciences, including theology, must possess a historical character that is the presupposition for creative insight and the necessity of scientific construction.[42] "Without exact historical knowledge of the past," Lücke asserts, "we could not conceive and duly value anything novel (Neugeschaffenes) in the sphere of theology, and could not even recognize whether and to what extent it is something new." This same principle holds for biblical hermeneutics which must regard each new insight as constituted by "a historical substance to which the novel element (das neuhinzugekommene) organically joins itself."[43] Lücke develops this Schellingian idea, which anticipates his later exposition of the two-moment interpretive schema in further reflections on creative production in theology. Once again, Lücke turns to Schelling's *Vorlesungen*, though now specifically to that work's occasional reflections on art, as a resource for understanding the theological task. "Moreover, if we follow Schelling in naming the divine power of production in humanity the power of art," he states,

> then we must say the same thing about the science of theology that Schelling truly and correctly has noted of science in general—"that whoever has not brought the same higher impulses, with which the artist calls forth from raw materials the image of his soul and of his own invention, to bear on the perfect construction of the image of his science in all details to the point of perfect unity with the ideal, has not completely fathomed the science."[44]

Here Lücke employs the same Schellingian analogy for the interpretive enterprise that Hans Frei proposed as a likely influence on Schleiermacher's hermeneutical axiom. And while there is every reason to think that their shared interest in Schelling's philosophy would have led Schleiermacher, Lücke, and Drey to encounter this analogy in the *System's* discussion of art, all three at least met this analogy in their respective readings of the *Vorlesungen*.[45]

Schelling's aesthetic version of the axiom on authorial understanding, then, offers the most likely, primary influence on Lücke's 1817, and Schleiermacher's and Drey's 1819 versions of the axiom,[46] with Lücke's 1817 formulation providing a noteworthy secondary influence on the language and notional specificity of Schleiermacher's and Drey's 1819 formulas. We shall now turn to a consideration of the importance of these influences for Drey's hermeneutics of tradition.

Hermeneutics, Tradition, and the
"Productive Other"

Schelling's likely influence on Drey's account of the hermeneutical task sheds light both on Drey's theological anthropology and on the role that anthropology plays in his understanding of tradition. If the contributions of the theologian to the process of unfolding tradition can be understood, as Drey suggests, in analogy to the hermeneutical act, then the interpretive *Nachconstruiren* that the theologian offers to the church as a living reconstruction of the ecclesial past presupposes a dialogical understanding of the self in which difference—in insights, truth-claims, and finally in selves—is productive of meaning. Just as the exegete's interpretation requires an act of "transforming oneself into a foreign writer" in order to offer an interpretation that raises the wisdom of distant times, places, and persons to contemporary meaning, so too, by implication, does theological interpretation that promulgates the tradition require the theologian's self-transformation into the "other" of the ancient past in order to bring the otherwise dead letter of orthodoxy to reconstructed life. To accomplish this act of hermeneutical revivification, the theologian must turn to the "other" of the present ecclesial community in order to discern in the developing experiences of contemporary Christians moments of truth and value that might stand in continuity with past manifestations of the *Reich-Gottes-Idee* in history. The theological act of interpreting the ecclesial past and present would seem to involve, in Drey's view, an imaginative act of empathy in which a productive encounter with another—both past and present and at once past and present—is a condition for the reconstructed animation and continuity of belief that Christians call tradition. For Drey, tradition as a theological judgment seeking the truth of the divine ideas in history is an act of ecclesial understanding whose unity is drawn from and dependent upon the rich pluralism in faith among believers throughout the ages.

Schelling himself expressed the importance of what we might call the "productive other" in his *System* of 1800, as he did consistently in his early writings.[47] The self, Schelling suggests, might be imagined as purely objective self-intuition (*Selbstanschauung*) and yet, so imagined, the self only would be capable of acts of intuition that never broke through to consciousness itself. The ground of consciousness, he insists, "cannot lie within the self (*im Ich selbst*). ...Consequently, the ground we seek beyond the individual can only lie *in another individual*."[48] The very nature of human consciousness, one might say, manifests itself in its own dialogical character that submerges itself intuitively in the individuality of the other only to emerge from it into the moment of reflexivity or, in Schelling's parlance, the possibility of transcendental truth. Drey's understanding of the hermeneutics of scripture and, by analogy, tradition proceeds from this Schellingian understanding of the developing self whose freedom and creativity (as a free act) presuppose the meaningfulness of the other as a context for their realization.

In the broader context of Drey's theology of tradition, the productive other with whom the interpreting self empathizes and whose individual meaning the interpreting self reconstructs is finally personal, and ultimately the productive other is the personal God whose providential love unfolds in the historical manifestation of the *Reich-Gottes-Idee*. But mediately, the productive other is pluriform, taking shape in the freely developing faith of believers past and present whose words and deeds, beliefs and worship are instantiated in the church's dogmas and flourish in contemporary lives. In Drey's judgment, tradition itself is *"lebendig"* in and as the free belief, action, and practice of individual Christian believers. But the universal pattern or, in Hinze's image, narrative of tradition becomes *"lebendig"* in and through the developing freedom and creativity of a believer who can recognize in "others" opportunities for discerning the productive other of the Spirit of God and who can reconstruct from these multiple encounters a historical continuity faithful to the universal and developing divine plan. Tradition, in this conceptualization, manifests the universal truth of God as necessary and absolute, and in its utter comprehensiveness as God's eternal idea of the Kingdom, but not to the exclusion of the conditions of its manifestation in time, space, and the manifold others that might be productive of its intelligibility.[49]

Considering Drey's theology of tradition in light of his Schellingian hermeneutics enables us to appreciate even more its extraordinary contributions to the character of modern theology itself, such as the idea of tradition as a development and the creative role of the theologian in its promulgation. In concluding we should not fail to note that Drey's hermeneutics of tradition yields another idea that by now is axiomatic for modern theology—the flourishing of truth, and even specifically of Christian truth, in times, places, persons, and circumstances that by their very nature are local. Certainly there is a legitimacy to Gadamer's concern that the Romantic configuration of the two-moment schema psychologizes interpretation to such a degree that the particularities of effective history vanish in the experiential homology of an empathy already on the way to the higher understanding of the contemporary interpreter. In the context of the German Enlightenment, however, Schelling's efforts to speculate on the coinherence of the absolute and the relative, the ideal and the real, and the eternal and the temporal constituted a remarkable intellectual breakthrough that, for all its attention to the infinite, required an unprecedented philosophical regard for the contingencies of historical existence as themselves indispensable manifestations of divine truth. Hermeneutically, this intellectual orientation appears most pointedly in Schelling's account of artistic creativity. In Drey's theological hermeneutics, this Schellingian sensibility appears in the interpretive expectation that a universal understanding unfolds in the encounter with a local, particular, and, in Drey's word, "foreign" truth, whose limitations offer and perhaps even occasion a truthful horizon of far greater expanse.

Modern theologies might be characterized by the authority they accord experience, alongside scripture and tradition. But as postmodern theologies never tire of pointing out, "experience" often is constructed in modern theologies as a false universal, as an abstraction that serves ideologies and power relations, and that fails to name the infinitely local conditions under which experiences really occur. It should not surprise us that Johann Sebastian Drey's theology of tradition, in its Idealistic concern for a universal ecclesial experience expressed as the universal tradition of the church, remains ever in need of the cautionary judgments of postmodern criticism. Is it not surprising, however, that Drey's appreciation of the "productive other" in his hermeneutics of tradition anticipates, however vaguely, sensibilities akin to those at work in the postmodern theologies of our own day?

NOTES

1. Josef Rupert Geiselmann, *Lebendiger Glaube aus geheiligter Überlieferung: Der Grundgedanke der Theologie Johann Adam Möhlers und der katholischen Tübinger Schule*, 2nd ed. (Basel/Wien: Herder, 1966), pp. 120f. See, also, idem, *Die katholische Tübinger Schule: Ihre theologische Eigenart* (Freiburg: Herder, 1964), pp. 23f.

2. Bradford E. Hinze, *Narrating History, Developing Doctrine: Friedrich Schleiermacher and Johann Sebastian Drey* (Atlanta, GA: Scholars Press, 1993).

3. Johann Sebastian Drey, *Kurze Einleitung in das Studium der Theologie mit Rücksicht auf den wissenschaftlichen Standpunct und das katholische System*, ed. F. Schupp, (Tübingen: Heinrich Laupp, 1819; rpt. Darmstadt: Wissenschaftliche Buchgesellschaft, 1971). Hereafter cited as *Kurze Einleitung*. This work has recently been translated into English: *Brief Introduction to the Study of Theology: With Reference to the Scientific Standpoint and the Catholic System* (Notre Dame Studies in Theology, 1), trans. M.J. Himes, (Notre Dame: Univ. of Notre Dame Press, 1994).

4. "...der Impuls zu weitern Entwickelungen und zu näherer Bestimmung der Begriffe noch nur von Einzelnen ausgehen kann... (*Kurze Einleitung*, p. 172, Par. 259). Drey speaks only of Christian doctrine but, by implication, the view expressed here would apply to other manifestations of ecclesial development.

5. Ibid.,p. 38, Par. 60.

6. Ibid.

7. Ibid., p. 37, Par. 59.

8. Ibid., p. 29, Par. 47.

9. Ibid., p. 43, Par. 69.

10. Ibid., p. 1, Par. 1.

11. Ibid., p. 3, Par. 6.

12. Ibid., pp. 5, 6, Par. 10.

13. Ibid., p. 7, Par. 12.

14. Ibid., p. 162, Par. 240.

15. Ibid., p. 67, Par. 100.

16. Ibid., p. 68, Par. 102.

17. Ibid., p. 170, Par. 256.

18. "Der Ausleger muss sich ganz an die Stelle seines Auctors setzen, sich so zusagen in ihn verwandeln, und nun von neuem construiren, was jener ursprünglichproducirte; dies heisst man nachconstruiren. In der Fähigkeit also sich selbst ineinen fremden Schriftsteller zu verwandeln, liegt der Beruf des Auslegers zuseinem Amte..." (Ibid., p. 109, Par. 161).

19. Drey himself proposes this analogical relationship between biblical and theological hermeneutics: "So bleibt auch hier das Geheimniss der Auslegung noch immer die Kunst sich in seinen Schriftsteller zu verwandeln und den Act seines Schreibens nachzuconstruiren..., aber dieser Act ist nun ein über die Grammatik erhabener, die Kunst eine heilige. Der religiöse, und zwar der christlich religiöse Sinn ist eine not hwendige Eigenschaft wie eines guten Theologen überhaupt...so auch des Exegeten" (Ibid. , p. 116, Par. 173).

20. "Die divinatorische ist die welche indem man sich selbst gleichsam in den andern verwandelt, das individuelle unmittelbar aufzufassen sucht. Die comparative sezt erst den

zu verstehenden als ein allgemeines, und findet dann das Eigenthümliche indem mit andern unter demselben allgemeinen befassten verglichen wird" (Friedrich D. E. Schleiermacher, *Hermeneutik*, 2 ed., ed. H. Kimmerle [Heidelberg: Carl Winter Universitätsverlag, 1974], p. 105).

21. "...die Rede zuerst eben so gut und dann besser zu verstehen als ihr Urheber" (Ibid., p. 83).

22. Nico Schreurs, "Johann Sebastian Drey und Friedrich Schleiermacher: Ein Forschungsbericht," in *Revision der Theologie—Reform der Kirche: Die Bedeutung des Tübinger Theologen Johann Sebastian Drey (1777–1853) in Geschichte und Gegenwart*, ed. A.P. Kustermann (Würzburg: Echter Verlag, 1994), p. 140.

23. Schleiermacher, *Hermeneutik*, p.75; Drey, *Kurze Einleitung*, p.viii.

24. For a discussion of the influence of Schleiermacher's theological encyclopedia on Drey's conception of doctrinal development, see John E. Thiel, *Imagination and Authority: Theological Authorship in the Modern Tradition* (Minneapolis: Fortress Press, 1991), pp. 63–90.

25. "...jeden einzelnen Gedanken mit seinem Verhältnis zur Idee des Ganzen zugleich richtig aufzufassen, und so den Akt des Schreibens nachzukonstruiren... (Friedrich Schleiermacher, *Kurze Darstellung des theologischen Studiums zum Behuf einleitender Vorlesungen*, ed. H. Scholz [Leipzig: A. Deichert'sche Verlagsbuchhandlung, 1910; rpt., Darmstadt: Wissenschaftliche Buchgesellschaft, 1973], p. 54, n. 2). Hereafter cited as *Kurze Darstellung*.

26. Schleiermacher's axiom on understanding the author better than the author himself appears in his earlier lectures on hermeneutics before 1819. The handwritten "aphorisms" on hermeneutics from 1805 and 1809/10 include a sketch for a course that lists the topic "Verständniss...des dem Schriftsteller eigenthümlichen indem man [als] Leser ihn nachconstruirt" (Schleiermacher, *Hermeneutik*, p. 33), and a later aphorism defines the hermeneutical goal as "Von den Schriftsteller besser verstehen als er selbst" (Ibid., p. 50). Schleiermacher's handwritten notes for his first offering of the lectures in the Winter semester of 1809/10 state: "Man muss so gut verstehen und besser verstehen als der Schriftsteller" (Ibid., p. 56). These earlier formulations, however, do not mention the hermeneutical first moment of empathetic identification with the author that appears for the first time in the lectures of 1819 and that reflects Schleiermacher's development of the tasks of technical or psychological interpretation in those lectures. Gadamer thinks of Schleiermacher's axiom in terms of its 1819 conceptualization, since it is that conceptualization that he judges a deficient counterposition to his own.

27. Hans-Georg Gadamer, *Truth and Method*, trans. G. Barden and J. Cumming (New York: Crossroad, 1975), pp. 171–72, 518 n. 43.

28. Ibid., p. 172.

29. Ibid., p. 518 n. 43. Here Gadamer also accords the status of "transitional" figure to Friedrich Schlegel. Schlegel is indeed a particularly strong candidate for influence on Schleiermacher's general axiom, as Hermann Patsch has argued so effectively. As Patsch shows, Schlegel's reflections on a "Philosophie der Philologie" from 1797 include the maxim "Kritisiren heisst einen Autor besser verstehn als er sich selbst verstanden hat" ("Friedrich Schlegels 'Philosophie der Philologie' und Schleiermachers frühe Entwürfe zur Hermeneutik," *Zeitschrift für Theologie und Kirche* 63 [1966]: 456–57). Manfred Frank, following not Patsch but Walter Benjamin, also regards Schlegel as an important influence on Schleiermacher's formula. Manfred Frank, *Das individuelle Allgemeine: Textstrukturierung und -interpretation nach Schleiermacher* (Frankfurt am Main: Suhrkamp Verlag, 1977), p. 359. One wants to make more of this influence as one recalls that in 1797/98 Schlegel and Schleiermacher shared living quarters in Berlin. Yet, Schlegel does not speak of empathetic identification with the author as Schleiermacher does in his 1819 version of the axiom. Moreover, Schlegel's above-quoted maxim was only published posthumously and so could not have influenced Drey.

30. Hans W. Frei, *The Eclipse of Biblical Narrative: A Study in Eighteenth and Nineteenth Century Hermeneutics* (New Haven: Yale Univ. Press, 1974), p. 295.

31. "...scheint der Künstler, so absichtsvoll er ist, doch in Ansehung dessen, was das eigentlich Objektive in seiner Hervorbringung ist, unter der Einwirkung einer Macht zu stehen, die ihn von allen andern Menschen absondert, und ihn Dinge auszusprechen oder darzustellen zwingt, die er selbst nicht vollständig durchsieht, und deren Sinn unendlich ist" (Friedrich Schelling, *System des transscendentalen Idealismus* [1800], in *Schellings Werke*, vol. 2, [Munich: C.H. Beck'scheVerlagsbuchhandlung, 1958], p. 617). Hereafter cited as *System.*

32. Ibid., p. 620.

33. Frei, *The Eclipse of Biblical Narrative*, p. 296.

34. Franz Schupp has recognized Schelling's influence on Schleiermacher's and Drey's hermeneutics, but not on the problem of textual grounding for Schleiermacher's and Drey's 1819 hermeneutical formulas. See Franz Schupp, *Die Evidenz der Geschichte: Theologie als Wissenschaft bei J.S. Drey* (Innsbruck: Universität Innsbruck, 1970), pp. 57–63.

35. Friedrich Schleiermacher, *Fr. Schleiermacher's Briefwechsel mit J. Chr. Gass*, ed. W. Gass (Berlin: Georg Reimer, 1852), p. 130.

36. Friedrich Lücke, *Grundriss der neutestamentlichen Hermeneutik und ihrer Geschichte zum Gebrauch für akademische Vorlesungen* (Göttingen: Vandenhoeck und Ruprecht, 1817). Hereafter cited as *Grundriss.*

37. Ibid., p. 85. This passage, and its continuation in the following quote, unmistakably bear the influence of Schleiermacher's *Kurze Darstellung* (see the text for note 25 above), although Lücke's text, unlike Schleiermacher's, makes explicit mention of empathetic identification with the author ("*dieselbe* Geisteskraft und Erkenntnissform, aus der sie [die Schrift] hervorgangen ist..."). We should note that the *Kurze Darstellung's* treatment of exegetical theology was Lücke's only exposure to Schleiermacher's hermeneutics prior to 1817. Heinz Kimmerle lists Lücke as a transcriber of the 1832/33 lectures on hermeneutics (Schleiermacher, *Hermeneutik*, p. 180 n.2), but Wolfgang Virmond corrects this view by showing that Lücke never had occasion to hear Schleiermacher lecture on hermeneutics before or after 1817. See Wolfgang Virmond, "Neue Textgrundlagen zu Schleiermachers früher Hermeneutik," in *Internationaler Schleiermacher-Kongress Berlin 1984*, vol. 1, ed. K. Selge (Berlin: Walter de Gruyter, 1985), p. 577 n. 6.

38. Lücke, *Grundriss,* p. 86. Lücke concludes this paragraph by describing further this higher interpretive moment: "Alle Functionen dieses Nachconstruirens aber sind unter der historischen Erkenntnissform begriffen" (Ibid.). Two paragraphs earlier in his presentation, Lücke had proposed that the New Testament, like any other writing, possesses a "logical" dimension in its content, a "grammatical" dimension in its external form, and a "historical" dimension in which both the logical and the grammatical "zu einem Ganzen vereiniget" (Ibid., p. 85). Lücke's placement of the interpretive act of *Nachconstruiren* under the "historische Erkenntnissform" expresses his view that this act, in its exegetical application, conceives the logical and the grammatical, content and form, as a comprehensive whole, "als eine von allen andern durch bestimmte Merkmahle unterschiedene Offenbarung der Religion, und zwar als ein universalhistorisches Factum..." (Ibid.).

39. "Das vollkommenste Verständniss aber des neutestamentlichen Kanons kann nur demjenigen geöffnet werden, der mit der neutestamentlichen Sprache und Zeit auf das innigste vertrauet ist, um die äusseren und inneren Formen und ihre Verhältnisse zu einander auf das deutlichste zu erkennen, der in beständiger Vollendung und Heiligung seines christlichen Gemüthes durch die kirchliche Gemeinschaft begriffen ist, um das religiöse Element immer reiner und vollkommener herauszuscheiden, der Geistesgewandtheit genug besitzt, um sich in die Individualität aller neutestamentlichen Schriftsteller mit Leichtigkeit und Gewissheit zu versetzen, der sich seiner Seelenverwandtschaft wenigstens mit Einem der neutestamentlichen Verfasser bewusst ist, um den Act des Nachconstruirens wenigstens in dem Einen auf das vollkommenste zu vollbringen, und der sich endlich durch historisches Studium universalhistorischen Sinn und Tiefblick genug erworben hat, um die Idee des Ganzen, die *Christliche* Offenbarung, im Gegensatz gegen jede andere, als solche, vollkommen zu begreifen" (Ibid., pp. 86–87)

40. The only explicit reference to Friedrich Lücke in Drey's writings occurs in the *Apologetik* where Drey refers in passing to Lücke's 1829 review of Sack's book on apologetics. Johann Sebastian Drey, *Die Apologetik als wissenschaftliche Nachweisung der Göttlichkeit des Christenthums in seiner Erscheinung*, vol. 1 (Mainz, 1838; rpt. Frankfurt: Minerva G.M.B.H., 1967), p. 139 n. 2.

41. In a short commentary on the paragraph devoted to his version of the hermeneutical formula, Drey writes: "Von dem Ziele und Verfahren der Auslegung ist die neuere Definition der Hermeneutik hergenommen, dass sie ist die Kunst die Gedanken eines Schriftstellers im Verhältnisse zu ihrer Idee des Ganzen aufzufassen, und den Act seines Schreibens nachzuconstruiren" (Drey, *Kurze Einleitung*, p. 109, Par. 161). Drey could have found this formulation either in Schleiermacher's *Kurze Darstellung* or in Lücke's *Grundriss*. See note 37 above. Drey would have been kept abreast of the new developments in hermeneutics by his Ellwangen and Tübingen colleagues Peter Alois Gratz (1769–1849), professor of New Testament, and Johann Georg Herbst (1787–1836), professor of Old Testament and co-editor with Drey of the *Theologische Quartalschrift*.

42. Lücke, *Grundriss*, p. 59 (pagination specific to the "*Akademische Einleitungsreden*"). Lücke cites the 1813 edition of Schelling's 1803 work. The passage can be found in Friedrich Schelling, *Vorlesungen über die Methode des akademischen Studiums*, in *Schellings Werke*, vol. 3 (Munich: C.H. Beck'sche Verlagsbuchhandlung, 1958), pp. 247–48: "Die neuere Welt ist in allem...schon alt und erfahren." Hereafter cited as *Vorlesungen*.

43. Lücke, *Grundriss*, p. 60.

44. Ibid., pp. 69–70. The Schelling text cited here can be found in Schelling, *Vorlesungen*, p. 263.

45. Schleiermacher reviewed the *Vorlesungen* for the *Jenaische Litteraturzeitung* in 1804. The review is reprinted in Friedrich Schleiermacher, *Aus Schleiermacher's Leben: In Briefen*, vol. 4, ed. W. Dilthey (Berlin: Georg Reimer, 1863; rpt. Berlin: Walter de Gruyter, 1974), pp. 579–93. Drey refers to the *Vorlesungen* in *Kurze Einleitung*, p. 57.

46. Naming Schelling as the primary influence on Schleiermacher's and Drey's 1819 formulations of the two-moment interpretive schema should not suggest that Schelling is in some reductionist manner an exhaustive influence on Schleiermacher's and Drey's hermeneutics. For a thorough study of the intellectual background to Schleiermacher's hermeneutics, see Reinhold Rieger, *Interpretation und Wissen: Zur philosophischen Begründung der Hermeneutik bei Friedrich Schleiermacher und ihrem geschichtlichen Hintergrund* (Berlin: Walter de Gruyter, 1988). For a consideration of the intellectual background to Drey's hermeneutics, see Schupp, *Die Evidenz der Geschichte*, pp. 51f. There are, of course, important respects in which Schelling's general influence regarding this interpretive idea should be qualified. Reinhold Rieger has noted that Schleiermacher's "Bestimmung der Hermeneutik kommt den Äusserungen Schellings in seinen Vorlesungen über die akademischen Studiums von 1803 sehr nahe." And yet, Rieger qualifies, there are important differences. While Schelling, for example, sees the productive value of individuality "nur in der unendlichen Totalität aller Individuen," Schleiermacher regards "die Endlichkeit des Wissens [als] nicht aufhebbar" (Rieger, *Interpretation und Wissen*, pp. 336–37), a qualified appropriation of

Schelling that would apply to Drey as well.

Another possible textual influence on Schleiermacher's and Drey's 1819 accounts of the interpretive act is Friedrich Ast's *Grundlinien der Grammatik, Hermeneutik und Kritik* (Landshut: Jos. Thomann, 1808). Schleiermacher refers to this work in his 1829 *Akademiereden* (Schleiermacher, *Hermeneutik*, pp. 123–56), though usually to distinguish between the nuances of Ast's comparative method and his own. Drey makes no reference to this work, though in his third unpublished manuscript on dogmatics Drey refers to Ast's 1807 *Geschichte der Philosophie im Grundriss* (Johann Sebastian Drey, *Praelectiones dogmaticae* [1821/23–1834], pp. 88–89; I am grateful to Abraham P. Kustermann for supplying this reference), and so was familiar with his writing. Although Ast refers to the constructive moment in understanding as a "Nachbilden des schon Gebildeten" (Ast, *Grundlinien*, p. 187), he does not speak of a moment of empathetic identification in which the interpreter becomes the author. Rather, Ast tends to see the ancient author and the author's work as expressions of the spirit (*Geist*) of their age, which the contemporary interpreter strives to understand. Indeed, Ast's specific discussion of understanding an ancient author presumes that one does so by answering historical questions concerning the author's life and times (Ibid., pp. 183–84). In any case, the possible influence of Ast on Schleiermacher and Drey best would be understood, as is Lücke's, within the scope of Schelling's primary influence, since Ast's hermeneutics shows him to be the student of Schelling that he was. See Harald Wagner, *Die eine Kirche und die vielen Kirchen: Ekklesiologie und Symbolik beim jungen Möhler* (Paderborn: Schöningh, 1977), p. 65.

Françoise Breithaupt, et al., underestimate Schelling's influence on Schleiermacher's hermeneutics drastically by asserting that by 1805 Schleiermacher had reversed Schelling's hermeneutical orientation. The authors attend only to Schelling's version of Kant's formula on understanding the author in his *Propädeutik der Philosophie* (1804), and do not refer at all to the substance of Schelling's interpretive position as presented in these pages. The authors also make too much of Schleiermacher's self-professed "Abweichung" from Schelling in his *Jenaische Litteraturzeitung* review of 1804, and as noted by Schleiermacher in a September 6, 1805, letter to Gass (Schleiermacher, *Fr. Schleiermacher's Briefwechsel mit J. Chr. Gass*, pp. 31–32). A deviation, however, does not a reversal make. See Françoise Breithaupt, Alain Brousse, Alain Deligne, Ann Desbordes, "Was heisst die hermeneutische Formel: 'Die Rede zuerst eben so gut und dann besser zu verstehen als ihr Urheber'?", in *Internationaler Schleiermacher-Kongress Berlin 1984*, vol. 1, pp. 601–11. One does well to follow Rieger's judicious distinctions on the Schelling-Schleiermacher relationship, and his observations also can inform our understanding of Drey's appropriation of Schelling.

47. In the *Vorlesungen*, for example, Schelling expresses this insight as follows: "Alles Produciren ruht auf einer Begegnung oder Wechseldurchdringung des Allgemeinen und Besonderen. Den Gegensatz jeder Besonderheit gegen die Absolutheit scharf zu fassen, und zugleich in demselben untheilbaren Akt jene in dieser und diese in jener zu begreifen, ist das Geheimniss der Produktion" (Schelling, *Vorlesungen*, p. 264).

48. Schelling, *System*, pp. 632–33.

49. It is interesting to consider that Drey's two-moment hermeneutical schema appears in his later theology in his development of the idea of inspiration, where the divine Spirit, now conceived in the role of interpreter, transforms itself, so to speak, into the human spirit and brings forth from it something new. See Johann Sebastian Drey, "Grundsätze zu einer genauern Bestimmung des Begriffs der Inspiration," *Theologische Quartalschrift* 3 (1821): 615–55, esp. 618–24. Cf. Drey, *Die Apologetik*, 1: pp. 232f.

4

The Holy Spirit and The Catholic Tradition

The Legacy of Johann Adam Möhler

— BRADFORD E. HINZE —

Johann Adam Möhler (1796–1838) is rightly honored for his historical investigations of the Catholic tradition. Although he is a professed historical, and not speculative, theologian, his works resound with apologetic and dogmatic passion and intent. The many writings of his short career attest to a profound desire and commitment to develop an ever more comprehensive analysis of the Catholic tradition in length, breadth, and depth. His long view of the Catholic tradition, acquired by his disciplined studies of the history of Christian beliefs and practices, was inspired by German romantic and idealist conceptions of history. He combined a great reverence for the apostolic and patristic heritage of the church with a willingness to acknowledge, if not promote, the ongoing development of the Catholic tradition.

Möhler's historical outlook on the Catholic tradition was enriched by a breadth of vision afforded him by a multifaceted ecclesiology. His view of the church reflected a deeply spiritual and liturgical sensibility as well as an institutional insight sharpened by the study of church history and canon law. Most importantly, his ecclesiology elicited an attentiveness to the roles of various groups within the church in the traditioning process: not only the hierarchy and theologians, but the entire believing community. He patiently reflected upon the relationships of individual bishops to local communities, the episcopacy working in concert, and the pope's relation to bishops and local churches. He affirmed episcopal authority without being Febronian or Gallican and defended papal authority without embracing an extreme Ultramontanist position. Möhler appreciated the importance of the bonds of ecclesial communion for the life of the church and for the proper functioning of hierarchical leadership, organically understood. This long historical and broad ecclesial vision nurtured in Möhler a depth of perception and analytic grasp of many aspects of the traditioning process at work: inner and outer, spiritual and institutional, affective and cognitive, subjective and objective, ideal and real.

The genuine achievement of Möhler's work is not without its enigmas, ambiguities, and limitations, a number of which will concern us later. This essay will concentrate on one enigma at the very center of his work that has long fascinated his interpreters: the changes in Johann Adam Möhler's treatment of the Holy Spirit and the Catholic tradition. It is a simple fact that Möhler's early work, *Unity in the Church or The Principle of Catholicism: Presented in the Spirit of the Church*

Fathers of the First Three Centuries (1825), gave great attention to the Holy Spirit as he deliberated on the nature of the church and tradition, whereas his later works championed a vigorous incarnational orientation, beginning with *Athanasius the Great and the Church of His Time* (1827), and culminating in *Symbolism or Exposition of the Doctrinal Differences Between Catholics and Protestants as Evidenced by Their Symbolical Writings* (1832). Alongside of this change from a Spirit-centered to a Word-centered ecclesiology, there is a correlative shift in emphasis in his treatment of tradition. The earlier work concentrates on the dynamism of the inner communal life of the church in advancing the identity and mission of the church, while the latter places a greater emphasis on the defense of and adherence to the external and objective manifestations of the church and the authority of the hierarchy.

The fact that there is a transition may be easy to ascertain, but its significance is more difficult to determine. It is commonly contended that Möhler matured in his outlook: his first book appeared in 1825 when the author was a mere 29; with a certain youthful energy and vagueness, and sharing a romantic predilection for beginning with human subjectivity and its social constitution, he focused on the Spirit's role in tradition. But this emphasis was soon replaced by a new clarity as the role of Jesus Christ, the Incarnate Word of God, became increasingly central and determinative in his treatment and defense of the objective norms and teachings of the Catholic Church. The catalysts for his change are debated; some posit philosophical factors, others more religious and theological. But the basic line of interpretation is hard to dispute. As Möhler continued his scholarly career, he also shifted in outlook, gained precision, and became more conservative, which is to say he gave great weight to the authority of the church's hierarchy in the tradition of the Catholic Church, especially as it functioned to secure the church's stable identity.

Möhler's transition can be clarified, but fundamental questions still lurk in the background: Is there a waning presence, a marginalization of the Spirit in Möhler's understanding of tradition? And if there is a diminishing role for the Spirit in Möhler's view of tradition, or at least a repositioning of the Spirit's role within a predominantly christocentric framework, what difference does it make for an overall assessment of his treatment of the church's traditioning process?

In order to address these questions, this investigation will proceed in three parts. Part I will set up the problematic by considering the history of reception and interpretation of Möhler's work, and especially the contributions of Josef Rupert Geiselmann and Yves Congar. Part II will review the basic transitions in Möhler's positions on the Holy Spirit and Catholic tradition. Finally, Part III will use Möhler's understanding of the pneumatological and incarnational nature of the Catholic tradition in order to pay tribute to the lasting significance of his work, but it will also provide a framework for exploring some of its limitations.

Remarks on the History of Reception and Interpretation

Möhler's lamentably short career, which ended at the age of 41, would have been impressive in its productivity even without his immensely popular book on comparative symbolics, *Symbolism*. Both his first book, *Unity in the Church* (1825), and his second one, which investigated Athanasius and the church's struggle against Arianism (1827), were respectable pieces in their own right.[1] They established his reputation as the kind of scholar who combines solid scholarship with deeply felt ecclesial concern. But it was *Symbolism*, which first appeared in 1832, that spread his reputation far and wide as a defender of the Catholic faith. This book's publication record is remarkable; it went through 5 editions in 6 years, was reprinted sixteen times before World War I, and was translated into Latin, Italian, French, English, Dutch, Swedish, and Polish.

It was Möhler's *Symbolism* more than any of his other works that left its mark on Catholic theology in the second half of the nineteenth century and during the first half of the twentieth century. Why was it so influential? This work offered a dignified defense of the Catholic Church's theological anthropology, sacramental theology, and ecclesiology not only in comparison with various branches of Protestantism, but also in contrast to modern rationalists and naturalists, and the current variations on Sabellianism, pantheism, and Gnosticism. Möhler offered a confessional approach to Catholic identity that was stately and scholarly, which seemed well suited to this challenging period in the church, academy, and society.

In particular, it was the christocentric ecclesiology of *Symbolism* and especially its view of the church as "the permanent (or ongoing) Incarnation" (*die andauernde Fleischwerdung*), a position already suggested in his work on Athanasius in 1827, that was of singular importance. This concept of an ongoing Incarnation undergirds Möhler's emphasis on objective tradition, and warrants his defense of the outward, institutional, and dogmatic character of the church's identity, and of the infallibility of the church.

The pervasive influence of Möhler's incarnational approach to ecclesiology and tradition has been ascertained in the work of many notable theologians.[2] Möhler made a lasting impression on his students at Tübingen and one student in particular, Johannes Kuhn, carried on his legacy there.[3] Probably more significant was his influence on the Roman school of theology associated with Giovanni Perrone, Carlo Passaglia, and Clemens Schrader during the middle of the nineteenth century, and carried on by Johann Baptist Franzelin.[4] Möhler's theology continued to have an effect on theologians at the end of the nineteenth century and the beginning of the twentieth, notably Matthias Joseph Scheeben and Karl Adam.[5] Moreover, it seems plausible to posit the ongoing, if diffusive and indirect, influence of Möhler's incarnational approach to church and tradition evident, down through the middle of the twentieth century, as the genuine and undisputed point of consensus, in the work of Karl Rahner, Edward Schillebeeckx, Henri de Lubac, and Otto Semmelroth.[6] During the 1950s theologians pursuing distinct programs—not only neoscholastic theologians, but also advocates of a return to biblical and early Christian sources and proponents of a new engagement with modern Contintental philosophies—

agreed on an Incarnation-centered christology and on an incarnational and sacramental approach to the church. And this consensus is, at least indirectly, a reflection of the momentous reception of Johann Adam Möhler's later work.

This consideration of the reception of Möhler gives rise to two questions: How are we to interpret Möhler's work and its lasting significance? And specifically how are we to understand his earlier Spirit-centered ecclesiology in relation to his later incarnational ecclesiology? We turn to Geiselmann and Congar to begin to address these questions.

Josef Rupert Geiselmann was the great twentieth century advocate of "The Catholic Tübingen School" and especially of Möhler's approach to tradition as providing a viable alternative to the regnant neoscholasticism.[7] He made this appeal in large part by developing a compelling historical interpretation of Möhler's theology. For Geiselmann Möhler was a classicist and traditionalist, but he was neither a restorationist nor an extreme ultramontanist. He was influenced by romantic and idealist philosophies, but he was neither the precursor of Catholic modernism nor an authoritarian right-wing Catholic Hegelian.[8] In Geiselmann's judgment, Möhler helped the Catholic Church move beyond a stagnant, abstract, and authoritarian understanding of tradition, while avoiding the perceived deficiencies of modernist and liberal views. Möhler forged his views of tradition and the integrity of Catholic identity as he critically engaged various forms of Protestant theology, as well as theologians influenced by modern rationalism, deism, and pantheism, and the particular version of traditionalism and fideism espoused by Louis Bautain.

Yves Congar sustained a wider range of scholarly commitments than Geiselmann over the course of his career, but he gave considerable attention to the importance of Johann Adam Möhler's theology.[9] Beginning in his essays in the 1930's, Congar was interested in the significance of Möhler for ecumenical relations with the Orthodox and Protestants. Over the years he also affirmed the value and significance of Möhler's understanding of tradition, the Holy Spirit, and of his communion ecclesiology as rich resources for theology in the second half of the twentieth century. Congar confessed that "in him [Möhler] I found a source, the source, which I directly used. What Möhler had done in the 19th century became for me an ideal toward which I would aim my own reflections in the 20th century."[10]

Geiselmann and Congar agreed on a number of valuable aspects of Möhler's treatment of tradition: his interpretation of the Council of Trent on the gospel, scripture, and tradition; his retrieval of a biblical and patristic approach to the nature of the church, tradition, and theology; and his development of the distinction between objective and subjective tradition. Both gave special attention to Möhler's earlier *Unity in the Church* and its importance for a communion ecclesiology; and by so doing they both attempted to do what Möhler could not do: reincorporate the insights of his earlier work within the frame of reference provided by his later work.

Congar also expressed, however, grave reservations about an incarnational ecclesiology that thinks of the Church as "a continuing Incarnation" wherein the divine and the human are hypostatically united "according to which, as the Church is Christ's body so its mouth would be Christ's own, and all that it says would come from Christ." This "excessively physical treatment of the theme of the body is to be found in Möhler (*Symbolik*, § 36), then in Perrone, and in Passaglia and Schrader." Congar came to the conclusion that without the proper distinctions this incarnational view of the church leads to "a certain ecclesiological Monophysitism."[11]

In Congar's later treatment of the Holy Spirit, he returns to his concerns about the proponents of an incarnational ecclesiology. "At the beginning of the nineteenth century, Möhler provided, in his book *Die Einheit* (1825), a radically pneumatological ecclesiology, but he later refused to prepare a new edition of this work, and what was preserved of his teaching is taken from his later work *Symbolik* (1832), with its resolutely Christological ecclesiology, in which the Church is seen as a 'continued Incarnation.' This idea dominated the Roman School through the nineteenth century."[12] When Congar bemoans the fact that "the Holy Spirit has sometimes been forgotten," it is telling that his key examples are two figures who continued the legacy of Johann Adam Möhler's incarnational ecclesiology, Matthias Joseph Scheeben and Karl Adam.

Spirit and Word in Tradition

There is a fundamental transition that occurs in Möhler's work: from a Spirit-centered to a Word-centered understanding of the church and tradition. This shift in emphasis is substantial, but it is not absolute. Möhler's early work is accurately called Spirit-centered because it accentuates the importance of the Holy Spirit in understanding the nature of the church and tradition, even though it still maintains the basic christological, i.e., christocentric, tenets of the Christian faith.[13] Alternately, his later work is Word-centered in its formulation of the nature of the church and tradition, although the Spirit's work is occasionally considered.

In *Unity in the Church* Möhler admittedly inverts the order of salvation—Father, Son, and Spirit—and "begins with the Holy Spirit" because, as he explains, the agency or work of the Spirit is "temporally first in our becoming Christians," for the Spirit "guides us to the Son, and the Son to the Father" (77, 3). And how does the Spirit bring this about? Neither through abstract concepts, nor through the imposition of institutional norms and regulations, but rather by bringing forth new life in the human heart. In this work the Spirit engenders a new incorporation, a new communal life that expresses its identity in liturgy—especially Eucharistic communion, in scriptures, in doctrine, and in episcopal leadership.

Möhler's early intersection of Spirit, life, and organic community features certain Pauline and Johannine biblical traditions, and patristic writings from the first three centuries that build on these biblical traditions. These classical themes powerfully coalesce with German romantic and idealist convictions about the organic character of the self and community, which account for various prominent motifs in his writings: his preoccupation with the origin and development of a community in terms of inner and outer influences on these life-like structures; the dynamic relationship between individual parts and corporate wholes; the romantic interest in individuality as a source of identity and creativity and as the matrix for the romantic concepts of *Volksgeist* and *Gemeingeist*; and the related understanding of organic leadership.[14]

One could say that for a number of important figures this organic preoccupation in nineteenth-century Germany was born of the Spirit. That is to say, the concept of "the Spirit" was a generative or a correlative principle for organic discourse in romantic writers, like Novalis (Friedrich von Hardenberg) and Friedrich Ast, and in idealist thinkers, preeminently Hegel; the important exception is Schelling, who viewed nature and history in organic and dynamic terms but without using the language of Spirit. Their writings provided a rich milieu not only for Möhler, but also for the theologians who initially influenced him most: J. S. Drey, Friedrich Schleiermacher, and church historian August Neander.[15]

The overarching structure of *Unity in the Church* conveyed the inner and outer manifestations of Christain life: "one Spirit, one body" (Ephesians 4:4). Part 1 treated the inner mystical and communal life as source of unity, love, and holiness; the egoistic and sectarian spirit that threaten this unity through heresy; and the genuine diversity and individuality that thrives within this unity. Part 2 examined the outer corporate expressions of unity through personal communion between people and bishop, in a metropolitan diocese, in episcopal collegiality, and papal primacy.

The Holy Spirit is the source of faith and life in the individual and in the corporate individual, the church, the body of Christ. The Spirit enables individuals to receive the church's proclamation, not only to be affected by the divine power, but to participate essentially in the divine life, and to form a living unity, a mutual exchange, with other believers in the church. The Spirit is thus considered the driving force in the individual's personal life of communication with God and in the life and mission of the church.

Möhler's concentration on the Spirit in the life of the church results in giving a certain priority of importance and time in the process of becoming Christian to the "inner" personal and relational character of faith in relation to "outer" matters of doctrine and institutional authority. "Inner faith is the root of the external; . . . it is given before the external" (§ 8). Positing this order of inner and outer matters of faith is not intended to neglect doctrines and institutions, but rather is offered to set these various issues in a certain relationship, order, and proportion. Indeed, the Spirit is presented as the source of faith and life, but Möhler also acknowledges that the life of faith entails receiving a truth that is given, in and from Jesus Christ and through the church.

This mutual dependence and reciprocity between inner participation in the divine life within a community and outer revelation communicated through the church is not demonstrated, but it is axiomatic for Möhler. Moreover, closer examination reveals a dialectical tension or paradox in this formulation: the axiom of mutual reciprocity between inner and outer grants temporal priority to outer over inner in the process of Christian becoming, although it also posits temporal priority to inner in this process, with the outer viewed as the subsequent embodiment of this life giving Spirit in doctrine and institution. This tension or paradox is obscured because only once does he accentuate the priority of the outer over the inner, whereas the entire work displays the temporal priority of the inner over the outer. This complexity may be attributed to the fact that Möhler's interest in Christian becoming encompasses both the historical origins of Christianity and the origins of Christian conversion in every historical era, which intersect in this work.

The crucial instance manifesting Möhler's Spirit-centered approach to tradition, with precedence granted to inner over outer, is found in his definition of Christian doctrine as "the conceptual expression of the Christian Spirit" (96,23). This approach assumes the reciprocal relationship between the inner life of the community and outer doctrinal forms, but it can leave the impression that doctrinal forms are secondary or derivative.[16] Such a judgment is neither intended, nor implied. Möhler never sought to undermine the authority of church doctrines and institutions, only to make them intelligible and compelling.

His Spirit-centered construal of the organic relation between the inner communal life of faith and outer doctrines warrants four major tenets of Möhler's initial understanding of tradition.[17] First, and most importantly, the nature of revelation is conceived in terms of a vital communal process. He criticizes the *sola scriptura* principle of the Reformers for failing to grasp the richness of this process.[18] But he also rejects the formula that revelation is contained partly in the scriptures and partly in tradition, which was not adopted at Trent, but survived as a commonly-held opinion. Revelation must first of all be conceived in terms of "the living speech" and "the living gospel" which issued forth in the establishment of a new Christian life through the Spirit (§§ 12, 14, 16). "The living gospel, ever proclaimed in the church . . . stretches forth to the whole spirit of Christianity, [and] to individual doctrines" (§ 12, n. 66). This view of revelation derives from one principle: the Spirit precedes the letter. Tradition and scripture are expressions of the same Holy Spirit and the same living gospel (§ 16). The inner life of the church precedes scripture and is expressed in scripture, as "the earliest steps in the embodied tradition" (§ 12, n. 66).

Second, Möhler's Spirit-centered and organic approach to revelation yields a developmental understanding of doctrine and correlatively an historical hermeneutic of tradition. Here he shifts his attention from the social genesis of the Bible and church doctrines to their communal reception, interpretation, and development. "The biblical words are revelations of the Holy Spirit, but they are only understandable to the person to whom the Spirit has already communicated itself" (§ 8). "Since Christianity is seen as a new divine life given to people, not as a dead concept, it is capable of development and cultivation . . . The inner unity of life must be preserved or it will not always be the same Christian Church; but the same consciousness develops, the same life unfolds itself ever more, is always more specific, makes itself always clearer" (§ 13). Möhler finds this organic development manifest in the writings of Paul and John and "in glorious bloom in the great synods." While questions about the deficiencies of such an organic view of doctrine merit attention which we cannot provide here, the chief advantage of such an approach to church doctrine is that it subtly moves between divine origins, identity in the midst of change, and eschatological growth into full identity.

Third, Möhler's treatment of doctrine, as the expression of the Spirit working through the life of the community, establishes a framework for distinguishing heretical egoism and sectarianism from legitimate individuality and diversity in the church. Egoism and legitimate individuality in matters doctrinal are fundamentally different (§ 40). The difference becomes clear by evaluating particular contributions in relation to the corporate whole through which the Spirit works. "If anyone initiated an egotistical development, its rejection was based finally on tradition that was nothing other than an agreement with the continuing faith of the church and the resulting demonstration of the novelty of that development" (§ 11; also see §§ 13, 17). The heretical principle is egotistical and sectarian and has as its source an alien spirit, guided by a freedom of study, sometimes a kind of rationalism, released from the bonds of tradition. Gnosticism and Protestantism provide his key examples (§ 30).[19]

The Catholic principle, on the other hand, is one of unity and communion, effectively combining the truth of faith and love (§ 18); it has its source in the Holy Spirit, and its term in the very unity of God (§§ 27, 30). This dynamic unity of the church thrives on the gifts of the Holy Spirit bestowed on individuals, and requires that these gifts be freely developed and integrated into the corporate whole for the good of the whole (§ 26). "Since the church can have in it members of differing individualities, the needs of all can be satisfied. . . . All together form a great organic whole enlivened by one Spirit. Single individuals grow and the whole flourishes. No constraint of individuality comes from the Spirit of the Catholic Church. Rather, she forms individualities in virtue and power" (§ 42). Möhler's high esteem for individuality extends to individual collectivities: historical periods, cultures, races, peoples, and families (§ 46). Here is evidence of the romantic concept of *Volksgeist*— a spirit that inspires the identity of a group. Each of these instances of individuality holds the prospect of contributing to the diversity that distinguishes the catholicity of the church, but each also carries the risk of egoism and sectarianism that subverts the work of the Spirit in the church.

Möhler capitalizes on a musical trope when treating legitimate individuality and diversity in the church: diverse voices and instruments are needed to produce the glorious harmony of Christianity (§ 40). By contrast, egoists and sectarian groups lead to cacophony and discord. This metaphor is quite effective, but it elicits a question: by celebrating the symphonic truth of Catholic Christianity, does Möhler suppress tension, conflict, and dialectical movement in the life of the church in the interest of the melody and harmony orchestrated by the hierarchy (what he calls "the conductor's wisdom")? Möhler's renowned distinction provides his response: egoistic and sectarian cacophony is a *contradiction* (*Widerspruch*) that destroys harmony and unity, whereas an *antithesis* (*Gegensatz*) contributes to a harmonious unity (§ 46). Heresy is a contradiction incompatible with Catholic faith, whereas antitheses are "life forces" that push the Catholic tradition toward a "higher unity." Catholicism included all heresies before they became separated from the organic community of faith, but, for Möhler, it is possible that what is now a heretical contradiction can become a true antithesis through a renewed desire for communion and unity. This entire discussion of diversity, unity, and discord in the church, its dialectical tension and process, conveys Möhler's depth of vision, and his generosity and openness for reconciliation, but these traits are often obscured by his dominant tone, which is blatantly apologetic and at times polemical.

The fourth and culminating feature of his Spirit-centered approach to tradition is his advocacy of a communion ecclesiology as the necessary precondition for dynamic unity and historical continuity in development. The Holy Spirit's communication with all believers results in a genuine participation in the divine life, which "stands in the closest relationship to Catholicism's characteristic mode of grasping the Eucharist. The Spirit that penetrates and gives life to all believers must in this way unite them to a greater life of the whole, beget a spiritual community, and bring forth a unity of all" (§ 1). The Spirit is given to all, but the gifts of the Spirit differ, including the gift of episcopal office. Charisms and office are not set in tension, but are united as gifts of the same Spirit (§ 53). The agency of the Spirit is visibly manifest in the communion between all individual parts within the organic body of Christ: believers and their bishop; between local bishops; collegiality among the total episcopate; and between the church and the Primate, the bishop of Rome. The hierarchy thus serves the Spirit at work in the entire community by opposing heretical egoism and articulating genuine Catholic identity.

Möhler writes in *Unity* of the Holy Spirit as the source of personal faith and life, and as the source of the common life and common spirit of the community. His way of speaking of the Spirit repudiates both a Deistic remoteness and a monistic immanentism; the Spirit is transcendence-in-immanence, a personal and communal power that is also a divine person in the Trinity (§ 26; 428, n. 26). The divine transcendence of the Holy Spirit in the Trinity is here decisively affirmed, but it will not be fully developed until later.[20]

The major publications that followed *Unity in the Church*, proceeded in a historical sequence—post-Nicene, medieval, and reformation: a book on Athanasius, a series of articles on Anselm, and then his comparative symbolics on the differences between Catholicism and classic Protestantism. Each had its own integrity as an historical study, but all offered comments on his own modern period.

His book *Athanasius the Great and the Church of his Time Especially in the Struggle with Arianism* (1827) is an important transitional work. In it he gave considerable attention to the Holy Spirit and to the doctrine of the Trinity, but its chief significance for our purpose is that as he ponders Athanasius's achievement he begins to develop an incarnational ecclesiology. To put it bluntly: Athanasius's christology displaced Möhler's earlier pneumatology. Möhler's study of Athanasius provided not only the context, but also the positive impetus for his newly developed focus on the Incarnation. It is also evident that a negative stimulus was provided by the concentration on "Spirit" in the increasingly influential dogmatics of Schleiermacher.[21] While preparing *Unity in the Church* Möhler came to realize the threat of losing the transcendence of the Holy Spirit by speaking of "the Spirit of the community" (*Gemeingeist*). His work on Athanasius's critique of Arianism and Sabellianism considerably sharpened his argument on this point.

Möhler's discussion of the Holy Spirit in his Athanasius book affirmed basic tenets of *Unity*, but also moved decisively beyond them. He reiterates several themes found in *Unity* about the role of the Spirit as the source of the life of faith and the corporate life of the church. His communion ecclesiology is also in evidence; bishops who were not in communion with the faithful were a significant factor contributing to the controversies which followed the Council of Nicaea (441). What is most significant and fitting for a work devoted to Athanasius and to this period of history is that he gives great attention to the establishment of the full divinity of the Holy Spirit and the Spirit's coequal status with the Father and Son, which makes the Spirit worthy of veneration; Arianism and Sabellianism are the correlative heretical contradictions to this orthodox faith.[22] New attention is also given to various ways the Spirit is spoken of in the New Testament, many of which are found in Athanasius' *Letter to Serapion*, e.g, the baptism of the Lord and the baptismal reception of the Spirit that makes believers children of God who can cry out Abba, Father.[23]

Athanasius's courageous defense of the doctrine of the Incarnation against considerable opposition after the Council of Nicaea is highlighted in this work. From this history Möhler derived reassurance and insight for the struggle with modern-day Sabellians like Friedrich Schleiermacher.[24] Athanasius' context and its relevance for Möhler's own, in which the church was struggling to reestablish and preserve its identity against opposing forces, served as Möhler's impetus to envision the church as the ongoing Incarnation. In his own words: "Athanasius stood with all the roots of his life, which were also inclined to spread so deep and so wide, planted in the church: he always contemplated within the community of the church and on its past. For, he taught, Christ has united himself most intimately with the church, just as with humanity, with which he constitutes a person, so that it [the church] is, as it were, Christ himself" (110). And again: "The entire church is in him [Christ], in his power. He is the point of origin, and just as everything is included in the origin, so the entire church is in him. The church is, as it were, . . . the development of Christ in time" (266). Möhler concluded that, in contrast to Paul of Samosata who denied that the Word of God had really become flesh, Athanasius fully realized that "This is my body" clarified the union between the divine and the human, not only in Christ, but in the church (564). Now an important work of the Spirit of God is to help believers to comprehend the difficult doctrine of the Incarnation (466).[25]

The Spirit of God is needed not only to understand the Incarnation; in three different essays that appeared in the years 1827 and 1828, Möhler stressed that priestly celibacy is a gift of the Spirit of God.[26] Möhler's treatment of Athanasius and Anselm devoted considerable attention to the importance of their ascetic lifestyles, including celibacy, for fulfilling their difficult missions. He implies that the pneumatological source of priestly celibacy provides an important rebuttal to the critique of this discipline, offered allegedly in the name of Enlightenment rationalism and human rights. One can infer that Möhler regarded the critique of mandatory celibacy as another example of egoism and sectarianism, although not heretical in the strict sense.[27] Möhler's treatment of the priestly celibacy tradition offers another instance of his understanding of the Spirit active in history.

Symbolism provides the fullest statement of Möhler's incarnational or Word-centered ecclesiology and his revised understanding of tradition.[28] Möhler identifies the church on earth as "the visible community of believers, founded by Christ," which has as its sole objective to exist for the redemption and sanctification of humankind, "by means of an enduring apostleship" and "under the guidance of his Spirit" (§ 36). The visible church of Christ, the apostles, and the Spirit are all important, but, as he goes on to explain, it is the visible church of Christ that takes precedence:

> Thus, in this great, important, and mysterious work entrusted to a visible society of men, the ultimate reason of the visibility of the church is to be found in the Incarnation of the Divine Word. . . . The visible church, from the point of view here taken, is the Son of God himself, everlastingly manifesting himself among men in a human form, perpetually renovated, and eternally young—the permanent Incarnation of the same, as in Holy Scriptures, even the faithful are called 'the body of Christ.' . . . As in Christ the divinity and the humanity are to be clearly distinguished, though both are bound in unity, so is He in undivided completeness perpetuated in the church (§ 36).

This shift from a Spirit-centered to a Word-centered ecclesiology corresponds to a change in his treatment of inner and outer manifestations of tradition. The mutual dependency of inner and outer, which we found in *Unity*, remains axiomatic in *Symbolism*, but the priority of importance and the temporal priority in the process of Christian becoming is given to outer manifestations. The official teachings and the teaching authority of the episcopacy and the pope come first. This transition was already established in his book on Athanasius. In *Symbolism* its significance becomes clear; this shift represents Möhler's changed understanding of the proper relationship, balance, and order of outer and inner dimensions of tradition.

The doctrine of the Incarnation thus reveals for Möhler the distinctive nature of the church as a visible institution, and warrants the teaching authority of the hierarchy. Divinity and humanity are united in the Incarnate Son of God and cannot be separated, and on this basis one can speak of an exchange of properties. Thus we read: "If the divine—the living Christ and his Spirit—constitute undoubtedly that which is infallible, and eternally inerrant in the church; so also is the human infallible and inerrant in the same way, because the divine without the human has no existence for us; yet the human is not inerrable in itself, but only as the organ and as the manifestation of the divine" (§ 36). The agency of the Spirit in the church's teaching office is here acknowledged, but it is the unity of the divine and the human in the Incarnation that provides the predominant framework for his treatment of the hierarchy. As we read in his section on the hierarchy, "The primary view of the church as a divine and human institution is here evinced in a very striking way" (§ 43).

Clearly, the Spirit is not absent in *Symbolism*.[29] However, the role of the Spirit is displaced in large part because Möhler's overarching argument against Martin Luther, and by extension against all of the Reformers, is that the doctrines *sola fides* and *sola Scriptura* rest on a *solus Spiritus Sanctus* doctrine. This means, on the one hand, in matters of personal faith, that Luther failed to recognize the role of human cooperation with the Holy Spirit. On the other hand, in matters ecclesial, Luther ended up accentuating the inner inspiration and testimony of the Holy Spirit in the interpretation of the Scriptures, and the priesthood of all believers to the exclusion of the exterior, incarnational, institutional, and objective character of the

visible Catholic Church.[30] The problem could not have been more obvious for
Möhler: "The meaning of the doctrine, the Word became flesh, the Word became
man, was never clear to Luther's mind" (§ 48). And that meaning is predominantly
ecclesiological. By accentuating the incarnational character of the church and its
importance for the authority of the hierarchy, and giving precedence to outer aspects over inner aspects of tradition, Möhler's treatment of the agency and efficacy
of the Spirit was subtly altered. His early work had concentrated on the Spirit's role
in the genesis and development of personal and communal faith. His later work
highlights the agency of the Spirit in defending the objective body of teachings of
the hierarchy, now spoken of as objective tradition, and in the act of receiving the
official teaching of the church by believers, now described as subjective tradition.
Personal participation in the divine life and in the organic community are still affirmed but they are resituated. The Protestant threat of the individual interpretation
of the Scriptures and Christian doctrine in the name of the inspiration and inner
testimony of the Spirit is now placed over against an incarnational ecclesiology and
the Johannine motif of the Spirit of truth, which is the truth of Christ, who preserves
the church against all odds and leads people to follow in the way of truth.

    The question arises: does Möhler's new theology of tradition imply a bifurca-
tion, wherein the Incarnation of the Son of God justifies the genesis of doctrine
through the teaching of the church's hierarchy, while the Holy Spirit enables the
believer to receive and appropriate this message? Does his new formulation dimin-
ish the role of the Spirit in the church's learning and teaching, in the development
and transmission of doctrine in the entire church? Is the Holy Spirit left to inspire
the defense and reception of the christocentric truth of the tradition taught by the
teaching office?

    This kind of bifurcation seems belied by the following passage, which refers to
the dynamic interplay between the Incarnation and Pentecost in the formation of
the church:

> Since the Word of Christ (taken in its widest signification) found, together with
> his Spirit, its way into the circle of men, and was received by them, it has taken
> shape, put on flesh and blood; and this shape is the church, which accordingly
> is regarded by Catholics as the ecclesial form of the Christian religion itself. As
> the Redeemer by his Word and his Spirit founded a community, where his
> Word should ever be living, he instructed the same to this society, that it might
> be preserved and propagated.(§ 36)

But even if no such strict bifurcation of the roles of the Word and the Spirit, and no
diminishment of the role of the Spirit is intended, it must be seriously asked whether
Möhler is not restricting the way the Spirit operates in the church in the traditioning
process.

    Still, even after Möhler embraces a Word-centered ecclesiology, and gives
precedence to outer over inner and objective over subjective, he continues to
affirm the basic features of his earlier formulation. (1) Scripture and tradition are
both necessary and mutually condition one another. (2) Doctrinal development,

generally speaking, is affirmed. (3) Heretical egoism and sectarianism contradicts acceptable forms of individuality, which include both expressions of individual persons and collective wholes (*Volksgeist*).[31] And (4) there is a profound reaffirmation of ecclesial communion, which is a gift of the Spirit bestowed at Pentecost, who brings the apostles and disciples into "one accord"(§ 37). Just as the Word takes flesh, so the Spirit took an outward shape.

One could examine these basic components of Möhler's position and conclude that although there has been a change of emphasis: from Spirit to Word, and from inner to outer aspects of the church's tradition, the details of his position on the nature of tradition have remained the same. But that verdict would fail to comprehend an important change in how tradition and especially doctrinal development are articulated in relation to his communion ecclesiology. Möhler no longer begins with the Spirit and the entire community in the generation of these doctrines. Rather the visible church, through its hierarchy, infallibly teaches. So while all the basic contentions are maintained, the way the community generates, transmits, develops, and receives doctrines is construed differently. His defense of objective tradition is intended to set forth the stable identity of the Catholic tradition not only against Protestant alternatives, but also against the rationalists and pantheists of his day. He still professes the importance of individuality and antitheses within this tradition. But despite this, his mature communion ecclesiology is in the final analysis "governed" in the sense of "constricted" by the teaching authority of the hierarchy and the Spirit's mission in the entire community is in effect reduced to enabling an obedient reception of this tradition.[32]

Assessing the Legacy of Möhler
for the Twenty-First Century

Johann Adam Möhler stands as an important figure in modern Catholic theology. But in what role is he cast? Is he, as Walter Kasper argues, "the forerunner of modern Catholicism"?[33] Or, as Joseph Ratzinger describes him, "the great reviver of Catholic theology after the ravages of the Enlightenment?"[34] Or does the theology of Möhler and its reception provide, as Johannes Brosseder contends, an obstacle to the future of theology?[35] This kind of debate about Möhler's identity and significance is nothing new: during the twentieth century he has been cast as neo-Protestant, proto-modernist, right-wing Hegelian, integralist, and the voice of moderation in an age of extremes. The interpretations of Möhler are no longer so divergent; extremely polemical and one-sided views have been discredited.

Nevertheless, Möhler's legacy remains ambiguous. On the one hand, he can be viewed as promoting a modern or post-Enlightenment approach to theology that begins with a socially constituted subject and that advances a historical understanding of Christian tradition. He was also an important advocate of a revived communion ecclesiology and pneumatology, and harbinger of ecumenical theology. On the other hand, his contribution can be viewed as classicist or traditionalist; he can be presented as one who never fully confronted modernity but reacted against it. And for all his care in developing a robust ecclesiology engaging the entire church, it can be argued that his work had the effect of promoting ecclesiological monophysitism, the modern increase in the power of the hierarchy, and a polemical and triumphalistic posture in ecumenical relationships. As a result of this ambiguity, his heirs in the twenty-first century will need to develop the ability to perceive both sides of Johann Adam Möhler's legacy: its genuine achievements and its real limitations.

When we consider the positive bequeathal of Möhler to the twenty-first century, it would be wise to follow the path prepared by Geiselmann and Congar. As we have found, Möhler pioneered an historical approach to the Catholic tradition that is rich and discriminating, committed to Catholic identity, and alert to and protective of the borderlines with Protestants, other religions, and social movements. His incarnational and sacramental approach to the entire church and to the hierarchy is of lasting significance, as is his treatment of ecclesial communion and diversity. Each of these contributions must now be rethought in light of developments in pneumatology[36] and in terms of an ecclesiology that is as pneumatological as it is christological and trinitarian.[37] The task is not to choose between a Spirit-centered or a Word-centered ecclesiology, but to clarify the trinitarian missions and relations of Spirit and Word active in the entire church. Consequently, the challenge is not to read Möhler's works in reverse order, or to harmonize his early and later works, but to think the unthought thoughts left in his work, and so to continue to work through his achievement, and as a result to move beyond it. This can be illustrated in a number of areas, which can only be identified here.

As we have seen, Möhler's later writings accentuated the role of the Spirit at work in the teaching office of the hierarchy and in the ecclesial reception of this teaching. He never wavered in affirming the transcendence and divinity of the Holy Spirit as a person in the Trinity. However, he did not fully incorporate his earlier discussion of the role of the Spirit in the communal genesis of traditions, nor was he inclined to reflect on how the Spirit works in the entire community through individuals and groups in advancing doctrinal developments and in serving as a catalyst for the reform of ecclesial traditions. Certainly for the later Möhler the Spirit is an active agent both in individuals drawing them into the divine life and into the common life of the body of Christ as well as in official acts of the hierarchy. The individual either acts in harmony with the corporate whole, enhancing its melody line, or is egoistic and sectarian. But what about the role of individual prophets, sages, and scholars, and distinctive theological traditions and local communities in the learning and teaching process of the church's tradition? Are there not times when individual critical and creative voices challenge the church for the sake of the whole and when communities find ways to inculturate the living Gospel in local churches that can teach the universal church something about the fullness of faith? Must these contributions be discredited as expressions of egoism and sectarian pathos? The deepest impulses in Möhler's work invite those in the twenty-first century to be open to the voice of the Spirit at work not only in the practice of the teaching office of the hierarchy and in ecclesial reception, but also in the larger processes of doctrinal development and ecclesial reform, as well as in the voices of individuals and discrete groups who have a contribution to make to the whole and so should be consulted by the hierarchy.

How are we to conceive of the gifts of the Holy Spirit and the ministerial offices in the church? In Möhler's early work, individual charisms and ecclesial office are viewed as complementary works of the Spirit. In his later work, priestly celibacy was defended as a gift of the Spirit in response to contemporary attacks. This raises an obvious question: can we not continue to affirm Möhler's conviction that the tradition of male celibate clergy is a gift of the Spirit, and at the same time be open to the many gifts of the Spirit, of married clergy and celibate clergy, of female as well as male clergy, for the future vitality of the corporate community? Unavoidably, the tradition of a male celibate clergy will be a contested issue in the twenty-first century, and Möhler's legacy will continue to be used to support the long-standing discipline of the church. But the question is, if we are truly open to the agency of the Spirit in the church, can we not think both *with* Möhler's position on priestly celibacy and *beyond* it?

Möhler's contribution to ecumenical theology has been viewed as pioneering, but it has also been criticized.[38] He is credited with advancing an honest comparison of Catholic and Protestant beliefs. However, his conception of reconciliation between the denominations seemed to require a Catholic conquest. While he occasionally acknowledges the legitimacy of the critical response of the classical reformers to the excesses of the "individual" character of medieval theology, he also confesses in his correspondence that there is a polemical edge in his treatment, evident throughout his career. Möhler's critique of the Protestant Reformers for focussing too much on the doctrine of the Holy Spirit is accompanied by an apparent unwillingness to consider the possibility that the Spirit of truth and holiness had actually inspired Protestant individuals and the local communities that received their teachings. His dialectical approach affirms the Catholic substance, but negates the Protestant principle, and as a result he offers an *Aufhebung* in which Catholic "identity" is uncomplemented by Protestant insights. He advances an ecumenical goal without a viable means to move toward reconciliation. His hermeneutical approach to doctrinal formulas is hard pressed to move people beyond confessional texts to envision how these various doctrinal perspectives shed some light on dense and commonly-loved realities. The question is whether a renewed theology of the Spirit can serve as a stimulus to ecumenical reconciliation. As Möhler indicated, a *Widerspruch* (contradiction) can become a *Gegensatz* (antithesis) by virtue of a desire for unity in the church. Could a greater openness to the Spirit foster the conversion of desires and promote reconciliation through common acts of repentance?

To complete this reflection on the future of Johann Adam Möhler's contribution to the doctrine of the Holy Spirit and Catholic Tradition, we return to Möhler's impact on the Tübingen tradition of theology. It is widely recognized that the programmatic emphasis on the revision of theology and ecclesial reform in tradition associated with J. S. Drey and J. B. Hirscher was jettisoned or least curtailed with the growing influence of Möhler's theology at Tübingen. There was a "Möhlerian turn" at the Catholic school at Tübingen.[39] The older school recognized a place for public opinion in the church, theological criticism of hyperorthodoxy as well as heresy, and individual creativity in the development of doctrine, whereas Möhler became increasingly associated with a more confessional brand of theology that left little room for open criticism and creativity in service to the church. Drey's model of theological revision and ecclesial reform gave way to Möhler's advocacy of traditionalism and ecumenical polemics.[40] These two trajectories of thought— Drey's and Möhler's—in the Tübingen tradition betray a faultline or an uneasy alliance in modern Catholic theology. The post-Vatican II period has demonstrated that this faultline or uneasy alliance between revisionists and traditionalists is still volatile. We conclude with this question: would a more fully developed under- standing of how the Holy Spirit and Jesus Christ work in concert in the church and in Catholic tradition enable us to incorporate Möhler's commitment to a strong Catholic identity with Drey's insight that the defense of a strong Catholic identity requires ongoing theological revision and ecclesial reform?

NOTES

1. *Unity in the Church or The Principle of Catholicism Presented in the Spirit of the Church Fathers of the First Three Centuries*, ed. and intro. Peter C. Erb (Washington, D.C.: Catholic University of America, 1996); *Die Einheit in der Kirche oder das Prinzip des Katholizismus dargestellt im Geiste der Kirchenväter der drei ersten Jahrhunderte*, ed., J. R. Geiselmann (Cologne and Olten: Jakob Hegner, 1957). Paragraph and page numbers will be given in the text. Page numbers will given to the English edition first and then the German edition, e.g., (77, 3). *Athanasius der Große und die Kirche seiner Zeit, besonders im Kampfe mit dem Arianismus* (Frankfurt am Main: Minerva GmbH., 1973 of the second edition of 1844).

2. For an overview see Harald Wagner, "Johann Adam Möhler: Fakten und Überlegungen zu seiner Wirkungsgeschichte," *Catholica* 43 (1989):195–208.

3. For Möhler's influence at Tübingen see Rudolf Reinhardt, "Die Katholisch-theologische Fakultät Tübingen im ersten Jahrhundert ihres Bestehens. Faktoren und Phasen der Entwicklung, in *Tübingen Theologen und ihre Theologie*, ed. R. Reinhardt (Tübingen: J.C. B. Mohr [Paul Siebeck], 1977), pp. 1–42; On Kuhn, see J. R. Geiselmann, *Die lebendige Überlieferung als Norm des christlichen Glaubens: Die apostolische Tradition in der Form der kirchlichen Verkündigung—das Formalprinzip des Katholizismus dargestellt in Geiste der Traditionslehre von Joh. Ev. Kuhn* (Freiburg: Herder, 1959).

4. Walter Kasper, *Die Lehre von der Tradition in der Römischen Schule (Giovanni Perrone, Carlo Passaglia, Clemens Schrader)* (Freiburg: Herder, 1962). Franzelin's work is treated in Congar's book, *Tradition and Traditions* (London: Burnes & Oates, 1966), p. 197;

5. Matthias Joseph Scheeben, *The Mysteries of Christianity* (St. Louis, MO: Herder, 1946); Karl Adam, *The Essence of Catholicism* (New York: MacMillan, 1929). On incarnational ecclesiology in Weimar Germany, see Thomas Ruster, *Die verlorene Nützlichkeit der Religion: Katholizismus und Moderne in der Weimarer Republik* (Paderborn: Schöningh, 1994), pp. 394–399.

6. Karl Rahner, "The Theology of Real Symbol," *Theological Investigations* vol. 4 (New York: Seabury Press, 1974); *The Church and the Sacraments* (New York: Herder and Herder, 1963); Edward Schillebeeckx, *Christ the Sacrament of the Encounter with God* (New York: Sheed and Ward, 1965); Henri de Lubac, *Catholicism: the Common Destiny of Man* (San Francisco: Ignatius, 1988); Otto Semmelroth, *Die Kirche als Ursakrament* (Frankfurt a/M: J. Knecht, 1953).

7. See Leo Scheffczyk, "Josef Rupert Geiselmann—Weg und Werk," *Theologische Quartalschrift* 150 (1970): 385–395. Among Geiselmann's many works on Möhler see,

Lebendiger Glaube aus geheiligter Überlieferung. Der Grundgedanke der Theologie Johann Adam Möhlers und der katholischen Tübingen Schule (2nd edition, Freiburg: Herder, 1966); "Der Wandel des Kirchenbewusstseins und der Kirchlichkeit in der Theologie Johann Adam Möhlers," in *Sentire Ecclesiam*, eds. Jean Daniélou and Herbert Vorgrimler (Freiburg: Herder, 1961), pp. 531–675.

8. Geiselmann's interpretation of Möhler effectively discredited Vermeil's interpretation of Möhler as a precursor to Catholic Modernism and Eschweiler's overemphasis on the influence of Hegel on Möhler's later theology; see E. Vermeil, *Jean-Adam Möhler et l'école catholique de Tubingue (1815–1840): Étude sur la théologie romantique en Wurtemburg et les origines germaniques du modernisme* (Paris: Librairie Armand Colin, 1913); Karl Eschweiler, *Joh. Adam Möhlers Kirchenbegriff. Das Hauptstück der katholischen Auseinandersetzung mit dem deutschen Idealismus* (Braunsberg Pr: Herder, 1930).

9. See the reflections and bibliography in Pablo Sicouly, "Yves Congar und Johann Adam Möhler: Ein theologisches Gespräch zwischen den Zeiten," *Catholica* 45 (1991): 36–43.

10. Cited in Pablo Sicouly's essay from J. Puyo, *Une vie pour la vérité. Jean Puyo interroge le Père Congar* (Paris: Le Centurion, 1975), p. 48.

11. *Tradition and Traditions*, p. 312, and note 1. This critique was originally suggested by Philipp Marheinecke in *Ueber Dr. J. A. Möhler's Symbolik . . . : Eine Recension* (Berlin, 1833), pp. 24–28, which was also cited by F. C. Baur in *Katholicismus und Protestantismus* (2nd edition; Tübingen, 1836), p. 536.

12. *I Believe*, 1:154f, also see 1:22.

13. Harald Wagner prefers to speak of Möhler's early christocentric pneumatology; *Die eine Kirche und die vielen Kirchen: Ekklesiologie und Symbolik beim jungen Möhler* (Munich: Schöningh, 1977), p. 92. There is no doubt that Möhler affirmed the christocentric character of the Christian faith (*Unity*, preface, §§ 7, 8, 36, 51, 64). Nevertheless, it is appropriate and clarifying to speak of his transition from a Spirit-centered to a Word-centered ecclesiology.

14. Möhler also uses a romantic and idealist distinction between the ideal and real (e.g., *Unity* §§ 31–32, 46). The distinction between objective Christianity and subjective Christianity is drawn in *Unity* (§§ 10, 16, 37, 51), but it becomes pronounced in his later writings.

15. For influential sources, see Harald Wägner, *Die eine Kirche*, pp.56–134; Geiselmann, e.g., *Legendiger Glaube*, pp. 324–341.

16. George Lindbeck has identified this kind of approach as an experiential-expressivist approach to doctrines because doctrines are described as outer expressions of inner experiences; *The Nature of Doctrine* (Philadelphia: Westminister, 1984). He associates this position with Friedrich Schleiermacher among others. It might be suggested, using Lindbeck's terms, that Möhler changed from being an experiential-expressivist to a doctrinal-propositionalist. Whatever merits this proposal might have, in my judgment Lindbeck's description of the expressivist position does not adequately present the reciprocal or dialectical relationship between inner and outer in Schleiermacher's formula, nor does it accurately designate Möhler's. See my discussion in *Narrating History, Developing Doctrine: Friedrich Schleiermacher and Johann Sebastian Drey* (Atlanta, Georgia: Scholars, 1993), pp. 93–104.

17. Each of the these four claims about tradition can be traced back to Möhler's "Pragmatic Glimpses," (1823 or 1824) and his lectures on canon law (1823) and on church history (1823, 1826–7).

18. See the comment on Protestants and tradition in the earlier version of *Unity* § 16, n. 83.

19. In *Symbolism* Möhler explores the affinity between Protestantism and Gnosticism, § 27.

20. An observation is in order: In this earlier work there are passages where Möhler pushed the identification of the inner Spirit with the outer body of the Church so far as to leave apparently little room for the role of the human. So, for example, he says that "doctrine cannot and must not be viewed as a human work, but as the gift of the Holy Spirit" (§ 10, see also § 52a). This identification left him open to the charge of ecclesiological monophysitism, a charge that is leveled against his Word-centered ecclesiology as well. This is not surprising in that there is a structural similarity between Möhler's early Spirit-body paradigm and his later Word-flesh paradigm, both of which emphasized unity, at least potentially, at the expense of distinction. For the Spirit-body paradigm see *Unity*, §§ 1, 49.

21. There is no clear evidence that Hegel's philosophy of Spirit was a motivating concern for Möhler in his shift, even though he knew of Hegel's work when these changes occurred. A negative impetus was supplied by the Catholic criticisms of his *Unity in the Church* by Bonn theologian Georg Hermes and the Archbishop of Cologne, Ferdinand August Graf Spiegel, see Hubert Wolf, *Ketzer oder Kirchenlehrer? Der Tübinger Theologe Johannes von Kuhn (1806–1887)* (Mainz: Matthias-Grünewald-Verlag, 1992), pp. 38–49.

22. Möhler's treatment of the Spirit in this work merits more attention than we can give it here. His treatment of the Spirit follows Athanasius' procedure in his contra-Arian writings and letters. Athanasius' Incarnation-centered approach to the Spirit—that as the Son is proper to the Father, so the Spirit is proper to the Son—is reflected in Möhler's new approach. In the words of Athanasius, "The Father does all things through the Word in the Holy Spirit;" *The Letters of Saint Athanasius Concerning the Holy Spirit*, p. 135, also see pp. 34–43, esp. pp. 128–9, 132, 170–171, 184. As R. P. C. Hanson describes: according to Athanasius' opponents, the *tropici*, if the Spirit is 'from God,' why is he not called a Son? "Athanasius cannot answer this, because he has almost no concept of the Spirit's function except to be a kind of understudy of the Son;" *The Search for the Christian Doctrine of God: The Arian Controversy 318–381* (Edinburgh: T. & T. Clark, 1988), p. 751, see pp. 738–790.

23. New motifs in Möhler's treatment of the Spirit in *Athanasius* which can be found in Athanasius' letter to Serapion include: the relation between the Holy Spirit and the human soul and body (e.g., 40–1, 58–61); prophecies concerning the Son (36, 284, 352, 564); the Spirit of truth (271, 351–2); spirit of falsity versus the Spirit of Truth (503); Spirit of freedom of the children of God, not of slavery (378, 443, 469).

24. Möhler devotes twenty pages to Schleiermacher's view of the Trinity and the problem of Sabellianism, 272–299; His disagreements with Schleiermacher had already been articulated in the notes in *Unity*, but here are developed. The most salient argument reads: The Catholic Church "will never deny that the Spirit of the whole, its public spirit (*Gemeinsinn*), its solidarity (*Gemeingeist*), and all the truth and glory it is endowed with, is an effect of the Holy Spirit; but it will never say that the Spirit of the whole is the Holy Spirit, the divinity itself.... Never has the common feeling (*Gemeingefühl*) that has always been with the Holy Spirit in the Church, been declared to be the Holy Spirit" (*Athanasius*, 291). On these issues, see Michael J. Himes, "'A Great Theology of Our Times': Möhler on Schleiermacher," *The Heythrop Journal* 37 (1996):24–46; and Dennis M. Doyle, "Möhler, Schleiermacher, and Communion Ecclesiology," *Theological Studies* 57 (1996): 467–480.

25. *Athanasius* also reflects a shift in focus on the question of tradition. It is the credal formulation of the Council of Nicaea, the outer teaching of the hierarchy as an objective tradition rather than its subjective and inner origins, and its defense by Athanasius that concern Möhler.

26. *Athanasius*, p. 376; "Anselm, Erzbischof von Canterbury." *Theologische Quartalschrift* 9 (1927): 487–492; "Beleuchtung der Denkschrift für die Aufhebung des den katholischen Geistlichen vorgeschriebenen Cölibates," *Der Katholik* 8 (1828): 1–32, 257–297 (pagination error, page 288 is followed by 249).

27. See Stefan Lösch's treatment of "Möhler und die schwäbisch-Bayerische Antizölibatsbewegung 1830–1832" in *Prof. Dr. Adam Gengler 1799–1866: Die Beziehungen des Bamberger Theologen zu J.J.J. Döllinger und J. A. Möhler* (Würzburg: Schöningh,

1963), pp. 215–252; and Rudolf Reinhardt, "Neue Quellen zu Leben und Werk von Johann Sebastian Drey," in *Tübinger Theologen und ihre Theologie*, ed. R. Reinhardt (Tübingen: J.C.B. Mohr [Paul Siebeck], 1977), pp. 117–166.

28. Johann Adam Möhler *Symbolik oder Darstellung der dogmatischen Gegensätze der Katholiken und Protestanten nach ihren öffentlichen Bekenntinisschriften*, 2 volumes, critical ed., Josef Rupert Geiselmann (Darmstadt: Wissenschaftliche Buchgesellschaft, 1958–60). English translation by James Burton Robertson, *Symbolism: or, Exposition of the Doctrinal Differences between Catholics and Protestants as Evidenced by their Symbolical Writings* (London: Catholic, 1843). I will use Robertson's translation with some modifications. Paragraph numbers will be cited. When page numbers are required, English page numbers will be followed by the German page number, e.g., (§ 36, 250, 384).

29. Möhler considers the Spirit in each of the sections of *Symbolism* devoted to anthroplogy, sacraments, and ecclesiology, but especially in the latter. Lutheranism is based on Luther's spirit, Catholicism on Christ's Spirit (§ 36); Word and Spirit are the source of the infallibility of the Catholic Church—"through the medium of the Spirit" the truths of the Church are believed and the institutions are observed (§ 36); the Spirit of truth, of Christ, the eternal truth, works through the authority of the Church, "if Christ is to be a true determining authority for us" (§ 37; 260, 397); the Spirit is present in diversity and individuality, but it is not stated that the Spirit is the inspiring source of individuality as an agent for the good of the whole Church (§ 37; 266–7, 305–6; § 42, 292, 441); each nation or group affirms the infallibility of its *Volksgeist* as does the Church in a more eminent sense, which has Christ's Spirit (§ 38; 274–5, 416). Luther's problems with the Spirit are brought to their extreme form with the Protestant sects, which are compared to Montanists, Novatians, Donatists (§ 54), and the "brothers and sisters of the free spirit," who claimed independent inspiration and freedom from ecclesiastical authority (§ 58).

30. *Symbolism*, §§ 44–48; pp. 306, 308, 311, 313, 315, esp. 323–6.

31. On *Volksgeist*, see *Symbolism*, §§ 37, 39; on individuality, see §§ 40, 42.

32. Three avenues from Möhler's literary remains merit further attention: (1) *Neue Untersuchungen der Lehrgegensätze zwischen den Katholiken und Protestanten* (Mainz, 1854); (2) "Sendschreiben an Herrn Bautain, Professor der philosophischen Facultät zu Straßburg," *Theologische Quartalschrift* 17 (1835):421–453; (3) his lectures on Pauline epistles and the Gospel of John given between 1835 and 1837.

33. Walter Kasper, "Johann Adam Möhler—Wegbereiter des modernen Katholizismus," *International Katholische Zeitschrift* 17 (1988):433–443.

34. Joseph Cardinal Ratzinger, *Church, Ecumenism, and Politics* (New York: Crossroad, 1988), p. 4.

35. Johannes Brosseder, "Möhler's Romantic Idea of the Church: Its Problems in the Present" *Philosophy and Theology* 3 (1988):161–171.

36. For an overview of this renaissance, see Bernd Jochen Hilberath, *Pneumatologie* (Düsseldorf: Patmos, 1994).

37. The assets and limitations of Möhler's approach to christology are as significant as the pneumatological issues we have explored, as is shown by Michael Himes, "Divinizing the Church: Strauss and Barth on Möhler's Ecclesiology." Besides the renewal of pneumatology, 20th century work on christology and on the perichoresis of persons in the Trinity have contributed to a richer understanding of the nature and mission of the church beyond Möhler's achievement.

38. Besides works by Congar and Geiselmann, see Heinrich Petri, "Katholizität in der Sicht Johann Adam Möhlers und ihre Bedeutung für den Ökumenischen Dialog," *Catholica* 42 (1988): 92–107; Hans Friedrich Geisser, "Die methodischen Prinzipien des Symbolikers Johann Adam Möhlers. Ihre Brauchbarkeit im ökumenischen Dialog," *Theologische*

Quartalschrift 168 (1988):83–97; Reinhold Rieger, "Johann Adam Möhler–Wegbereiter der Ökumene? Ein Topos im Licht neuer Texte," *Zeitschrift für Kirchengeschichte* 101 (1990): 267–286.

39. Rudolf Reinhardt, "Die katholisch-theologische Fakultät Tübingen im ersten Jahrhundert ihres Bestehens. Faktoren und Phasen der Entwicklung," *Tübinger Theologen und ihre Theologie*, 1–42; Hubert Wolf, *Ketzer oder Kirchenlehrer, pp.* 12, 68–71.

40. Of course Drey's emphasis on historical theology and Catholic identity left its mark on his one time student Möhler, but Möhler was not in total agreement with Drey's understanding of tradition and theology. Drey influenced Möhler's understanding of historical theology under the mutual influence of Schelling and Schleiermacher. There is also evidence that Drey in his later work *Apologetik* which appeared after Möhler's *Athanasius* and *Symbolism*, was influenced by Möhler's confessional approach and incarnational ecclesiology—e.g., there is no longer any explicit discussion of the need for a theological critique of hyperorthodoxy. On the relationship between Drey and Möhler, see Geiselmann, *Lebendiger Glaube*, pp. 294–298, and passim; Harald Wagner, *Die eine Kirche*, pp. 114–118, 265–270.

5

Divinizing the Church

Strauss and Barth on Möhler's Ecclesiology

— MICHAEL J. HIMES —

Modern ecclesiology was born in the shift from viewing the church as the bearer of the mystery of Christian faith to recognizing it as itself part of that mystery. Certainly the work of Johann Adam Möhler was central to that shift within Catholic theology. In the brief course of his active career, a mere fifteen years from his first publications in 1823 to his death in 1838, he moved from a pneumatocentric ecclesiology to a Christocentric one. Much can and has been written about the reasons for this development and the trade-offs in switching from a Spirit-centered to an incarnational way of treating the church's nature and mission. Two of Möhler's most distinguished Protestant critics offered perceptive observations which help to clarify one of the ecclesiological problems which he left unresolved. Interestingly, both critics raised their objections to Möhler's treatment of the church while attacking Friedrich Schleiermacher.

Two Critics: Strauss and Barth

Möhler's *Symbolik*[1] provoked comment and criticism from several noted theologians at the time of its publication. The most elaborate criticism and the one that stirred Möhler to write an extended reply was that of Ferdinand Christian Baur, but Karl Immanuel Nitzsch of the University of Bonn and Philipp Konrad Marheineke of Berlin both wrote booklength critiques. Perhaps the most significant Catholic criticism came from Anton Günther in Vienna who reviewed the debate between Möhler and Baur.[2] But two other important figures, one of Möhler's century and one of our own, have made especially interesting observations bearing upon Möhler's ecclesiology—D. F. Strauss and Karl Barth. Strauss' comment is merely a brief remark: "So Möhler could derive the sole-redemptive Popish Church with no greater difficulty from the Christian consciousness than Schleiermacher could his Redeemer. He could give the Christian consciousness a form, in which it seemed interchangeable with the modern principle of progress."[3] Barth's discussion of Möhler is part of a longer critique of the Catholic understanding of tradition in which he uses the Tübingen school as an example.[4] To understand Möhler's ecclesiology a little more deeply, it is helpful to look first at Barth's criticism and then at Strauss's.

Karl Barth

After the first publication of *Symbolik*, Baur insisted repeatedly that Möhler had bought so deeply into the intellectual world of his time that the Catholicism which he sought to defend was, in fact, his own creation bearing little resemblance to the Catholic doctrinal positions found, for example, in the Tridentine decrees. Indeed, Baur had charged, Möhler took over many of his most basic and characteristic positions from Friedrich Schleiermacher.[5] Möhler had been rankled by this charge of "Schleiermacherising" five years before *Symbolik* and had replied that what appeared distinctive in Schleiermacher was the result, in fact, of the latter's "Catholicizing" tendencies.[6] On this Karl Barth wholeheartedly agrees with Möhler.

> It was really a waste of time for Protestant critics of Möhler's system to accuse him of "Schleiermacherising" and to charge him with transmuting Catholic doctrine. Möhler himself had already given the answer: Why should we not speak rather of a catholicising of Schleiermacher?; which means that we have to weigh the possibility that in availing himself of his ideas and formulations, Möhler did represent Catholic doctrine, and in doing so understood Schleiermacher at the deepest possible level and rightly applied him in this way. And do we not have to admit that he is right? The Catholic and the idealistic interpretation of Christian history both do go back to the same conception. They are at one in what ultimately emerges and is expressed in Möhler: in the identity of the Church and its faith and its Word with the revelation which is its basis.[7]

So Barth sees Möhler as being in the mainstream of Catholic thought. Baur and others who pointed to his resemblance to Schleiermacher were right but merely displayed their own lack of understanding of Schleiermacher. They failed to recognize what Möhler, "who knew Schleiermacher particularly well," according to Barth, saw at once; at bottom Schleiermacher, like idealist thinkers in general, was Catholic. If anything Möhler is "a definite Catholic improvement on Schleiermacher."[8]

The question, however, is not whether Baur understood Schleiermacher but whether Barth understood Möhler. Both the Catholic in Tübingen and the Protestant in Berlin "started from the distinction between faith and doctrine, spirit and letter, hidden root and visible shoot, pious self-consciousness and outward ecclesiasticism in the life of the Church, i.e., of revelation." Möhler's advance on Schleiermacher, according to Barth, is that "the two elements are now shown to be originally coordinated with each other, so that the Catholic conclusion that we must listen to the Church can now be understood *a priori* from within."[9] That is an excellent statement of Möhler's achievement in his first book, *Einheit in der Kirche*.[10] But Barth seems unaware that the perspective of the 1825 work and that of the later Möhler in *Symbolik* are very different. He quotes from the two books indiscriminately, making no attempt to place the citations in their very dissimilar contexts. Thus Barth depicts Möhler's final position as "the identity of the Church and its faith and its Word with the revelation which is its basis." Since that revelation is divine self-communication, Barth understands Möhler as holding the final identity of the church with the divine. If he were referring only to *Einheit in der*

Kirche, he might very well be correct, for in his first book Möhler was hard put to maintain the distinction between the Christian *Gemeingeist* and the Holy Spirit.[11] The 1825 work did open the possibility of simply making the church into the incarnate Spirit. But from 1827 on, Möhler's entire effort is taken up with the attempt to preserve the integrity of the divine and the human.[12] Thus *Symbolik* shifts from the notion of the church as the incarnate Spirit to that of the incarnate Son as the basis of the church precisely because the traditional Chalcedonian understanding of hypostatic union allows the church to be fully human as well as divine.[13]

But even if Barth has simplified the issue by failing to distinguish the various stages of Möhler's developing thought on the church, and even if we grant that Möhler had recognized the problem to which Barth points and tried to avoid it, we can ask whether Möhler succeeded. Certainly he carefully preserved the integrity of the human within the church. The Christian community is thoroughly human, as can be seen in its organization on the two balancing principles of episcopalism and papalism. But Barth sees this as a mere inconsistency in Möhler's working through of his ecclesiology. It was simply that "the question had not yet been finally made clear, where that Church which is identical with revelation, i.e. where that mouth which declares revelation, where that authority of the Church which is identical with the authority of the Word of God, has to be sought and heard *in concreto*."[14] For despite his attempt to distinguish the divine and human elements in the church, did Möhler not simply identify the church with God's self-communication in Christ when he called it "the Son of God manifested among human beings in human form in a continuous manner, ever renewed, eternally rejuvenated, his ongoing incarnation, just as the faithful are called in holy scripture the body of Christ?"[15]

There can be no question that Möhler at first sight leaves himself open to this charge of identifying Christ and the church. Even his one-time student Johannes Evangelist Kuhn admitted that Möhler's description of the church as an "ongoing incarnation" could seem "a dogmatic exaggeration."[16] But did Möhler actually make this identification?

J. R. Geiselmann points to an interesting statement on the relation between Christ and the church made in the first edition of *Symbolik* in 1832 and retained in all the subsequent editions.[17] The context is Möhler's discussion of the Catholic doctrine of the Eucharist and the Mass.

> But now to develop more clearly the Catholic perspective we must anticipate a few remarks in the treatment of the church. Viewed from one aspect, the church is, in a kind of a living image [*auf eine abbildlich-lebendige Weise*], Christ manifesting himself and working through all ages, and consequently it eternally preserves and continues without interruption his redemptive and salvific activities.[18]

Here the church is not *identified* with Christ but *functions* for Christ as his living image. It is the tool which Christ employs in his work of redemption. That position is continued in the properly ecclesiological sections which follow the discussion of the Eucharist. When writing of the incarnation as the ultimate ground of the church's visibility, Möhler states, "This was decisive for the character of those means through which the Son of God after his withdrawal from the eyes of the world would still work in the world and for the world."[19] The church is clearly an instrument in which and through which Christ's activity is continued. To be such an instrument, however, it must be suited to its task. That task is the re-establishment of the proper God-man relation and so requires as its means a visible society in which the divine and the human elements are related in that proper balance, inseparable but unmixed. The instrument then must be modeled upon Christ, as indeed every human being must be related to God in accord with the model of the relationship of the divine and human natures in Christ. As that does not mean that every Christian is an instance of hypostatic union, so neither does it follow that the church is an incarnation of the divine.

The clearest demonstration that Möhler did not intend the church to be understood as itself a divine incarnation is his ready admission of the presence of evil in the church. Sounding very much like Schelling and his teacher Johann Sebastian Drey, he rejected the separation of the ideal and the real in treating the church. Catholics know, he wrote, "that the idea is not ordinary reality, and *vice versa*; but they also know that, where no idea lies at the foundation of the real, there is as little truth as where nothing real corresponds to the idea."[20] The idea in question is a church in which the divine and human are united inseparably but unconfusedly, a church modeled upon the incarnation as described in the Chalcedonian formula. If that church is not "real," if it is not in some way realized in the world, then there is no church at all, and the redeeming work of Christ grinds to a halt. But the church which does exist and which is the realization of that "ideal" church is not a *perfect* realization of it. That fact invalidates neither, for the existing church which is not in some measure the realization of the ideal has no truth, and the ideal church which has no correspondence to reality has no existence. But to admit that the church is not the full and perfect realization of the ideal is simultaneously to admit that the human element in the church is not yet perfectly coordinated to the divine. For in Christ, who has been made like us in all things except sin, human nature is perfectly responsive in its relationship with the divine. But in the church the human element, united with the divine on the model of the relationship established in Christ, is not sinless. Möhler's willingness to admit this means that he does not intend the church to be understood as in fact a divine incarnation but rather as analogous to the incarnation.[21]

Although Barth failed to recognize the stages of development within Möhler's thought and the very decided changes which his theology underwent in the course of that development, he did see what Kuhn called "the dogmatic exaggeration" of identifying the incarnate Son with his church. Others, too, made that mistake as Kuhn's comment shows. But the fact that a mistake is made by more than one renders it no less a mistake. For Möhler in *Symbolik* the incarnation remains the foundation, the origin, and the model for the church, but the church is related to Christ as an image and as an instrument. One must view the church within and against the light of the incarnation if one is to understand it. But Möhler does not *identify* it with the incarnation.

D. F. Strauss

Like Barth, Strauss believed that Möhler understood Schleiermacher very well. But he thought that Möhler had used Schleiermacher for his own purposes quite contrary to the Protestant theologian's intention. Strauss's criticism of Schleiermacher's Christology is well-known. While respecting Schleiermacher's work as the only serious and thorough attempt to construct a Christology beyond the language of "nature" and "person," he argued that Schleiermacher had moved illegitimately from Christian consciousness to the historical Jesus. Schleiermacher had defined Christianity as "a monotheistic faith, belonging to the teleological type of religion, and [which] is essentially distinguished from other such faiths by the fact that in it everything is related to the redemption accomplished by Jesus of Nazareth."[22] Thus, by what amounted to a variant of *post hoc ergo propter hoc*, he had to trace what is distinctive in the consciousness of the Christian community to Christ. This yielded the Christ of Christian faith. "If, then, this Christ was a necessity for Schleiermacher as a pious man, and if he believed that as a theologian he could hold fast to him scientifically at the same time, then his dealing with the gospel story must be oriented to ascertaining just this picture of Christ."[23] So Strauss could charge that Schleiermacher "derived" his Redeemer from Christian consciousness and that Möhler followed this pattern with his church. Believing that what is intrinsic to the faith of the Christian could come only from his participation in the church, Möhler simply located in the church as he constructed it all of the hopes and strivings of believers. If Strauss is right, Möhler's refusal to dissociate the real from the ideal would explain his identification of this ideal church which answers the needs and desires of Christians with the historical Catholic Church and so provide the counterpart to Schleiermacher's identification of his Christ of faith with the historical Jesus.

Quite apart from the justice or injustice of Strauss's criticism of Schleiermacher, the question here is whether his reading of Möhler is accurate. At the risk of making the Berlin professor a battlefield for Strauss and Möhler, it may prove helpful to note the latter's final judgment on Schleiermacher. It is found in the epilogue to *Neue Untersuchungen* when Möhler responds to Baur's claim that, whereas Catholicism allows objectivity to suppress subjectivity and classical Protestantism allows subjectivity to triumph over objectivity, the Protestantism of their day allowed both their proper weight thanks especially to the new direction given theology above all by Schleiermacher. This new direction consists in making Christian consciousness the center of systematic theology. This consciousness is possible only in the context of the community of faith, but, as Möhler emphasizes, Schleiermacher makes it stand superior to both scripture and symbolical books in that both must be interpreted only in accord with it. Baur thought that one might compare it to the contemporary Catholic view of tradition. But Möhler sees little or no basis of comparison. "Schleiermacher places himself in the same relation to Christian objectivity as an oriental despot to the laws of his realm."[24] This is why he can in his *Glaubenslehre* twist citations from scripture and previous confessional statements "with horrifying arbitrariness" to make them corroborate his own spinning out of Christian consciousness. Luther, at least in his early career as a reformer, had his "voice of the Spirit" as an interpretive principle, Zwingli his "experience of the heart," the Anabaptists "interior revelation," the Quakers "inner light," and Schleiermacher "Christian consciousness." The difference is that "he expressed himself with the utmost clarity in his striving for scientific form without fear of its results, and with the skill and judgment which are the product of his extraordinary talent and his vast multifaceted learning as well as of the spirit of the nineteenth century." Möhler's respect for Schleiermacher's accomplishment as a theologian is evident even when, in reply to Baur, he is forced to criticize him. But he professes himself astonished that Baur could praise Schleiermacher for balancing objectivity and subjectivity in his formulation of Christian doctrine.

Indeed, had it not been for his communal sense and, Möhler shrewdly remarks, his unpopularity with so many Protestant churchmen, Schleiermacher could have been a sectarian within the German Reformed community. For "his idealism denied all objective foundations" and forced many to recognize that, despite the Protestant confessional statements of the past, scripture alone cannot be the standard for faith. Schleiermacher will have to end by holding one of two conclusions if he seriously wants to maintain Christian consciousness as the center of faith. Either he will have to admit that "Christian consciousness is the source of the doctrine of faith, and then all objectivity has disappeared in Protestantism," or

> since the central point of a doctrine (or of a system of doctrine) can only be another doctrine, and in Christian systematics the doctrine of the person of Christ is the central point, we would once more lose the external historical Christ, and the doctrine of the Christ within, i.e. that each in his own person is the Son of God, would become the center around which systematics moves, and doctrinal theology itself would become the reflection of pious emotions.[25]

> The subject must swallow up the object, and the Christian community must fashion Christ in its own image.[26]

The immediate concern here is not with Möhler's view of Schleiermacher but with Strauss's view of Möhler. And it is interesting to note that at the conclusion of *Neue Untersuchungen* Möhler's criticism of Schleiermacher exactly coincides with Strauss'. Does Möhler himself then fall under that criticism?

Section 37 of *Symbolik*, a lengthy section on the church added in the second edition (1833), might well be understood as an attempt to derive the church from the consciousness of believers. In that section Möhler attempted to illustrate the correspondence between the church and the intellectual, volitional, and emotional needs of human beings who are in process of discovering the God-man relation. But section 37 was added in the second edition as a complement to section 36, in which the church is derived from the incarnation understood precisely as an event which comes to humanity, not emerging from it. Indeed, as Möhler is at considerable pains to point out, a visible church is necessary precisely because that God-man relation which is established in and by Christ "came from outside of human beings, and, of course, first to the apostles in whom the Kingdom of God was founded by the Word of God speaking to them in a human way from outside themselves, so that it penetrated into them from without."[27] What has happened in Christ is not something which can emerge from within humanity. It breaks in upon us from without. It is a revelation within history. Just as the fact "that Carthage was captured by Scipio Aemilianus is known to us only through ancient historians, and our own internal processes of thought give us not the slightest hint of it,"[28] so too one cannot deduce the fact of the incarnation from consciousness. The existence of the church is derived from that event. But then it too confronts the consciousness of believers. It is no more deduced from that Christian consciousness than is the fact of the Christ.

Strauss criticized Schleiermacher for avoiding the acceptance of the New Testament miracles as purely supernatural while not eliminating the basic miracle of the appearance of a sinless Jesus with fully developed God-consciousness in history.[29] Although God-consciousness is intrinsic to human beings as such, the perfection of Jesus in this regard in quality and degree is such that it can be explained only by a direct act of God. But in the panentheist universe such an activity has no place. In a particularly relevant passage for the present purpose, Strauss draws out the consequences of this in Schleiermacher's thought.

> The divine in Christ is to relate to his individual human life the way the Holy Spirit as the divine element is related to the Christian communal life in the church. Still, there is a difference—in Christianity, as in every single Christian, that which emerges as actual decision and deed is always imperfect, infected with sin; in Christ, to the contrary, "that which appears as human was indeed also single, definite as well as limited, but in its human form was to be explained purely on the basis of the divine in him," and was perfect and sinless. This means that the relation of the divine and the human in Christ is to be thought of like the same relation in the church, yet totally differently; in common life we would think ourselves victims of a hoax if someone talked us into something in this way.[30]

This position on the relationship of Christ and the church which Strauss credits to Schleiermacher seems remarkably similar to the position which we find in Möhler. In both the distinction between the relation of the divine and human in Christ and that same relation in the church consists in the fact that in Christ the human was perfectly coordinated and obedient to the divine whereas in the church that ordering of the human to the divine is not yet perfected. Strauss regards this as incomprehensible in Schleiermacher on the grounds that the presence of the divine in Jesus is not of a different order from that presence in any other human being. It could not be, for in Schleiermacher's panentheist system the divine is so joined with the natural which exists within it that, although differences of degree and intensity of divine presence may be conceivable, differences of kind are not. But Schleiermacher has left room for "a miraculous fact."[31] He had carefully prepared in the introduction to the *Glaubenslehre* for the Christological doctrine to be expounded later by noting that "the appearance of the Redeemer in history is, as divine revelation, neither an absolutely supernatural thing nor an absolutely superrational thing."[32] The possibility of the fullness of God-consciousness appearing within a human being, even to the extent that it could be regarded as "a veritable existence of God in him,"[33] cannot be claimed as supernatural in the sense of an abrogation of natural laws in a particular instance. Were it so claimed, the Redeemer would not be a human being at all. The possibility of the appearance of one in whom there would be "a veritable existence of God" must be regarded as natural. But the one in whom God-consciousness would be perfect must, as a human being, have been conditioned by the whole of history with all its sinfulness. Thus the appearance itself of the Redeemer, the *fact* of that appearance, not its possibility, must be regarded as miraculous. Schleiermacher expresses this as the fact that Jesus "must have entered into the corporate life of sinfulness, but he cannot have come out of it."[34] In his lectures on the life of Jesus, Schleiermacher suggests that it as precisely the astonishing fact of his own sinlessness, the complete harmony of his sensuous life with his God-consciousness, which led Jesus to "the consciousness of a specific difference between himself and all other men."[35] Thus Schleiermacher is not subject to Strauss's strictures on this point while at the same time affirming the uniqueness of Jesus and his "specific difference" from all others. Accordingly, he can also speak of the divine and human in Christ as united in a way both like and unlike the union of the Holy Spirit and the church.

Although Strauss might well have regarded Möhler's position as cruder and more "supernaturalist" than Schleiermacher's, he could not have questioned its consistency. For the primary difference between the way in which Möhler uses the relationship of the divine and the human in Christ to explain the relationship of the divine and the human in the church and the way in which Schleiermacher does so rests upon their differing attempts at formulating the God-man relationship. Strauss wrote of Schleiermacher's attempt that the latter had recognized that:

> a divine nature will always degrade the human, with which it is to constitute a single person, to a mere appearance; on the other hand, human nature is quite capable of containing the existence of the divine within it, if only this divine is not conceived as a nature with its own knowledge, will, and so forth, alongside the human.[36]

Having recognized this important distinction, Schleiermacher accepted the necessary condition, quite rightly according to Strauss. When Schleiermacher equates the divine in Christ with the Holy Spirit in the church, he maintains that the humanity of the church is not endangered.

> But why can one assume a divine element only here in the church, without dissolving the continuity of the human? For this reason: Because in this the divine is thought of not in the form of an actual distinct consciousness but only as what lies at the base of the common consciousness, only as the energizing power at the inmost center, in contrast with which we understand everything which externalizes itself as purely human. If we think of the divine in Christ according to this analogy, then we no longer think of it in personal terms, no longer as a divine being united with the human, but only as an effective impulse working on it, that is, as a heightening of its natural powers, especially of its

God-consciousness, which we assume in Christ to be something absolute, powerful, and exclusively determinative of all aspects of life.[37]

To demonstrate that Strauss is not completely just to Schleiermacher would take us far afield. This passage does, however, serve to point to that which differentiates Schleiermacher and Möhler so clearly on this issue. For Schleiermacher the distinction between the divine in Christ and the divine in the church is an economic distinction, that is, a distinction in the way in which God is related to humanity. On that economic level, the distinction is real and the uniqueness of Christ is preserved. But that distinction reflects no distinction immanent to the divine pole of the God-man relation. The relativity of the immanent Trinity, which Möhler found in 1827 was necessary to preserve the integrity of the human in the God-man polarity, allowed him to affirm not only real distinctions between the ways in which divinity and humanity were united in Christ and in the church, but also real distinctions in both the divine and the human poles of that unity. The union of the Son with human nature in Christ is hypostatic, a unique relationship. Far more important at this moment than exploring what this had meant in the traditional Chalcedonian formula is noticing the direction in which Möhler seems to point. The additions and revisions in the successive editions of *Symbolik* between its publication in 1832 and its author's death six years later as well as his defense of his book against Baur's attacks all demonstrate that the nature-supernature relation or, as he sometimes framed it, the God-man polarity, is central to Möhler's thought and not least his ecclesiology. The primary concern in the development of his thought from 1827 on was the maintenance of the integrity of the human, a concern which demanded his defense of the doctrine of the immanent Trinity. In this respect the Tübingen theologian was both pointing toward and laying the groundwork for the suggestions advanced regarding the Trinitarian doctrine in our century by Karl Rahner who noted that incarnation is to be understood as a term designating that form of self-communication characteristic of the second person of the Trinity.[38]

An Unresolved Problem in Möhler's Ecclesiology in Symbolik

The criticisms raised by Strauss and Barth serve to draw attention to a problem in Möhler's ecclesiology. In *Symbolik* Möhler employed the incarnation as the framework in which to understand the church so that he could affirm both the integrity and the interaction of the divine and the human. But he clearly did not wish to claim the church as an instance of hypostatic union. Indeed, he became acutely sensitive to the danger implicit in his formulations in *Einheit in der Kirche* of interpreting the church as a hypostatic union of the Spirit and the community. But how the church can be a fit instrument for the continuance of Christ's work, i.e., a society which reflects the proper God-man relation, without itself being the relationship established in Christ, i.e., hypostatic union, remains unresolved in Möhler's work. The importance of Strauss' brief comment on Möhler is that, in taking seriously the Tübingen theologian's placement of the doctrine of the church within the framework of Christological thought, he forces us to confront the major gap in

Möhler's work, the absence of a carefully worked-through Christology. That absence also sheds further light on Barth's fundamental criticism that Möhler divinized the church.

The lack of a sustained Christological reflection in Möhler's writing is not surprising. First, Möhler was not a systematic theologian and so was not called upon by his academic work to produce a synthesis in which so important an element as Christology could not be bypassed. Second, but related closely to this first consideration, Möhler's published work during his lifetime basically consisted of three books: *Einheit in der Kirche* (1825), *Athanasius der Grosse* (1827), and *Symbolik* in its various editions (1832-38). There were, of course, numerous reviews and articles, some of them quite lengthy, such as the study of Anselm of Canterbury.[39] Many of these, however, were called forth by specific events about which the author wished to comment, e.g., his intervention in the Bautain affair[40] or his remarks on the clash between the Catholic Church and the Prussian government over marriage legislation.[41] *Neue Untersuchungen* is a defense and explanation of *Symbolik* and should not be regarded as a distinct work. Thus Möhler's three principal literary products are a patristically based study of ecclesiology, an investigation of the Arian controversy, and a book on comparative dogmatics. It is not a matter of astonishment then that we should find little direct reference to Christological questions. Third, Möhler died at the age of forty-two but in fact produced no major work after 1835, save for the uncompleted fifth edition of *Symbolik*, because of his failing health. His productive life as a writer was, in effect, finished by his fortieth birthday. The brevity of his career makes it remarkable not that he should have failed to concern himself with a major issue in theology but that he succeeded in contributing importantly to any. And, fourth, the date of the last significant publications of Möhler's work in his lifetime is noteworthy. For 1835 also saw the appearance of Strauss' *The Life of Jesus Critically Examined.*

"What if ...?" is a fascinating but usually unproductive game, at least when clues are few. It seems unlikely that Möhler could have avoided being drawn into the debate surrounding Strauss' book had his health been better and his life longer. Strauss was a student of Baur and a familiar figure at Tübingen. If Möhler's controversy with Baur had continued, it seems reasonable to imagine that his attention would have been drawn to Strauss as an example of those aspects of contemporary Protestant thought to which he most objected in Baur. But more important, Strauss' work raised the question which the historical theologian Möhler could not possibly have avoided, the relationship of the Christian faith and history. Would Möhler have been led by participation in the Life of Jesus debate to devote greater attention to Christological questions?

The very mootness of the question raises an interesting point. The "quest for the historical Jesus," which was given such impetus by the appearance of Strauss' study, occurred after Möhler's time. This suggests an important element in Möhler's Christology—or, rather, the lack thereof. What is most obviously missing from Möhler's work is any reference to the *life* of Jesus. The incarnation plays a decisive role in the working out of the God-man relation in Möhler's thought, but appeal is always made to the fact of Jesus, not his career. Möhler's Christological focus is the incarnation, not the life, death and resurrection of Jesus. The story, the fate and the glorification of Jesus are treated, at most, as the verification and manifestation of the incarnation. In this view, the significance of Jesus is who he is, not what he does. If the effecting of the divine-human person in the incarnation is made the sole focus of attention, the death of Jesus can become merely the working-out of the consequences of the existence of the God-man, and the resurrection can be reduced to a warrant for belief in the incarnation. The vocation, career, message, death and glorification of the historical Jesus can be rendered unimportant when the establishment of the hypostatic union in the Christ of the Chalcedonian formula is seen as the center of Christian faith. Möhler did not reject the historical Jesus for the Christ of faith. He simply devoted his attention to the latter.

That decision on Möhler's part is especially ironic in an historian. For exclusive concentration on the Christ of dogma leads to an interpretation of the incarnation as the divine assumption of human nature but fails to appreciate the divine assumption of human history. Perhaps the central role of the notion of living tradition which he had learned from Drey inclined Möhler to assume too easily that the classical dogmatic tradition exhaustively translated the scriptural witness to the salvation worked in Jesus. If so, the "quest for the historical Jesus" might well have introduced him to a more broadly biblical Christology.

Had that happened, what difference might it have made to his Christocentric ecclesiology? The descending Christology which finds its most balanced expression in the Chalcedonian formula has undeniably had a monophysite bent in the history of Christian thought. If the incarnation establishes in its perfection the God-man relation in the union of the divine and human natures in Jesus, then his actions, his choices, his final self-gift to the Father have no constitutive meaning. He has a human nature without a human history, and the now familiar problems arise of the state of his human consciousness, knowledge and will. The bias of such a Christology is necessarily toward the divine pole in the God-man relation. The accuracy of Strauss' judgment is attested by the history of the mainstream of Christological thought and Christian piety, that "a divine nature will always degrade the human, with which it is to constitute a single person, to a mere appearance."[42] If this is the context of one's Christology, if indeed this is the inherent bias of the Chalcedonian formula, then making that formula the foundation of ecclesiology will tend, however much one tries to preserve the integrity of both the divine and human elements in the church, to eclipse the latter. Möhler saw that rooting ecclesiology in Christology would provide the doctrine of the church with the proper formulation of the God-man polarity. But clearly a biased Christology will produce a biased ecclesiology. Since Möhler began with the formula of Chalcedon, which has in fact often been interpreted with a monophysite bias since the fifth century and which must, by its employment of the static concept of "nature," prove weighted toward the divine, he inevitably if unintentionally, ended up with an ecclesiology biased toward monophysitism.

This is the element of truth at the heart of Barth's criticism of Möhler. Although Barth failed to appreciate the marked difference between Möhler's understanding of the church in *Einheit in der Kirche* and in *Symbolik*, his charge that

Möhler identified "the church and its faith and its Word with the revelation which is its basis" comes close to the truth. We have noted Kuhn's worry about Möhler's "dogmatic exaggeration." Although Möhler did clearly decline to identify the church with Christ, nevertheless the question must arise why such astute readers as Barth and Kuhn could interpret his final position in that fashion.

In seeking to escape the implication of a divinized church inherent in his early panentheism in the style of Schleiermacher, Möhler took the Chalcedonian Christological formula as the basis for ecclesiology. Ironically, however, the monophysite bias of the interpretation of that Christology easily leads to precisely what he had set out to avoid, a divinized church. The root of this divinization of the church is no longer a panentheist identification of God's Spirit with the Christian *Gemeingeist*, but the *communicatio idiomatum*, the logical translation of hypostatic union, the claim that attributes of either nature can be affirmed of the one person. This *communicatio* extends to the church in Möhler's Christocentric ecclesiology, leading to the affirmation that the church is sinless. Möhler acknowledged the reality of evil within the church, of course. He wrote of the sinfulness which affects even those occupying positions of leadership, e.g., popes, bishops, priests, "who unconscionably and indefensibly failed in those areas dependent precisely on them to establish a better way of life" or who, "through scandalous behavior and living, extinguished the still glimmering torch which they should have kindled." Such sinful leaders "hell has devoured." But however sinful the members of the community, including its leaders, might be, he insisted that the church itself is "forever pure and eternally undefiled."[43] Thus he presents us with a church of sinners but a sinless church.[44]

In accord with the suggestion that Möhler's Christology is too static, too much an ontological and too little an historical understanding of Jesus, we should note that the *communicatio idiomatum* may function in the same way but mean something quite different in various Christological perspectives. In a descending Christology, such as that which Möhler presumed in the Chalcedonian formula, the *communicatio* is a given, a logical consequence of the hypostatic union. In an ascending Christology which takes the life, death and resurrection of Jesus as its focus, the *communicatio* is an achievement, a reality finally proclaimed in triumph. An ecclesiology built upon the first Christological stance seems inevitably to tend toward the identification of the divine and the human elements in the church from its inception. As the very thought-form, a union of natures, dictates an essentially static view in which, on the level of Christology, the salvation worked in Christ is effected without, indeed prior to, any freely determined act on Jesus' part, so on the level of ecclesiology, the church may expand but not, in any decisive or significant way, develop. Thus the humanity of the church's members, which can entail sin, error, cowardice, etc., may be affirmed, without really affirming the humanity of the church. For if the church *qua* church is truly a human community and not merely a community of human beings, then the church *qua* church must be subject to the vicissitudes of history. But it is precisely history which is absent from the static conceptual world of "natures." An ascending Christological stance, however, must allow the historically conditioned personality of Jesus, developing over time, its full weight. This is not to accord dominance to time over being but to assert the mutuality of their relation. This introduces the category of history into the *communicatio idiomatum* in such a way that, without prejudicing the complementary insight which gives rise to various forms of descending Christology, full weight can be given to the events by which Jesus became established as the Son of God in power. An ecclesiology shaped in accord with such a Christology must allow for the historically conditioned process by which the church becomes more manifestly the story of the communion of the Spirit within human society.

This insistence on the history of the church as a fully human history which not only coincides with but realizes the dealing of God with history at large is very much more in accord with Möhler's language about the church as a "living image" of Christ which functions as the instrument of the Lord but is not identified with him.[45] The *communicatio idiomatum* cannot be employed in ecclesiology as it is in Christology. Jesus' history is complete; he is established in power as the Christ. But the church's history is not complete; it is still a pilgrim on the way to being what it will be when it comes to full stature, the body of Christ.[46]

Möhler's presumption of a descending Christology which was framed in terms of a union of natures rather than as an ultimately significant history and his failure to critique that presumption, a critique which might well have been demanded of him had he lived a few more years, shaped his Christocentric ecclesiology in such a way that, despite his constant endeavor to guarantee the integrity of the human element in the church, the church emerges as an institution which at key points seems to be preserved from the vicissitudes of history and so appears more or less than human. This was not some covert escape into supernaturalism on Möhler's part, still less a move toward a politic ecclesiastical conservatism. It was simply the state of the question as he left it at his death.

NOTES

1. Johann Adam Möhler, *Symbolik, oder Darstellung der dogmatischen Gegensätze der Katholiken und Protestanten, nach ihren öffentlichen Bekentnisschriften* (Mainz, 1st ed., 1832). Subsequent revised and enlarged editions appeared in 1833, 1834, 1835 and 1838, containing significant expansions and substantial alterations. The critical edition is by Josef Rupert Geiselmann in two volumes (Köln: Jakob Hegner, 1958–1960). The English translation is by J. B. Robertson, *Symbolism or Exposition of the Doctrinal Differences between Catholics and Protestants as Evidenced by Their Symbolical Writings*, 2 vols. (London, 1843).

2. F. C. Baur, *Der Gegensatz des Katholicismus und Protestantismus nach den Principien und Hauptdogmen der beide Lehrbegriffe mit besonderer Rücksicht auf Hrn. D. Möhler's Symbolik* (Tübingen, 1834); K. I. Nitzsch, *Eine protestantische Beantwortung der Symbolik Dr. Möhlers* (Hamburg, 1835); P. K. Marheineke, *Über D. J. A. Möhlers Symbolik oder Darstellung der dogmatischen Gegensätze* (Berlin, 1833); A. Günther, *Der letzte Symboliker. Eine durch die symbolische Werke Doctor J. A. Möhler's und Doctor F. C. Baur's veranlasste Schrift* (Vienna, 1834).

3. D. F. Strauss, *Gesammelte Schriften*, 12 vols. (Bonn, 1876–1877), 2:222, quoted in K. Barth, *Church Dogmatics*, trans. G. T. Thomson and H. Knight (Edinburgh: T. and T. Clark, 1956), 1–2:563.

4. Barth, *Church Dogmatics*, 1–2:560–572.

5. F. C. Baur, *Der Gegensatz des Katholicismus und Protestantismus*, 2nd enlarged edition (Tübingen, 1836), pp. 60f.

6. [Johann Adam Möhler], review of *Über das Verhältnis der Theologie zur Philosophie. Eine Abhandlung* by Adam Gengler, *Theologische Quartalschrift* 9 (1827): 514f. All reviews in the *Theologische Quartalschrift* were unsigned at that time.

7. Barth, *Church Dogmatics*, 1–2:563.

8. Barth, 1–2:561.

9. Ibid.

10. Johann Adam Möhler, *Die Einheit in der Kirche oder das Prinzip des Katholicismus, dargestellt in Geiste der Kirchenväter der drei ersten Jahrhunderte* (Tübingen, 1825). The critical edition was edited and annotated by Josef Rupert Geiselmann (Köln: Jakob Hegner, 1957). The English translation by Peter C. Erb is *Unity in the Church or The Principle of Catholicism Presented in the Spirit of the Fathers of the First Three Centuries* (Washington, D.C.: The Catholic University of America Press, 1996).

11. See the discussion of this point in Michael J. Himes, "'A Great Theologian of Our Time': Möhler on Schleiermacher," *The Heythrop Journal* 37:1 (January, 1996): 24–46.

12. This can be see in Johann Adam Möhler, *Athanasius der Grosse und die Kirche seiner Zeit, besonders im Kampfe mit dem Arianismus*, 2 vols. (Mainz, 1827), in which he extensively criticized what he understood to be Schleiermacher's failure to distinguish between the Christian *Gemeingeist*, the communal spirit of the Christian church, and the Holy Spirit; see Himes, pp. 31ff.

13. On the factors influencing the development of Möhler's ecclesiological thought from *Einheit in der Kirche* through the various editions of *Symbolik*, see Michael J. Himes, *Ongoing Incarnation: Johann Adam Möhler and the Beginning of Modern Ecclesiology* (New York: Crossroad, 1997).

14. Barth, 1–2:565.

15. Möhler, *Symbolik*, 1:389.

16. J. E. Kuhn, *Katholische Dogmatik*, 1–1: *Einleitung in die katholische Dogmatik*, 2nd ed. (Tübingen, 1859), p. 101, n. 1.

17. Möhler, *Symbolik*, 2:633f.

18. Möhler, *Symbolik*, 1:353.

19. Möhler, *Symbolik*, 1:388.

20. Möhler, *Symbolik*, 1:408.

21. If it is true that Barth's reading of Möhler is understandable—and Kuhn's comment indicates that *Symbolik* was similarly read even by sympathetic nineteenth-century Catholic readers—it is also true that others recognized Möhler's real intention. Giovanni Perrone saw his point within a decade of Möhler's death; see G. Perrone, *Praelectiones theologicae*, 9 vols. (Rome, 1835–1842), 8:28–31, quoted by Roger Aubert, "La géographie ecclésiologique au XIXe siècle," *L'ecclésiologie au XIXe siècle*, ed. by M. Nédoncelle (Paris: Cerf, 1960), p. 35:

Non defuerunt tamen qui, ulterius progressi, sibi in Ecclesia quandam veluti Incarnationis continuationem videre visi sunt. Justa hos, Christus Deus-Homo voluit in ea perfectam sui imaginem ac similitudinem relinquere, in qua et per quam ipsemet vivere quodammode videretur, ac nobiscum etiam post visibilem suum in coelum ascensum conversari. Haec propterea societas, Christum prae se ferens, ut ipsi loquuntur, divino-humana est, subsistens in *unitate* personae cum utriusque naturae *communicatione*; quo fit ut elementum, ut vocant divinum pervadat ac penetret elementum humanum, ipsumque regat ac dirigat, alat ac veluti informet, unitatemque ex utroque constituat. Quod divinum in hac persona morali seu societate inesse dicunt, constituit partem ejus formam exteriorem ac visibilem sive corpus, quo velut organo anima exterius se prodit ac manifestat. ...

Dummodo haec rite intelligantur, prout natura similitudinis exigit, nihil reprehendendum in iis conspicimus, imo ad Ecclesiae naturam et constitutionem explicandam valde hanc ideam conferre existimamus, eaque uti non abnuimus.

Perrone was certainly thinking of Möhler for he refers to section 36 of *Symbolik*. It is clear, too, that the Roman theologian understood Möhler's thinking, for, in that note, he rejects the opinions of those who would reproach such an ecclesiology with "nescio quem pantheismum." Pantheism is precisely what Möhler had come to fear in his early pneumatocentric ecclesiology in *Einheit in der Kirche* which had come very close to making the church into the incarnation of the Holy Spirit.

22. Friedrich Schleiermacher, *The Christian Faith* (hereafter referred to as *Glaubenslehre*), 2nd ed., trans. by H. R. Mackintosh and J. S. Stewart (Edinburgh: T. and T. Clark, 1928), p. 52.

23. D. F. Strauss, *The Christ of Faith and the Jesus of History: A Critique of Schleiermacher's "Life of Jesus,"* trans. by Leander Keck (Philadelphia: Fortress Press, 1977), p. 35.

24. Johann Adam Möhler, *Neue Untersuchungen der Lehrgegensätze zwischen den Katholiken und Protestanten. Eine Vertheidigung meiner Symbolik gegen die Kritik des Herrn Professors Dr. Baur in Tübingen*, 2nd rev. and enl. ed. (Mainz and Vienna, 1835), p. 417.

25. Möhler, *Neue Untersuchungen*, 2nd. ed., pp. 418f.

26. The context of these statements should be kept in mind if one is to evaluate fairly Möhler's attitude toward Schleiermacher. At the point cited in *Neue Untersuchungen* Möhler was engaged in giving Baur what he hoped would be the *coup de grâce* in their debate and so had to state his case in strong terms. If anything is to be made of this passage in regard to Möhler's judgment of the man whose thought had been so influential in his own earlier work, attention should be paid to the expressions of admiration and respect which appear even in this very polemical atmosphere. In fact, Möhler seems too clever in his reduction of Schleiermacher's position to an "idealism" which denies "all objective foundations." But he can be partially absolved from the charge of deliberately distorting his great contemporary's thought. Strauss, after all, understood Schleiermacher as attempting to derive Christ from Christian consciousness, and he had the advantage of having read the latter's lectures on the life of Jesus, a benefit denied to Möhler in that they were not published until twenty-six years after his death and thirty years after the death of their author. But it was clear, nevertheless, from Schleiermacher's *Kurze Darstellung des theologischen Studiums zum Behuf einleitender Vorlesungen* (which Möhler almost certainly knew) that he accorded critical historical study of the gospels an important place. The hinge of the relationship between these critical studies and the doctrine of the Redeemer set forth in the *Glaubenslehre* is Schleiermacher's insistence that the person and the work of Christ cannot be separated from one another. The former is centered on his being the *Urbild*, the archetype, of humanity, the latter on his being its *Vorbild*, humanity's exemplar. His exemplarity is discovered in the power exercised upon us and communicated to us by his self-revelation in word and deed in which, Schleiermacher argued in his lectures on the life of Jesus, we find that he is the archetype.

27. Möhler, *Symbolik*, 1:483.

28. Möhler, *Symbolik*, 1:459.

29. Strauss, *The Christ of Faith and the Jesus of History*, pp. 83–99.

30. Strauss, *The Christ of Faith and the Jesus of History*, p. 26.

31. Schleiermacher, *Glaubenslehre*, 2nd ed. trans., p. 381.

32. *Glaubenslehre*, 2nd ed. trans., p. 62.

33. *Glaubenslehre*, 2nd ed. trans., p. 385.

34. *Glaubenslehre*, 2nd ed. trans., p. 381.

35. Friedrich Schleiermacher, *The Life of Jesus*, ed. by Jack C. Verheyden, trans. by S. MacLean Gilmour (Philadelphia: Fortress Press, 1975), p. 100.

36. Strauss, *The Christ of Faith and the Jesus of History*, p. 24.

37. Ibid. The quotation from Schleiermacher is a very loose citation of *The Life of Jesus*, p. 97.

38. Karl Rahner, *The Trinity*, trans. by Joseph Donceel (New York: Herder and Herder, 1970), pp. 24–33.

39. "Anselm, Erzbischof von Canterbury. Ein Beitrag zur Kenntnis des religiös-sittlichen, öffentlich-kirchlichen und wissenschaftlichen Lebens im elften und zwölften Jahrhundert," *Theologische Quartalschrift* 9 (1827):435–497, 585–664, and 10 (1828): 62–130; republished in *Dr. J. A. Möhlers gesammelte Schriften und Aufsätze*, ed. by Johann Joseph Ignaz Döllinger, 2 vols. (Regensburg, 1839–1840), 1:32–176.

40. "Sendschreiben an Herrn Bautain, Professor der philosophischen Facultät zu Straßburg," *Theologische Quartalschrift* 17 (1835): 421–453; republished in Möhler, *Gesammelte Schriften*, 2:141–164.

41. "Über die neueste Bekämpfung der katholischen Kirche," *Münchener Politische Zeitung*, January 29–30 and February 15–17, 1838, pp. 149–151, 154–156, 241–242, 254–256; republished in Möhler, *Gesammelte Schriften*, 2:226–243.

42. Strauss, *The Christ of Faith and the Jesus of History*, p. 24.

43. Möhler, *Symbolik*, 1:410–411.

44. Johann Auer has described this position as ecclesiological Nestorianism; see Johann Auer, *The Church: The Universal Sacrament of Salvation*, trans. by Michael Waldstein, ed. by Hugh M. Riley (Washington, D.C.: The Catholic University of America Press, 1993), p. 466:

In order not to deny what is unholy and evil in the Church, more idealistic thinkers will think they owe it to their pious thinking about the Church to distinguish between "the Church" as the holy bride of the lamb and "Christians" in the Church as poor and wicked failures. However, this would separate the mystical body of Christ from the new people of God, which leads to a Nestorian erroneous image of the Church and misses the reality of the Church, just as Nestorius destroyed the reality of the historical Christ.

I think that what Auer sees as Nestorian is, in fact, better described as the opposing classical Christological heresy, monophysitism. The swallowing-up of the human into the divine within the church leads to the insistence on its sinlessness as an institution. At least, this is what happened in Möhler's case.

45. Möhler, *Symbolik*, 1:353.

46. It should be noted that eschatology is not a category employed by Möhler prior to *Symbolik*. It might well be argued, however, that the path to a more eschatological framing of the "sinful church /holy church" question was opened by the anthropology which Möhler developed in the course of the various editions of *Symbolik* and in *Neue Untersuchungen* under the pressure of his on-going debate with Baur. A working-out of the question based on just such an anthropology can be seen in Karl Rahner, e.g. "The Church of Sinners," "The Sinful Church in the Decrees of Vatican II," and "The Church and the Parousia of Christ," all in *Theological Investigations*, vol. 6, trans. by Karl-H. and Boniface Kruger (Baltimore: Helicon Press, 1969), pp. 253–312. There is also a study by Anselm Moons, "Die Heiligkeit der Kirche nach J. A. Möhler," *Wissenschaft und Weisheit* 18 (1955): 81–94 and 175–191, which, while it raises some interesting points on this issue, is very weak in terms of placing the question within the larger framework of Möhler's thought.

6

Idealistic Hermeneutics in Theology

Remarks on Baur,
Möhler, and Schleiermacher

— REINHOLD RIEGER —

In the first half of the 19th century, theology was influenced by philosophy both because philosophy itself had theological interests and because theology was involved in philosophical discussion. Further, theology was based on principles which took their origin in philosophical systems, so that the various types of theology can be analyzed with regard to general concepts and principles, which are not specific to one particular subject or field of knowledge. These concepts can be called categories because of their universality, simplicity, and fundamental character. The examination of the various types of theology in this period can use these categories to describe these types in general terms, which show their connection with philosophy. This method of categorical analysis of types of theology is not a projection or arbitrary application of concept, which originates in the mind and in the time of the historian; on the contrary, this method uses only the terms and concepts of its subject because the theologies in question used these concepts themselves. The result of such analysis may be an abstract typology of theologies, which can parallel a typology of philosophies in the same period. This approach may provide the key for the attempt to understand how various kinds of hermeneutics shape theology in particular ways.

If we accept this method we may find, with some simplifications, that in the first half of the last century in Germany there were three mainstreams of hermeneutics and three corresponding types of theology depending on three kinds of philosophy. These three philosophical strands are connected with the names of Kant, Schelling, and Hegel. The parallel theologies related to these philosophies are represented by Schleiermacher, Möhler, and Baur.

I

To begin with Ferdinand Christian Baur (1792–1860), we can demonstrate that he is convinced of the dependence of theology on philosophy, even when theology is seen as essentially an historical examination of the Christian religion. In his first book, *Symbolism and Mythology* (1824), he states that, "without philosophy history remains eternally dead and silent."[1] Only philosophy can reveal history because historical phenomena are conditioned by philosophical ideas. So Christian belief, which is based on historical events, must be analyzed by the application of philosophical methods and concepts. In theology, historical and systematic methods are not separate but interdependent; the systematic form of theology is related to historical research, while the historical form of theology is determined by systematic principles.[2] Consequently, faith and knowledge are not an opposition; on the contrary, belief must be justified and reconstructed by knowledge. The principles of Christian faith and belief cannot be justified by faith and belief themselves; rather, they must be grounded in ideas and concepts, which have priority in relation to religious symbols.[3]

This idealistic conception of theology found in Baur's first work achieves its decisive form in the adoption of Hegel's system of absolute idealism. Whereas Schleiermacher tries to separate philosophy from faith, Hegel insists that the task of philosophy is to give religion its true self-conception and to elevate faith into knowledge. For Hegel, faith and knowledge, religion and philosophy have the same content and so differ only in form. The subject of religion and of philosophy is the same, namely the eternal truth in its objectivity, the Absolute.[4] Religious belief in an external contingent history cannot be the goal of theology. The sensuous form of religious belief must be transmuted into a spiritual and intellectual form, in which the content of religion achieves self-awareness. The justification of this transformed belief cannot be sensuous but must be spiritual or intellectual through the return of spirit from its sensual historical manifestation to its own adequate form in intellectual consciousness. "The true Christian content of faith must be justified by philosophy, not by history."[5] Thus, the highest level of the Christian religion is the philosophy of religion, in which everything merely historical and sensual is transformed into the intellectual, the conceptual, the ideal. The content of religion receives its truest and most adequate expression in the conceptual form of knowledge. This process of transforming religion into philosophy is regulated by the "law of identity."[6] In the Christian philosophy of religion, theology and philosophy are identical, and theology obtains its true form and its justification in the philosophy of religion.

In this idealistic approach to religion, the way of understanding religious manifestations within history is regulated by philosophical hermeneutics. This way of understanding starts with the distinction of form and content and supposes that the same content can find expression in different forms. The intellectual, conceptual content is not merely identical with its historical form and manifestation. The task of interpretation is to reduce the various forms to their one content, the phenomena to the idea, representations to a concept. According to idealistic hermeneutics, the concept is the adequate form of the historical content, which is in itself intellectual and conceptual. And so an identity of form and content is attained in the concept. The theological interpretation of the Christian religion must reduce its historical forms, its belief, to their conceptual content, i.e., the philosophical idea, in order to overcome the difference and contradiction between form and content in history and to reach identity, while at the same time justifying the plurality of historical forms.[7] For Baur, the method of interpretation, which enables this reduction of historical form to the idea on which it is based, is allegoresis. Allegoresis is the "artificial mediation of the speculative and the historical," by means of which the figurative form reflects the true speculative content.[8] Allegoresis is the neces-

sary result of the idealistic conception of the relation between history and philosophy. This conception presumes that the substance of history is the idea, the concept, and that history must be understood, therefore, by way of allegory, in which
the sensual form represents the spiritual content that is its true essence. The interpretation of historical forms as allegory makes it possible to harmonize religious
images and narratives with philosophical conceptions, so that the literal content of
the former receives a different figurative sense.[9] The literal sense of Holy Scripture
is interpreted as a symbol whose sensual and external pictures are transformed by
a higher sense into their true spiritual substance: the concept. This transformation
takes place by way of a dialectical process of negation of the immediate sense and
the negation of the negation in the conceptual sense.[10] The allegorical method
approximates its subject, because the method as a kind of knowledge also turns its
subject into a kind of knowledge. This speculative identity of method and subject
generates a knowledge of knowledge, which leads to self-awareness of knowledge
and the absolute mediation of it with itself, i.e. the absolute knowledge in the
absolute identity of subject and object. The goal of interpretation is the reduction
of differences and contradictions into absolute identity of form and content, subject and object. Historical forms become mere phenomena and appearances, which
can only be understood as the representations of the unity of the absolute philosophical idea.

At this point, the question may arise: how is this allegoresis related to the
historical and critical method which Baur uses as a historian? Does historical
criticism not exclude an allegorical interpretation of historical testimonies? Is it not
a contradiction to emphasize on the one hand a merely historical point of view and
to postulate on the other the allegorical point of view? Can Baur maintain both
historical objectivity and a philosophical approach to religion? Baur describes his
point of view as a purely historical approach with which he intends only to comprehend the historical data in their pure objectivity.[11] The concept of historical objectivity seems to mediate between the two opposing positions. Baur defines the
critical method as the intention to treat nothing which is only subjective as the pure
objectivity of the thing itself.[12] The historian must free himself from one-sided
subjective opinions and place himself in the objectivity of the thing itself. Thus
history is not reflection of historian's own subjectivity; rather, he is only the mirror
in which the historical phenomena are perceived in their true and real shape.[13]

The term "objectivity" refers to the true substance of history, not the plurality
of surface appearances but the deeper principle of life of the historical subjects
which determines historical evolution. This substance is the spirit of history which
moves and organizes historical phenomena. Participation in this spirit is the criterion of historical investigation. "Only when the essence of the spirit represents
itself with its inner moving and evolving and progressively increasing self-awareness in historical description is the true objectivity of history comprehended."[14]
Historical investigation is objective only when its object is represented in the
investigation and is transformed from the objective state, i.e., passivity, into the
subjective state, i.e., activity, and the investigating agent becomes like his object.
This position is rooted in the idealistic conception of history as the Absolute

Spirit's process of self-discovery through the plurality of appearances. Accordingly, all temporal changes must be understood as necessary and essential elements by means of which the concept moves itself and, driven by the negativity of all contingent historical forms, separates the essential from the nonessential in the ever increasing value of the pure idea and so becomes able to comprehend itself in its own inner essence through all the factors of its evolution.[15] For Baur, this speculative conception of history is the principle of historical criticism. He does not accept, therefore, the accusation that he is not able to harmonize his speculative position with the critical method in theology. There can be no opposition between speculation and criticism, since criticism can only understand historical manifestations on the basis of a speculative conception of history. Only within this perspective can history become the self-discovery of the present by means of the past, which is the divine destiny of history. The conscious human spirit must search for the true substance within all the changing flow of temporal forms, i.e., the substance which has overcome all preceding factors and integrated them as necessary conditions of itself into itself.[16] This process of the spirit's self-discovery in the external historical manifestations leads to absolute knowing, the evolution of which requires historical mediation as a necessary element.

Historical understanding participates in the self-development of the concept through historical manifestations, so that the understanding itself is moved by the concept as the substance of these manifestations. In this way, the historical method attains the objectivity of its subject and constitutes a unity with it. So Baur postulates the identity of the method of the history of dogma and the objective way of dogma itself. The historian of dogma must follow the path of evolution of dogma in its immanent moving, in order to comprehend one factor as a necessary condition of the other and all of them together as the unity of the concept. Thus, in the history of dogma, each dogma comes into relation to itself and posits its content externally in an objective form so that it can comprehend itself and develop its self-awareness.[17] The history of dogma itself is part of the evolution of dogma and contributes to the evolving self-awareness which the spirit in the form of dogma undergoes. Dogma is the spirit in its self-objectivization by means of self-mediation through the opposition of subject and object. In the concept of a thing which is the subject of historical knowledge, subjective knowledge of that thing and its objective nature are unified. The knowing subject and the known object have their identity in the concept of the thing.[18] Historical understanding overcomes the difference between it and its subject and leads to unity and thus to an identity with it.

If historical investigation is itself part of the objectivity of history, its manner of proceeding must be constituted by a speculative method which comprehends the moving principle of history. Baur defines this speculative method as participation in the objective process of the investigated subject and the attempt to follow it through all its moments of self-development. The presupposition of such a method is that history is a connection of all its parts in a rational unity which human reason can therefore comprehend. Without this speculative method, historical investigation remains on the surface of history. By contrast, the historian's real task is to reconstruct the "eternal thinking of the eternal spirit, whose product is history."[19]

This conception of theological hermeneutics differs from Schleiermacher's hermeneutics which attempts to understand the sense of a text in relation to the individual consciousness of its author. By contrast Baur postulates a hermeneutics, in which the individual and the particular are comprehended nearly as factors in the development of the general and the absolute. This hermeneutics tries to understand the thinking and doing of individuals as parts of the process of the self-development of the universal spirit who must overcome all oppositions as limits to self-awareness.[20] Historical research must clarify this general connection of all things in a historical universal; it must discover the unity of sense in sensuous plurality. Interpretation of historical data participates in the process of the development of its subject and so becomes an inner factor in it. Thus, interpretation is not an external approximation to its subject but an internal development of it by means of which the subject reflects itself in the interpretation and generates its self-awareness.

The critical method is the way in which speculation distinguishes between the subjective and the objective. This differentiation is necessary in order not to confuse the subjective with the objective and not to put the subjective in place of the objective.[21] The critical method distinguishes the subjective from the objective and thus provides the necessary condition for the speculative comprehension of the real unity of both in absolute knowledge. Thus, the critical method is a factor in the development of speculative method.

Baur's hermeneutics is based on two abstract concepts, the two categories of identity and speculation. The concept of speculation designates the path to the spiritual or intellectual sense of all of history, of which individual events are parts. The concept of identity expresses the relation between the opposing poles of knowledge and understanding, between subject and object of interpretation. Identity is the condition and the aim of interpretation, and in this conjunction of condition and aim identity is realized once again.

II

For Schleiermacher, too, theological hermeneutics is based on philosophical principles, but for quite other reasons. This is the case not because theology is actually philosophy of religion, as Baur would have said, but because in Schleiermacher's eyes, theological and philosophical hermeneutics are one and the same. There is only one kind of hermeneutics, which possesses a philosophical foundation and a philological method, and it is not specific to one subject or field of knowledge. This universal hermeneutics is a philosophical discipline allowing for various applications to various subjects, one of which is sacred scripture.[22] From another perspective, hermeneutics is universal because it is not restricted to specific kinds of difficulties in understanding a text, but is called into play whenever a sentence or text is uttered: "Misunderstandings arise by themselves but understanding is to be sought systematically."[23]

The philosophical status of hermeneutics rests on the correspondence of speaking and understanding and on the interdependence of speaking and thinking. Every act of understanding is the reverse of an act of speaking, and speaking is the externalization of thinking. Therefore, hermeneutics is related to the theory of language and to the theory of thought.[24] Hermeneutics depends on rhetoric and grammar because thought is realized only in the form of language. Understanding cannot attain the level of pure thought without linguistic mediation because the sense of every utterance must be expressed once again in the form of speech, i.e., in sensual form. Content, thought, concepts are only accessible through sensual expression. Therefore, understanding never leaves the sphere of language, and there is never a point where interpretation becomes unnecessary.

For Schleiermacher, the theory of knowledge and dialectics demonstrates that thinking depends on the sensuality of the particular subject and of the act of thinking itself. Although the concepts used in thinking and knowing are universal, their actual form always possesses individual characteristics because they are expressed in a specific language. Thinking reaches its goal only linguistically or semiotically; signs, e.g. language, give the thought its determination.[25] If pure thought is to become determinant, i.e., if one is thinking of some determinant thing, at least inner speech is required.[26] Knowledge, therefore, depends on the interpretation of signs and never reaches the pure concept as such without the use of signs. To know something means to understand the linguistic expression by which it must be represented. Thinking is completed in speaking, and because speaking must be intelligible, thought is always related to the task of interpretation. Thus, thinking cannot happen apart from the understanding of its own expression. "No one is able to think properly without the intention of being understood."[27] Thinking is knowing only if it is communicable and capable of being understood by others. The ability to be understood is a condition for the generality of knowledge. Thus, knowledge depends on speaking and understanding. Dialectics depends on rhetoric and hermeneutics, and rhetoric and hermeneutics require dialectics.[28] Dialectics and hermeneutics are interdependent.

The interaction of dialectics and hermeneutics results from the interaction of thinking and speaking. Dialectics resolves thinking into speaking, while hermeneutics resolves speaking into thinking.[29] Hermeneutics, as the art of understanding particular expressions of thought, transforms these particular expressions by means of universal concepts into a form in which they can be integrated into the thinking of the understanding subject. Hermeneutics helps to control the relativity of thinking, i.e., the individuality of its expressions. Thus, hermeneutics has an essential function for philosophy, especially for dialectics as the theory of knowledge. The common formation of concepts by and within a language depends on the ability of the understanding to resolve linguistic forms into the universal forms of thought. Schleiermacher calls this the "reconstruction" of speech.[30] This reconstruction is possible only approximately, never totally, because the subject cannot become identical with the object.

In contrast to Baur, Schleiermacher regards understanding as a relation between subject and object, with no possibility of overcoming the difference between them totally. The conscious subject attempts to understand his counterpart and employs common terms and universal concepts for this purpose but is never able to establish a total identity with him. The individuality of the object cannot be dissolved; it can only be reconstructed approximately. The key difference between subject and object remains. Thus, Schleiermacher follows the theory of knowledge of Kant, who emphasized the difference between the subject and the object in itself, although he developed a theory of categories as subjective conditions of knowledge which constitute the object as a phenomenon.

For Schleiermacher, interpretation is an art because the application of the rules of interpretation cannot be gained from the rules themselves but requires a creative act.[31] Because of the distinct essences of the objects, interpretation must employ rules and methods to reconstruct their sense. But method does not automatically yield reconstruction; linguistic virtuosity or a talent for language and understanding must be applied, i.e., a sense for analogy and difference, as well as an ability to judge human nature.[32] This means that the difference between subject and object is treated reflectively, not speculatively in the manner of Hegel. Speculation claims to reach the identity of the subject and the object, whereas reflection accepts the difference between them and articulates it. Reflection is the condition for interpretation as the creative reconstruction of sense.

According to Hegel, the philosophy of Kant is based on reflection, not on speculation, because Kant maintains an unresolvable duality of two principles of knowledge, namely, reception and production, perception/intuition and concept, phenomenon and the thing in itself. This duality is also found in Schleiermacher, when he distinguishes between the subject of interpretation and its object as two distinct poles in the process of understanding around which the circle of interpretation revolves with the aim of approximation, but without the ability to reach identity. This relation of subject and object requires of the interpreter receptivity to perceive the structure of the sensual phenomenon and productivity to reconstruct the sense that is expressed by sensual forms. This duality of reception and production can never be dissolved and reduced to one or the other or to an identity of both. The relation of the two is never merely an opposition; it has the nature of reflection because the two are interdependent and one requires the other. This is the structure of identity in difference.

Analogously to Kant's duality of perception and thinking, Schleiermacher distinguishes between two aspects of interpretation, the grammatical and the psychological. The grammatical aspect has to do with the sensual side of the object of interpretation, which must be perceived by the senses. In this aspect interpretation must attain to the system of language which is the condition for the expression of thought. In contrast, the psychological aspect deals with the conceptual side of the object of interpretation which must be reconstructed in the form of concepts. In this aspect, interpretation must attend to the subject's system of thought which is the context of the individual utterance. The grammatical aspect is the real, the psychological aspect the ideal pole, corresponding to the relation of form and content.[33] Grammatical interpretation analyzes the particular form of a text, its style, while psychological interpretation analyzes the particular content of a text, its sense. Style and sense are never separated from each other; sense is expressed by means of style, and style is formed by sense. Thus grammatical and psychological interpretations are interdependent. The process of understanding is an "oscillation" between them.[34]

The interdependence of these two aspects has as its consequence the fact that the solution of the task of understanding would be achieved by a perfect treatment of either aspect, because the other aspect would be perfectly represented within the first, i.e., it would not become superfluous but would be integrated wholly in the other aspect.[35] So, one can imagine that we might understand a text linguistically or grammatically so well that one also succeeds in understanding the psychological individuality of its author. The condition for this would be that all difficulties of grammatically interpreting the text are solved. Or, were the psychological individuality of an author perfectly understood, the grammatical aspect of his utterance would also be perfectly intelligible. But, of course, this is an interpretive ideal which is only approximately reached by way of that art which always creates anew the individual sense of its object. In fact, the linguistic aspect presupposes the psychological; it is impossible not to connect both aspects because otherwise the connection of speaking and thinking would be dissolved and a continuous reading would be rendered impossible. Any claim to perform a grammatical interpretation separately and in itself is a mere fiction.[36] Once again, Schleiermacher uses the method of reflection to describe the process of understanding as composed of two distinct aspects which are related to one another in such a way that the one could not operate without the other and operates only by integrating the other. The act of interpretation is divided into two distinct moments, which are related to one another in such a way that the one depends on the other. This results not in a speculative unity or identity of the two, but in a dynamic interrelation between them.

Grammatical interpretation is the art of finding the sense of a text by means of language and its rules for the generation of such texts.[37] Interpretation moves from the general rules of linguistic meaning to their specific application and to the particular sense of the text in question. This transition from the indeterminate to the determinant in interpretation is an infinite task.[38] This is because the object of interpretation possesses an individual quality which can only be known approximately and hypothetically.

The aim of interpretation can only be achieved approximately, never totally or perfectly. The approximation is attained by two methods, the divinative and the comparative. The first attempts to grasp the particular sense of the text by the fiction of identification with or transformation into the author of the text to be understood. The second starts with a general concept of the sense of the particular text and attempts to identify it further by comparison with other instances of the same general concept. The two methods are inseparable and interdependent because divination attains a degree of certitude only by comparison with general concepts so as to avoid mere fantasy, and comparison requires divination in order to attain the unity of sense and avoid separating the general from the specific.[39] Once again, Schleiermacher uses a reflective model to determine the relation of the two methods of psychological interpretation.

The individual qualities of style and sense make it impossible to reconstruct them in purely conceptual form. Such reconstruction must be based on perception and must find a new particular representation.[40] Thus, comparison is insufficient for interpretation because it remains in the domain of generality. It requires completion by divination, the creation of the particular sense. Divination, of course, is not real identification with the author of the text; its result is not the real identity of thinking and concept, but a fictional exchange of roles between the author of the text and its interpreter. The interpreter imagines the role of the author, puts himself in the author's position, and reconstructs the generation of the text. For Schleiermacher, this distinction between the author as object and the interpreter as subject does not allow the perfect unity or identity of spirit which Hegel postulates; the interpreting subject, however, allows his object, the author of the text, to be transformed fictively into a function of the subject in order to reconstruct the author's activity in the production of the text. The fictive character of this understanding has as its consequence the fact that the interpretation can never claim a necessity of hermeneutical insight, but in most cases only the probability of divination.[41] The fictive immediateness of this divinatory process remains in the real state of difference. This difference cannot be really, but only fictionally, dissolved.

The difference between the author and the interpreter is partially, but never absolutely, dissolvable. If the author and the interpreter had exactly the same thought and expressed it in precisely the same language, there would be no task of interpretation. If they think utterly differently, it would be impossible to achieve understanding, even if they share the same language. But this opposition never exists in fact; there is always only a certain degree of difference of thought between author and interpreter; this is the precondition for interpretation. Every intentional act of understanding assumes that this difference can be dissolved to some degree if the reasons and qualities of the difference are analyzed. But this task has its difficulties.[42] In spite of "divinatory daring," lack of understanding can never be dissolved absolutely.[43]

Schleiermacher describes the task of understanding as an act designed "to understand the speech first in the same way and then better than its author."[44] He explains this by saying that, because we do not have immediate knowledge of the mind of the author, we must bring to awareness that of which the author himself was unaware. Here it becomes clear that Schleiermacher's notion of hermeneutics is not a psychological one interested in exploring the mind or the soul of the author through his texts, but is instead directed toward the sense of the text as such as the product of the author. Genetic reconstruction of the sense of the text yields knowledge of that of which the author was not aware; this is the specific task of interpretation.[45] Another reason for this surplus of interpretation is the creative aspect of understanding. Because interpretation cannot attain total identity with the sense of the text, it must employ a creative divination of that sense in a process of never-ending approximation. The task of understanding is infinite, and so interpretation necessarily goes beyond the mind of the author. The sense of the text itself is infinite because it has a history of effect and interpretation which goes beyond the knowledge of its author.[46] The claim to understand the text better than the author makes clear that interpretation cannot conclude with the (fictional) identification with the author but is more than mere identity; it recognized the consciousness of difference which cannot be dissolved because it constitutes the individuality of the author as well as the individuality of the interpreter and of the text between them.

It is clear that Schleiermacher's conception of hermeneutics is based on the principle of difference between the subject and the object of understanding and on the reflective relationship of opposing aspects which constitutes the method of interpretation. He follows the Kantian theory of knowledge. Reflection recognizes and deals with difference but does not dissolve it. Reflection shows that opposites are related to one another and that each is logically dependent on the other but not in the process of identification. Because of the principle of difference at the heart of the method of reflection, Schleiermacher's hermeneutics is fundamentally opposed to the hermeneutics of Baur and Hegel in which the principle of identity lies at the heart of the method of speculation.

III

A third position which stands between that of Baur/Hegel and Schleiermacher/Kant is that of Johann Adam Möhler. He criticizes Baur's method of speculation, but accepts the principle of identity, and he rejects Schleiermacher's principle of difference, but employs the method of reflection. Thus, he seems to maintain a middle position, a middle course between the two extremes. By claiming the principle of identity, he wants to avoid the residue of uncertainty in understanding which is the result of Schleiermacher's hermeneutics. By maintaining the method of reflection, he tries to avoid the speculative construction of history in the manner of Baur who runs the risk of dissolving individuality in the general process of the mediation of the absolute spirit. Unlike Baur and Hegel, Möhler wishes to begin with concrete historical life and rejects speculation on the basis of the concept alone. Unlike Schleiermacher, he insists on the dogmatic conditions of theological hermeneutics and so rejects a universal hermeneutic. In short, with regard to the two principle hermeneutical concerns we have discussed, namely, the alternative between the principles of identity and of difference and that between the methods of speculation and of reflection, Möhler holds a position between Baur and Schleiermacher; he shares the principle of identity with Baur and the method of reflection with Schleiermacher.

Möhler's first book, *Unity in the Church or the Principle of Catholicism Presented in the Spirit of the Church Fathers of the First Three Centuries* (1825), demonstrates that, for him, unity as the identity of spirit is the principle of both Catholicism and of his theology. Although like Schleiermacher he is convinced that Christianity is found in life and spirit, unlike Schleiermacher he insists on a real identity of sense and not merely a fictional one. Identity is based in a unity of spirit which has its origin in the coming of Jesus Christ and the community of the apostles. This spirit is permanently present in the church, and the church is defined by unity with this spirit. The giving of the spirit was immediate for the apostles and communicated to them a new principle of life, which is mediated by them to the whole. The vital energy of the church reproduces itself in its tradition.[47] Tradition is the reproduction and transmission of the principle of Christian life; thus, Christianity is not a mere concept but determines a person's whole life and is only understandable if lived. Unity exists in and through life which is given constantly and immediately by the divine spirit and which is conserved and reproduced through the loving interrelation of the faithful.[48]

Tradition is the criterion by which the relationship of any phenomenon to the Christian life is judged in respect of its identity with or difference from union with this life and its principle. A deviation is recognized and refuted when its novelty is demonstrated. Heresies do not stand in continuity with apostolic origins and emerged in later periods. For Möhler the role of tradition is not to prove the truth of Christian doctrine, but to repudiate alien developments which destroy identity with the church and its spirit. Tradition can also demonstrate the identity of the Christian consciousness of individuals with the consciousness of the whole church.[49]

Möhler emphasizes that the identity of consciousness within the church does not mean that there is a mere static stability but that, on the contrary, this identity is the basis and condition of the development of Christian life.[50] Unlike Hegel, Möhler rejects any idea of individuality's dissolution within the process of history. The individual must be preserved as a vital element in the life of church. Because the life of the individual is grounded in his uniqueness, this uniqueness must not be absorbed in the whole. In order to form the living organism of the Christian community, individuals must be animated by an identity of spirit. Grounded in this identity, Christian life develops into various forms which represent one spirit in a plurality of expressions.[51] Individuality is the true form of the spirit, but it is not the spirit in itself, because individuality is connected with sensuality and finiteness.[52] The spirit develops within the forms of individuality, but individuality only makes sense as an expression and development of the spirit and its unity.

In this context, Möhler distinguishes two kinds of difference: opposition and contradiction. Opposites are legitimate developments and variations within the unity of the spirit in the history of the church, whereas a contradiction stands outside this unity and negates it. Legitimate opposites are products of the life of the church itself, but contradictions are separations and deviations which reject a positive relation with the life of the church.[53] Here Möhler employs the reflective method on three levels: first, he describes Christian history as a development of opposites which reflect each other in such a way that one requires and presupposes the other; second, he distinguishes two kinds of difference, opposition and contradiction, which stand in a relation of reflection to the degree that one can be compared with the other; third, he describes some historical phenomena as purely negative contradictions to the unity of the church, which is an abstract kind of reflection insofar as negation reflects affirmation and vice versa. On the first level there is positive reflection through variety within unity, and so, he claims, the reflected opposites are integrated within the whole of Christian unity. This is possible only because he treats individuality as a sensual realization and mediation of the spirit, not as spiritual in itself. On the third level, a negative reflection is supposed by contradiction and mere negation, which violates unity.

This distinction between opposition and contradiction helps Möhler to distinguish between legitimate developments and variations within the church and illegitimate plurality. The first is found in the various historical movements and phenomena of Christian doctrine, custom, and worship, which realize unity in plurality. The second, plurality without unity is the essence of heresy. Heresy is a contradiction to the church, but the elements of truth within heresies come from the church. Thus, the church is an unconscious unity prior to the separation of heresies, and a conscious unity after that separation. But while the separation exists, the church stands in a relation of contradiction to heresies, just as heresies are in contradiction to one another.[54]

For Möhler, contradiction, mere negation, and separation characterize the principle of heresy. Heresy is the result of egoism and individualism and has no true essence or being because it lives only within the individual and not in the unity of Christian life which has an objective ground and is the source of true essence and being. In its separation from the unity of spirit, heresy is a negation not only of this unity but of itself as well, i.e., heresy is engaged in a permanent battle with itself in a permanent self-dissolution. Heresy is self-contradictory. Möhler observes that in modern times this trait of heresy is called Protestantism. By contrast, Catholicism is eternally affirmative, positive, true, because it remains in a relation of identity and unity with the spiritual life originated in Jesus Christ and handed down by the apostles.[55] Möhler distinguishes Catholicism and heresy by relating them to abstract principles, the principle of identity and the principle of difference, which are contradictories in a purely negative reflection, because they stand in no positive relation to one another. And so, as heresy departs from unity with the church, it also departs from any positive essence and existence based on the Christian spirit. For this reason, heresy is excluded from history because it is not really existent.

For Möhler, the demand for freedom of investigation is a consequence of heresy, because heresy supposes that Christianity is or could be lost. Separation and discontinuity seem to insist on free theological investigation in history and exegesis. The historical view of Catholicism, which is concerned with continuity of doctrine in the church, is replaced by mere speculation.[56] Möhler emphasizes that human consciousness has a twofold aspect; a contemplating, reflecting aspect and a contemplated, acting, living aspect. The latter supplies the material for the former. So the Christian must have consciously received the Christian faith and lived it before he can reflect upon it. There must be material before Christian investigation can begin. Otherwise, the desire to arrive at Christianity as a conclusion remains vain. If heresy supposes that the reality of Christianity does not exist and so wants to go in search of it, then it cannot preserve Christianity as an already living reality, but only as a mere thought or concept which becomes the starting point for speculation. Thus, heresy regards the Christian as, in fact, a non-Christian, because the essence of Christianity is yet to be sought. When it demands that the church acknowledges its full freedom of investigation, it in fact insists that the church does not know Christianity and should, therefore, regard itself as non-existent. But this means that it demands that the church contradicts itself, insofar as the church would simultaneously be and not be. Catholicism, on the other hand, grounds its investigation on the foundation of its Christian consciousness, and so Catholicism is really free to investigate and does not choose between truth and error, but simply judges the latter. Heresy can attain no more than a state of indifference between freedom and bondage, because it is only in process of becoming free and is not yet in possession of freedom and because it might even erroneously become unfree.[57] Möhler maintains that heresy's demand for freedom of investigation demonstrates its self-contradictory character. By contrast, Catholicism is self-consistent because it is based on the principle of identity. Every Catholic investigation of Christianity presupposes the truth of its object.

For Möhler, one consequence of heretical freedom of investigation is the principle of "scripture alone," because heresy claims to investigate and develop Christianity by separating scripture from tradition and basing its investigation on scripture in isolation. To this principle of "scripture alone" Möhler opposes the claim that the Christian church is not based on scripture alone because Christianity existed in the mind of Jesus and of the apostles before it received conceptual, spoken, or written expression. Before the letter existed, the spirit was at work. The precondition for understanding the letter of the text is to possess the spirit and to participate in it through unity with it. Identity in the spirit animates the church continuously throughout its history. Whoever has received the spirit from the church will recognize himself in the historical forms of the spirit and will understand those forms. This means that the spirit encounters itself in understanding its self-expressions, because it lives both in the interpreter and in the object of interpretation. Thus, it is impossible to understand the scriptures outside the church. If the existence of the spirit and of the church are equivalent, the spirit would have to be outside itself were it possible to understand the Bible, which is its effect, outside the church. For Möhler, the principle of "scripture alone" results in contradictions. So he maintains that the church explains the Bible and that possession of and participation in the spirit is required for its interpretation. The Bible is the revelation of the Holy Spirit, and it can be understood only if the spirit has been communicated to the interpreter. "Only the spirit gives the spirit, only life gives life, but the letter never gives the spirit and death never gives life."[58] Scripture separated from interpretation is nothing but an empty letter. The sense of the scripture is found only by a spiritual act.[59] The question whether tradition is of equal value with or subordinate to scripture must be rejected because it is based on erroneous presuppositions. There is no opposition between tradition and scripture. They are not merely parallel but are interrelated and interdependent.[60] Thus, the principle of "scripture alone" presupposes an opposition between scripture and tradition, which opposition results from the principle of difference, the heretical principle.[61]

Möhler emphasizes that Christianity cannot be grounded on critical and hermeneutical principles because the Christian religion long existed without hermeneutic rules. The reason for this is that life always precedes rules, and rules without life are empty. Only when problems in Christian living, i.e., controversy with heretics, required reflection on the reasons for their rejection did hermeneutical rules develop.[62] According to Möhler, only in Catholicism was there an historical-grammatical interpretation of the Bible; outside the church, allegorical-mystical interpretation was dominant. He explains this by defining hermeneutics as the inverse of logic. Logic cannot be used heuristically, and hermeneutics has no criteria for evaluating the sense of its object. Hermeneutics yields only an aggregate of thoughts, opinions, and doctrines, but cannot judge their truth. Historical-grammatical interpretation is insufficient, therefore, and requires the criterion of Christian spirit which is found in dogmatics. As Sacred Scripture, the Bible should not be interpreted in the same manner as secular scripture; if it is, the result will be merely secular. The Bible must be understood by a dogmatic interpretation, corresponding to the spirit of its object.[63] The presupposition for understanding sacred scriptures is participation in the spirit which produced scriptures and which is also the church's spirit. Spirit precedes the letter, and the spirit within the apostles as authors of the New Testament is eternally present within the church. The interpreter possesses this same spirit and is thus able to understand its product, the scriptures. The spirit encounters itself in the process of interpretation.[64] As a result, the subject of interpretation becomes object in reflection, and the object of interpretation becomes subject which reflects itself by means of the interpretation. For Möhler, the identity of the spirit in the subject and object of interpretation results in an exchange of roles between the subject and the object, i.e., between the interpreter and the text. Against the objection that in this dogmatic interpretation and the Christian investigation of history the spirit of the interpreter finds itself in its object and so is not objective, Möhler responds that this transformation is not an alienation of the object, because both the interpreter and the object have originated from the same spirit of the church. The church has first communicated itself to the interpreter, and he then returns this communication to the church. Thus the church itself describes itself and explains its essence through the process of interpretation; the church is its own interpreter and uses its members to effect this self-interpretation. In this respect, according to Möhler, the interpretation of the sacred scriptures is the self-reflection of the spirit of the church.[65]

The principle of identity, which is essential for Catholicism, determines not only the object of investigation, scripture or the history of church, but also the method of investigation, the interpretation which participates in its object and makes self-reflection possible. Consequently, interpretation is only successful in essential unity with its object. Critical distance in interpretation, the distancing of free investigation from its object, must fail because it places investigation outside the sphere of its object. An external interpretation is self-contradictory insofar as it simultaneously claims to discover its object and tries to keep distance from it, so that it cannot reach unity which is the condition of knowledge. Möhler resolves the problem of knowledge in the case of interpretation by emphasizing the principle of unity and identity and by denying the capacity of critical rationality to deal with the object of understanding. This denial is the result of Möhler's combination of the principle of identity with the method of reflection, because reflection cannot achieve the identity of subject and object, as would be the case with the principle of identity combined with the method of speculation. Möhler wants to maintain the principle of identity on the one hand and the method of reflection on the other, but the first allows him to reject any critical and skeptical distancing of the subject from the object, while the second requires precisely that distancing. The demand for identity and the use of reflection will not harmonize, because reflection presupposes the relationships of negation and difference which should be overcome by the principle of identity. Thus, Möhler's theory is aporetic and fails in its attempt to navigate between Baur's integrationalism of absolute speculation and Schleiermacher's renunciation of absolute understanding.

That the method of reflection is essential for Möhler is shown by his analysis of oppositions within the church as he reflects on its unity and his treatment of heresy as a mere negation of unity. In the first case opposites are seen to be legitimate developments of ecclesial unity through the use of positive reflection, while in the second case, the opposition of church and heresy is construed as a mere contradiction throughout the use of negative reflection. Its negativity excludes heresy from being and thus from history, so that Möhler deprives it of real historical existence. Once again, the combination of the method of reflection with the principle of identity has disastrous consequences, because Möhler is forced to assess some historical phenomena as merely negative and nonexistent and so excludes them from history.

IV

In the first half of the nineteenth century, there were in theology two hermeneutical streams influenced by idealism: a hermeneutics of reflection and a hermeneutics of speculation. Another way of classifying hermeneutics is through the use of the concepts of identity and non identity. These two classifications or typologies are not totally coextensive but only partially so, specifically in the cases of Baur and Schleiermacher, where we find a speculative hermeneutics of identity in the one and a reflective hermeneutics of non identity in the other. The overlapping of the two typologies is represented in the approach of Möhler, whose hermeneutics is based on reflection, not on speculation, but a reflection of identity, not of nonidentity. Thus, Möhler stands between the other two types, and we have three forms of hermeneutics in theology. The first, that of Baur, is influenced by the absolute idealism of Hegel, the second, that of Möhler, perhaps by the objective idealism of Schelling, and the third, that of Schleiermacher, is related to the philosophy of sensuality of Leibniz, Baumgarten, and Kant.

We may ask whether at that time it was necessary for theological hermeneutics to be idealistic, in that the subject of theology is regarded as ideal, spiritual, only accessible through intellectual or spiritual ideas and forms. But is not Schleiermacher's hermeneutics a counterexample, because it renounces the attempt to reach an identity between the interpreter and the text? What about his method of divination; is it not a subjective idealistic attempt to realize identity? Then, what about Baur's historical method, is not his idealistic theory undermined by the realism of historical criticism? And what about Möhler's idealistic objectivity, is it something other than a subjective option? We may well ask whether all three positions are not based on presuppositions which endanger their coherence and consistence. Baur's allegorical hermeneutics presupposes the real objectivity of history, while he attempts to understand it speculatively as an ideal process. Schleiermacher's divinatory hermeneutics presupposes the identity of the interpreter and the author while he seems to renounce this identity. Möhler's Catholic hermeneutics presupposes the truth of Catholicism alone while he cannot really exclude its negation, heresy. Baur's position is endangered by historical criticism which he uses as a method of interpretation. Schleiermacher's position is endangered by the idealistic goal of identity, which he reaches by his method of divination. Möhler's position is endangered by Catholicism's self-negation because the use of negative reflection in defining Catholicism creates its negation.

All three types of theological hermeneutics cannot avoid aporias. Although Baur's position which combines the principle of identity with the method of speculation can embrace all historical phenomena in the process of the historical mediation of the absolute idea, it risks losing the otherness and individuality of its objects. Although Schleiermacher's position, which combines the principle of difference with the method of reflection, can understand all historical data as objectively given facts of history in their individuality which remains over against the subject, it is forced to renounce absolute knowledge and understanding and restrict itself to divination, supposition, or hypothesis. Although Möhler tries to avoid these aporias in the other two positions by taking the principle of identity from one and the method of reflection from the other, he too cannot escape an aporia because he pays for his seeming middle course by a historical dualism of existing and non-existing phenomena. The aporetical character of Möhler's position seems more dangerous than of the two because, in his treatment of history, he is forced to accept a dualism between existing and non-existing realities which appears contradictory, while the other two positions—if we prescind from their presuppositions—are consistent in themselves.

This way of analyzing these three types of theological hermeneutics is not unique to recent scholarship; it is analogous to critiques offered by nineteenth century theologians, most especially by these three opponents themselves. Möhler, for instance, accuses Baur of treating Catholicism and Protestantism speculatively as mere relics and of dissolving them in the universal process of the divine spirit's self-development.[66] With regard to Schleiermacher, he rejects his concept of Christian consciousness as a mediation of subjectivity and objectivity and regards his position as subjective idealism destructive of all objectivity.[67] For his part, Baur regards Möhler's position as a rejection of historical truth, because his judgment of the absolute truth of Catholicism relegates other Christian communities to the status of mere appearances. The absolute opposition between Catholicism and Protestantism results from a one-sided affirmation of one historical alternative and leads to a docetic dualism.[68] Thus, each embraces a diagnosis of the aporias of the two alternative positions, so that the three are interrelated critically with one another.

What we have seen in theological hermeneutics is a special instance of the problems and aporias of a general theory of knowledge. What is the relation between the subject and object of knowledge? Is it characterized primarily by identity, or by difference, or by mediation? Is the speculative method allowable or even necessary for the theory of knowledge, or must it use a reflective method? What is the relationship between the principles of identity and of difference and the methods of speculation and of reflection?

And there is the still further question of the difference between theological knowledge and knowledge of non-theological objects. This question has found different answers in each of the three types of theology we have seen. Baur and Schleiermacher for different reasons do not maintain that there is a significant difference; Möhler emphasizes the very different nature of theological knowledge which has its own unique presuppositions.

NOTES

1. Ferdinand Christian Baur, *Symbolik und Mythologie oder die Naturreligion des Alterthums* (Stuttgart, 1824), p. xi: "Ohne Philosophie bleibt mir die Geschichte ewig tot und stumm." Recent investigations on Baur are published in: *Historisch-kritische Geschichtsbetrachtung. Ferdinand Christan Baur und seine Schüler*, ed. Ulrich Köpf, (Sigmaringen: Thorbecke, 1994.)

2. Cf. Ferdinand Christian Baur, *Die Epochen der kirchen Geschichtsschreibung* (Tübingen, 1852), p. 5.

3. Cf. Ferdinand Christian Baur, "Abgenöthigte Erklärung gegen einen Artikel der evangelischen Kirchenzeitung," in *Tübinger Zeitschrift für Theologie* (1836), reedited in *Historisch-kritische Untersuchungen zum Neuen Testament* (Stuttgart - Bad Cannstatt, 1963), pp. 301, 304.

4. Cf. Ferdinand Christian Baur, *Die christliche Gnosis oder die christliche Religions-Philosophie in ihrer geschichtlichen Entwicklung* (Tübingen, 1835) p. 669.

5. Ibid., p. 696: "Der wahrhafte christliche Glaubensinhalt ist durch die Philosophie zu rechtfertigen, nicht durch die Geschichte." Cf. p. 714.

6. Ibid., p. 699f.

7. Cf. ibid., p. 718.

8. Ibid., p. 41: "künstliche Vermittlerin des Spekulativen und Historischen."

9. Ferdinand Christian Baur, *Kirchengeschichte der drei ersten Jahrhunderte,* 3rd ed. (Tübingen, 1863), p. 179.

10. Cf. Baur, *Gnosis*, pp. 93–96.

11. Baur, *Kirchengeschichte*, vi-vii: "Mein Standpunkt ist mit einem Worte der rein geschichtliche, auf welchem es einzig darum zu tun ist, das geschichtlich gegebene, so weit es überhaupt möglich ist, in seiner reinen Objektivität aufzufassen."

12. Ferdinand Christian Baur, *Lehrbuch der christlichen Dogmengeschichte* (Stuttgart, 1847), p. vii: "nichts, was nur subjektiver Natur ist, für die reine Objektivität der Sache selbst zu halten."

13. Baur, *Die Epochen,* p. 247.

14. Ferdinand Christian Baur, *Die christliche Lehre von der Versöhnung in ihrer geschichtlichen Entwicklung* (Tübingen, 1838), p. vi.

15. Ibid., pp. vi–vii.

16. Ibid., p. vii.

17. Baur, *Lehrbuch,* p. 8.

18. Ibid., p. 18.

19. Ferdinand Christian Baur, *Die christliche Lehre von der Dreieinigkeit und Menschwerdung Gottes in ihrer geschichtlichen Entwicklung* (Tübingen, 1841), p. xix: "die ewigen Gedanken des ewigen Geistes, dessen Werk die Geschichte ist, in sich nachzudenken."

20. Ibid., p. xx.

21. Baur, *Lehrbuch,* p. vii.

22. Friedrich Schleiermacher, "Über den Begriff der Hermeneutik," in *Hermeneutik und Kritik*, ed. Manfred Frank (Frankfurt: Suhrkamp, 1977), p. 311. On the philosophy of Schleiermacher, cf. Heinrich Scholtz, *Die Philosophie Schleiermachers* (Darmstadt: Wissenschaftliche Buchgesellschaft, 1984) and Reinhold Rieger, *Interpretation und Wissen. Zur philosophischen Begründung der Hermeneutik bei F.D.E. Schleiermacher* (Berlin: de Gruyter, 1988).

23. Schleiermacher, *Hermeneutik und Kritik*, p. 92: "dass sich das Missverstehen von selbst ergibt und das Verstehen auf jedem Punkt muß gewollt und gesucht werden."

24. Schleiermacher, *Hermeneutik und Kritik*, p. 76: "Da Kunst zu reden und zu verstehen (korrespondierend) einander gegenüberstehen, reden aber nur die äussere Seite des Denkens ist, so ist die Hermeneutik im Zusammenhang mit der Kunst zu denken und also philosophisch. ... dass jeder Akt des Verstehens die Umkehrung eines Aktes des Redens ist."

25. Schleiermacher, *Hermeneutik und Dialektik*, p. 411.

26. Schleiermacher, *Dialektik*, ed. L. Jonas (Berlin, 1839), p. 491.

27. Schleiermacher, *Dialektik*, ed. R. Odebrecht (Darmstadt: Wissenschaftliche Buchgesellschaft, 1976), p. 126: "Man kann nie ordentlich denken, ohne das Streben zu haben, verstanden zu werden."

28. Schleiermacher, *Hermeneutik und Kritik*, p. 76.

29. Schleiermacher, *Dialektik*, ed. L. Jonas, cited in *Hermeneutik und Kritik*, p. 411: "Auslegungs- und Übertragungskunst ist Auflösung der Sprache in Denken; Dialektik ist solche Auflösung des Denkens in Sprache, dass vollständige Verständigung dabei ist."

30. Ibid., p. 411: "Kunst, die Rede oder Schrift des Menschen völlig nachzukonstruieren."

31. Schleiermacher, *Hermeneutik und Kritik*, p. 81.

32. Ibid., p. 81f.

33. Ibid., pp. 77–79.

34. Schleiermacher, *Hermeneutik*, ed. Heinz Kimmerle, 2d ed. (Heidelberg: Carl Winter Universitätsverlag, 1974), p. 56: "Mannigfaltige Oscillation zwischen beiden."

35. Schleiermacher, *Hermeneutik und Kritik*, p. 80: "Die absolute Lösung der Aufgabe ist die, wenn jede Seite für sich so behandelt wird, dass die Behandlung der andern keine Änderung im Resultat hervorbringt, oder, wenn jede Seite für sich behandelt die andere völlig ersetzt, die aber ebensoweit auch für sich behandelt werden muss."

36. Ibid., p. 164.

37. Schleiermacher, *Hermeneutik*, p. 57: "die Kunst aus der Sprache und mithülfe der Sprache den bestimmten Sinn einer gewissen Rede zu finden."

38. Schleiermacher, *Hermeneutik und Kritik* p. 101: "Das Wahre ist, dass das Übergehen vom Unbestimmteren in das Bestimmte bei jedem Auslegungsgeschäft eine unendliche Aufgabe ist."

39. Ibid., p. 169.

40. Cf. Schleiermacher, *Hermeneutik*, p. 115.

41. Schleiermacher, "Über den Begriff der Hermeneutik," in Schleiermacher, *Hermeneutik und Kritik*, pp. 317–319. Schleiermacher criticizes F.A. Wolf who claims necessity for hermeneutical insight. But partially Wolf himself acknowledges "mehr divinatorische als demonstrative Gewissheit" in hermeneutics.

42. Schleiermacher, *Hermeneutik und Kritik*, p. 178, "In jedem Verstehenwollen eines anderen liegt schon die Voraussetzung, dass die Differenz auflösbar ist. Die Aufgabe ist, in die Beschaffenheit und Gründe der Differenzen zwischen dem Redenden und Verstehenden genauer einzugehen. Dies ist schwierig."

43. Schleiermacher, "Über den Begriff der Hermeneutik," in Frank, p. 327.

44. Schleiermacher, *Hermeneutik und Kritik*, p. 94: "Die Aufgabe ist auch so auszudrücken, - die Rede zuerst ebensogut und dann besser zu verstehen als ihr Urheber."

45. Schleiermacher,"Über den Begriff der Hermeneutik," in Frank, p. 325.

46. Schleiermacher, *Hermeneutik und Kritik*, p. 94: "Die Aufgabe ist ... eine unendliche, weil es ein Unendliches der Vergangenheit und Zukunft ist, was wir in dem Moment die Rede sehen wollen."

47. Johann Adam Möhler, *Die Einheit in der Kirche oder das Prinzip des Katholizismus dargestellt im Geiste der Kirchenväter der drei ersten Jahrhunderte*, ed. Josef Rupert Geiselmann (Köln: Hegner, 1957), pp. 5, 8, 10.

48. Ibid., p. 21: "Einheit der christlichen Kirche: sie besteht durch ein unmittelbar und immer durch den göttlichen Geist bewegtes, sich durch liebende Wechselwirkung der Gläubigen erhaltendes und fortpflanzendes Leben."

49. Ibid., pp. 33, 39.

50. Ibid., p. 43.

51. Ibid., p. 114.

52. Ibid., p. 146.

53. Ibid., pp. 152–157. Möhler cites the 'Bruno' of Schelling (152).

54. Ibid., pp. 154–157.

55. Johann Adam Möhler, "Pragmatische Blicke," in *Nachgelassene Schriften* I, ed. Rudolf Reinhardt 1 (Paderborn: Bonifatius, 1989), pp. 50, 62.

56. Möhler, *Die Einheit in der Kirche*, p. 59.

57. Ibid., pp. 64–66; cf. "Pragmatische Blicke," pp. 40–43.

58. Ibid., p. 25; cf. "Pragmatische Blicke," p. 37.

59. Ibid., p. 51.

60. Ibid., p. 53.

61. Ibid., p. 62. On the relation between Möhler and Baur cf. Reinhold Rieger, "Reflexion und Spekulation. Prinzipien zur Deutung des Konfessionspluralismus bei J.A. Möhler und F.C. Baur," *Münchener Theologische Zeitschrift* 45 (1994), pp. 247–270.

62. Ibid., p. 79.

63. Ibid., p. 80; "Pragmatische Blicke," p. 39.

64. Möhler, *Einheit,* p. 24.

65. Ibid., p. 328.

66. Möhler, *Neue Untersuchungen der Lehrgegensätze zwischen den Katholiken und Protestanten* (Mainz, 1834), p. 527.

67. Ibid., p. 523.

68. Ferdinand Christian Baur, *Der Gegensatz des Katholizismus und Protestantismus nach den Prinzipien und Hauptdogmen der beiden Lehrbegriffe* (Tübingen, 1833), p. 422.

7

Doctrine as Symbol

Johann Adam Möhler in Dialogue
with Kant and Hegel

— STEPHEN FIELDS, SJ —

The "Introduction" to Johann Adam Möhler's great work *Symbolism* offers a definition of the book's title, which indicates the method that Möhler uses to advance his argument. According to Möhler, symbolism means:

> the scientific exposition of the doctrinal differences among the various religious parties opposed to each other, in consequence of the ecclesiastical revolution of the sixteenth century, as these doctrinal differences are evidenced by the public confessions or symbolical books of those parties.[1]

This statement contains two distinct but interrelated meanings of symbolism. The first defines symbolism as a theological method: the systematic exposition of doctrinal differences between Catholics and Protestants.[2] Indeed, this method already enjoyed an extensive history prior to Möhler's use of it.[3] The second meaning of symbolism indicates the sources to which the method will be applied: the public confessions of Western Christianity, such as the decrees of the Council of Trent and the Articles of Smalcald. Thus, the title of the book and the name of its method are derived from considering Christianity's public decrees as symbols.

Möhler's statement that symbolism as a method is derived from considering the decrees of the denominations as symbols raises a provocative philosophical question that *Symbolism* itself does not address: How are these decrees constituted as symbols? Turning to Möhler's wider corpus for an answer, the first part of this essay shows that religious doctrines can be understood as symbolic when they are interpreted in light of Möhler's metaphysics of ecclesial history and his model of human reason. The essay's second and third parts then bring Möhler's notion of symbolism into dialogue with the symbol-theories of two of his contemporaries, the Idealist theory of Kant and the Romantic theory of Hegel. Part two shows that Möhler's notion of symbolism charts a middle course between Idealism and Romanticism, whereas part three shows that Kant's and Hegel's symbol-theories can be used to amplify and further develop Möhler's theory.

Möhler on the Symbolism of Doctrine

Möhler grounds the symbolism of religious confessions or doctrines in a metaphysics of ecclesial history, that is itself implicitly symbolic. In positing this metaphysics, Möhler wishes to navigate between two erroneous and opposing views. On the one hand, he wishes to avoid the pagan view of antiquity that, knowing nothing of Providence, reduces history to an irrational fatalism. On the other hand, he wishes to avoid those Idealists who reduce history to strict rational necessity and who thereby undermine the graciousness of God and the freedom of humanity.[4] His theory seeks, therefore, to synthesize two realities: the spontaneous contingency of human action in history and the divine teleology that, guiding and shepherding history, provides history with its ultimate meaning.

Accordingly, Möhler's synthesis centers on the notion of "organic evolution." Existing within time, the church constitutes a living consciousness that develops by dialectically resolving the challenges presented to it by historical contingencies. Although the church is a unified organism that retains its substantial identity through the successive resolutions of crises, its doctrines and institutions, which constitute its empirical manifestations, must necessarily be changed and modified. Sometimes, for instance, under pressure from hostile forces, one of the church's constitutive elements may assume a disproportionate importance and thereby require a future curtailment.[5] Crucial for Möhler, the organic evolution of the church's visible manifestations is derived from an "internal force" that must actively respond to external exigencies.[6] If, for example, a particular institution dies because it fails to respond to current needs after having served well for a period of time, the historian may conclude, says Möhler, that the institution was not essential to the church's identity.[7]

The internal force that drives organic evolution is not reducible to a form of human self-consciousness, although human rationality is an important factor in Möhler's notion of organic evolution. Rather, the internal force is derived ultimately from the Trinity, from Christ's Incarnation, a mission received from the Father that the power of the Holy Spirit continues in time.[8] According to Möhler, "the Church is Christ acting and manifesting himself through the ages."[9] In history, the Son of God continues "to appear in human form" because the church represents "his permanent incarnation."[10] Just as humanity is "won again to God" by the merits of the sufferings, works, doctrines, conduct, and death of Christ that remain undivided from the God-man, so the church derives its inner life undivided from the Son and communicates this life undivided to the doctrines and institutions that historically emanate from it.[11] Möhler's metaphysics of ecclesial history thus reconciles the transcendent and the immanent, divine teleology and historical contingency, by a twin ontological participation. The organic life of the church's internal force is derived from Christ's organic unity with God, whereas the church's doctrines and institutions that empirically appear through the ages are derived from, and reciprocally act upon, the life of the church's internal force.

Möhler's model of human reason follows from his theory of this twin ontological participation. The analytical and synthetical powers of the mind, *Verstand* and *Vernunft*, function in tandem. Whereas *Verstand* examines the empirical data in order to establish a sequence of historical events, *Vernunft* must penetrate the sequence in order to discern the intelligibility immanent in it. This penetration must first diagnose patterns in the sequence that partially explain the events. But beyond this diagnosis, *Vernunft*, enlightened by faith that believes in the immanence of Providence in history, must further discern in the sequence something of the divine causality that sustains history and leads it to its perfection in Christ.[12] This second task does not imply, however, that Möhler's notion of *Vernunft* aims fully to encompass history by reason.[13] On the contrary, *Vernunft* for Möhler endeavors more modestly to grasp the phases of the church's organic evolution in their interdependent unity and to measure their relative importance and particular contributions.[14]

The ecclesial historian who embraces this model of reason knows that, because history is partially conditioned by human freedom, it will inevitably escape the full comprehension of human intelligence. Furthermore, this historian knows that, because God is history's ultimate ground, human reason must submit to the inscrutability of the divine mind. Nonetheless, because history does not fully explain itself but leaves open many questions including the question of its final destiny, the historian can affirm that the laws of reason themselves demand "something eternal that will stand over the temporal; they demand that the divine be grasped in the human."[15] If history is implicitly religious, it follows that the principles of divine revelation, far from being externally imposed upon history, are a necessary complement to the use of *Vernunft* in historical investigation.[16]

Möhler's metaphysics of the internal force that drives the church's organic evolution implicitly constitutes ecclesial history as an "intrinsic symbol." In intrinsic symbolism, the reality that the symbol signifies needs the symbol in order for the reality to become itself. The medium thus constitutes an essential element of the structure of the signified reality.[17] Intrinsic symbols sharply contrast with "extrinsic symbols" in which the relation between the signified reality and the symbol is arbitrary or accidental.[18] Extrinsic symbols, such as national flags and traffic signals, merely point to their signified realities without ontologically constituting them.[19]

Möhler's theory of ecclesial history may be considered intrinsically symbolic because history makes present in time and space the saving work of the Incarnation. Ecclesial history is the empirical medium in which the Holy Spirit maintains the living presence of the God-man. If history is thus essential to the divine economy of salvation, the church's internal force that animates history mediates the activity of the Spirit to ecclesial doctrines and institutions. As a result, these empirical manifestations, however much they are historically conditioned, are implicitly consecrated as intrinsic symbols of the internal force. Doctrines thus embody a paradoxical synthesis: they are eternally true, yet they are expressed in changing forms. Möhler explains this paradox by distinguishing between the objective and the subjective senses of doctrine.

The objective sense of doctrine means that the church at its inception received the immutable divine revelation in its full truth.[20] This truth, the source of all subsequently formed doctrines, necessarily must evolve because, as Möhler says, the Word of God lives perpetually "in the hearts of believers."[21] Accordingly, the subjective sense of doctrine means that the church is able to unfold the objective revelation. As its self-consciousness matures, the church gains clearer and more distinct insights into the truth that it received.[22] The abiding immutability in these evolving insights is guaranteed by the Holy Spirit who, present throughout ecclesial history, cannot admit of contradiction.[23] As new insights emerge through the church's internal force, the church, using its authoritative organs, incorporates as doctrines what it discerns to be authentic.[24]

Möhler's notion of doctrine's subjective sense makes it clear that human self-consciousness plays an important role in his metaphysics of organic evolution. The form of doctrine is necessarily expressed in concepts and images. Although this form is temporal, perishable, and exchangeable, Möhler takes care to observe that, when subjective doctrines articulate objective revelation, the inner truth of the revelation perdures.[25] The difference between, for instance, the language of the Gospels about God and the Nicene dogma of the Trinity is "formal" not substantial. The difference applies only to the conceptual formulation of the revelation.[26]

Möhler does not comment directly on the extent to which doctrines that have been defined by the church in one age may be revised by it in another. On the one hand, the logic of the internal force, together with Möhler's statements about the exchangeability of subjective formulations, suggests that the church is free to modify, even to retract, what it has defined. On the other hand, his avowal that the Holy Spirit, who cannot err, is the animator of the church's definitions suggests otherwise. Given that Möhler's comments on the development of doctrine intend to restate the canon of Vincent of Lérins, which affirms the abiding consistency of the church's doctrines, the second position seems more likely to be Möhler's.[27]

If his metaphysics of ecclesial history can be considered intrinsically symbolic, so can Möhler's theory of doctrine that follows from it. Doctrine is intrinsically symbolic for Möhler because its subjective sense, its historically conditioned form, expresses its objective sense, the immutable revelation received by the church at its beginning. Doctrine develops as the Christian consciousness matures in its understanding of revelation. The objective revelation, which is the reality symbolized, needs, therefore, the subjectively expressed doctrine, which is its symbol, in order more to become itself. Although divine revelation does not require the church's doctrines in order to be true, it does need them in order for the Christian consciousness to recognize and appropriate the depth of its truth. This recognition, conditioned by the need for an organic consciousness to evolve, is nonetheless animated by the internal force that, under the guidance of the Spirit, leads the church to its telos, the fullness of Christ.[28] In sum, Möhler's understanding of doctrine as intrinsically symbolic, however implicit, explains why finite human concepts and images can represent a divine surplus of meaning that transcends their finite symbolic form.[29]

Möhler strongly affirms the importance of the forms of rational self-consciousness as factors in the organic evolution of doctrine. Accordingly, not only is his view of doctrine's intrinsic symbolism derived from his metaphysics of ecclesial history; it also corresponds to his model of human reason. In this model, the categories of *Verstand* function in the service of a metaphysically constituted *Vernunft*. As an ontological propaedeutic, the categories of *Verstand* organize empirical data into an intelligible form. *Vernunft* is the penetration of intelligence into the intelligible; it discloses pattern and meaning in this form. This disclosure is a result, not only of the metaphysical power of *Vernunft*, but of *Vernunft* enlightened by faith, which is thereby graced with some insight into the divine teleology that sustains the temporal order. Nonetheless, *Vernunft* does not fully comprehend time by unfolding it according to a strictly immanent necessity. *Vernunft* for Möhler preserves something of the apophaticism strong in the Catholic view of God's relation with the world. According to this view, all positive or kataphatic manifestations of the divine discernable in creation must be followed by negations. These deny that God's identity is co-equal with any or all of the predicates affirmable of Him.[30] As a result, *Vernunft*, although efficaciously endowed with metaphysical insight and graced with faith, fails exhaustively to disclose the divine intelligibility.

Corresponding to this model, doctrines, as intrinsic symbols, are both metaphysical and nonreducible. As metaphysical, they import real knowledge of God that *Vernunft* can apprehend and articulate. Although their form consists of historically conditioned concepts and images, the finitude of this form implicitly carries the immanence of the Spirit's activity. As nonreducible, doctrines cannot be rendered by *Vernunft* into a more univocal form that would allow the objective revelation they express to become more transparent to *Vernunft*. Although *Vernunft* acting in the church under the Spirit's direction can gain further insight into previously expressed doctrines, that insight remains necessarily symbolic. Conditioned by time and space, doctrines cannot articulate with full intelligibility the reality that they nonetheless ontologically represent.

Kant and Hegel on the Symbol

Möhler's view of the doctrinal symbol as metaphysical and nonreducible charts a middle course between the Idealist symbol-theory of Kant and the Romantic symbol-theory of Hegel. According to Kant, the symbol cannot claim to represent real content about the divine because metaphysics only regulates *Vernunft*; it does not constitute it. Nonetheless, the symbol is not reducible by either *Vernunft* or *Verstand* to a more univocal form of knowledge. Kant's theory centers on the notion of *hypotyposis*, a process that brings a type, an intuition, under a form, a rational concept, and thereby concretizes, exhibits, and represents it.[31] An intuition is "any presumed awareness or experience of an object."[32] *Hypotyposis* can be either symbolic or schematic.[33] In schematic *hypotyposis*, an intuition directly corresponds to object. Through schematism, the imagination synthesizes data that are intuited through sensation into an image. The image is then presented to the categories of *Verstand*, which in turn bring the image under a determined concept that adequately or directly exhibits the intuition.[34]

In symbolic *hypotyposis*, however, the mind possesses ideas or concepts to which no sensible intuitions directly correspond because empirical data are either unavailable or inadequate for their exhibition. These concepts are "only thinkable by the reason," and they constitute the matter of religious doctrines.[35] Religious doctrines according to Kant, consist of three rational products: the ideas of pure reason (God, the soul, the world); the postulates of practical reason (God, freedom, the soul's immortality); and aesthetic ideas (such as love, envy, and death). Although the ideas of pure reason and the postulates of practical reason are conditions for the possibility of thought, the mind remains ontologically agnostic about their existence even while maintaining a cognition of them.[36] The aesthetic ideas are intuitions that the imagination freely works up from the material supplied by nature, which they creatively surpass. These intuitions also include religious notions like hell, eternity, creation, and the kingdom of the blessed.[37]

The ideas that are symbolized, whether they be aesthetic, practical, or purely rational, occasion much thought, Kant observes, without the possibility of being determined by schematism.[38] Nonetheless, although these ideas cannot be directly represented, they can be exhibited indirectly when they come under the direction of aesthetic judgment. This faculty, a spontaneous and creative power of reason, seeks to represent these intuitions according to their purpose.[39] This representation requires judgment to supply for the intuition which cannot be directly exhibited another intuition, retained in the mind, which can be directly exhibited. The supplied intuition, a determined concept, constitutes the symbol.[40]

Citing an example of how symbolic *hypotyposis* proceeds, Kant explains how either a living body or a hand mill can symbolize a monarchical state. The mind perceives that an analogy links the intuition that cannot be directly exhibited (a monarchical state) with two directly exhibitable intuitions (a living body and a hand mill). The selection of the directly exhibitable intuitions as symbols for the monarchical state is a result of reason's seeing a common purpose in the symbol and its referents. Accordingly, a living body symbolizes a monarchical state if national laws hold sway over it. In this case, the monarchical state, like a living body, is organically interdependent. A hand mill symbolizes a monarchical state if an absolute will rules it. In this case, the monarchical state, like a hand mill, is an inert automaton.[41]

Kant contends that a mere similarity between the symbol and its referent does not constitute the *hypotyposis*. Rather, the symbol is constituted by the common purpose that intrinsically unites the concepts. This union occurs when the subject reflects "upon these two things [the symbol and its referent] and their causality."[42] The mind fuses the common purposiveness with the original characteristics of the directly exhibitable concept. Because these characteristics become identical with the import that the concept bears as a symbol, these characteristics thus explain how the concept becomes a symbol.[43] The symbol exhibits a surplus of meaning in the characteristics of the directly exhibitable concept because they carry their own purpose together with that of their referent, which they indirectly represent.

Symbolic *hypotyposis* is not only a function of judgment; it is also conditioned by the imagination. The imagination is productive, according to Kant, because it can play with the material it intuits through sensation.[44] Together with the power of judgment, this play explains genius, whether it be aesthetic, humanistic, or even scientific. Judgment and the imagination spontaneously work on the ideas that are not directly exhibitable, creatively seeking other intuitions that will represent them.[45] Symbolizing is thus at the core of theology. Ideas such as God, soul, freedom, creation, redemption, blessedness cannot be expressed except in symbols. When the ideas of pure reason and the postulates of practical reason are indirectly exhibited, the determined concepts that constitute their symbols are impoverished when compared to their referents, because no sensible intuition is available for them. By contrast, when the other religious ideas that Kant subsumes under the aesthetical ideas are indirectly exhibited, their symbols expand the data of intuition, because no sensible intuition is adequate for their content. Accordingly, in symbolizing, the imagination, "as the author of arbitrary forms of possible intuition," stretches the understanding beyond its determining powers in order "to quicken" it.[46] Kant offers no further insight into the creative genius that drives *hypotyposis*, contending that it is "an art concealed in the depths of the human soul, whose real mode of activity nature is hardly likely ever to allow us to discover."[47]

Like Möhler's doctrinal symbol, Kant's symbol is non-reducible. It is non-reducible because reason has no power directly to schematize pure reason's ideas, practical reason's postulates, or the aesthetical ideas. Nonetheless, the determined concept that indirectly exhibits its referent bears the intelligibility of reason on the one hand and the creativity of the imagination on the other hand. Accordingly, Kant asserts that knowledge of God mediates between anthropomorphism and Deism.[48] Although knowledge of God is indirectly represented in a sensuously intuitable concept, it is not anthropomorphic. The symbol's referent is linked to its symbol by a rational faculty, the purposive power of judgment.[49] Similarly, although religious knowledge cannot be directly represented or schematized, it is not Deistic. The ideas of pure reason and the postulates of practical reason are intrinsically, even if indirectly, linked to directly intuitable concepts through judgment's purposiveness.

In contrast to Kant's view of the symbol, the metaphysical structure of Möhler's doctrinal symbol bears a similarity to the Romantic symbol-theory of Hegel.[50] Nonetheless, although both Möhler's and Hegel's theories are metaphysical, Hegel's view of *Vernunft*, unlike Möhler's, reduces the symbol to a more univocal form of knowledge. The symbol for Hegel is a product of representation (*Vorstellung*), the dimension of human intelligence that comprises the acts of recollection, imagination, and memory. Representation builds on the previous moment of intelligence, intuition, which constitutes the multiple data of sensation into the unity of a substance.[51] In intuition, intelligence raises the data of sensation into an externally existing object.[52] In representation, intelligence raises intuition to a higher level of interiority so that, in the symbol and the sign, intelligence can be posited "in itself in an externality of its own."[53]

Recollection, the first moment of representation, elevates the substance unified in intuition into an image; recollection thus renders the substance subjectively "mine." This elevation is a result of the interior spatio-temporality of the subject who universalizes it; subjectivity frees the intuited datum from the immediacy of exterior space and time. This freedom allows the substance further to be incorporated into intelligence. As immediately mine, however, the image possesses only a formal subjectivity. Because it is lodged in the "darkness" of the subconscious, it becomes representation proper only when negated, dislodged, brought to "light" by a fresh intuition. When the image is dislodged from the subconscious, intelligence is then able to determine it. The image becomes distinct from immediate subjectivity on the one hand and from the intuition that dislodges it on the other.[54]

The distinctive determination of the image occurs because intelligence perceives a common universal, a general idea, in the dislodged image and the intuition that dislodges it. This perception allows the image to be subsumed under the universal; thus, in a more enriched form, the image is presented consciously to intelligence. In recollection, both the image and the intuition that dislodges it verify each other by comparison and contrast. Although they participate in the same general idea, they are nonetheless distinctive images. This verification means that neither the general idea nor the images that participate in it have achieved full independence. Accordingly, verification must be elevated by intelligence.[55]

Imagination, the second moment of representation, negates the verification and intensifies the opposition between the dislodged image and the image that dislodges it. The reproductive function of the imagination gives the dislodged image greater independence; reproduction frees the image from dependence on verification and subjects it to voluntary recall. The associative function of the imagination further interiorizes this recall. Association allows the whole range of ideas that can be recalled to be connected to one another according to the similarity they share. As a result, the recalled image, now capable of association with other recalled images, depends even less on the external objectivity of the sensation that intuited it. Nonetheless, because the image has not yet attained the level of full subjectivity but continues to be determined, at least partially, by objectivity, the image requires further elevation by intelligence.[56]

The creative function of the imagination definitively negates the general idea's dependence on the verification of recollection. The general idea and the images that precipitate its cognitive awareness are now free of their necessary association with each other. Accordingly, the general idea can be freely associated with a range of images other than those that precipitated its cognitive awareness. For its part, the image is now so enriched by subjectivity that it can be individuated and posited by intelligence as a symbol and a sign of a general idea. In positing these forms, subjective intelligence represents itself in its own objective other. The symbol is constituted as an object by intelligence in order for intelligence to realize itself in it.[57] Thus manifested as "self-uttering," intelligence creates its own intuitions that embody it.[58]

Although both the symbol and the sign export subjective rationality, the symbol depends on objectivity more than the sign. As a representation of the general idea, the symbol consists of an intuition whose sensuous qualities correspond in some fashion, however creatively, to the general idea. Accordingly, the symbol still retains in its sensuous form an attachment to external objectivity. As a result, Hegel asserts that the symbol is less adequate than the sign as a representation for intelligence. Consequently, because it remains tied to the finite, the symbol is impoverished and must yield to the sign.[59]

The sign renders intelligence free of the need to express itself in a sensuous medium. In the sign, the relation between the general idea and its representation is arbitrary. Thus, language for Hegel is the consummate sign. In language, intelligence exercises a fuller authority to harness media that are more independent than the symbol of any inherent relation to external objectivity. Nonetheless, since intelligence must still harness some medium other than its pure self when it utters the sign, even the sign must yield to a more elevated form of intelligence.[60]

Möhler in Dialogue with Kant and Hegel

Bringing Möhler's notion of doctrine as a symbol into dialogue with the symbol-theories of Kant and Hegel reveals that Möhler's notion of intrinsic symbolism charts a middle course between Idealism and Romanticism. Like Kant's symbol and unlike Hegel's, Möhler's symbol is rationally non reducible. But like Hegel's symbol and unlike Kant's, Möhler's is metaphysically constituted. Although Möhler thus offers a critique of both Kant and Hegel, still their symbol-theories can be used to amplify Möhler's. Kant's and Hegel's theories can be used additionally to help explain *Symbolism's* understanding of the difference between Protestant and Catholic views of the doctrinal symbol.

Möhler observes that Catholic doctrines, as confessional symbols, do not derive their authenticity from theologians. Doctrines pre-exist theologians because Catholicism distinguishes between "peculiar opinions and the common doctrines declared by the Church."[61] As a result, no Catholic dogma can be referred to any particular thinker as its author.[62] By contrast, the distinction between theological opinion and official doctrine does not obtain in Protestantism, whose "whole system," claims Möhler, "is only an individuality exalted into a generality." As a result, the theological writings of the individual Reformers "perfectly coincided, in their opinion, with the dogmas themselves."[63]

The impact of personal temperament on Protestantism's doctrinal symbols is nowhere more pronounced, says Möhler, than in Luther. More than in Melanchthon, Calvin, or Zwingli, in Luther

> [t]he peculiar emotions of his spirit, out of which his system gradually arose, ...the rational construction of his doctrine by the exhibition of his feelings...[are] of high significance to one, who will obtain a genuine scientific apprehension of Protestantism as a doctrinal system....[64]

At times, Luther's views seem "the sport of momentary impressions and transient moods of mind."[65] Accordingly, Möhler concludes that "the Protestant articles of faith are so interwoven with the nature of their original production in the mind of Luther...that it is utterly impossible to sever them."[66] Among the official Lutheran symbols cited by Möhler, the Formulary of Concord, Luther's two catechisms, and the Smalcald Articles especially manifest this interweaving of doctrine with Luther's mind. In them, ecclesial dogma becomes "equally subjective" with their genesis in Luther's reason, imagination, and affectivity.[67]

Möhler's critique of Lutheran symbols can be further explained by using Kant's account of symbolic *hypotyposis*. Observing that theological genius especially manifests itself in symbolizing, Kant argues that rational judgment and the imagination must work in tandem in order creatively to find intuitions that can indirectly exhibit religious intuitions. In the search for symbols, the imagination, as the author of arbitrary forms that surpass nature, stretches the categories of *Verstand* beyond their determining power. Accordingly, although symbolic *hypotyposis* is driven by genius, when the imagination is strongly influenced by emotion and mood, the symbols it exhibits can be eccentric, arbitrary, oblique, even strange and odd in their indirect relation to the intuitions they seek to represent. The spontaneous play of the imagination can overpower judgment's purposiveness that links the characteristics of the symbol to those of its referent. The imagination can thus undermine the appropriateness of the concept selected as the indirect exhibition of the religious intuition.

In the case just described, the symbol becomes inadequate, even incomprehensible, as an expression of its referent. Accordingly, in Kantian terms, Möhler seems to accuse Luther of an idiosyncratic *hypotyposis* caused by his failure to bring his imagination under the discipline of rational judgment. Although a genius, Luther, in creating doctrinal symbols, allows affectivity to subdue judgment's purposiveness when he seeks indirectly to exhibit religious intuitions. And his disordered *hypotyposis* necessarily infuses the spirit of all the Lutheran symbolical confessions.

Möhler indicates that the strong influence of affectivity on the imagination must be overcome in order that the influence of idiosyncracy on theological symbolizing can be obviated. "Truth and falsehood," he says, "can be enclosed at the same time in feeling, and it is only possible to distinguish them on a higher level of the life of the mind."[68] Nonetheless, the representations exhibited by idiosyncratic symbolizing can aid the church's organic evolution of authentic symbols. These are produced by the dialectic that heresy, inappropriate symbols, stimulates within the church's internal force, its self-consciousness. "The deeper insight of the human mind into the divine revelation in the Church," Möhler affirms, "seems determined by the struggles of error against Christian truth."[69]

So long as heretical views are not articulated boldly and believed widely, the church is reluctant to refute them in a doctrinal symbol, because the church itself does not possess a clear and exhaustive understanding of the beliefs under question. But sustained and pervasive heresy provokes controversy, and controversy evokes renewed symbolizing in human minds. Heresy thus effects in the church's consciousness a crystallization of what the church has believed, however implicitly, since its origin. Accordingly, the church's internal force, constituted by the community immersed in its living tradition, matures into a certitude about its questioned beliefs. When this evolution occurs, beliefs are posited as doctrines in order to distinguish them from mere theological opinions.[70]

As Möhler affirms, idiosyncratic symbols must be overcome by a higher intelligence. This intelligence is the faculty of a metaphysically constituted *Vernunft* in individuals as it collectively aggregates under the Spirit's guidance into the self-consciousness of the church. The "original material" for doctrinal symbols, contends Möhler:

> after having been subjected to the repeated workings of the human mind, now presents itself under an appearance which is the product of successive modifications. It remains the original, yet it is no longer the same; there is identity in essence, diversity in form.[71]

The notion of doctrinal development that these comments outline finds a further philosophical explanation in Hegel's account of representation.

Analogous to Hegel's notion of intuition, the revelation received by the church at its origin is possessed only latently before heresy forces it to develop. Although the church possesses revelation as a unity, revelation is lodged inchoately within the church's self-conscious beliefs. Analogous to recollection, heresy constitutes a fresh intuition that dislodges the latent belief, thereby bringing it more clearly into the church's purview. This dislodging allows the church to grasp the deeper truth implicit in its original belief, a truth that the heresy partially and inadequately grasps. When the church sees this truth, it comes to recognize the original belief precisely as original and the heresy precisely as heresy.

Analogous to Hegel's concept of the reproductive imagination, further controversy intensifies the opposition between the original belief and the heresy. Analogous to the associative imagination, more reflection allows the original belief to be seen as part of a nexus of beliefs that the church clearly recalls and asserts. Analogous to the creative imagination, reflection finally produces an independent ecclesial consciousness of the original belief. As such, the belief can be posited in human concepts, in a language that often bears the influence of the heresy's language while remaining free of its idiosyncratic relation to the original belief.[72]

Analogous to Hegel's notion of a sign, therefore, a doctrine constitutes the church's original belief brought clearly into its consciousness through a dialectic engaged by heresy. This clearly conscious belief is then expressed in a signifying form chosen by the church's internal force as the representation of its belief. The church's doctrines are thus its self-utterings, because in them the church posits its own consciousness in a form that it determines. Accordingly, Möhler can affirm that a doctrine is identical in essence to the originally received revelation, although diverse in form, because a metaphysical unity links the three elements of the dialectic that develops a doctrine: the received revelation, the clear consciousness of it that heresy precipitates, and the doctrinal form that represents it.

In sum, although analogous to Hegel's metaphysics of representation, the metaphysical unity of Möhler's doctrinal symbol emerges from his own metaphysics of twin participation and his own model of human reason. On the one hand, doctrines derive from the church's self-consciousness, which is animated by the life of the Trinity. On the other hand, human reason, although constituted by an ability to apprehend and to articulate something of the divine teleology in history, possesses no individual protection from idiosyncracy in these endeavors. *Vernunft* must therefore actively participate in the church's internal force if it wishes authentically to contribute to, and benefit from, the divine truth that revelation embodies.

NOTES

1. Johann Adam Möhler, *Symbolism or Exposition of the Doctrinal Differences Between Catholics and Protestants as Evidenced by Their Symbolical Writings*, trans. James Burton Robertson, 5th ed. (London: Thomas Baker, 1906), p. 1; originally published as *Symbolik oder Darstellung der dogmatischen Gegensätze der Katholischen und Protestanten nach ihren öffentlichen Bekenntnisschriften*, 5th ed., 2 vols. (Mainz: Kupferberg, 1838), ed. Josef Rupert Geiselmann (Darmstadt: Wissenschaftliche Buchgesellschaft, 1958), p. 17. Unless noted otherwise, citations to *Symbolik* are taken from volume 1 of Geiselmann's 5th edition, and translations of this edition are taken from Robertson's 5th edition.

2. For a further definition, see *Symbolism*, pp. 1–2; *Symbolik*, pp. 17–18.

3. For this history, see Josef R. Geiselmann, "Zur Einführung," *Symbolik*, pp. 44–54.

4. Edmond Vermeil, *Jean-Adam Möhler et l'école catholique de Tubingue (1815–1840)* (Paris: Librarie Armand Colin, 1913), pp. 155–56.

5. Johann Adam Möhler, *Gesammelte Schriften und Aufsätze*, ed. Johann J. I. von Döllinger, 2 vols. (Regensburg, 1839–40), 2: 273–77, cited in Vermeil, p. 156.

6. Johann Adam Möhler, *Theologische Quartalschrift* (1826): 434; [Hereafter *TQ* (1827): 487–88; *Gesammelte Schriften* 1: 68f, cited in Vermeil, p. 157.

7. *TQ* (1826) 430–32; *TQ* (1827) 73; cited in Vermeil, p. 157.

8. See Johann Adam Möhler, *Die Einheit in der Kirche oder das Prinzip des Katholizismus dargestellt in Geiste der Kirchenväter der drei ersten Jahrhunderte*, ed. E. J. Vierneisel (Mainz: Matthias Grünewald, 1925), p. 24, cited in Gustav Voss, "Johann Adam Möhler and the Development of Dogma," *Theological Studies* 4 (1943): 420–444 at 428; see also Joseph Fitzer, *Moehler and Baur in Controversy, 1832–38: Romantic-Idealist Assessment of the Reformation and Counter-Reformation* (Tallahassee: American Academy of Religion, 1974), p. 19.

9. Johann Adam Möhler, *Symbolik*, 4th ed., 2 vols. (Mainz: Kupferberg, 1835) 1: 301, cited in Hervé Savon, *Johann Adam Möhler: The Father of Modern Theology*, trans. Charles McGrath (Glen Rock: Paulist, 1966), p. 95.

10. *Symbolik* (4th ed.) 1: 335, cited in Savon, p. 95.

11. *Symbolik*, p. 277; *Symbolism*, trans. Robertson, 3rd ed. (New York: Catholic Publication House, n.d.), p. 178; cited in Fitzer, *Moehler and Baur*, p. 41.

12. Fitzer, *Moehler and Baur*, p. 17.

13. See Möhler, *Gesammelte Schriften* , 2: 269–71, cited in Vermeil, p. 156.

14. *TQ* (1826): 324–25; *Gesammelte Schriften* 2: 281–85; *TQ* and *GS* cited in Vermeil, p. 160.

15. Johann Adam Möhler, "Die Idee der Geschichte und Kirchengeschichte," in *Geist des Christentums und des Katholizismus: Ausgewählte Schriften katholischer Theologie im Zeitalter des deutschen Idealismus und der Romantik*, ed. J. R. Geiselmann (Mainz: R. Oldenbourg, 1940), pp. 391–96 at 392, cited in Fitzer, *Moehler and Baur*, p. 17.

16. Fitzer, *Moehler and Baur*, pp. 17, 19.

17. Karl Rahner, "The Theology of the Symbol," *Theological Investigations* 4, trans. Kevin Smyth (Baltimore: Helicon, 1966), pp. 221–52 at 225; originally published as "Zur Theologie des Symbols," in vol. 4 of *Schriften zur Theologie*, 16 vols. (Einsiedeln: Benzinger, 1954–84).

18. Ibid., p. 225.

19. Louis Dupré, *The Other Dimension* (New York: Seabury, 1979), pp. 105–07.

20. Möhler, *Die Einheit*, pp. 24, 325, cited in Voss, "Development of Doctrine," pp. 428, 430.

21. *Symbolik*, 9th ed. (Mainz: Kupferberg, 1884), p. 357; *Symbolism*, p. 279; cited in Voss, "Development of Doctrine," p. 428.

22. Voss, "Development of Doctrine," p. 429.

23. *Die Einheit* (1925), p. 24, cited in Voss, "Development of Doctrine," p. 428.

24. *Die Einheit* (1925), p. 33, cited in Voss, "Development of Doctrine," p. 429.

25. *Die Einheit* (1925), p. 22; *Symbolik* (9th ed.), pp. 369–71; *Symbolism*, pp. 289–90, cited in Voss, "Development of Doctrine," pp. 430–31.

26. *Symbolik* (9th ed.), p. 368; *Symbolism*, p. 288, cited in Voss, "Development of Doctrine," p. 434.

27. Voss, "Development of Doctrine," pp. 434–44.

28. *Die Einheit* (1925), p. 33, cited in Voss, "Development of Doctrine," p. 429.

29. See Rahner, "Theology of the Symbol," p. 225, who cites Friedrich Theodor von Visher, "Das Symbol," *Altes und Neues* (Stuttgart: A. Bonz, 1889); see also Dupré, *Other Dimension*, p. 108.

30. For a study of the principles of apophatic predication as laid out by (Pseudo) Dionysius, see Bernard McGinn, *The Presence of God: A History of Western Christian Mysticism* (New York: Crossroad, 1994), pp. 157–82 at 173f.

31. Immanuel Kant, *Kritik der reinen Vernunft* (1781), *Gesammelte Schriften* 4, 15 vols. (Berlin: Royal Prussian Academy of Scineces, 1902–13), p. 145; see the 1787 ed., in *Werke* 3, 11 vols., ed. Ernst Cassirer (Berlin: B. Cassirer, 1912–23), pp. 184–85. ET: *Critique of Pure Reason*, ed. N. Kemp Smith (New York: St. Martin's, 1965), p. 185. Hereafter, the 1781 ed. is cited as A, the 1787 ed. as B, and the ET as First *Critique*. See also Marcia Moen, "The *Critique of Judgment* and Its Legacy," in *New Essays on Kant*, ed. Bernard D. den Ouden and Marcia Moen (New York: P. Lang, 1987), pp. 251, 253–54.

32. A, p.109; First *Critique*, p. 137.

33. Immanuel Kant, *Kritik der Urteilskraft* (1793), *Werke* 5, section 59; ET: *Critique of Judgment*, trans. J. H. Bernard (New York: Hafner, 1951), p. 197. Hereafter, the ET is cited as Third *Critique*.

34. A, pp. 140–145; B, pp. 179–185; First *Critique*, pp. 182–185, see also Moen, "Legacy," p. 253; and Donald W. Crawford, *Kant's Aesthetic Theory* (Madison: University of Wisconsin, 1974), p. 83.

35. *Kritik der Urteilskraft*, p. 59; Third *Critique*, p. 197.

36. For the mind's generation of the three ideas of *Vernunft*, see A, pp. 584–668; B, pp. 612–96, First *Critique*, pp. 495–549; see also Kant, *Kritik der praktischen Vernunft*, *Gesammelte Schriften* 5, p. 134; ET: *Critique of Practical Reason*, trans. Thomas K. Abbott (London: Longman, Green, 1954), p. 232.

37. *Kritik der Urteilskraft*, p. 49; Third *Critique*, pp.157–158. For a further discussion of the aesthetical ideas, see Crawford, *Aesthetic Theory*, pp.118–124.

38. *Kritik der Urteilskraft*, p. 49; Third *Critique*, p.157.

39. Moen, "Legacy," pp. 246, 265; J. H. Bernard, "Translator's Introduction," Third *Critique*, pp. xvii–xviii.

40. *Kritik der Urteilskraft*, p. 59; Third *Critique*, pp. 197–198.

41. *Kritik der Urteilskraft*, p. 59; Third *Critique*, p.198.

42. *Kritik der Urteilskraft*, p. 59; Third *Critique*, p.198.

43. Wilbur M. Urban, *Language and Reality* (London: G. Allen and Unwin, 1939), p. 423.

44. *Kritik der Urteilskraft*, p. 22; Third *Critique*, p.77.

45. For more on Kant's conception of genius, see *Kritik der Urteilskraft* , pp. 46–47, Third *Critique*, pp.150–153.

46. *Kritik der Urteilskraft*, p. 22, 49; Third *Critique*, p. 77, 157, 160.

47. A, p.141; B, p.181; First *Critique,* p. 183.

48. *Kritik der Urteilskraft,* p. 59; Third *Critique,* p.198.

49. Moreover, knowledge of God is not anthropomorphic because it is "cognized" even though it is not schematized (*Kritik der Urteilskraft,* p. 59; Third *Critique,* p.198).

50. Scholarly disagreement exists about the extent of the influence of Romantic metaphysics on Möhler. For a discussion of Schleiermacher's and Schelling's influences on *Die Einheit in der Kirche,* see Fitzer, pp.15–16 and Henry Nienaltowski, "Johann Adam Möhler's Theory of Doctrinal Development: Its Genesis and Formulation" (Doctoral dissertation abstract: Catholic University of America, 1959), pp. 6–8. For Möhler's alleged dependence on Hegel, see Karl Eschweiler, *Johann Adam Möhlers Kirchenbegriff* (Freiburg-im-Breisgau: Herder, 1930) passim. For rebuttals of Eschweiler's thesis, see Yves M. J. Congar, "Sur l'évolution et l'interprétation de la pensée de Moehler,"*Revue des sciences philosophiques et théologiques* 27 (1938): 205–12; and Martin Preis, Review of K. Eschweiler *supra, Zeitschrift für katholische Theologie* 56 (1932): 101–03. For the plausible argument that Möhler's debt to Romanticism is derived less from individual thinkers as such and more from the reaction against the rational ahistoricism of the Enlightenment that he shares with them, see A. Minon, "L'attitude de J. A. Moehler dans la question du développement du dogme," *Ephemerides Theologicae Lovanienses* 16 (1939): 328–82 at 362–67; and Vermeil, pp. 1–8.

51. Georg W. F. Hegel, *Enzyklopädie der philosophischen Wissenschaften im Grundrisse* (1830), ed. Friedhelm Nicolin and Otto Pöggeler, *Philosophische Bibliothek* 33 (Hamburg: F. Meiner, 1969) section 449. ET of *Enzyklopädie,* Part 3, "Philosophie des Geistes": *Hegel's Philosophy of Mind,* trans. William Wallace [together with the *Zusätze* in Boumann's text (1845) trans. A. V. Miller] (Oxford: Clarendon, 1971), p. 199. The *Zusätze* are not printed in Nicolin and Pöggeler, but in Boumann. Boumann's edition of them is reproduced, together with a parallel ET, in *Hegel's Philosophy of Spirit,* trans. and ed. Michael J. Petry, 3 vols. (Dordrecht and Boston: D. Reidel, 1979). Hereafter, the *Enzyklopädie* is cited as EPW and *Hegel's Philosophy of Mind* as PM.

52. EPW, p. 448Z; PM, pp. 199–200 [Z=*zusatz*].

53. EPW, p. 452; PM, p. 202.

54. EPW, pp. 452–43Z; PM, pp. 203–205.

55. EPW, pp. 454–54Z; PM, pp. 205–206.

56. EPW, pp. 455–55Z; PM, pp. 206–209.

57. EPW, pp. 456–457 passim, 457Z; PM, pp. 209–212.

58. EPW, p. 457; PM, p. 210.

59. EPW, pp. 456–457 passim, 457Z; PM, pp. 209–212.

60. EPW, pp. 457Z–459; PM, pp. 212–214.

61. *Symbolism,* p. 7; *Symbolik,* p. 25.

62. *Symbolism,* p. 6; *Symbolik,* p. 24.

63. *Symbolism,* p. 8; *Symbolik,* p. 26.

64. *Symbolism,* p. 6; *Symbolik,* p. 24.

65. *Symbolism,* p. 10; *Symbolik,* pp. 37–38.

66. *Symbolism,* p. 7; *Symbolik,* p. 24.

67. *Symbolism,* p. 7; *Symbolik,* p. 24.

68. *Symbolism* (4th ed.), pp. 1, 73, in Savon, p. 82.

69. *Symbolism,* p. 291; *Symbolik* (9th ed.), p. 371, in Voss, p. 433.

70. *Symbolism,* pp.7, 118–19; *Symbolik,* pp. 25, 186–87; see also Voss, "Development of Doctrine," p. 433.

71. *Symbolik* (4th ed.), pp. 1, 375, in Savon, *Father of Modern Theology* p. 96.

72. *Symbolism,* p. 290, *Symbolik* (9th ed.), pp. 370f, cited in Voss, "Development of Doctrine," p. 434.

8

Kingdom of God–Church–Society

The Contemporary Relevance of Johann Baptist Hirscher,
Theologian of Reform

——HERMANN J. POTTMEYER——

Johann Baptist Hirscher was for a long time overshadowed by the other Tübingen theologians. His analysis of modernity and his theoretical and practical program have developed some exceptional interest as the next millennium approaches. His theology aims at a reform that makes the Church better able to move into the future, its preaching more credible, and the social relevance of Christianity clearer.

Hirscher as Theologian of Reform

The very reasons for this diminution are indicative of his importance as a theologian of reform. It was the triumph of Ultramontanism and of Neoscholasticism that led to the repression of Hirscher's theology. Josef Kleutgen, one of the most important advocates of Neoscholasticism, attacked Hirscher in the same breath with Georg Hermes and Anton Günther, and one of Hirscher's writings on reform was placed on the Index. The period of reform Catholicism awakened a new interest in Hirscher. In the period leading up to Vatican II he was rediscovered initially as a contributor to catechetics. When Vatican II approved of reform concerns that were also his, it contributed to a renewal of attention to the whole of Hirscher's theology. The first adequate presentations and assessments of his theology were published only after the Second World War.[1]

This current cultural amnesia is in striking contrast to the high esteem which Hirscher enjoyed in his lifetime. Many regarded him as "the teacher and leader of Catholic Germany" and counted him, along with Möhler, among the best known and most effective theologians of his age.[2] But he was not the adherent of any party and for this reason was at that time already controversial. One group considered him not liberal enough; the other thought of him as "a prosecutor and reformer" of the church, who was calling for a revolution in the church, and even as "an enemy of Rome."[3] As a result, he fell between two stools.

This description of his fate at the time already gives us an idea of his present-day relevance. The call for reform, for a more credible proclamation of the Gospel and a more credible form of the church itself in today's world, is becoming ever more urgent. Prior to Vatican II many thought the church had reached its perfect and definitive social form at the end of the nineteenth century, but the Council was aware that the church is in fact the people of God on its way to the complete and perfect kingdom of God. The history of the church is part of the coming of the kingdom of God, which is already present but not yet complete.

"Reform" of the church is understood in three ways today. Some, wittingly or unwittingly, think of reform as an adaptation of the church to the age; they confuse the Holy Spirit with the spirit of the times. Others understand reform as a withdrawal of the church into itself; they confuse the church as such either with the church of the nineteenth century or with the church of the first century. Both conceptions of reform lack an understanding of the church as the people of God on a journey, for they locate the perfect church in the early period or in the nineteenth century or in the present day.

A third group takes seriously the pilgrim nature of the church. They understand that the church is an historical entity. They attempt to discern the strengths and weaknesses of the church in each age, and then to place themselves firmly in the present time and learn from the past how to structure the present-day church. In this effort they ask two critical questions. What is the form in which the church can best carry out its mission at the present time? And: What developments in the present age are signs of the oncoming reign of God or, as Vatican II puts it, "signs of the times," and what developments in the church and in society are opposed to the reign of God and hinder its coming?

This third approach to understanding the "church as in need of constant reform" *(Ecclesia semper reformanda)* is the approach taken by Vatican II. The Council rediscovered the riches of the original tradition and of the tradition in its entirety and formulated the mission of the church in the present-day world. It did the first in the conciliar Constitution *Lumen gentium* and the second in the Pastoral Constitution *Gaudium et spes*. The two Constitutions therefore belong inseparably together. However, it also became clear at the Council that the three conceptions of reform rarely appear in their pure form; frequently they are intermingled.

The third conception of reform is also Hirscher's. In fact, his views offer a surprising parallel in both structure and content to Vatican II's conception of reform. Along with Johann Sebastian Drey, but also with other theologians of his day, he, like the Council, goes back to that which is at the center of the New Testament: the message of Jesus about the kingdom of God. In his suggestion to hold synods in which the laity participate, he, like the Council, harks back to the early church's practice of "communion." This, too, is a return to the original tradition.

But Hirscher also warns against a reform that appeals solely to the "letter" of the scriptures or aims at restoring the state of affairs that existed in the early church. For the Spirit of God, who advances the coming of God's reign intends to be active in the present.[4] The historical character of the church is taken seriously only when the church consciously takes its place in present-day society. "We must be part of our time if we are to have an effect on our time."[5] This self-positioning in time, in today's world, is thus the other pillar in Hirscher's conception of reform as in that of the Council. Like the Pastoral Constitution *Gaudium et spes*, Hirscher undertakes a critical and discriminating analysis of the age.

There is still another remarkable agreement with the Pastoral Constitution. Like the latter, Hirscher does not regard the social praxis of Christians as simply an application of Christian doctrine or dogma. In his view, social praxis belongs rather to the content of dogma, because it is the coming of God's reign, of which dogma speaks. But Hirscher is not speaking of either a simple accommodation to the age or an optimism regarding progress. The reader is reminded rather of the address with which Pope John XXIII opened the Council. Hirscher distances himself both from the fossilizers who see only dangers in anything new and from the progressivists who think that the new is always the better. Like Pope John, he distinguishes between "what is taught in the church" and "what is taught by the church," and therefore also between "the praxis in the church" and "the praxis of the church."[6] The former changes according to the challenge of the age, the latter is the abiding truth of the Christian faith or "the spirit of Christianity."[7]

Again, changes in teaching and practice to meet the needs of the day do not mean simply an external adaptation to the age in language, organizations, and forms of activity. The purpose of the changes is rather that believers who open themselves to the challenges of the age will have a fuller awareness of "the spirit of Christianity" because they have made the faith their own with conviction and that they will make this spirit the principle that guides their free self-determination.[8] Hirscher speaks of "making the faith subject-oriented" (Subjektivierung des Glaubens) through "freely adopted conviction."[9] According to Hirscher, involvement in the age leads to a deeper understanding of God, humanity, and the church, and one that gives a better answer to the questions of the time than an earlier understanding did.

We may, therefore, see Hirscher's concept of reform as summed up in the sentence: "We must build from inside out; no external changes and improvements will be of any help to us here."[10] "From inside out" means for Hirscher "from the Christian spirit in the person."[11] If believers are vividly aware of the reign of God in their hearts and minds and attest to it in their activity, then we share in "building" the kingdom of God here on earth or, as Hirscher puts it, the reign of God "in the individual and in humanity."[12] This is authentic reform of the individual, the church, and society.

In what has been said, a central concern of Hirscher has already become evident. In a secularized and pluralistic society, the faithful must come to think of themselves as responsible subjects of the church in the service of the kingdom of God and its coming. Consequently, Hirscher is opposed to "every kind of despotism in matters of faith and love," both within and outside the church, and he is for "the free shaping of all Christian life in light of it" (i.e., of the spirit of Christianity).[13] This concern is evidently even more relevant today than it was in Hirscher's time, and it finds expression everywhere in the world. But Hirscher bases his proposals for reform on a theological theory that provides him with the necessary criteria for judging what is to count as true reform. This theological theory also underlies his analysis of the modern age.

The Modern Age: Increasing Awareness of the Subject— Sign of the Coming Kingdom of God

What is described as "the anthropological turn" of the modern period is a new phase, in the process whereby human beings become subjects. It led to the scientific, social, and political revolutions of the eighteenth and nineteenth centuries. Human beings became increasingly aware of themselves as the active subjects of their own history, and thus aware of themselves and their world as historical. We recognize today that the modern period did not bring the absolute beginning of this process, as the feelings of the Enlightenment led it to believe for a long time. This was in fact only a new phase in the process whereby human beings become subjects. As far as European culture is concerned, this process began with the Greeks and was deeply influenced by Christianity. The thing that was new was simply that freedom, subjectivity, and history now became central themes; new, too, was the degree of consciousness of the subject that was achieved. To that extent, the modern age was truly a new phase.

Hirscher and other theologians of his time recognized, first, what was specific to the new situation and, second, the Christian heritage that was operative here despite a good many distortions of it. As a result, Hirscher comes to an affirmative but at the same time critical judgment on the modern age. What he calls "the spirit of the new age" is, in his view, nothing but "the moral spirit of Christianity" that has now awakened to historical "self-awareness" and is in a position to develop "Christian moral principles out of itself."[14] This spirit is the spirit of Christian freedom. Its self-awareness shows, negatively, in "removing and throwing away" everything that stands in the way of a free appropriation and activation of faith and love. This same spirit shows itself, on the positive side, as an "effort... to manifest itself more and more.... in the full purity of its essence"[15] and to shape the entire Christian moral life in free self-determination.[16] This "spirit of Christianity" is not an "abstract teaching," not a "mere doctrine," but, everywhere and always, "action and life."[17] According to Hirscher, then, it is the "spirit of Christianity" or the coming of the kingdom of God that is the driving force of history, even the history of the modern age.

But the "kingdom of evil" is also at work in the development of the modern age.[18] Hirscher laments the social and moral conditions of his day and warns of "revolution" and a "red republic." He sees "emancipation from God" and the "idolization of the human spirit" as the causes of moral decay.[19] The "external freedom" which human beings have secured for themselves cannot endure without "interior" or "moral" freedom.

When the revolution of March, 1848, and the Baden revolution of 1849 declared the state to be nondenominational, Hirscher realized quite clearly the consequences for society no less than for the church.[20] In the areas of socialization and communication the church now had to rely on itself. What sociologists today call the "churchification of Christianity" now began. For the church this meant it had to develop the social forms that would ensure it a broad social basis and keep it from being regarded by democratic society as either heteronomous or alien; to this end,

Hirscher suggested a revival of the synodal structure. For society the change meant the danger of losing the commonly accepted foundations of moral motivation. Both of these problems are even more real today than in Hirscher's time. In any case, Hirscher was convinced that in the long run society and church could not do without each other.

Instead of making the needed changes, the Catholic Church of the nineteenth century entrenched itself behind the ramparts in an attitude of defense against the modern age. Hirscher had explicitly warned against this reaction, because the church was putting itself in danger "of being dismissed by modern society as "antiquated" and as a "hindrance to the modern age."[21] Erwin Keller's judgment that "in many areas Hirscher was far ahead of his time"[22] seems to be an accurate judgement.

Hirscher's Theology: The Message of God's Kingdom as a Bridge between Faith and Modern Rationality

This analysis of the age brings out the concern of Hirscher's theology and of his proposals for reform. Hirscher realizes that after the Enlightenment and Kant the truth of the faith can no longer be substantiated, at least at the scientific level, by a direct appeal to the objective authority either of revelation or of the church. The simple acceptance of an authority-based faith must be replaced by a free faith that draws its life from personal conviction. This does not mean for Hirscher that faith is to be superseded by knowledge. The point is rather that to the positive data of divine revelation is to be added reflection which recognizes that the content of faith is something true and good even for reason. This is precisely what reason can see to be the case with Jesus' proclamation of the kingdom of God.[23] There is an intrinsic "evidence of Christian moral life" that illumines reason as well.[24] In the background here is obviously Hirscher's conviction that human reason develops through history and shares in the action of the Spirit of God in history.

Hirscher had to put forward his contrast between authority-faith and free faith in opposition to the ultramontane party and to Neoscholasticism. Kleutgen, for example, understood the modern age as nothing but "an impudent revolt against authority."[25] In his view, the objective authority of the church is the sole source of the certitude of faith. He justifies his return to the *Theology of the Distant Past (Theologie der Vorzeit)* on the grounds that its exclusive validity has been established by ecclesiastical authority. For this reason it is in the area of the problem of authority and freedom that Walter Fürst locates the cause of the nineteenth-century dispute over theological methodology.[26] Whereas in the eyes of the Ultramontanists the new claims of the subject and the modern freedom movement are simply forms of rebellion against the authority of God and the church, Hirscher and other theologians see the Christian heritage also at work in these phenomena, as well as the action of God in the history of humankind, of the God who calls human beings to freedom.

It may be added that Hirscher tried to overcome the unfortunate antithesis of heteronomy and autonomy, which has influenced modern thought down to today. Against a claim to autonomy which increasingly regarded itself as opposed to Christianity, Hirscher distinguishes a free human self-determination that is willed and brought about by God. He also stresses the point that to the extent that human beings are conscious of themselves as personal subjects, they also know themselves to be bound up in relationships to God and to their fellow human beings.

In opposition to rationalism, Hirscher thinks of theology as coming not from the self-knowing subject but from the believed object, that is, from the Logos who has appeared in history, from the person and message of Jesus Christ.[27] The knowing subject does, however, play a part. "Apart from reason there can be hearing but no understanding."[28] The extent to which Hirscher holds to the positivity of revelation can be seen in the fact that for him the comprehensive object of theology is not God in himself and in the abstract, as it is for a theology that starts with metaphysics, but God who reveals himself in history or, more concretely: the kingdom of God on earth. He therefore defines theology as "the science of God in Christ."[29] Here the idea of revelation as historical is thought out to its logical conclusions. But just as knowledge does not produce history and life but supervenes upon it in the form of understanding, so, too, theological understanding does not produce revelation and faith but continually lives out of these.

Theology, however, does not simply promote an understanding of the faith. Insofar as it helps in understanding the truth of the faith, it also promotes a faith based on responsible conviction and thus the free self-determination of the believing subject. According to Hirscher, it is necessary to get beyond an "empty verbal faith," any "enslavement to the letter," a barren "memorized theology" and arid "manual theology." On the contrary, the faithful must be brought "to challenge themselves . . . to lay claim to themselves and their entire lives, and to order these according to the truth." Hirscher is thus seeking the "conversion" of doctrine into life. He wants truth "for the sake of freedom" and "freedom guided by truth."[30] For Hirscher, "Truth is not words but life and action. It is found not where people write it down, read it, hear it, learn it, and retain it in memory, but where they use it and live it."[31] He talks, therefore, about an "orthodoxy of life," which is the goal of theology.[32] Theology is thus in the service of the individual's self-becoming as subject and of the coming of God's reign in humanity.

As Josef Rief in particular has shown, Hirscher's theology is not an intraecclesial theology. Rather it takes in the basic questions of modern society. Its aim is to respond to a question that is becoming ever more relevant: Where does a democratic society that is built on respect for human dignity have its ethical foundation? According to Hirscher, this foundation is threatened by "the attempt of human beings, in disregard of the incompleteness of this world, to think through their existence solely in terms of the possibilities of this world."[33] The relationship between human beings must not be thought of as purely economic or be determined by unrestrained self-interest. Over against these tendencies, Christianity makes possible a moral conception of freedom, one that alone is compatible with a radical, responsible self-determination of the human person. Hirscher, therefore, seeks a church that in its own relationships gives a credible example of what Christian freedom and participatory communication mean.[34]

The relevance and fruitfulness of Hirscher's conception of theology is clear not only in itself but also from the reception it is receiving today, whether with him as a source or independently of him. There is a striking similarity to the theology of liberation, which has found in the message of the reign of God a central motif that possesses both theological and social relevance.[35] Following the lead of Drey and Hirscher, the message of God's reign is also the central point of reference in the *Handbuch der Fundamentaltheologie*.[36] Seckler expounded this conception as the basis of a contemporary fundamental theology.[37] I for my part argued its importance in two areas: the criteriology for the credibility of Christianity[38] and the ecumenical question of the true Church.[39] This last suggestion has been taken up by Munich ecumenist Heinrich Döring as fundamental for a modern ecumenical "proof of Catholicism" (demonstratio catholica).[40] For the rest, Hirscher's conception of theology is in the line of Vatican II and of its axial documents *Lumen gentium, Gaudium et spes,* and *Dignitatis humanae.*

It is quite easy in fact to detach this conception of theology from the implications, inherited from late idealism, which it has in Hirscher and Drey, and, in addition, to deepen it from the viewpoints of biblical theology and social philosophy. The content of the message of God's reign, which forms the center of the gospel, offers, on the one hand, the criteria by which the internal credibility of Christianity in the form of the church is measured. On the other hand, the same content also grounds the external credibility of Christianity, since it can be shown, at the bar of contemporary reason, which is formed by society and history, to be a condition necessary for a society that is worthy of the human person.

The Kingdom of God on Earth: A Divine-Human Reality

Following Rief and Fürst, Max Seckler has investigated the kingdom of God as the central idea in the work of Drey and Hirscher.[41] In the process he has paid special heed to the "potential for the future" that their program contains. It was not an accident that Drey and Hirscher chose the kingdom of God as the central idea of their theology. This theme played an important role during the eighteenth and nineteenth centuries in Protestant theology, especially in Württemberg pietism, and in the philosophies of Kant, Fichte, Hegel, and Schelling. Consequently, it presented itself to Drey and Hirscher as a bridge between faith and reason. On the one hand, the kingdom of God is the center of the New Testament message; on the other, it provides philosophical reason with the ideas of freedom in the spirit and of the unity of all reality. At that time, then, the kingdom of God motif became "a signal of readiness for a reform that was in keeping with the times and Christian in its orientation."[42] This point of view emerges even more strongly in Hirscher than in Drey. The kingdom of God motif also moves into the background again in Möhler and the later Tübingen theologians. The distinguishing mark of Drey and Hirscher is not, however, that they take up the idea of the kingdom of God, but how they do this. Which elements in the message of Jesus make it suitable as a bridge to the modern mind?

The proclamation by Jesus of the kingdom of God gives meaning and purpose to the world as God's creation and to the entirety of history. It is God who gives them this meaning, but it is a meaning that at the same time fulfills the deepest longing of human beings and enlightens their moral reason. For as God himself is justice, freedom, and love, his kingdom is a kingdom of justice and freedom, peace and love. God thus gives himself to us in such a way as to establish personal relationships among human beings, as well as a society worthy of them, and this even now. It is a kingdom for human beings, but also and no less a kingdom of human beings. For the kingdom of God comes into existence precisely through their free collaboration. For this reason it is also a kingdom which they build under the guidance of their moral freedom and with the support of God´s action.[43]

Hirscher here understands history to be a history of divine revelation, a history of the coming of God's kingdom, and a history of a divine-human partnership that has its focal point in the incarnation of the Son of God. History thereby acquires a profoundly personal character. It is a history of personal and therefore also free relations between God and humanity and no less of human beings with one another.[44] In the course of this history human beings achieve a progressive knowledge of themselves, their freedom, their social nature, and a society worthy of humankind, at least if, at the same time, they seek communion with God. For this reason Hirscher is able to interpret the modern movement toward freedom as an expression of the coming of God's kingdom, although he rejects the distortion of the "turn to anthropology" into a "reduction to anthropology."

Max Seckler: "The kingdom of God is therefore to be understood as a process of the historicization of the reality of God, as an authentic self-communication of God in the process that is the universe." While Drey saw in this connection the central idea of Christianity and of theology and the bridge between faith and reason, Hirscher transposed it into a vision of Christian and, at the same time, secular praxis, thus interpreting the kingdom of God as divine-human activity. Hirscher's principal work is entitled "Christian Moral Theology as the Doctrine of the Realization of God's Kingdom in the Human Race" (*Die christliche Moral als Lehre von der Verwirklichung des göttlichen Reiches in der Menschheit*). He understands moral theology not as applied dogmatics "but as a doctrine of the conversion of the divine reality into human praxis; and in his vision of these connections he surpassed Drey in his intellectual achievement."[45]

God, Humanity, and Church in Light of the Message of God's Kingdom

In light of the divine-human structure of the kingdom of God Hirscher is also able to move beyond a distorted *understanding of God* on the part of Christians. As he correctly realized, one of the roots of modern atheism is the rejection of the autonomy of a God who alone acts and leaves no room for human freedom. To this one-sided theocracy the modern age opposed a no less one-sided claim of human autonomy or a one-sided anthropocentrism. Hirscher is therefore anxious that the kingdom of God is not to be understood as a theocracy in which God rules over subjects, but as a divine-human reality in which God takes human beings seriously as freely acting partners. For this reason Karl Frielingsdorf describes Hirscher's position as a "theo-anthropocentrism that conceives of human beings and their world in the light of God but also gives them an independent place in the economy of salvation."[46] This is fully in accord with the conception of revelation in the Constitution *Dei Verbum* (no. 2) of Vatican II. By means of this understanding of God and the corresponding understanding of the human person Hirscher surmounts the unfortunate antithesis of autonomy and heteronomy in the relationship of human beings with God, an antithesis that has played such a determining role in modern thought. This approach also means for Hirscher a deeper understanding of the doctrine of the Trinity and of pneumatology.

The divine-human character of the economy of salvation also plays a decisive part in Hirscher's *ecclesiology,* which is notably different from that of Möhler.[47] Both ecclesiologies have a common starting point, but each develops differently. The well-known development from his *Einheit* to his *Symbolik* allows Möhler increasingly to unify subjective faith, objective tradition, and the church and to emphasize objective authority; this development has led to his being accused of an ecclesial monophysitism. Over the years, Hirscher, like Möhler, lays an increasing emphasis on the Christological dimension of the church alongside the pneumatological and, therefore, also on the role of apostolic office. But, unlike Möhler, he maintains a more critical difference between the kingdom of God and the church; he also stresses the collaboration of the faithful in shaping and developing the tradition of the faith. Tradition is not simply divine; it is divino-human. It must always be interpreted in light of its true spirit and meaning and find the expression appropriate to each period. The faith must never be confused with its temporally conditioned forms of expression. Because of the necessary subjective appropriation of the objective tradition the church is necessarily "collegial" (to use Hirscher's term). Therefore, he argues for a collegial decision-making or a dialoguing church. Respect for the personhood and dignity of the faithful is, in his view, the primary duty of the church; the formation of community is only the second.

The development of Hirscher's ecclesiology can be summarized as follows: His original, primarily pneumatological view of the church as a community of subjects is later completed by a Christologically based view of the church as sacrament (to use our present-day language). But the church is a sacramental subject only through the activity of its members, who are real subjects in the church. While for Möhler the locus of the certainty enjoyed by believers is the objective authority of tradition and the church, this locus remains for Hirscher the conscience of the faithful insofar as this makes the objective truth of the reign of God subjective or real for the believing subject.[48] In this process the faithful are guided by the common faith of the church.

It is obvious that Hirscher's conception of the church provides a better basis for the *Ecclesia semper reformanda* than Möhler's does. It also explains why Möhler's ecclesiology initially enjoyed a greater success than did Hirscher's. For Möhler's emphasis on ecclesiastical authority made him more acceptable in an age of ultramontanism, although his ecclesiology, too, promoted renewal. Hirscher's ecclesiology is today seen as newly relevant. In a more consistent way than Möhler, Hirscher understands the church to be the community of the people of God on its journey through history. The church is not an end in itself but is to serve the coming of the reign of God in every age and society. Hirscher speaks more clearly than Möhler does of the active and responsible role that all believers have in the church.

Max Seckler and Eugen Biser speak of a "turning point in the history of the faith" as being in the offing today, i.e., "a shift of level, in the consciousness of faith, from a faith identified with obedience to a faith based on experience and understanding."[49] If this is so, then Hirscher's theology has a future. It is especially suited to reactivate the Vatican II reform that has begun to flag. It can help to reconcile the modern age and its valuable human accomplishments with Christianity and the church.

This help takes the form of a twofold clarification. Hirscher's theology shows modern society and the church that their alleged opposition rests on a misunderstanding, namely, that the reign of God proclaimed by Jesus means a theocracy which leaves no room for human freedom. Furthermore, in light of the internal contradictions of the modern age that are intensifying at the end of our millennium and that have led to the greatest mass murders in history and are threatening the future of our planet, Hirscher shows that the hope which inspires the modern age, that of a society worthy of the human person, has its basis in the message of Jesus. For the coming of the reign of God is the meaning and goal of history, and God invites us to collaborate in its realization.

NOTES

1. Franz Xaver Arnold, *Dienst am Glauben. Das vordringliche Anliegen heutiger Seelsorge* (Freiburg: Herder, 1948); Adolf Exeler, *Eine Frohbotschaft vom christlichen Leben. Die Eigenart der Moraltheologie Johann Baptist Hirschers (1788–1865)* (Freiburg: Herder, 1959); Josef Rief, *Reich Gottes und Gesellschaft nach Johann Sebastian Drey und Johann Baptist Hirscher* (Paderborn: Schöningh, 1965); Johannes Stelzenberger, "Das Menschenbild Johann Baptist Hirschers," in *Theologie im Wandel* (München: Wewel, 1967), pp. 565–581; Erwin Keller, *Johann Baptist Hirscher. Wegbereiter heutiger Theologie,* ed. Heinrich Fries and Johann Finsterhölzl (Graz: Styria, 1969); Karl Frielingsdorf, *Auf dem Weg zu einem neuen Gottesverständnis. Die Gotteslehre des J.B. Hirscher als Antwort auf das säkularisierte Denken der Aufklärungszeit* (Frankfurt: Knecht, 1970); Erwin Keller, "Johann Baptist Hirscher (1788–1865)," in *Katholische Theologen Deutschlands im 19. Jahrhundert,* ed. Heinrich Fries and Georg Schwaiger, vol. 2 (München: Kösel, 1975), pp. 40–69; Josef Rief, "Kirche und Gesellschaft. Hirschers kritische Analysen und Reformvorschläge der vierziger Jahre," in *Kirche und Theologie im 19. Jahrhundert. Referate und Berichte des Arbeitskreises Katholische Theologie,* ed. Georg Schwaiger (Göttingen: Vandenhoeck & Ruprecht, 1975), pp. 103–123; Walter Fürst, *Wahrheit im Interesse der Freiheit. Eine Untersuchung zur Theologie J.B. Hirschers (1788–1865)* (Mainz: Grünewald, 1979); Max Seckler, "Die Reich-Gottes-Idee bei J.B. Hirscher und in der Tübinger Schule," in *Glaube als Lebensform. Der Beitrag J.B. Hirschers zur Neugestaltung christlich-kirchlicher Lebenspraxis und lebensbezogener Theologie,* ed. Walter Fürst (Mainz: Grünewald, 1989), pp. 12–31.

2. Walter Fürst, *Wahrheit,* p. 62.

3. *Historisch-politische Blätter* 24 (1849): 272; 26 (1850) II: 194–198; Walter Fürst, "Von innen heraus. Zur Aktualität der Frage Johann Baptist Hirschers: Wie soll das Christentum in der Gegenwart unter uns lebendig werden?," *Theologie der Gegenwart* 33 (1990) : 82–83.

4. Johann Baptist Hirscher, *Erörterungen über die großen religiösen Fragen der Gegenwart,* III (Freiburg: Herder, 1855), pp. 95–96; Walter Fürst, *Wahrheit,* pp. 428–429.

5. Johann Baptist Hirscher, *Besorgnisse hinsichtlich der Zweckmäßigkeit unseres Religionsunterrichtes* (Freiburg: Herder, 1863), p. 87: "Wir müssen inner unserer Zeit stehen, um auf unsere Zeit zu wirken."

6. Johann Baptist Hirscher, *Antwort an die Gegner meiner Schrift: Die kirchlichen Zustände der Gegenwart* (Tübingen: Laupp, 1850), p. 79; Walter Fürst, *Wahrheit,* p. 428.

7. Johann Baptist Hirscher, *Die christliche Moral als Lehre von der Verwirklichung des göttlichen Reiches in der Menschheit,* vol. I (Tübingen: Laupp,^{5}1851), p. 78; Walter Fürst, *Wahrheit* , p. 447.

8. Johann Baptist Hirscher, *Die christliche Moral,* vol. I (Tübingen: Laupp, ^{4}1845), p. 61; idem, *Katechetik* (Tübingen: Laupp, 1831), pp. 421, 474, 493–494.

9. Peter A. Schleyer, "Hirscher und seine Ankläger," *Zeitschrift für Theologie* 9 (1843): 443.

10. Johann Baptist Hirscher, *Die kirchlichen Zustände der Gegenwart* (Tübingen: Laupp, 1849), p. 1: "Wir müssen von innen heraus bauen, alle äußeren Umwandlungen und Verbesserungen werden uns da nicht helfen."

11. Walter Fürst, "Von innen heraus bauen," p. 83.

12. Johann Baptist Hirscher, *Die christliche Moral,* vol. II (Tübingen: Laupp, ^{5}1851), p. 1; Walter Fürst, *Wahrheit,* p. 477.

13. Johann Baptist Hirscher, *Die christliche Moral,* vol. I (^{4}1845), p. 61; Walter Fürst, *Wahrheit,* p.430.

14. Johann Baptist Hirscher, *Die christliche Moral,* vol. I (^{2}1836), p. 58; Walter Fürst, *Wahrheit,* pp. 316, 429, 446–447.

15. Johann Baptist Hirscher, *Die christliche Moral,* vol. I (^{2}1836), p. 59; Walter Fürst, *Wahrheit,* pp. 429–430.

16. Walter Fürst, *Wahrheit,* p. 447.

17. Johann Baptist Hirscher, *Die christliche Moral,* vol. I (^{5}1851), p. 74; Walter Fürst, *Wahrheit,* p. 316.

18. Walter Fürst, *Wahrheit,* pp. 468–476.

19. Johann Baptist Hirscher, *Die Notwendigkeit einer lebendigen Pflege des positiven Christenthums in allen Klassen der Gesellschaft* (Tübingen: Laupp, 1848), p. 16; idem, *Die socialen Zustände der Gegenwart und die Kirche* (Tübingen: Laupp, 1849), pp. 11, 15–16; Walter Fürst, "Von innen heraus bauen," p. 84.

20. Walter Fürst, *Wahrheit,* pp. 248–249; idem, "Von innen heraus bauen, " pp. 86–87.

21. Erwin Keller, *Johann Baptist Hirscher,* p.19.

22. Ibid., p. 20.

23. *Hirschers nachgelassene kleinere Schriften,* ed. Hermann Rolfus (Freiburg: Herder, 1868) 10–12; Walter Fürst, *Wahrheit* 352.

24. Walter Fürst, *Wahrheit,* pp. 573–575.

25. Josef Kleutgen, *Die Philosophie der Vorzeit,* vol. I, (Innsbruck: Rauch, ^{2}1878), p. 4.

26. Walter Fürst, *Wahrheit,* p. 283.

27. Johann Baptist Hirscher, *Die christliche Moral,* vol. I (^{2}1836), p. 139.

28. Ibid.; see Walter Fürst, *Wahrheit,* p. 353.

29. Johann Baptist Hirscher, *Die christliche Moral,* vol. I (^{2}1836), p. 1.

30. Walter Fürst, *Wahrheit,* pp. 365–366.

31. Johann Baptist Hirscher, *Betrachtungen über die sonntäglichen Evangelien des Kirchenjahres,* vol. II (Tübingen: Laupp,^{5}1848), p. 115.

32. Johann Baptist Hirscher, "Über einige Störungen in dem richtigen Verhältnisse des Kirchenthums zu dem Zwecke des Christenthums," *Theologische Quartalschrift* 5 (1823): 246.

33. Josef Rief, *Kirche und Gesellschaft*, p. 110.

34. Walter Fürst, *Wahrheit*, p. 248.

35. Max Seckler, "Das Reich-Gottes-Motiv in den Anfängen der Katholischen Tübinger Schule (J.S. Drey und J.B. Hirscher), *"Theologische Quartalschrift* 168 (1988): 280–281.

36. *Handbuch der Fundamentaltheologie*, ed. Walter Kern, Hermann J. Pottmeyer and Max Seckler, 4 vols. (Freiburg: Herder, 1985–1988).

37. Max Seckler, "Fundamentaltheologie: Aufgaben und Aufbau, Begriff und Namen," in ibid. vol. 4, pp. 451–514.

38. Hermann J. Pottmeyer, "Zeichen und Kriterien der Glaubwürdigkeit des Christentums," in ibid. vol. 4, pp. 373–413.

39. Hermann J. Pottmeyer, "Die Frage nach der wahren Kirche," in ibid. vol. 3 (Freiburg: Herder, 1986), pp. 212–241.

40. Heinrich Döring, "Demonstratio catholica," in *Den Glauben denken. Neue Wege der Fundamentaltheologie*, ed. Heinrich Döring, Armin Kreiner and Perry Schmidt-Leukel (Freiburg: Herder, 1993), pp. 147–244.

41. Max Seckler, "Das Reich-Gottes-Motiv in den Anfängen der Katholischen Tübinger Schule," pp. 257–282.

42. Ibid., p. 265.

43. Walter Fürst, *Wahrheit*, pp. 221, 227, 351, 418–419.

44. Ibid., pp. 232–233.

45. Max Seckler, "Das Reich-Gottes-Motiv von den Anfängen der Katholischen Tübinger Schule," p. 269.

46. Karl Frielingsdorf, *Auf dem Weg zu einem neuen Gottesverständnis*, p. 146.

47. Josef Rief, *Reich Gottes und Gesellschaft*, pp. 378–403; Walter Fürst, *Wahrheit*, pp. 399–413.

48. Johann Baptist Hirscher, *Die christliche Moral*, vol. I ([2]1836), pp. 177–181, 204, 382–383; Walter Fürst, *Wahrheit*, pp. 403–404.

49. Max Seckler, "Das Reich-Gottes-Motiv in den Anfängen der Katholischen Tübinger Schule," p. 276; Eugen Biser, *Glaubenswende Hoffnungsperspektive* (Freiburg: Herder, 1987).

9

The Problem of Revelation in the Theology of Johannes Evangelist von Kuhn

— ZACHARY HAYES, OFM —

Among the most philosophically sophisticated Roman Catholic theologians in Germany during the nineteenth century, the figure of Johannes Evangelist von Kuhn (1806–1887) stands out. Being well-trained in philosophy, Kuhn approached the major theological issues with a sharp and penetrating mind.[1] This paper discusses his attempt to come to terms with an issue which, by any standard, is foundational to a theological epistemology; namely the question of the nature, possibility, and limits of revelation. We shall first point out some of the highlights of the cultural context within which Kuhn approached his task as a systematic theologian. Within this broader context, we shall then comment briefly on his personal background. This will be followed by some reflections on the development of Kuhn's philosophical position. Finally, we shall speak about the specific elements which enter into his understanding of religious experience and revelation.

Broader Context

It is understandable that for any well-educated European of the early nineteenth century, the question of revelation might have appeared simply as the foundational problem for theology. This becomes clear from at least two perspectives.

First, at this time theology was beginning to feel the impact of critical studies on the biblical text. Lessing had published fragments of Reimarus' comments on the problem of Jesus and the New Testament. David Strauss, from the Protestant faculty of Tübingen, had published his *Leben Jesu*. Clearly the impact of critical studies was beginning to eat away at the authority of the biblical text. More and more the Bible began to look like a human product. It would become ever more difficult to discern what it might mean to use such familiar words as *inspiration* or *revelation* in any sense that could make a helpful distinction between the Bible and other significant literature.

Second, the early nineteenth-century was the time of the great German philosophies of the *Geist*. Hegel, Fichte, Schelling were living realities, and their philosophies reflected and reinforced the spirit of the times. These philosophies were all great dialectical structures for interpreting the dynamics of universal history. But more to the point, they were emphatically focused on the dynamics of consciousness, conceiving it as moving—in one way or another—from levels of total lack of differentiation to ever greater levels of self-awareness. The reality of the Absolute and its movement from unconscious to conscious existence was seen to be intimately tied to the history of emerging human consciousness. It will be remembered how intimate this relation was seen to be if we recall how readily these philosophies were felt to lapse into pantheism or pure immanentism.

It is clear that, abstracting from everything else in this period of revolutionary turmoil, these two cultural factors would raise serious questions for any claim about a divine revelation or about a religious message that is not simply the unfolding of the immanent dynamics of human, religious consciousness. Yet the epistemological claims of Christian theology are centered around the Christian claim about a supernatural revelation of God to humanity focused in the person of Jesus of Nazareth.

Clearly Christian theological language about revelation is an attempt to give an account of how Christians believe they come to know what they claim to know about God, humanity, and the world in terms of the Christian religious tradition. While Christian revelation is not totally a cognitional question, there are clearly cognitional claims involved. And the Roman Catholic theological tradition has held, over the centuries, that the supernatural order is not in basic conflict with the order of nature. If this conviction is translated into the theology of revelation, it leads to the conviction that, while supernatural revelation in fact transcends the range of unaided human reason, yet there need be no basic conflict between natural knowledge and supernatural knowledge, at least in principle.

One cannot think of supernatural revelation in cognitive terms without asking how the religious mode of knowing is related to other modes of human knowing. Hence, one cannot give a serious account of the nature of Christian revelation without probing deeply into the structures of human knowledge and consciousness.

Personal Background

Against this broader background it will be helpful to point out some factors in Kuhn's personal history. First, after completing the ordinary study program for ordination expected for students of the diocese of Rottenburg, Kuhn worked for a doctorate at the University of Tübingen not in theology but in philosophy. His pre-ordination studies at Tübingen would have included work with well-known figures such as J.G. Herbst, J.S. Drey, J.B. Hirscher, and J.A. Möhler. His initial study of philosophy was done on the work of F.H. Jacobi, and he received the doctoral degree in philosophy at Tübingen in 1830. Subsequently he lectured on exegesis at Giessen from 1832 to 1837. He then lectured on exegesis from 1837 to 1839 at Tübingen until his appointment to the chair of dogmatic theology in 1839 as the successor to J. S. Drey. From this period came the first edition of his *Katholische Dogmatik*.[2] Finally, with the exception of his years in the political arena (1848–1852), he was engaged as a systematician until the end of his academic career which saw the publication of the second edition of his *Katholische Dogmatik*[3] and his treatment of grace.[4] He retired from his career as a lecturer at Tübingen in 1882 and died just five years later in 1887.

Stages in his Thought

Philosophical Orientation

Kuhn is an interesting figure in the sense that his career virtually spans all the great movements—philosophical, political, and ecclesial—of the nineteenth century. He was born in 1806 and died in 1887. Throughout the whole of his academic career, he was deeply concerned to engage the major philosophies of the age in critical discussion from a theological perspective. This would include Enlightenment, German Idealism, Romanticism, and historical studies, all of which left a mark on Kuhn's theological output.

Our sense of his philosophical orientation can be sharpened a bit by pointing out that one of his major concerns was to give a critical account of faith and the science of faith. As a philosophically trained theologian, he was deeply aware of the implications of Kant, Fichte, Schelling, and Hegel for the entire theological venture. He did not hesitate to delve into the most fundamental questions of human consciousness and knowledge.

The direction which his thought was to take is laid out provisionally in two early works. The first is his early study on the philosophy of Jacobi.[5] The second is an article treating the nature of speculative theology which is entitled "Über den Begriff und das Wesen der speculativen Theologie und (oder) Philosophie."[6] In these early works, Kuhn argues for the need to find a way between two philosophical extremes, that of total *a priorism*, and that of uncritical empiricism. As regards the first, Kuhn argues that this orientation tends to treat purely speculative knowledge and knowledge drawn from sense experience as two incompatible forms of knowledge. It is clear where the preference lies when one takes into account the fallibility of sense knowledge involved in any appeal to experience. With the second, he is concerned with views such as Jacobi's appeal to direct, immediate experience as the source of truth and certitude. But this view seemed unable or unwilling to move from what Kuhn saw as a kind of blind intuitionism to a more critical, self-conscious level of reflection.

Kuhn sympathizes with Jacobi to a degree. All extreme forms of Idealism seem to involve the conviction that the world of human subjectivity is really closed in on itself and cannot be acted on by God *from outside*. There can be no knowledge about God as transcendent Being since any pure knowledge which is logically consistent can exist only when thought remains totally immanent to consciousness. It is the fatal error of *a priorism* to claim that such is, indeed, the limit of significant cognitive claims. Jacobi's response to this position had been the appeal to an immediate intuition of the Absolute. Schelling had respect for this aspect of Jacobi's thought and saw it as reminiscent of Schleiermacher's notion of *Gefühl*. It was precisely this issue that proved to be the point of departure for Kuhn's study of Jacobi. In this context, Kuhn himself came to speak of a sort of intuition as the starting point of knowledge. He used the term *faith* to describe this, and he spoke of it as the way in which we come to some contact with the Absolute and as the source of all knowledge.

Thus, Kuhn agreed with Jacobi that some form of faith must be seen as the beginning of all knowledge. But he disagreed with both Jacobi and Schleiermacher in that he was not willing to allow faith to remain at the level of an irresponsible trust or feeling. From the start, this *faith* has the tendency to show itself to be reasonable. At this point we notice a conviction that is characteristic of Kuhn's predecessor, J. S. Drey; namely, the basic concern for the nature of theology as a *Wissenschaft* has a legitimate authority. There is, argues Kuhn, an unconscious cognitive element which he calls an initial *bewusstes Glauben*. This must be drawn to the level of conscious and critical awareness. The attempt to do this leads to what Kuhn calls a *gewusstes Glauben*.[7]

This process provides the opportunity for faith to show in what sense it may be seen as responsible and coherent. But in the end, faith cannot be dissolved fully into knowledge. If it were possible to do this, it would make God into a mere creation of human thought or an object that stands at the disposal of the human mind. Kuhn attempts to argue that the very nature of our knowledge makes it clear that God stands over-against us and independent of us, and that God is active in leading human existence in history. The consciousness of this is expressed in what we know as religion. Religion, therefore, is rooted in the receptive capacity in human nature for the divinity that reveals itself both in nature and in history.

Kuhn's philosophical orientation is an attempt to embrace two interrelated moments in a unity: the immediate moment of awareness and the mediate moment of reflection and representation. Experience and speculation, therefore, must be seen not as two opposed forms of knowing, but as two interrelated moments of one process of human knowing. The two philosophical extremes discussed by Kuhn have made the mistake of taking these two interrelated moments of knowledge and treating them as though they were contradictory to each other. Kuhn's response is an attempt to show that every act of human understanding in fact embraces both the immediate moment of awareness and the mediate moment involving reflection and representation.[8]

As a result of his study of Jacobi, Kuhn is led to distinguish between *Grundbewusstsein*, and *abgeleitetes Bewusstsein*. With this terminology Kuhn intends to designate, first, the direct encounter of consciousness with reality. At this level, consciousness is independent of or prior to any form of representation (=*Vorstellung*). Thus the term *Grundbewusstsein* refers to the primal unity of consciousness prior to any differentiation between subject and object. The I and the not-I are given in one unified and undivided act of consciousness.[9] This is, for Kuhn, the truth which Jacobi represents.

But consciousness and knowledge have not yet been adequately accounted for. Immediate experience is mediated at the level of objectified knowledge. The mind has the power to objectify the not-I and to shed light on the differentiation between the I and the not-I. At this second level, which involves reflective thought, it becomes clear that all discursive thought—if it is to be true—will be an unfolding of what is given first in *Grundbewusstsein*. Thus, through a process of mediation involving representation (=*Vorstellung*) and concept (=*Begriff*), the move is made to *abgeleitetes Bewusstsein*. Mediation is indispensable, but mediation is based on *Grundbewusstsein*, and hence on experience. And what is given there is the reality of the I and the not-I in what is at first a relative identity and comes to be known as an objective and essential difference through reflective thought.[10]

Here Kuhn hopes to have provided ground for the critique of major streams of philosophy which seem too one-sided. At the same time, he has set up the framework for certain themes that are characteristic of his theology. Such themes are: the relation between *Glauben* and *Wissen*, not only with respect to theology but with respect to all forms of human knowledge; the relation between philosophy and theology in an appropriate dialectical relationship; and the relation between nature and grace.[11] We merely mention them here, and we pass on to the specific question of revelation.

Revelation in the Strauss Affair

From epistemological foundations such as these, Kuhn was able to shape his theology of revelation. One of the first areas in which we can discern this is in his discussion of David Strauss' *Leben Jesu.*[12] Kuhn took up the challenge of Strauss as an exegete with a strong philosophical background. With the eye of the philosopher, Kuhn moves away from the level of symptom to what he considers the real problem in Strauss' argument.[13] This, says Kuhn, is really a false philosophy of history. The problem is not critical exegesis as such, but a problematic philosophy of history which Kuhn attributes to Hegel, or at least to Strauss' reading of Hegel. Independently of the problem with Strauss, it seems clear that, at least at this stage of his development, Kuhn saw Hegel's philosophy of history to be pantheistic.[14] The central issue in Strauss' interpretation of the Scriptures as Kuhn sees it is that of the relation between fact to Idea, or of history to Spirit.[15] In Strauss' reading of Hegel, there is no intrinsic relation between the Absolute and the historical facts in which the Absolute has revealed itself in history. The facts are simply the occasions that let loose certain Ideas. Once the Ideas have been let loose, the facts can be discarded as worthless, just as the skin of a snake is discarded.[16]

As this philosophy of history was applied to the reading of the New Testament, it was taken by Strauss to mean that it makes no difference for the truth of certain Ideas whether they are based on history or are purely mythical. What is important about the life of Jesus is the Christ-Idea. Once this has been unleashed in the consciousness of humanity on the occasion of Jesus' life, that life itself becomes unimportant. In fact, that life has been transformed into a non historical myth through the creative powers of the unconscious *Geist* of the community. One is invited to think of this much as one understands the emergence of the sagas of a people. In the end, it makes no difference whether or not the Christ-Idea is based on history or myth. What is important is the Idea itself.

In response to this, Kuhn maintains a tighter relation between Idea and historical fact. The factual really embodies the Ideal. "It would be just as difficult to separate the Idea from the truth of the fact as it would be to separate the fact from the truth of the Idea."[17] If one does not see the truth embodied in history as grounded in the reality of the Absolute Spirit, there remains only the alternative that such truth is drawn from the finite spirit; that is, from one's own head. And in fact, Kuhn argues, this is the case with Strauss. Strauss' philosophy of revelation reconstructs history in such a way that history corresponds fully to the ideas of

Strauss. It is, indeed, Strauss who has created a myth, and not the authors of Scripture.[18] This understanding of the relation between history and Idea, first treated in the context of the Strauss-controversy, will emerge again in the two editions of Kuhn's *Katholische Dogmatik*. But before we move to that, we shall look at his early discussion of Schelling's philosophy of revelation which would be important in the development of Kuhn's own position.

Revelation in the Criticism of Schelling

In a series of three articles,[19] Kuhn discusses the problematic character of Schelling's philosophy under the rubrics: negative philosophy; positive philosophy; and the philosophy of revelation. Here the problem is discussed in terms of the relation between reason and revelation, or between natural revelation and positive religion. It is Kuhn's concern to argue that, if revelation is not to be thought of as simply opposed to human nature, then there must be some positive point of contact in human nature to which revelation can address itself. But this should not be taken to mean that the sort of *a priori* knowledge which can be drawn from the analysis of reason itself—so much a concern of Enlightenment philosophy—defines the ultimate limits of the cognitive claims that may be made in the name of revelation. We think here of the problem intimated in the title of Kant's discussion of *Religion within the Limits of Reason Alone.*

Precisely in this problematic area, Kuhn finds the philosophy of Schelling to be very questionable. In his attempt to delimit the range of reason with respect to revelation, Schelling had worked with the distinction between theoretical Ideas and factual realities. The same Idea may be known, first as a purely theoretical possibility, and second as a factual reality. While revelation must, in some way, transcend reason, according to Schelling, this will be not in terms of the actual content of Ideas, but in terms of the manner in which the Ideas are known. Revelation does indeed have its origin in God. But the content of revelation may be derived as purely theoretical possibility in an *a priori* way from reason. What is added through history is the factual reality given through the historical enactment of the theoretical Idea. From this base it becomes clear how, from one perspective, Schelling can speak of the transcendence of revelation over reason, and yet, from another perspective, can hold that the content of revelation is entirely understandable by reason.

This is understandable against the background of what Kuhn had earlier described as a philosophy of the *a priori*. If the range of knowledge is defined in reference to that which can be deduced *a priori* from the human mind and its innate structures and laws, then empirical experience is excluded from the start as a meaningful source of knowledge. But empirical experience is precisely what is involved in the biblical claims concerning a revelation in historical events. In its strict form, therefore, the philosophy of the *a priori* excludes in principle any valid claims to truth on the part of Christianity that could not be made on the basis of "pure reason alone."[20]

Schelling recognized this problem. He developed his negative and positive philosophy as an attempt to deal with the question. The negative philosophy represents the movement of the human mind to the Absolute. Since the Absolute always remains outside this dialectical process of the mind, the dialectic itself reveals not the reality of the Absolute but the exigence of the mind for the existence of the Absolute.[21] The final fruit of the mind's reflection is indeterminate and negative; it is the pure Idea of the Being.

But the move from this purely conceptual level to the knowledge that this pure Being is not a mere concept but is real—which is the beginning of the positive philosophy—this move cannot be a necessary extension of pure thought. The move can be made only by an act of the will,[22] that is, by an act of faith. Schelling's argument reflects the conviction that there is a purely rational knowledge prior to any knowledge of the real. Purely rational, or *a priori*, knowledge is deduced strictly from reason alone. Reason itself is incapable of extending beyond this limit since it deals only with possible being. Specifically, the best of unaided human effort culminates in the theoretical concept of pure Being.

After this strenuous effort of reason, there remains only the possibility that an act of faith can open up the knowledge of the real. Thus, human knowledge ultimately culminates in faith. Thus, we come to one of Schelling's basic principles: all knowledge of the real rests on thinking and willing together.[23] Pure being prior to all potency is beyond all thought and experience. We can only postulate it by an act of the will, which, in essence, is an act of faith. While we can arrive at the theoretical concept of a personal God from reason, we cannot know from this concept alone that such a God exists. It is only an act of faith which makes possible the movement from the concept of a personal God to the affirmation of God's real existence.

In summary, for Schelling the relation between reason and historical revelation involves the following. What is known by reason as an *a priori* possibility is known in its real existence only from the experience of history. It is the function of reason to deduce the content of revelation as possible.[24] Since revelation, conceived in this way, is divine in origin but not in terms of its content, it follows that, once revelation has been given by God, its content can be thoroughly understood by reason.[25]

It is from this base that Schelling proceeds to interpret the major Christian dogmas in a way that reflects his conviction that these dogmas should be thoroughly understandable to human reason. While Shelling claims he is not offering a new content for these doctrines but merely expanding the limited concepts of traditional Christianity to match the divine[26] Kuhn sees the results to be a fundamentally new content which amounts to a purely pantheistic philosophical system.[27] Just as Hegel was found to be inadequate in the case of Strauss, so Schelling is found to be inadequate here. He has placed too much confidence in philosophy. The mercurial development of his own philosophical positions and the history of philosophy at large ought to serve as a warning against such an approach.[28] In this discussion with Schelling, the lines are set for the final reflection of Kuhn on the question of revelation. This will take us eventually to the treatment found in his *Katholische Dogmatik*, especially in the second edition.

Elements in a Theology of Revelation

Our discussion up to this point provides a background for a discussion of the fundamental elements which, in Kuhn's approach, would have to play into any critical theology of revelation. We single out the following:

a) The historical dimension.

b) Natural and supernatural revelation.

c) Supernatural revelation as history.

d) Christological dimension of revelation.

e) Philosophy of history, philosophy of religion, and philosophy of Christianity.

The Historical Dimension

We have seen the role that the philosophy of history played in Kuhn's discussion of Strauss. Throughout his literary career, Kuhn remained firmly convinced of the foundational significance of history for Christian theology. "Geschichte ist der Grundcharakter und gleichsam das Urelement des Christenthums."[29] He was convinced that Christianity presents the human mind with an object that can be identified neither with the reality of the outer world of cosmic reality, nor with the interior world of human consciousness. If the revelation lying at the base of Christianity is fundamentally tied to history, then the object of speculative theology—in its most basic sense—is history; not only the history of the original revelation, but that of the ongoing Christian community.[30]

It is because of its fundamental bond between Christian revelation and history that speculative theology cannot be satisfied with any form of philosophical *a priorism*. What is needed to carry out the task of Christian theology is an adequate speculative philosophy of history. Here we are dealing with a theme that is native to the great philosophies of history of the nineteenth-century. Kuhn's own view involves a critical use of Hegel and Schelling, as well as of Wilhelm von Humboldt.[31] Specifically, Kuhn is impressed with Von Humboldt's view that the study of history is aimed at the contemplation of the spiritual reality that breaks forth into history. The more basic impulses of history come not from the empirical realities of the world but from Ideas that lie beyond the realm of the finite. These penetrate all of history and provide the power and the goal of history. The goal of history, then, can only be the realization of the Idea from every perspective and in all forms through humanity. It is the contemplation of the hidden power of the Idea that opens the way for the human spirit to move toward that unifying goal toward which it naturally strives.[32]

Kuhn reformulates the Romantic notion of the Idea in terms of an intelligent, transcendent causality or teleology in the context of a philosophy of history that is clearly reminiscent of Schelling and Hegel. Yet he employs their work in a critical way. The decisive difference between Kuhn and the great Idealists lies in the fact that, for Kuhn, the truth with which philosophy and theology are concerned is a truth that is given to or presented to humanity. It is not simply and totally the product of creative, speculative human thought.

When the divine Spirit reveals itself to us, speaking in historical facts which our spirit dissolves into Ideas, the primal relation of Spirit to history is so close that "it would be just as difficult to separate the Idea from the truth of the fact as it would be to separate the fact from the truth of the Idea."[33] The divine reality is the ultimate source of the Ideas that move history, and only a speculative philosophy of history can move beyond the empirical level to disclose the true nature of the Ideas.

In a sense, Kuhn's view may sound very similar to the Hegelian philosophy of history. There is, however, a basic difference. For Hegel, history is the necessary self-objectification of the Absolute. For Kuhn, however, the world of history is characterized not so much by necessity as by freedom, both on the part of God and on the part of humanity. While history is, in a sense, the self-objectification of God, it is not an objectification that is necessary for the unfolding of the self-consciousness of God. On the contrary, it is an entirely free work of God's self-revelation to humanity, and it is directed to the free response of human beings. Though God and humanity are intimately related to each other, the divine Spirit that calls forth and sustains history is in no way to be identified with the human spirit. History is, for Kuhn, the arena in which divine and human freedom are in constant interaction. When the element of divine freedom is added to what has already been said about revelation in historical acts, we may conclude with Kuhn that, if God freely reveals the mystery of the divine to humanity not only in the universal flow of history but also in particular acts within history, then these acts as salvific will never be separated from the salvific truth revealed in them. Divine Idea and revelatory historical act constitute an inseparable unity.

Natural and Supernatural Revelation

Kuhn's discussions about revelation attempt to cut between all forms of extreme supernaturalism, (fundamental, biblical orthodoxy) and all forms of rationalistic *a priorism*.[34] For biblical orthodoxy, the very text of the Scriptures is literally the word of God. For *a priorism*, only that which can be inferred from the structures of rationality can be called the word of God. If an historical revelation is, indeed, involved in Christianity, one must hold at least the possibility that there may be more in its content than can be derived *a priori* from reason. On the other hand, if Christianity is not to be judged irrational, the truth of historical revelation must bear some positive relation to human reason. If historical revelation is called supernatural both because of its source in God and because, in principle, it can provide a content that transcends "the limits of reason alone," one must ask about the relation between the natural and the supernatural.

Revelation in its broad sense refers to the fact that God proceeds from inaccessible light (1 *Tim.* 6, 16). In some way God is presented in another being so that the divine reality may be recognized by the eye of the spirit.[35] Using the ancient metaphor of light, Kuhn describes the human experience of revelation as a process of gathering the rays of light sent out by God. By gathering these rays, the human mind comes to form an idea of God (=*Gottesidee*). This Idea can be expressed in anthropological terms as the sense that humanity is fundamentally directed to God and stands at God's disposal.

Thus, when viewing the question of revelation from the perspective of nature and spirit, Kuhn speaks of a primal revelation (=*Uroffenbarung*) grounded in the very structure of creation. God is revealed in all the works of creation, but above all in the crown of creation—the finite spirit—which is a likeness of God's own being. It is in the finite spirit that we find the eye capable of recognizing God in all the divine works, but above all in itself; for God is most clearly reflected in the finite spirit (Rm. 1: 19–20).[36] To avoid any form of deistic understanding, Kuhn emphasizes that creation must be understood inseparably together with the providence and sovereign ruling power of God. God not only creates the world, but is intimately present to it not only as a power from outside, but as a mystery that penetrates the world interiorly. "In Him we live and move and have our being" (Acts 17: 26–27). By reason of God's essential presence to the world, God is the light that illumines all human beings from the beginning (Jn.1:4). By reason of this primal revelation situated in the very nature of created reality, the human person carries within itself the idea of God, but not yet as a conscious, articulated concept of God.

Kuhn's understanding of the *Gottesidee* and the *Uroffenbarung* can best be understood against the background of his understanding of the Adamic revelation. Kuhn envisions the original situation of Adam as one of great intimacy with the divine involving an immediate awareness of God. This intimate form of relation was the original intent of God in creating humanity. As a result of the Fall, humanity's consciousness of God was no longer immediate but dependent on the consciousness of something other than God. Humanity's consciousness of God has been severely weakened. In order that the purpose God had in creating would not be totally frustrated, God engages humanity in a history of self-revelation with the intent of restoring the original bond of union.[37]

The notion of a *Gottesidee* in post-Adamic history, then, refers to a sort of preconceptual consciousness of God contained within human consciousness. Here we discern the background discussion which Kuhn had carried out with Jacobi and Schelling. This *Gottesidee* is not an articulated concept of God but an immediate awareness contained in and together with the immediate intuition of reality and the human self. The distinction between immediate and mediate consciousness first developed in Kuhn's discussion of Jacobi provides the tools for distinguishing and explicating the levels of God-consciousness in the human subject. The most basic level corresponds to that of immediate consciousness, and is located at the level of what Kuhn calls *Vernunft*.[38] *Vernunft* here refers to the general receptive capacity of the mind. It is distinguished from *Verstand*, the reflective procedure through which the immediate consciousness is raised to the level of mediated self-consciousness. As mediation enters in, the immediate awareness of God may be brought to the level of an articulated concept of God (= *Gottesbegriff*). Thus, while God is never a categorical object of knowledge, the divinity is known indirectly and transcendentally in the analysis of human self-consciousness.

With this understanding of a *Gottesidee*, we are on the way to comprehending Kuhn's understanding of the *Uroffenbarung*. This term, for Kuhn, refers not simply to a revelation given once and for all at the beginning of human history (as in the Adamic revelation of the Bible), but to a revelation that is given wherever we are dealing with intelligent, human beings. The *Uroffenbarung* is given in the human experience of the world and above all in humanity's experience of itself.[39] The Idea that lies at the root of all revelation is the Idea of God. But the Idea of God is not known in all its inner moments and in full clarity at all times and places. The awareness that this God wishes to enter into personal relations with humanity evolves through history.

If nature precisely as nature is a source of revelation, it is so only to a limited degree. A clearer understanding of God is to be found in humanity, created in the likeness of God.[40] In his *Leben Jesu*, the revelatory significance of humanity is discussed at several levels. First, in terms of human nature precisely as nature, humanity stands at the highpoint of created nature.[41] But when it is viewed only in terms of nature, humanity is but a virtual revelation that awaits to be unfolded in the history of human life.[42] Here Kuhn reflects a sort of *Lebensphilosophie*. It is through the history whereby human nature unfolds its inner dynamic that the virtual revelation of human nature is unfolded more explicitly. And it is within the broader movement of human history generally that biblical history must be situated.

The concern with human history generally focuses on what Kuhn sees as the essential content of human life: the search for the true, the good, and the beautiful. This quest is embodied in science, art and ethical activity.[43] It is from these areas that Kuhn argues for an understanding of history as a highly ordered movement dynamically orientated to a definite goal. The principle that unifies history into this orderly movement cannot be the individual or finite consciousness. It must be a transcendent reality. Together with Jacobi, Kuhn describes this as "an unchanging, objective *Vernunft*," which is the higher, objective regulator of the human *Vernunft*.[44] The highest meaning of life rests on the conjunction of the objective and the subjective *Vernunft*. This may be seen more specifically as the conjunction of an objective world-order of divine origin with human freedom. When a human agent grasps the point of divine providence and becomes its active agent in the moral movement of the world, that person becomes the organ of divine revelation in a special way that moves beyond any reflection on the world of nonhuman nature alone. Such a person performs a significant service in the authentic, spiritual development of humanity. Kuhn singles out Moses and John the Baptist as examples of this.[45]

Following a tradition that runs through his Tübingen predecessor, J. S. Drey, back to Lessing, Kuhn uses the metaphor of *education* to express the relation between natural and historical revelation.[46] While in Lessing, this metaphor was given an emphatically rationalist interpretation, Kuhn interprets the metaphor in harmony with the argument we have just sketched. Kuhn takes the metaphor to mean first that God does, indeed, "teach" humanity through history and not simply through the structures of human reason. Both the realm of nature and the realm of history provide objects of knowledge, and the full perfection of human consciousness depends on our openness to both.[47] Second, the metaphor suggests that

God teaches in accordance with particular levels of human development. Therefore, there is a multiplicity of forms and levels of revelation as indicated in the
epistle to the *Hebrews* (Heb. 1:1).[48]

Supernatural Revelation as History

It is within his broad vision of history that Kuhn situates the significance of
biblical history. It should be clear from the above that we should not expect biblical
history to provide a *totally* new revelation about God that is not somehow anticipated at least virtually at the level of *Uroffenbarung*. Indeed, this seems to be the
case.

It is important to point out that the entire issue of biblical history is situated
explicitly in an infralapsarian world. In the most general terms, this specific religious history offers the possibility of rediscovering and re-establishing the original
intent of God given in the reality of creation but obscured through the reality of sin.
That is, from the beginning God created with a view to realizing the most intimate
sort of relation between God and humanity. Though the Fall intervenes and breaks
the bond which God had originally established, the specific history of biblical
revelation has the task of bringing that original intent to consciousness again and
leading to its realization as the truly fulfilling relation between God and creation. To
specify this a bit more clearly, we might say that while we are created for a profound
relationship with God, our experience of ourselves in our fallen condition might
never lead to an awareness that such a relation is, in fact, God's salvific intent and
the only way in which we may ultimately find fulfillment. This intent of God cannot
be simply deduced from the structures of reason. It may be possible for us only
through the free history of God's self-disclosure.

Thus, while Kuhn will argue that there must be a positive point of contact
between natural and the supernatural revelation, he will not be satisfied with any
solution that suggests history can reveal nothing that cannot be derived *a priori*
from reason itself. It is possible that, without history, reason reflecting on its own
intrinsic structures and laws might never come to an understanding of the *salvific
intent* of God. It is at least theoretically possible that humanity would never come
to an adequate awareness of this without taking history into account. As in philosophy, the Absolute cannot be known in a specific concept except through the
mediation of the relative, so the salvific intent of God cannot be known explicitly
except through the mediation of this historical revelation. At least in this sense,
Kuhn argues, we must be willing to accept the possibility that history generally,
and the biblical history specifically, may offer "new objects" of knowledge.

Christological Dimensions

From Kuhn's perspective, the whole of history with its natural and supernatural revelation—all that is of enduring value in human life and religion—is but a
preparation for and an introduction to the messianic figure of Jesus Christ. The
incarnation is the culmination and summation of all other levels of revelation.[49]
From the Christological perspective, Kuhn can interpret the entire process of revelation teleologically. It is an historical process through which a humanity *thor-*

oughly pleasing to God is actualized so that this humanity is united with God perfectly and immediately. In Christ the highest act of divine governance in the world and the most noble human moral development coincide.

Because of this conjunction of the human and the divine, Christ is seen as the high-point in the development of humanity and, as such, he is the bearer of the supreme revelation to and for the human race. It is clear that this line of revelation directed to Christ is related intrinsically to the original revelation. While the revelation in Christ may be described as new in terms of its basis, its execution, and its means, its goal rests in the restoration and ultimate fulfillment of the original, God-intended relation between God and creation.[50]

While Kuhn maintains the unsurpassability of the revelation that has taken place in Christ, he disagrees both with the philosophical rationalists and with the radically orthodox supernaturalists as to how this is to be understood. Both of these positions maintain that if the revelation in Christ is unsurpassable, then there can be no development after Christ. In the case of the rationalists, this would lead to the conclusion that the claim of unsurpassability is unacceptable because it stands in contradiction to the philosophical principle that the fullness of truth is found at the end of history. Obviously history did not end with Christ. In the case of the extreme supernaturalists, the claim of unsurpassability was accepted but it was taken to mean that there could be no development after Christ. Therefore, the developments of subsequent church doctrines, dogmas, and structures come in for criticism.

Kuhn's theory is an effort to maintain the unsurpassability of Christ and to explain the legitimacy of development in subsequent church history. On this point, Geiselmann sees a basic shift in orientation from the earlier Romantic theories of development, including that of Kuhn's predecessor at Tübingen, J.S. Drey, and perhaps even in the writings of Kuhn himself.[51] The Romantic theories generally were inclined to see development as a quiet, interior, dream-like process. Kuhn's theory, in its final form, emphasizes the fact that at least at its most important moments, the development of the faith-consciousness of the Christian community takes place in the full light of the spirit.[52] In this respect it reflects something of Hegel's philosophy of spirit. Where there is spirit, there is the *Anstrengung des Begriffs*. Spirit moves to concept through struggle. This is the case with pre-Christian history. It is perhaps more emphatically the case with the history of the church itself. Christian faith-consciousness after the appearance of Christ is not a static condition. Rather, it is a history of development through a real dialectic called forth by positions and counter-positions. It is a dialectical process conditioned by opposing conceptions of Christian truth. This is grounded in the very nature of historical revelation. For when the divine Spirit of revelation encounters the objective spirit of an age, it enters into a living relation with the dominant spiritual, ethical, and religious impulses of that age.[53] To ignore this history is as unnatural as it is mindless and ungrateful.

In general terms, Kuhn holds a formal or objective development involving change, development, and progress at the level of human awareness, and at the level of means and forms of expression. Since form is the objectification of content,

Kuhn speaks of a formal or an objective development. And since objectifications are the means of moving from immediate awareness to mediated knowledge of reality, the objectifications of revelation correspond to a growing knowledge of the divine truth which remains always unchanging in itself.

Philosophy of History, Philosophy of Religion, and Philosophy of Christianity
For Kuhn, as we have seen above, the task of the philosophy of history is principally to discover, express, and explicate the highest reality at work in history. And if that highest principle of history is located at the level of Ideas grounded in the Absolute, it becomes clear why Kuhn is inclined to identify the philosophy of history with the philosophy of religion. The highest principle in history is that whereby humanity is bound with a level of reality other than the empirical. Philosophy of history at its best, therefore, deals with that which pertains essentially to the religious impulse of humanity. In this sense, the philosophy of history is in essence a philosophy of religion, or *Religionslehre*.[54]

Now, since from the beginning of history—or from the Fall—the real, historical form of the religious dimension has always included the historical revelation given by God to establish or to reestablish a lasting union between humanity and God, and since this historical revelation deals with the most fundamental meaning of religion, it is an easy step to identify the philosophy of religion with the philosophy of revelation.[55]

At this level, Kuhn's view about nature and history as objects of knowledge leads him to an understanding of this identity that differs fundamentally from those of Hegel or Schelling. Rather than limit the range of knowledge to the *a priori*, Kuhn holds that the range of knowledge must include the open and unfinished evolution of history. The philosophy of religion and of revelation, therefore, is in principle broader in intent and in extension than was envisaged by any form of *a priorism*.[56]

Since God's revelation in Christ is the high-point and center of the entire history of revelation, the philosophy of Christianity is the high-point of the philosophy of religion. It is, in turn, the essence of the philosophy of history. That with which the philosophy of history is concerned finds its highest actualization and expression in the revelation of Christ.[57] For Kuhn, the Christ-Idea expresses the free divine intent which undergirds the entire mystery of creation and history.[58] It follows that the principal task of the philosophy of Christianity or speculative theology is to clarify all of reality from the basic fact of Christian revelation: the incarnation of the eternal Word. The task of speculative theology is to offer a scientific presentation of the Christian revelation as something fully historical in its fullest unity, totality, and completeness.[59]

The preceding reflections indicate that, in Kuhn's view, there is, indeed, a development of revelation. What is unchangingly true in revelation from the beginning is God and the divine salvific intent. What develops in history is not the divine truth itself but human knowledge of the divine together with human forms of objectification and expression of its perceptions of the divine truth.[60] As a process that has reached its high-point in the revelation embodied in Jesus Christ, revelation remains a living, effective reality in history following Christ. At this point, it becomes an issue of the knowledge of revelation and the many objectifications of it that constitute the tradition of the Christian community of faith.

As this theory of revelation allowed Kuhn to see the phenomenon of religious consciousness universally as both positively and negatively related to Christianity, it provided the underpinnings also for his understanding of the historical evolution of the Christian community in its juridical, liturgical, and doctrinal forms. We will not pursue this issue here since it is, in essence, the problem of tradition. It is sufficient for our purposes here to point out that the principles on which Kuhn's understanding of tradition is based are laid out in his theology of revelation. It is, at its core, a developmental theory of revelation and tradition based on principles worked out over many years of philosophical and theological analysis; a theory which attempts to respect both the more critical understanding of consciousness and the increasingly historical understanding of Scripture and of church doctrine.

CONCLUSION

Kuhn's discussion of revelation, as we have presented it, reflects the Tübingen respect for Christian tradition as well as the concern for dialogue with the concerns of modernity. For Kuhn, such an orientation provides the means through which the unwarranted claims of uncritical Christian pietism as well as excessive views of philosophers may be subjected to helpful criticism. Kuhn's concentration on basic questions of epistemology is clear evidence of his willingness to take seriously the legitimate problems raised by the modern movement in philosophy even while subjecting the philosophical positions to fundamental criticism.

Kuhn's emphasis on history likewise reflects the conviction of Drey and Möhler that systematic theology will be a scientific reflection on the meaning of history. In Kuhn this conviction finds perhaps its most articulate expression in the nineteenth-century. This becomes clear already here in the treatment of revelation. It would become even more obvious in a fuller treatment of the specific themes of his *Dogmatik*, particularly in the later edition.

If the scientific nature of a theological style becomes more apparent at the level of systematic theology, the work of Kuhn serves as an outstanding effort of a Catholic systematician to deal with the claims of tradition and those of the modern experience in a scientific way. His work is an apologetic in the best sense of the word. Despite the problems which some of his contemporaries saw in his work, in retrospect one could hardly accuse Kuhn of having sold out to the modern spirit in its anti-Christian dimensions. But, without doubt, the quality of his work is conditioned deeply by his willingness to engage the issues of modern philosophy critically on its own grounds. In this sense, his work stands as a significant anticipation of some of the best Roman Catholic theology in the second half of the twentieth-century. And when we look to the future, whatever postmodernism might eventually come to mean, it is to be hoped that it will not mean the rejection of the critical turn that proved to be so important in the work of Kuhn.

NOTES

1. Kuhn is frequently described as the sharpest mind of the nineteenth-century Tübingen faculty. Cf. P. Schanz, "Zur Erinnerung an Johann Evangelist von Kuhn," in *Theologische Quartalschrift* [Hereafter ThQ.] 69 (1887): 531–598; esp. 532. Also, H. Fries, *Wegbereiter heutiger Theologie: Johannes von Kuhn,* ed. H. Fries & J. Finsterhölzl, (Graz, Wien, Köln; Styrria, 1973), p. 15, and K. Adam, "Die katholische Tübinger Schule zur 450 Jahrfeier der Universität Tübingen," *Hochland* 24, (1926–27): 581–601, esp. 593–601.

2. Tübingen, 1846.

3. Tübingen, 1859.

4. J. Kuhn, *Die christliche Lehre von der göttlichen Gnade* (Tübingen, 1868).

5. J. Kuhn, *Jacobi und die Philosophie seiner Zeit. Ein Versuch das wissenschaftliche Fundament der Philosophie historisch zu erörtern* (Mainz, 1834).

6. *ThQ.* 14 (1832): 253–304 and 411–444.

7. Cf. *Jacobi,* pp. x, 37; "Begriff und Wesen," art. 1, p. 278.

8. "Begriff und Wesen," art. 1, p. 278.

9. *Jacobi,* p. 37.

10. *Jacobi,* p. 412.

11. Cf. also: *The Problem of Revelation* "Glauben und Wissen, mit Rücksicht auf extreme Ansichten und Richtungen der Gegenwart," *ThQ.* 21 (1839): 382–503, esp. 382–385.

12. David F. Strauss, *Das Leben Jesu kritisch bearbeitet* (Tübingen,1835).

13. Kuhn's response to Strauss in the form of a book is *Das Leben Jesu wissenschaftlich bearbeitet* (Mainz, 1838). This book was preceded by "Von dem schriftstellerischen Charakter der Evangelien im Verhältnis zu der apostolischen Predigt und den apostolischen Briefen," *Jahrbücher für Theologie und christliche Philosophie,* ed. Kuhn, Lüft, Locherer, and Staudenmaier 6 (Frankfurt, 1836): 33–91; "Hermeneutik und Kritik in ihrer Anwendung auf die evangelische Geschichte," *Jahrbücher Für Theologie und Christliche Philosophie* 7(1836): 1–50.

14. Cf. J. Kuhn, "Das Leben Jesu. Selbstanzeige," *ThQ* 20 (1838): 564–575. Here Kuhn points out that his concern is not directly with critical exegesis as such, but with exegesis that bases itself on an unacceptable, pantheistic rationalism. This, in his mind, is the problem of Hegel's philosophy of history with its understanding of the place of religious consciousness in the broader historical context.

15. Kuhn, *Leben Jesu,* p. v.

16. Ibid.

17. Kuhn, *Leben Jesu,* p. vii.

18. Ibid.

19. "Die Schelling'sche Philosophie in ihrem Verhältnis zum Christenthum," *ThQ.* 26 (1844): 57–88, 179–221; 27 (1845): 3–39.

20. "Die Schelling'sche..." art. 3, pp. 8ff.

21. "Die Schelling'sche..." art. 1, pp. 86–87.

22. "Die Schelling'sche..." art. 2, pp. 180ff.

23. Ibid.

24. "Die Schelling'sche..." art. 3, p. 21.

25. Ibid., pp. 5ff.

26. Ibid., p. 32.

27. Ibid., p. 32.

28. Ibid., pp. 38–39.

29. "Begriff und Wesen," art. 1, p. 299.

30. Ibid., p. 264.

31. "Begriff und Wesen," art. 1, pp. 284–286.

32. Ibid.

33. *Leben Jesu*, p. vii.

34. *Katholische Dogmatik* (2 ed.), p.16.

35. *Katholische Dogmatik* (2 ed.), p.5.

36. *Katholische Dogmatik* (2 ed.), p. 6; also, *Leben Jesu*, p. 129.

37. "Begriff und Wesen," art. 2, pp. 413ff.

38. *Katholische Dogmatik* (1 ed.), pp. 5–65; (2 ed.), p.6; *ThQ*. 21 (1839): 392–4.

39. *Leben Jesu*, pp.129ff.; *Katholische Dogmatik* (2 ed.), pp. 5, 14.

40. *Katholische Dogmatik* (2 ed.), p. 5.

41. *Leben Jesu*, p. 129.

42. Ibid.

43. Ibid., p. 130.

44. Ibid., p. 134.

45. Ibid.

46. Cf. A. Schilson, "Lessing und die katholische Tübingen Schule," in *ThQ* 160 (1980): 256–277; W. Fehr, *The Birth of the Catholic Tübingen School: The Dogmatics of Johann Sebastian Drey* (Chico,CA: Scholars Press, 1981), pp. 57ff.

47. "Begriff und Wesen," art. 1, pp. 281–282.

48. *Katholische Dogmatik* (2 ed.), pp. 119–221.

49. "Begriff und Wesen," art. 2, p. 414; *Leben Jesu*, p. 136; *Katholische Dogmatik* (2 ed.), pp. 19ff.

50. *Katholische Dogmatik* (2 ed.) p. 120.

51. *Die lebendige Überlieferung als Norm des christlichen Glaubens dargestellt im Geiste der Traditionslehre Johannes Ev. Kuhns* (Freiburg: Herder, 1959), pp. 203ff.

52. *Katholische Dogmatik* (2 ed.), p. 149; T. O'Meara, *Romantic Idealism and Roman Catholicism* (Notre Dame: Notre Dame Press, 1982), p. 158, citing F. Wolfinger, *Der Glaube nach J. E. Von Kuhn* (Göttingen: Vandenhoeck & Ruprecht, 1972), p. 155.

53. *Katholische Dogmatik* (2 ed.), p. 149.

54. "Begriff und Wesen," art. 2, p. 412.

55. Ibid., p. 413.

56. Ibid., pp. 416–417.

57. Ibid., p. 418.

58. Cf. *Leben Jesu*, pp.129ff. for the deduction of the Christ-concept from reflection on the dynamic of human life.

59. "Begriff und Wesen," art. 2, p. 423.

60. *Katholische Dogmatik* (2 ed.), pp. 20–21 and 119–121

10

Beyond "Hierarchology"

Johann Adam Möhler and Yves Congar

— THOMAS F. O'MEARA, O.P. —

Introduction

Yves Congar is not only the leading ecclesiologist of our century and one of the most important theologians of topics touching the church since the Reformation and Trent. Congar's publications during the thirty years prior to Vatican II, containing so many creative ideas for the renewal of entire theological areas, argue that he was also the most important theologian leading up to Vatican II.[1] His lifelong theme of the church understood in history and in the present as the Spirit-directed Body of Christ active in diverse ministries and offices renewed both the theology and the practice of the church.

For Johann Adam Möhler, Yves Congar became an advocate, a channel, and a theological amplifier—all on a large scale. In the first third of this century, after a time of neglect outside of Germany, this French Dominican [2] with others reintroduced the German theologian and brought his ideas to an ecumenical council. The following pages sketch their intertwined destinies: a theologian reintroduced and a theologian inspired.

In 1930 Congar wrote down a kind of profession of his faith and vocation; it was to study the church in order to let "the true face of the church" assume its full reality.[3] The young Congar already saw that the ecclesial visage changed in history. In his autobiographical sketches Congar never failed to introduce prominently, if succinctly, the influence of the person and work of Johann Adam Möhler. "A leader in the renewal of Catholic theology in Germany in the nineteenth century,"[4] the German romantic theologian offered a thought which was "inexhaustible;"[5] *Die Einheit in der Kirche* was a "masterpiece."[6] The Tübingen theology was not a text for research but an ecclesiology for change. "As with other things, Père Chenu revealed Möhler to me. I found there a source, the source, which I needed....So what Möhler did in the nineteenth century became for me an ideal which would inspire and lead me to my own theology in the twentieth century....A great author is inexhaustible: his work presents itself for various re-readings."[7] Whether we are reading Congar's observations about Mohler from 1938 or 1973, the themes and enthusiasm remain much the same.

By the mid-1930s Congar was already publicly at work on the revitalization of broad areas of ecclesiology, a renewal which needed a new view of the church. Can one define the church? That was an early preoccupation of Congar, and his long labors to move beyond defining the church as a perfect, hierarchically formed institution never tired of repeating the alternative view in Möhler.[8] The organic approach of romanticism reached from Möhler, Franz von Baader, and F. A. Staudenmaier to Matthias Scheeben and L. Atzberger, and on to Friedrich Pilgram and Erich Przywara. Congar saw in that organic view of the church animated by the Holy Spirit a seminal perspective rich with implications: in short, "the theology of the future."[9] Already in 1934, looking at the reasons for the lack of faith in France, he had written:

> To every growth of humanity, to every bit of progress, to every extension of the human in any one of the domains of creation—whether of knowledge or action—there should correspond a growth of the church, an incorporation of the faith, an incarnation of grace, a humanization of God! The church is not a small social group, isolated, a separate entity remaining untouched among the evolving realities of the world. The church is the world insofar as it believes in Christ.[10]

But where to find a concrete ecclesiology expressing this vision? Its source would come not from a solitary transcendental analysis or a lonely existentialism but from a past theologian devoted to the theologies of the third century.

Making Johann Adam Möhler Known

French resources on the history of modern German Catholic theology and of its romantic restoration were, one suspects, sparse before 1930. Notable German books on Möhler appeared in the decades prior to 1940, namely, studies by S. Lösch, S. Merkle, K. Eschweiler and J. R. Geiselmann.[11] Was the thought of Möhler at all available to French theology before the published translation of *Die Einheit* in 1938? In fact, a number of articles led up to and celebrated the anniversary year of Möhler's birth in 1937. Congar and G. Rouzet wrote on Möhler and Orthodoxy in 1935 for *Irenikon*,[12] and the centenary year saw a few essays appear like that on Newman and Möhler by an Oratorian in Birmingham, England, Henry Tristram.[13] A Jesuit of the Fourviere faculty, Pierre Chaillet, was an important and early advocate of Möhler. In 1937 he published in the Paris Dominicans' *Revue des sciences philosophiques et théologiques* a two-part study on the school of Tübingen and its antecedents,[14] and that was succeeded in the following year by a study on living tradition published in an issue of the same *Revue* entitled "Hommage à J.-A. Moehler."[15] For the anniversary he published in 1939 a volume of essays including contributions by A.-D. Sertillanges, Gustave Bardy, Geiselmann, Lösch, Congar, Josef Jungmann, and Yves de Montcheuil.[16] Chaillet had a remarkable knowledge of German Catholic theology in the nineteenth century which could draw in figures like J. M. Sailer and Alois Gügler. In 1938 Congar published three articles on the Tübingen theologian, and we will return to them. "The importance of Möhler and of the school of Tübingen (which includes others) is to have opened or re-opened the consideration of a truly theological and supernatural view of the church."[17] Congar found some unusual parallels to the Tübingen school: for instance, in Francois de Salignac de la Mothe Fénelon. Through Fénelon, he thought, this idea of 'living tradition' had passed to Sailer and to Möhler.[18]

Congar said that the idea of the collection, *Unam Sanctam*, was born of two needs. On the one hand, the ecumenical movement had led to issues of ecclesiology; on the other hand, the idea of the renewal of the church involving the renewal of its theology and the understanding of its history of forms, was appearing on all sides but in a vacuum of resources. "The two areas called for basically the same response: an effort to conceive of a theology of the church which was truly grand, living, serious."[19] The collection was not to be limited to church history, apologetics, ecumenism, or missiology but was to include all that flowed from the mystery and the nature of the church. "I wanted to open the collection with a new translation of *L'Unité dans l'Eglise* of J. A. Möhler. This masterpiece, imperfect like so many masterpieces, represented something quite remarkable in the genre and spirit of what I hoped to do. Unfortunately, there were delays in the translation, and the first volume was my *Chrétiens désunis. Principes d'un 'Oecuménisme' catholique* which appeared in July, 1937..."[20] Nevertheless, *L'Unité de l'Eglise* is a parent, an intimation of the many books to come.[21] In his "Chronique" for 1938 Congar reviewed the published translation. The book "had been practically inaccessible to French readers... This is a profound book which illumines, synthesizes, and makes one think."[22] What are the basic elements he finds in Möhler?

> Some are disappointed in the thought of Möhler. They believed that the visible church was for him less an institution coming from Christ than a spontaneous product of the Spirit of love, and they made Möhler into a father of modernism in the style of Tyrell. This is an enormous error. If Möhler has at times too little marked the role and divine origins of the institutional element, that can be conceded. But *L'Unité* does not deny that element; it underlines that it is secondary....It remains that *L'Unité dans l'Église* is the treatise in which modern theologians of *De ecclesia* will find the most abundant source for that living and dynamic notion of the church which all, today, are seeking to restore.[23]

Congar was capable of describing the German romantic idealism attracting Catholic minds and movements after 1795. "Möhler assumes into this pneumatological perspective romantic ideas of organicism and communitarian life and even that of the *Volksgeist*."[24] Romanticism promotes integration rather than rationalism and separation; it recaptures a sense of the contemplation of the truths of faith, even while it introduces development and history. "It also conveys a sense of connections and a viewpoint of the living organism."[25] In his introductions to Möhler, Congar mentioned the Tübingen school begun by J. S. Drey and the inspiration of Schelling, but his knowledge of German philosophers was at that time probably largely limited to ideas taken from books on the theologians.[26] As is well known, through Drey and Möhler, Schelling's philosophy of an actualization of the ideal in the real in history joined with patristic insights to influence Roman Catholic theology. Schelling applied after 1800 his aesthetic pattern of the ideal shining forth in the real to Christianity. The *Lectures on Academic Studies*, when they turned to treat theology and Christianity, brought a number of fruitful ideas together. Christianity was, in contrast to religions of nature, a statement of incarnation, or of incarnation-in-history. "Hence Christianity's leading idea is God becoming incarnate."[27] The mysterious structures of nature and the objectification of the transcendental self led to an objective idealism and to a romantic idealism. Just as in science and art, so too in religion the ideal was manifest in the real. "The ideas of a religion in which the infinite is apprehended in the finite have to be expressed primarily in actually existing things. The actions and customs of the church "are held to be objectively symbolic on the ground that their significance can only be mystical." Far from being an unfree institution of antiquity outside of science and art, an important "symbol of God is the church as a living work of art."[28] For Congar, in *Die Einheit* the Tübingen theologian is under the influence of the organic philosophy of Schelling, the mystical immanentism of Schleiermacher, and patristic ideas. All this brings forth an ecclesiology different from one focused on the structure of hierarchy. "External structures do not create the intimate being of the Christian and they do not precede it: God raises them first from an interior need....The Spirit is inseparable from the visible organism to which it is linked, and the faithful live from it to the extent they are inserted into community."[29] While attention was given to the subject as spirit, to societies as organisms, to an expression of the ideal in finite forms, to history as permeating knowing and living. Möhler joined idealism to patristic motifs of eschatology, life, history, and spirituality. In Congar's view, however, Möhler left Schelling, but not as early as Congar thought, for some of the views of Hegel.[30] If that Catholic theology is concerned with "the lived," nonetheless, it has, in Congar's view in the 1940s, some limitations. "In the romantic school of Tübingen, insufficiently freed of German philosophical and theological idealism, theology appears as too concretely concerned with faith as lived in the church. The sources and objective criteria of theology are not sufficiently disengaged or elevated from the ordinary....The thought of the greatest among those at Tübingen is thoroughly orthodox. But their theology is conceived too much as an intellectual realization of what the church and the theologian in the church has received and by which it lives....In a word, theology is too much a science of faith and not enough a science of revelation."[31]

The discussion of Möhler in Congar's large historical works on theology or ecclesiology was usually counterpoised to various schools of positive theology, canon law, neoscholasticism, and a melange of all three in Roman schools or papal administration. They formed what Congar called "the situation" of the theory of the church prior to the Council. Congar, nonetheless, had found that the Tübingen theologian was not ignored by all the teachers in the Roman schools: "Through Passaglia, Schrader owed to him partly the theology of the church as Mystical Body, which he introduced into the first drafts of the schema *De Ecclesia* of the Vatican Council from 1869-1870."[32] Early on, for partly apologetic reasons, Congar found a similar "path" even in Dominican Thomists of the sixteenth century like Domingo Banez and Thomas de Vio, Cardinal Cajetan;[33] moreover, Congar stated that, while Möhler and Newman were pioneers, even Thomas Aquinas had been an anticipation. "The theology of the great masters, in first place that of Thomas Aquinas to whom I owe the foundation of my thought, is far from having nothing to say in the field which engages us."[34]

The young Dominican was working in a climate which was more open than that of the years after the anti-modernist document *Pascendi dominici gregis* of 1907, but which was still circumscribed as to encouraged themes and approaches. Apparently, even a translation of a book from a hundred years past, if it held a new ecclesiology, would attract attention in Rome. Jean-Pierre Jossua writes in his biography: "Father Congar [was] suspect as early as 1939 because he encouraged the "return to the sources" (which some—not without a certain 'flair' in a sense—deemed extremely dangerous)....The publication of Möhler's *Unity in the Church* in *Unam Sanctam* (1939) had almost caused trouble."[35] Congar recalled: "What I was writing [after 1935] displeased [Rome]. There was no heresy with which I could be accused, but I was suspect. When I published a translation of Möhler, I wasn't very popular in Rome; one imagined he was a precursor of modernism (that was not written but it was said in Roman circles), but I argued that this was absolutely false."[36] Perhaps Vatican circles correctly intuited that the ideas of Möhler and Congar would lead historical research and traditional theology to new perspectives full of ecclesial insights and pastoral innovations.

Möhler's Theology of the Church

In the centenary year Congar published three articles on the Tübingen theologian: particularly on *Die Einheit in der Kirche*. The longest piece sketched Möhler's life and writings and then surveyed the history of the reception of the German theologian.[37]

A second article focused on Möhler and patristics. "The Fathers are people," Congar began, "who more completely and more totally than others lived *in the church*."[38] They were not scholars or hermits but voices of the church. We hear echoes of romantic idealism as Congar continued: "To live *in the church*—that's to be a living part of an organic totality of which the Holy Spirit is the interior principle, in which the incarnation of Christ continues, and which Incarnates itself or 'gives itself a body' [Congar places in quotation marks "*se corporifie*"] in dogma, worship, and the social or hierarchical institutions."[39] The Spirit is both an objective reality and a subjective, active principle as it anticipates and furthers the activity of the church. Such a view of the life of the church in history when transposed to the realms of believing and knowing raises the idea of tradition. Among the fathers Möhler had found Athanasius to be a representative of his own themes, and his large work on Athanasius studied not just the Alexandrian bishop's struggles with authority but his theological method. Athanasius treated every Christian doctrine in its relationship to the essence of Christianity. What is that essence, Congar asked? God became man for our redemption. Thus Möhler too had rooted theology in the incarnation and pneumatology.[40] Congar moved on to the motif of organic vitality within history. The church's life is organic; it is rooted in a particular epoch with its proper forms. Congar stressed how Möhler's perception of diverse forms living in history, "organs of the Holy Spirit," permitted different understandings of the "essence" of Christianity. Unlike modern thinkers who searched for a single idea or a new term which would capture fully Christianity, for the fathers the essence is Jesus Christ, the divine really incarnate in the human.[41] That escapes one book or idea.

A third article related Möhler to the new ecumenical movement of the twentieth century, as yet unaccepted by Rome. Congar was struggling to develop a theology which would permit and draw Roman Catholic participation in the ecumenical movement. Möhler's trip as a young scholar to visit at important German universities historians, theologians, and philosophers—particularly Friedrich Schleiermacher, August Neander and Philipp Marheinke—was for him a revelation, and he called the German professors, "a decisive influence on historical work."[42] Congar found the inspiration and genius of Möhler mainly in *Die Einheit*. Through the originality of its sources and principles, by the depth and fecundity of its points of view, and by its integrative vision, the book contributed to a liberation of forms in Catholicism, which, when subsisting in an ossified style, obscure the reality they should bear. His later, more substantial *Symbolik* is not so creative, and in treating that later work Congar inevitably touched briefly on opposition and Hegel, and on how Möhler's response to the problem of heresy and schism within the church and churches had ecumenical value. "Unity! Reunion! Möhler noted often the immense joy with which the church saw a schism end in a communion restored; it was each time as if the church, which is a mystery of reconciliation and of unity, refound itself."[43]

If we ask what Congar drew from Möhler—others can inquire as to whether he was fully faithful to the German theologian—the Dominican himself repeated over decades the same perspective drawn from romantic idealism and the Greek fathers, both with links to Neoplatonism: a return to Christology and ecclesiology in the basic themes of the body of Christ and the animation of the Spirit, a theology of the organism of the church in history as an interpretation of and liberation for a diversity in ministries and all kinds of forms. A comparison of writings in the 1930s with those of thirty years later discloses little change in Congar's thought as he selected the same basic themes. Pages written at the time of the Council summed up these themes:

> Möhler proposed a different vision of the church which would develop under the sign of the Holy Spirit (in *Die Einheit*) and later under the sign of the incarnation (*Symbolik*). Nourished by the ancient fathers, Möhler restored (1) a pneumatological consideration of the mystical body beyond a Christological one (This point is quite sensitive and merits by itself a study), (2), an anthropology, a consideration of the perspective of the mystical body moving from within outwards to what constitutes the Christian living in communion with brothers and sisters. In the categories of scholasticism, one could say that Möhler had seen the church in the realm of its '*res*' or of Christian ontology before the consideration of the realm of its "*sacramentum*" or external structures; (3), Consequently, the activity of the ecclesial body animated by the Spirit of Christ was affirmed.[44]

Möhler's ecclesiology offered something quite different from the positive theologies and neo-scholastic writings offered before and after the 1830s. The latter
had seen the church, as Congar put it, not as the Body of Christ animated by the
spirit but "as a society or an organization where Christ intervenes at its origins as
the founder and where the Holy Spirit guarantees authority. Since they [Christ and
the Spirit] had given once and for all a superterrestrial quality to the institutions,
more interventions were not needed. Hence the celebrated formula with which
Möhler summed up the ecclesiology of the Enlightenment. *Gott schuf die Hierarchie
und für die Kirche is nun bis zum Weltende mehr als genug gesorgt.*"[45]

The incarnation is the pattern of the church, but the Spirit is the continuing
animator necessary to give it life. "After *Die Einheit* which exalts the *divine* principle of the church, Möhler drew out the Christological dimension in a study on
Athanasius and in the various editions of the *Symbolik*."[46] Exterior structures do
not create the intimate being of Christianity nor do they precede it, but they are
important. The aspects of society emphasized after the Enlightenment must be
balanced by institution and hierarchy. The church is the community of the faithful
vivified by the Spirit of love from Pentecost. The union of the divine and the human
is seen there under the form of a personal-substantial union of the Holy Spirit with
the believers. In his magisterial historical survey of ecclesiology, *L'Église de saint
Augustin à l'époque moderne*, Congar wrote that "the work of Möhler cannot be
reduced to ecclesiology but its ecclesiological part is central because his central
concern is the relationship of man and God: the church is the true reality of that
relationship."[47] The Tübingen school pondered anew the divine sources of the
church, Trinitarian missions which bestow both the Incarnation and the active
spirituality of the members.[48]

The Theology of Tradition

Ideas in themselves seminal are in a particular time fruitless for certain individuals but powerful for others.[49] One of the areas Congar particularly advanced
through his vocation of historical reappraisal was the theology of tradition. Here
Möhler was to play a special role, because for him the church led to tradition.
When Congar began his reconsideration of tradition, he found it held captive in
Catholicism by erroneous but widely held convictions: (1) tradition was static,
timeless, perennially full, and complete; (2) it was located in texts; (3) it was a
support for and an instrument of the papal magisterium. A deeper theology of
tradition had to show how tradition was not the same as the patristic writings
(Migne), nor the ensemble of writings from patristic theologians, councils, and
papal documents, (Denzinger), and also not the Roman magisterium. Also, (4) there
was the prejudice that any movement away from fixing tradition in patristic and
papal documents would lead to the Protestant "*sola scriptura*," and (5) that tradition would be absorbed in idealist philosophies and their offspring, Protestant
histories of dogma, where history would sweep away the content of revelation.
"For several years prior to that encyclical [*Humani generis* in 1950]...[there had

been] studies on tradition which went far to restore its ancient ecclesiastical meaning—so well understood by Möhler."[50] Möhler would unite the old and the new: "To summarize, for Möhler living tradition is what was called at the time of Trent 'the Gospel written in men's hearts' but understood within the framework of a theology of communion, and influenced as much by romanticism as by German idealism."[51] Tradition was not a handed-down collection of dogmas and books but the life of the church underlying diverse realizations which served the communication of the Gospel apart from Scripture.

An idea from Möhler—"This vital, spiritual force which we inherit from our ancestors and which is perpetuated in the church is interior tradition"[52] - found in Congar an imaginative elaboration. "The expression 'living tradition,'" Congar wrote in *Tradition and Traditions*, "was not invented by the Catholic school of Tübingen; but it is rarely found in patristic or papal texts."[53] It appears with the Catholic adversaries of the Reformation. Möhler himself was reacting to the Enlightenment, Baroque ecclesiology, and the false interpretation of Trent in terms of *partim-partim*. The explication of Spirit, tradition, and church belongs to "the writings of the Tübingen school, and in particular [to Möhler]. Möhler, so much inspired by the Fathers and employing many of their lines or thought, did not take this particular theology from them as such; it is his personal development."[54] Tradition proclaimed in the church extends to the whole spirit of Christianity and to all its doctrines. "Tradition contains and preserves everything; it is the Gospel living in the church."[55] Tradition like the church enjoyed a progress from interior presence to external expression, from the Spirit to its realized verbal and ecclesial forms, "a sort of progress from what was inside to what was outside, starting from the Spirit within which there is a constant striving to find an adequate expression."[56]

Equally important was the bearer and agent of tradition: not a past book or pope but an organically living collective self. Tradition was "a theology of communion by the Spirit given to the community, but not by the Spirit only....tradition is only one aspect, one application of this theology of communion."[57] *Die Einheit* gave an original importance to the Spirit and the community marked by development and history. "The aspect of development, still absent from the Tridentine affirmation about apostolic traditions, is clearly marked in Möhler's idea and already in Sailer's, provided it is understood that Möhler is concerned not with a purely dialectical development but with a development arising from the demands of Christian allegiance."[58] Congar in the second part of *Tradition and Traditions* concluded: "Möhler saw in Tradition that which effectively brings about the unity of the Church as the Church formed both by the teaching of Christ and by Pentecost: through the Spirit, the truth taught by Jesus Christ is gradually assimilated more and more intimately and, through love, becomes the inspiration towards communion. The Spirit creates, from within, the unity of the community, and also the organs or expressions of its special genius, i.e., its tradition. The heart of all these theological perspectives is the identity of the principle which acts throughout the Church's duration, and is at work in the activities by which it builds itself up, with that principle which was at work from the beginning in the revelation made to the prophets and the apostles, and in the saving actions of the incarnate Word."[59]

Congar went on to develop in that synthetic coda by drawing on theologians as varied as Jean Mouroux and Joseph Ratzinger the theology of historical and sacramental organic life. One senses his excitement over a new expression of an ancient theology that avoided "ecclesiological monophysitism every bit as much as nestorianism"[60] where the Spirit acts in the members of the church. The actions of the body of Christ in ongoing history is a spiritual "event" in each consciousness; Christians are not just witnesses to but bearers of tradition. "The whole ecclesial community is the organ of Tradition."[61] It would seem that the fundamental theology of the organic life of the church is the prior foundation for the more well known theology of tradition.

Tradition does find a prison of security in the promise of the Spirit and the magisterium but that stability exists to sustain the church in the upheavals of history and culture. "This tradition is living because it is not a thing exterior to living souls vivified by the Spirit."[62] Tradition, the whole life of the church, dialectical and organic, sustained a diversity of charisms and offices, perspectives and insights. Such a theology could liberate the church from being bound to one age, one technical language, one office. And, although the Christology of the Body of Christ is foundational, it should not be interpreted in a monophysite form as if offices and forms were mechanical instruments coming from Christ.[63]

An Organic Ecclesiology: Thirty Years after Vatican II

Congar did not publish Möhler's ideas simply as a contribution to the history of ecclesiology. They could serve, as he increasingly saw, as stimuli and principles of his ecclesiology of renewal. "The vision of the Council," Congar wrote retrospectively, "has been resolutely that of the history of salvation completed by eschatology."[64] In a volume honoring the Tübingen faculty in 1970 the French Dominican concluded: "Möhler can even today be a vital source—that is what he was for me over forty years ago."[65] Congar then would not mind our looking at his past dialogue with Möhler as it continues into the present time. Whether in 1938 or 1978 Congar's theology worked not solely to research the past but to understand it, to employ the history of theologies and church institutions for a future, more vital church. "It is certain, or at least quite probable, that Vatican II will condition the life of the church for a long time. That council incorporated a great density of faithfulness and wisdom coming from the entire church: it is an event of a Pentecostal type."[66] Jossua writes in a recent encomium: "Congar in no way remained fixed within the advances or the limits of the Council. From the very first broad reception of Vatican II there was a lively openness to rapid changes in ideas and praxis."[67] Congar, however, thought that the upheavals in the post-conciliar era had their roots not in Vatican II, but in the constrictive decades or centuries before it. "The years after the Council are a global phenomenon with world-wide dimensions. A crisis would have come anyway. The Council assisted its entry into the church by ending the isolation of the church, by giving a wider audience to the church, and by ending a monolithic institution protected by fictions. The present time is linked to the gigantic change which touches culture, the ways of life in society and the 'cohumanity' around the world."[68]

To prepare in 1970 for a consultation on a national pastoral council for the United States, a move blocked by Rome and only slightly realized later in an advisory council, I sent Yves Congar some questions about ecclesiology. At the conclusion of his answers he wrote: "It is astonishing how the post-conciliar period has so little to do with the Council...The post-conciliar questions are new and radical, and "aggiornamento" [now] means changes and adaptations to a new situation, assuming the principles of the original institution."[69] He mentioned in a later interview: "All the work of the Council is a half-way station."[70] Do the dynamic lines of Congar's employment of Möhler continue today? To Americans the influence of what might appear to be transcendental and historical ideas should suggest that the practical areas of ecclesiology, spirituality, liturgy, moral theology, and pastoral theology draw energy from historical and speculative sources and directions. The following pages look at some movements within contemporary Catholicism which are today facing the implications of subjectivity, process, communion, and history.

Beyond the Baroque.

Möhler was able to transcend an ecclesiology which was mechanical and juridical; his thought could "open (or re-open) a truly theological and incarnational ecclesiology. . .beyond the treatises of ecclesiology done in terms of papal *potestas* or apologetics."[71] Renewing the church in the twentieth century meant leaving behind an administrative style that combined the negative aspects of the Dionysian and medieval hierarchies with the centralization made visual in Baroque architecture. For some time, all had been absorbed into one teaching office whose language and conceptuality were held captive in a melange of canon law, Neoscholasticism, and what might be called "encyclicalese." Was it possible to pass beyond a church whose condition was that of a static monism and which was, from the point of view of authority, a "hierarchology"?[72] To accomplish this there had to be something different.

Congar was convinced that the exciting decades of the French church from 1930 to 1960 were not simply suggesting selected reforms but opening a new era.[73] Teaching at Le Saulchoir, Henri Feret, M. D. Chenu, and Congar developed a critique of a theological and ecclesiastical era they named "Baroque." Its characteristics were anti-Protestant in the style of the seventeenth century, antiliberal in terms of the period after the French Revolution, neoscholastic, and papalist. That ecclesiastical format Congar also called a Bellarminian juridicism.[74] "The benefit (of the Council) has taken mainly the form of a departure from Tridentinism.... It was a system which took in absolutely everything: theology, ethics, Christian behavior, religious practices, liturgy, organization, Roman centralization, the perpetual intervention of Roman congregations in the life of the church, and so on."[75] One might employ "Tridentine" for the structures of the centralist papacy during the centuries between Trent and Vatican II, but for the ensemble of the cultural life of the church, which is much more than the unoriginal administration of the Counter-Reformation, the term, "Baroque" is preferable. Regardless, at the end of the section on the Counter-Reformation in *L'Église de saint Augustin à l'époque moderne*, Congar described the institutionalized ecclesiology which had lasted almost four centuries. "We can note the ecclesiological aspect of Roman centralization, which is linked to a further important aspect. Trent had affirmed in the face of Protestantism that Christ is not solely a redeemer but that he is also a law-giver. In this line, even in its work at sustaining and demanding a kind of bishop who was truly pastoral, it favored the construction of a hierarchical order, but not one arranged around the Eucharist but around the "regime" of which Rome occupies the center and summit. Despite the admirable expansion of Christian life and pastoral ministry, an era of legalism began, replacing a somewhat theoretical ecclesiology. Finally an orthodoxy, not only of faith but of theology, is fixed by a kind of canonization of the conceptual and verbal system come down from scholasticism which from then to our own times has incorporated itself into catholicism."[76] The force of history furthered by biblical and patristic sources of salvation-history and its secular forms in German idealism let that time yield to a new era. "I believe that the novelty of Vatican II consisted largely in its acceptance of the historicity of the church, of scripture, etc."[77] Clearly, as the Dominican faculty foresaw in the 1930s, an era was coming to an end.

Through an Organic Ecclesiology to the World-Church.

It is clear that as a consequence of Vatican II, perhaps as a by-product of its liberation from an a-historical neo-Aristotelianism, Roman Catholicism is becoming what some would call "a world-church." Congar wrote in 1973: "People often ask me how I see the future of the church? It seems to me that it is necessary still to enlarge our viewpoints [to see] that the church is called to become in a new way a church of all peoples, called to recognized in a new and more profound way its genius for expressing itself in great cultures...."[78] Just as the period of time going back four centuries is partly coming to an end, so an expanding church has begun to leave a millenium-long Eurocentrism and to realize itself locally in modest ways. History has led to local church, and that organic church has multiplied ministry. In fact, Congar wrote fifty years ago that the awareness of being universal leads to becoming a truly universal church, and that in "every sphere, the church's potentialities are brought out by being actualized, and it is brought to self-understanding by events. That, after all, is the law of all living things."[79] Then in one of his last essays he described the destiny of our ecclesial era as a multi-cultural incarnation of the Spirit springing from "that fundamentally historical Pentecost,"[80] in which we all participate and live.

The church is seeking the diversity-in-unity which Congar found in Möhler. Authority, liturgy, and ministry are the most public areas emerging from an acceptance of organic diversity. In those three areas, whose moments the media over thirty years has monotonously presented as "crises," are found most of the changes and issues of the postconciliar era.

The past thirty years have witnessed a considerable number of discussions and conflicts over authority. Most of these have been between the central authority and other entities, which the Council encouraged to claim some independent role: for instance, bishops' conferences, individual dioceses, bishops, theologians, lay and theological associations, regions of the church, etc. One sees here the tension between Baroque centrism and the organic theology of Möhler and Congar. The challenge is obviously to develop beyond the rather primitive ecclesiastical logic dominant from 1860 to 1960 a sociology of shared knowledge, leadership, and communally held authority. The identification of the contributors to the process of decision-making in the church and the description of their roles is fundamental as is the exploration of the process, neither monarchical nor democratic, by which each finds some power and voice. But further discussions of tradition active today have been halted.

Ministry

After the Council Congar wrote: "The responsibility of witness and service flows from the Christian quality as such: thus there is mission in the broad sense, and this mission is equally incumbent on every Christian. All the disciples received the Holy Spirit and the gifts which render them responsible for God's cause."[81] Since 1965 the ministerial life of the church has passed rapidly beyond the forms of the seventeenth and nineteenth centuries and taken up, consciously or uncon-sciously, a ministerial praxis of the baptized rooted in the Body of Christ. "The Church is an organic reality in which members receive a gift to enable them to fulfill a particular function."[82] Renewal of the church involves passing beyond the single ministry (bishop, priest, pope), which had absorbed everything, but in a way which renders leadership important and challenging. While Congar spoke generally of many activities in the church, not surprisingly his examples and theology come from teaching. He said that most biblical ministries were about teaching, and that teaching and learning in hierarchy and laity loom large.[83] The seminal insights concerning universal activity in a church viewed as an organism are introduced in a general way, but understandably he did not imagine the contemporary, broad expansion of ecclesial ministries, mirroring the first century but now diversely real-ized in hundreds of local and regional churches.[84]

In 1953 Congar had written the first theology of the laity, *Jalons pour une théologie du laicat* (1953).[85] He began:

> It is not just a matter of adding a paragraph or a chapter to an ecclesiological exposition which from beginning to end ignores the principles on which a 'laicology' really depends. Without these [new] principles we should have, confronting a laicised world, only a clerical Church which would not be the people of God in the fullness of its truth. At bottom there can only be one sound and sufficient theology of laity, and that is a 'total ecclesiology'.[86]

Twenty years later, after the Council, he reexamined that work and concluded: "I have not written that ecclesiology."[87] The decades since the Council have been occupied with parochial and diocesan diversity in ministerial areas, which has its source in the gifts of the Spirit to the Body of Christ which become charismatically inspired public and ecclesial ministries, some ordained through baptism and others through further ordinations. The development from 1965 onward went ahead of ecclesiastical direction and theological reflection.

Congar addressed anew in 1972 laity and ministry to correct a vision "which at first was principally and spontaneously clerical."

> The church of God is not built up solely by the actions of the official presbyteral ministry but by a multitude of diverse modes of service, more or less stable or occasional, more or less spontaneous or recognized, and, when the occasion arises consecrated, while falling short of sacramental ordination. These modes of service do exist...mothers at home, the person who coordinates liturgical celebrations or reads the sacred text, the woman visiting the sick or prisoners, adult catechists....They exist right now, but up to now were not called by their true name, ministries, nor were their place and status in ecclesiology recognized.[88]

This is very different from the church in the 1950s when a few thousand out of millions shared in an ecclesially insignificant "apostolate" gingerly bestowed by bishops. That model changed. "It is worth noticing that the decisive coupling is not 'priesthood/laity,' as I used it in *Jalons*, but rather 'ministries/modes of community service'."[89] Congar gave a sketch of the model which would replace the bipolar division of clergy and laity. It is a circle with Christ and Spirit as ground or animating power upon ministries in community. He continued: "It would then be necessary to substitute for the linear scheme a scheme where the community appears as the enveloping reality within which the ministries, eventually the instituted sacramental ministries, are placed as modes of service of what the community is called to be and do."[90] The venerable model of clergy and laity is fully incapable of explaining what the church has already become in many parts of the world. As both Möhler and Congar glimpsed, the people of God and the animating Spirit of the church are open to and restless for the rush of diversity in unity.

Conclusion

To reread Congar is to be struck by his passion for the future. An eschatological confidence empowered the fearless examination of the force of history, a history which keeps the church alive but which from time to time sweeps some of its forms away. How often in his writings "*l'avenir*" appeared, and how different this view is from other directions in the twentieth century. Heidegger pronounced the end of metaphysics; Spengler divined the end of the West; and Bultmann presumed the end of belief in the supernatural; Schoenberg announced the end of the diatonic scale, and it would be impossible to list all those who have confirmed the end of art. Recently Francis Fukuyama proclaimed the end of history, and John Horgan the end of science. But like Möhler, Yves Congar and Vatican II are about beginnings, about the emergence of the new, about the future. This eschatology of each present moment is a gift; it is also a warning that Catholicism's vision still differs from modernity's shadow side of doubt and decline. That courageous belief perceives in the continuing presence of the Spirit in history a power which, though silent and invisible, is, nonetheless, real.

NOTES

1. Richard McBrien writes: "By any reasonable account, Yves Congar is the most distinguished ecclesiologist of this century and perhaps of the entire post-Tridentine era. No modern theologian's spirit was accorded fuller play in the documents of Vatican II than Congar's. Vatican II was a council of the church, and Congar has been a theologian of the church *par excellence.*" "Church and Ministry: The Achievement of Yves Congar," *Theological Digest* 32 (1985): 203. In the view of J. P. Jossua Congar is "a figure emblematic of the theology of the Council, perhaps the best known theologian of this century." "Yves Congar. La vie et l'oeuvre d'un théologien,"*Cristianesimo nella storia* 17 (1996):1. The biography by Jossua with its bibliography is helpful but it ends before 1970. Congar in writings or interviews gave several autobiographical sketches.

2. Möhler would have been surprised that his rehabilitation came from a French friar. Congar wrote: "Möhler was wrong in believing that the religious orders were finished and in rejoicing that the French Revolution has freed the church from that dead weight. Möhler did not distinguish between the religious orders which were in fact dead in the eighteenth century, and those which revived in a magnificent and faithful way in the nineteenth century," Y. Congar, *Vraie et fausse reforme dans l'église* (Paris: Cerf, 1950), p. 175 citing an important source for French scholars, E. Vermeil, *Jean-Adam Möhler et l'école catholique de Tubingue (1815–1840)* (Paris: Colin, 1913), p. 38. Indeed, Congar saw Lacordaire, the restorer of the Dominicans, as an exemplar of new and old directions in religious life after 1820, and as holding in his thought "instinctively" an idea or two of Möhler (*Vraie et fausse* 257).

3. Y. Congar, *Une Passion: L'Unité. Reflexions et souvenirs, 1929–1973* (Paris: Foi Vivante, 1974), p. 15. The following year in 1931 the French translation of Karl Adam's *Das Wesen des Katholizismus* appeared with the title, *Le vrai visage du catholicisme.*

4. "Y. Congar, Je crois en la sainte église [1938]," *Sainte Église* (Paris: Cerf, 1964), p. 11.

5. J. Puyo, *Une vie pour la verité. Jean Puyo interroge le Père Congar* (Paris: Le Centurion, 1975), p. 48.

6. Congar, *Une Passion: l'unité,* p. 48.

7. Puyo, *Une vie pour la verité,* p. 48.

8. The style of ecclesiological expressions in the century before Vatican II is treated in "Situation ecclésiologique au moment de 'Ecclesiam suam' et passage a une église dans l'itineraire des hommes," Y. Congar, *Le Concile de Vatican II* (Paris: Beauchesne, 1984), pp. 8ff.

9. "Y. Congar, Peut-on definir l'Église?" *Sainte Église,* p. 38f.; "Dogme christologie et Écclesiologie," *Sainte Église,* p. 98; "'Lumen Gentium' No 7, 'L'Église, Corps mystique du Christ" vu au terme," *Le Concile de Vatican II,* p. 149.

10. "Y. Congar, Une conclusion théologique a l'Enquête sur les raisons actuelles de l'incroyance," *La Vie intellectuelle* 37 (1935): 247.

11. J. R. Geiselmann, *Johann Adam Möhler. Die Einheit der Kirche und die Wiedervereinigung der Konfessionen* (Vienna: Herder, 1940) and an earlier, lengthy essay, "J. A. Möhler und die Entwicklung seiner Kirchenbegriff," *Theologische Quartalschrift* 112 (1931): 1 – 91. Congar's review began: "The book of Geiselmann abounds in precise details and gives a context to particular elements." Cited in "Chronique: Années 1939 – 1946," in *Sainte Église,* p. 564. The notes in Y. Congar, *Tradition and Traditions* (New York: Macmillan, 1967) indicate the importance of Geiselmann's writings for Congar (for instance, 221–3); see also Congar's bibliography of German works in *L'Église de saint Augustin à l'époque moderne* (Paris: Cerf, 1970), p. 418, and in *Tradition and Traditions,* pp. 194ff. The reports titled "Chronique" in *Sainte Église* are taken from Congar's surveys of theological areas published in *La Vie intellectuelle, La Vie spirituelle, Bulletin Thomiste*, and *Revue des sciences philosophiques et théologiques*.

12. Congar, "La Pensée de Moehler et 'ecclésiologie orthodoxe,'" *Irénikon* 12 (1935): 321ff.

13. Henry Tristram, "J. A. Moehler et J. H. Newman. La pensée allemande et la renaissance catholique en Angleterre," *Revue des sciences philosophiques et théologiques* 27 (1938): 184ff.

14. Pierre Chaillet, "L'esprit du christianisme et du catholicisme," *Revue des sciences philosophiques et théologiques* 26 (1937): 483ff. and 713ff.

15. Chaillet, "La tradition vivante," *Revue des sciences philosophiques et théologiques* 27 (1938): 161ff. Chaillet had traveled in Germany before the war; after the French defeat, he was active in the resistance, organizing groups hiding Jewish children from deportation and founding the anti-Nazi clandestine journal *Témoignage Chrétien*. See Renée Bédarida, *Pierre Chaillet. Témoin de la Resistance Spirituele* (Paris: Fayard, 1977); (see W. D. Halls, *Politics, Society and Christianity in Vichy France* (Oxford: Berg, 1995), pp. 136ff., 213.

16. Pierre Chaillet, *L'Église est une. Hommage à Moehler* (Paris: Bloud et Gay, 1939); see too, Chaillet, "Centenaire de Moehler. L'amour et l'unité. Le mystère de l'église," *Revue apologetique* (May, 1938); Chaillet, "La signification oecumenique de l'oeuvre de Möhler," *Irénikon* (March/April, 1938), and Chaillet "Le principe mystique de l'Unité," in the commemorative volume.

17. Congar, *L'Église de saint Augustin*, p. 423.

18. Congar, *L'Église de saint Augustin*, p. 388; similarly, *Tradition and Traditions*, p. 191. Curiously, Congar also claimed that the spirit of Bossuet lived on in Möhler's view of the vitality and sanctity of the church despite the sins of bishops (*Vraie et fausse*, p. 89). Congar mistakenly locates Sailer in the Tübingen school (for instance, *Tradition and Traditions*, p. 193).

19. Congar, *Une Passion: L'Unité*, p. 47.

20. Congar, *Une Passion: L'Unité*, p. 47f.

21. See E. Fouilloux, "Frère Yves, Cardinal Congar, dominican. Itineraire d'un théologien," *Revue des sciences philosophiques et théologiques* 79 (1995): 387.

22. J. A. Möhler, *L'Unité dans l'Eglise ou le Principe du Catholicisme d'après l'esprit des Pères des trois premiers siècles de l'Eglise*, translation by A. de Lilienfeld and introduction by P. Chaillet [*Unam Sanctam* 2], (Paris: Cerf, 1938); Y. Congar "Chronique: Annee, 1938," *Sainte Eglise*, p. 509.

23. Congar, "Chronique: Année, 1938," *Sainte Église*, pp. 509f.

24. Congar, *L'Église de saint Augustin*, p. 420.

25. Congar, *A History of Theology* (Garden City: Doubleday, 1968), p. 183.

26. "Drey introduced this ideal of organic unity in the plan of God into theology....He sees the church in the framework of the plan of God as the manifestation of the kingdom of God, the organ of his revelation, an organism sustained by the Spirit... with an influence of Schelling." Congar, *L'Église de saint Augustin*, pp. 418f. Drey's *A Short Introduction to the Study of Theology* observed: "Particular remarks, well worthy of attention, on a more scientific understanding of Christianity and a more scientific treatment of theology are found in Schelling's *Lectures on the Method of Academic Studies*." J. S. Drey, *Brief Introduction to the Study of Theology*, translated with an introduction and annotation by Michael J. Himes (Notre Dame: University of Notre Dame Press, 1994), p. 39.

27. Friedrich Schelling, *On University Studies* (Athens: University of Ohio Press, 1996), p. 89.

28. Schelling, *On University Studies*, p. 90; Schelling usually exemplified the idea of the organic either in nature as the realization of the odyssey of the absolute or in the state. See A. Hollerbach, *Der Rechtsgedanke bei Schelling* (Frankfurt: Klostermann, 1957).

29. *L'Église de saint Augustin*, p. 420.

30. *Vrai et fausse*, p. 239. "Certain pages show the dialectical point of view which Möhler, abandoning Schelling, has taken from Hegel and according to which he has constructed *Die Einheit*." "Chronique: Annees 1939 – 1946," *Sainte Église*, p. 564. "Möhler separated himself significantly from Schelling, whom his master Drey follows, for Hegel, and so had been able to avoid making the development of external oppositions in the church depend upon heresies." *Vrai et fausse*, p. 239.

31. Congar, *A History of Theology*, p. 184.

32. Congar, "Peut-on definir l'Eglise," *Sainte Église*, p. 38.

33. In Cajetan there is an anticipation of the ecclesiology of communion and of Möhler. Cajetan lays the foundation for the paths to the admirable theology of Catholic communion in J. A. Möhler. "Catholicité," *Sainte Église*, p. 161. Cajetan wrote: "The faithful, because they are moved by the Holy Spirit to the works of their spiritual life..., act as parts of one totality....Each faithful believes him to be a member of the church, and as a member of the church believes, hopes, ministers the sacraments, receives, teaches, learns, etc, and on behalf of the church does these things as a part of the whole to whom they [the activities] all belong." *Commentaria Cardinalis Caietani* on *Summa Theologiae* II–II, 39, 1 in Santi Thomae Aquinatis, *Opera Omnia*, Leonis XIII, P. M., edita, vol. 8 (Rome: Typographia Polyglotta, 1895), p. 307.

34. Congar, *Vraie et fausse*, p. 9.

35. J. P. Jossua, *Yves Congar* (Chicago: The Priory Press, 1968), p. 29. The Holy Office wrote the translation of Möhler should not appear, but diplomatic protests from the French embassy to the Vatican gained its publication; Bédarida, *Pierre Chaillet*, pp. 69ff.

36. Puyo, p. 100. See F. Leprieur, *Quand Rome condamne* (Paris: Cerf, 1989); T. O'Meara, "Raid on the Dominicans." The Repression of 1954," *America* 170 (1994): 8ff.

37. Y. Congar, "Sur l'évolution et l'interprétation de la pensée de Moehler," *Revue des sciences philosophiques et théologiques* 27 (1938): 129ff.

38. Y. Congar, "L'esprit des Pères d'après Moehler," *Vie Spirituelle, Supplément* (1938): 3.

39. Ibid., p. 3.

40. Ibid., p. 15f.

41. Ibid., p. 15f.

42. "La signification oecuménique de l'oeuvre de Moehler," *Irénikon* 15 (1938): 116.

43. Ibid., p. 129.

44. Congar, "'Lumen Gentium' No 7,' L'Église, Corps mystique du Christ, vu au terme de huit siècles d'histoire de la théologie du Corps mystique," *Le Concile de Vatican II*, pp. 148f. Congar in the 1970s looked back: "[Möhler's] vision was synthetic, vital, communitarian: it is in communion with other people that one reaches a culture whether that be a people or the church....He knew very well Irenaeus, Cyprian, Origen. He had empowered them to give a vision of a church as a spiritual organism animated by the Holy Spirit. He enriched this in 1832 in the *Symbolik* with a vision more christological." J. Puyo, *Une vie pour la verité*, p. 48.

45. *L'Église de saint Augustin*, p. 382f. The quote from Möhler is found in *Theologische Quartalschrift* 4 (1823): 497.

46. Congar, *L'Église de saint Augustin*, p. 421. Congar saw some affinity between Möhler's theology and eastern Orthodoxy; the influence of certain early Greek theologians on both is one reason, but there is also the common source of Schelling's thinking which was known in Russia after 1830. Congar wrote: "One has more than once linked the Catholic Möhler (at least the author of *Die Einheit*) with the orthodox and slavophile Khomiakov. In both an ecclesiology is sketched which is constructed with precision out of elements which the Counter-Reformation left in the shadows: pneumatological element and anthropological element, interior action of the Holy Spirit and the active part of the body of the faithful." "Chronique: Années 1939–1946," *Sainte Église*, p. 564; *Divided Christendom* (London, 1939) devoted pages to slavophile ecclesiology (208ff.); see S. Tyszkiewicz, "La théologie moehlerienne de l'Unité et les théologiens pravoslaves," in Chaillet, ed., *L'Église est une*, pp. 270ff.; S. Bolshakoff, *The Doctrine of the Unity of the Church in the Works of Khomyakov and Möhler* (London: The Society for Promoting Christian Knowledge, 1946); W. Setschkaroff, *Schellings Einfluss in der russischen Literatur der 20er und 30er Jahre des XIX Jh.* (Leipzig: Harrasowtiz, 1939; 1968); L. Müller, *Schellings Einfluss in Russland* (Stuttgart: Schmidt, 1949).

47. Congar, *L'Eglise de saint Augustin*, pp. 419f.

48. Congar, *L'Église de saint Augustin*, pp. 420ff.

49. Congar lists (*Tradition and Traditions*, p. 196) an essay by Gustav Voss, "Johann Adam Möhler and the Development of Dogma," *Theological Studies* 4 (1943): 420ff. It may be the only American essay on Möhler prior to Vatican II. The author, a professor at St. Mary's College in Kansas, was capable of finding and reading German sources. He illustrates the theological mentality of the time which sought for a timeless harmony between all sources dominated by the papal magisterium. "...His conception of the Church as an organic whole and a living community in which all the members have their specific functions and contribute to the development of the whole. This led him to understate somewhat the prominence we must necessarily concede to the *magisterium*. In thus judging him, however we must not forget that he lived at a time when Febronianism was still in the air, and furthermore, that he died years prior to the Vatican Council" (442f.). An interesting contrast with Congar's discovery of originality and inspiration is: "Möhler cannot claim any new discoveries" (443).

50. Congar, *A History of Theology*, p. 197.

51. Ibid., p. 194.

52. Congar citing *Die Einheit* (par. 3) in *Tradition and Traditions*, p. 194.

53. Congar, *Tradition and Traditions,* p.189.

54. Ibid., p. 339.

55. Ibid., p. 193.

56. Ibid., pp. 193f.

57. Ibid., p. 194.

58. Ibid., p. 195f.; see *Vraie et fausse* 249.

59. Congar, *Tradition and Traditions*, p. 340.

60. Ibid., p. 344.

61. Ibid., p. 324.

62. Ibid., p. 193f.

63. Ibid., p. 312. "Certain presentations of the idea of a 'continued Incarnation' are problematic" (312). Drawing on Geiselmann, Congar discussed J. Ev. Kuhn; he noted that Scheeben too, perhaps influenced by Kuhn, gave the entire church and not just the hierarchy a role in handing on tradition [*Tradition and Traditions*, p. 213]. In a criticism of the Tübingen school Congar speaks of "a certain exclusivism to the detriment of the hierarchical magisterium." *Tradition and Traditions*, p. 324.

64. Congar, "Situation au moment," p. 27. See Congar's interesting evaluation of Charles Journet's ecclesiology, which, the Dominican says, also has ties to Möhler; despite its many contributions it seems to lack a sense of history, eschatology, and an attention to the concrete externals of the church. "Chronique: Années 1939–1946," *Sainte Église*, pp. 567ff. and 659ff.

65. "Johann Adam Möhler, 1796–1837," *Theologische Quartalschrift* 150 (1970): 51.

66. Congar, "Regard sur le Concile Vatican II (à l'occasion du 20e anniversaire)," *Le Concile Vatican II*, p. 68.

67. Jossua, "Yves Congar," p. 9.

68. Congar, *Une passion. L'unité*, p. 109; Congar wrote: "I do not believe that the present crisis in the church is the result of Vatican II.... The realities that preoccupy us today were already present or beginning to appear in the 1950s and even in the 1930s." Congar, "A Last Look at the Church," in Stacpoole, *Vatican II Revisited by Those Who Were There* (Minneapolis: Winston, 1986), p. 351.

69. Private letter of 12. 9. 1970. "...The dominant values in our way of looking at the Church were changed by the Council. Vatican II was intentionally in continuity with the previous councils of the church and with tradition. Paul VI insisted on its continuity...." "Moving towards a Pilgrim Church," in A. Stacpoole, *Vatican II Revisited*, p. 129.

70. Puyo, *Une vie pour la verité*, p. 149.

71. *L'Église*, p. 423; see "La Signification oecuménique,. . ." pp. 121ff.

72. "Not a hierarchiology" *Jalons pour une théologie du laicat* (Paris: Cerf, 1953), p. 68f.; "Not a hierarchology," Congar, *Ministères et communion ecclésiale* (Paris: Cerf, 1971), p. 10. "The term, 'hierarchology' which I introduced in 1947 has since then been taken up a little widely." Congar, "Situation au moment," p. 13. Congar describes at some length his views on another theology of the Body of Christ, *Mystici Corporis* of Pius XII. He does not relate it to Möhler. Appreciative of its efforts to offer some new directions, the letter remains too ordered to the papacy and hierarchy and not to the full body of Christ, unrelated to Pauline exegesis, too captive to illustrating the members of the body in terms of religious life and sacraments (Congar, *L'Église de saint Augustin*, pp. 470ff.).

73. Peter Hünermann's words about the origins of the Tübingen school raise the theme of the future, for Schelling in the first lecture on university studies spoke of the birth of a new world. "We need to ask how these theologians who all pondered and dealt with German idealism in a basic way, heard the message of revelation in a new way and empowered this messages to become a fundamental way of thinking." "Der Reflex des deutschen Idealismus in der Theologie der katholischen Tübinger Schule," *Philosophisches Jahrbuch* 73 (1965/66): 51.

74. "Bellarmine (*Ecclesia est coetus hominum ita visibilis et palpabilis...*) is dominated by the need to be able to designate the church of Christ as well as to be able to say who is and who is not a member of the church.... In short, he deliberately pictures the church, even under its title of the Body of Christ, from the perspective of external elements, from the visible and externally verifiable. He goes very far in this sense. In the theology of the Counter-Reformation, however, the doctrine of the mystical body is not absent but it perdures in insisting on external elements and the social nature of the church.... The two currents run side by side." "'Lumen Gentium' No. 7, L'Eglise, Corps mystique du Christ," pp. 147ff.

75. Congar, *Fifty Years of Catholic Theology: Conversations with Yves Congar*, B. Lauret, ed. (Philadelphia: Fortress, 1988), pp. 3f.; see Congar, "Les théologiens, Vatican II et la Théologie," *Le Concile de Vatican II*, p. 81.

76. Congar, *L'Église de saint Augustin*, p. 368.

77. *Fifty Years of Catholic Theology: Conversations with Yves Congar,* B. Lauret, ed., p. 8; see "Les implications christologiques et pneumatologiques de l'ecclésiologie de Vatican II," *Le Council de Vatican II*, pp.171ff.

78. Congar, *Une Passion: L'unité*, p. 112.

79. "The Life of the Church and Awareness of its Catholicity," *The Mystery of the Church* (Baltimore: Helicon, 1965 [2nd edition]), p. 100. Congar in the "Avertissement" to the second edition in French noted that the two articles on Möhler originally from 1938 and published in the first edition as appendices have been omitted, "not having the same contemporary interest as they had in 1940." *Esquisses du mystère de l'église* [*Unam Sanctam* 8],(Paris: Cerf, 1953), p. 10.

80. Congar, "Les implications christologiques," *Le Concile de Vatican II*, p. 176. Congar cited Paul VI speaking in 1973: "The Christology and especially the ecclesiology of the Second Vatican Council should be followed by a new study and a new cult of the Holy Spirit, as an indispensable complement of the conciliar teaching." Paul VI, June 6, 1973 cited in Y. Congar, *I Believe in the Holy Spirit* 1 (New York: Seabury, 1983), p.172.

81. Congar, *Le Concile au jour le jour,* Session IV (Paris, 1966), p. 61; see *Tradition and Traditions*, pp. 329ff.

82. *Tradition and Traditions*, p. 321. "In leaving the Middle Ages and the Counter-Reformation we are leaving a legalism which has surrounded our ways of thinking since the end of the twelfth century. The consciousness of the church as it unfolds from the Council gives a primacy to the ontology of grace over the structures of law and authority which are in their place only as ministers at the service of a supernatural reality which is basically sacramental." "L'Avenir de l'église" (1964), *Écrits Reformateurs* (Paris: Cerf, 1995), p. 367.

83. In Congar's smaller version of *Tradition et Traditions* (Paris: Fayard, 1963), the theologian treats liturgy but mainly as teaching; on biblical ministries centered in teaching, see *Tradition and Traditions*, pp. 329ff.

84. Paul VI urged local churches to set up formally traditional ministries in parishes (*Ministeria quaedam*) and the new code of canon law speaks of them as an "ecclesiastical office." [CIC, canon 145.]

85. The previous ecclesiology was found in manuals like a text by Gerard Paris, widely used in the *studia* of the Dominican Order: the *Tractatus de ecclesia Christi ad mentem S. Thomae Aquinatis* (Malta: Muscat, 1949) presented the four causes of the church in Aristotelian language: the formal cause was the bishops; the efficient cause was Jesus, the Holy Spirit, and bishops; the final cause was heaven; the material cause, like clay for a statue, was everyone who was not a bishop, provincial, or pastor.

86. *Lay People in the Church*, p. xvi.

87. Congar, "My Path-Findings," p. 169.

88. Congar, "My Path-Findings," p. 181. He spoke of the basic equality of the baptised and of a diversity of services and offices which involves some inequality; at times he put "laity" in quotation marks. "Vision de l'église comme peuple de Dieu, " *Le Concile de Vatican II*, p. 114.

89. Congar, "My Path-Findings," p. 176.

90. Congar, "My Path-Findings," p. 178.

11

The Authority of the Church and the Problematic Nature of Modern Subjectivity in Johann Adam Möhler's *Symbolik*

— ANTON VAN HARSKAMP —

Why should we read a theological work from the past, in particular Johann Adam Möhler's *Symbolik*?[1] One of the seemingly plausible answers can be extracted from the writings of Y. M.-J. Congar, one of the modern catholic theologians who kindled new interest for Möhler from the 1930's through the 1950's in Europe. According to him, Möhler's work is of importance today for two reasons. In the first place, because Möhler opened a perspective in which the church was seen in a truly theological way—as an institution which ultimately is derived from a divine source, the Incarnation. The formation of the church is seen as the consequence of the mission of the Holy Spirit in which life is elevated to God and simultaneously humanized. In the second place, Möhler is extremely significant because of his supposed ecumenical intentions. Congar was convinced that the renewal of Catholic theology, at which he was aiming in his attempts to overcome the neoscholastic straitjacket of theology, was anticipated by Möhler, who was thought to demonstrate a real confrontation with Protestantism.[2] This latter conviction has become an ongoing theme in the recent interpretations of *Symbolik*.[3]

So the dominant answer among Catholic theologians to the opening question, is: Möhler must be read because of the impulses he gave to the renewal of ecclesiology and ecumenical theology. I shall try to make the case that as far as the actual significance of Möhler's *Symbolik* is concerned, it is time to drop this dominant view. My thesis is that the significance today of the book is not Möhler's majestic anticipation of the sacramental meaning of the church nor Möhler's views on Protestantism and on its differences with Catholicism. The significance of *Symbolik* for us, has to be located in Möhler's intuitive apprehensions of the aporias of modern subjectivity. These intuitive apprehensions lie underneath Möhler's ecclesiology and his theological anthropology, which is the basis of his rebuttal of Protestantism.

This essay aims at a reconstruction of these intuitions. To do so, I must mention the central theological issues in Möhler's development so that we may gain a tentative feeling for the particular catholic nature of his interest in the exposition of confessional differences. Then I must point to the sociopolitical and church-political context, in which *Symbolik* was published. Although written by an intentionally irenic and apolitical author, this book was composed to produce effects on a church-political and cultural level. This will help us to understand that Möhler, as Walter Kasper rightly observes, has to be considered as "an a-political church politician"[4] Then I shall elaborate Möhler's theological contribution to see the very demanding foundational function that Möhler is ascribing to the Roman Catholic Church.

Development

First we must touch on the nerve center of his first book, that masterpiece of catholic-romantic theological thinking, *Die Einheit in der Kirche*.[5] To get a proper idea of this book it is important to read the preface carefully. Möhler explains that the treatise begins, not with the center of the Christian faith, Jesus Christ, but with the Holy Spirit. Möhler wants to focus on the process of becoming a Christian. Therefore, he feels himself obliged to start with what comes first in time for the individual believer (cf. E., 3). So the point of issue for Möhler is the existential process of becoming a Christian. But in elaborating this point Möhler does not confine himself to the purely individual dimensions of this existential process. The overall structure of the book is determined by his view of the dynamism of the Holy Spirit. Using the range of patristic thought, Möhler indicates in a romantic-organological way of thinking how the mystical and invisible life of the Church as guided by the Holy Spirit is proceeding outward into the external formations of the Church. The book is, as F. Vigener once remarked, not only a learned book but above all a confession of faith[6] that the existential process of becoming a Christian first and foremost requires the identification of the individual consciousness with the consciousness of the whole church, above all through partaking in the reciprocal love of the faithful by the intuitive immediate vision ("unmittelbare Anschauung," cf. E., 12, 21). Essentially this means that the individual who considers himself an enlightened person, rationally striving for moral autonomy, discovers that true autonomy and real human development are only attainable by growing into the spiritual community of the church. In view of the dynamism of the Holy Spirit, we can understand that this growing into the spiritual community simultaneously implicates the subordination of the individual believer to the external and institutional forms of the actually existing Catholic Church (cf. E., 32, 98, 147).

All interpreters of Möhler, however, note the fact that he himself indicated that although *Einheit* had touched on several burning theological problems, it did not address them all in a satisfactory way. Looking forward to *Symbolik,* Two of those problems emerge. The first concerns the more exact determination of the relation between the external and visible dimensions of the church as well as her internal and invisible dimensions. For a long time the dominant view on *Einheit* was that the book stressed only the organological unfolding of the internal aspect of the church into the external aspect. The book was supposed to offer a one-way orientation. But this view is not correct. Möhler's organological way of thinking actually reveals something like a dialectical approach. The external dimensions of the church as caused by the inner dimensions, which in their turn are guided by the Holy Spirit, are also working causes themselves. There is a kind of interaction between the internal and the external dimensions (cf. E., 101).[7] Nevertheless, one must admit not

only that Möhler is not clear in elaborating the way, in which romantic organological thinking is mediated with idealist dialectical thinking, but also that his main
interest in *Einheit* is the way in which the individual is guided by the mystical
dimensions of the church. Basically the direction of his theological thinking in the
book was to search into the faith and acquaint the believer with the great all-
pervading mystical unity of the church. In *Symbolik*, Möhler is no longer concerned with the question *how to become* a Christian; he now deals with the question concerning which theological conditions are necessary so that one can *be* and
stay a Christian. Seen from that perspective, at first sight it seems as if he is arguing
in a somewhat more superficial way. For now he is apparently *not* interested in the
inner and mystical dimensions of the church. But this impression of superficiality
is false. Möhler simply presupposes that the church, in its visible dimensions,
constitutes the necessary habitat, in which the believer lives in accordance with
Christian truth. The question then becomes in what way we have to understand the
workings of the visible dimensions of the church. In other words, Möhler is looking
for the theological-transcendental status of the external dimensions. According to
him, these dimensions cannot be seen as purely historical and contingent expressions of the mystical. If that were the case, we would have to conclude that the
content of our belief is contingent too and that our faith is only a façade, which
never touches the inner dimensions of our spiritual life.

Every reader of Möhler's *Symbolik* knows that what is at stake here is the
meaning of the Incarnation. For Möhler the Incarnation not only comprises the
articulation of the ultimate Christian mystery, but also is the speculative means by
which one approaches the ways in which faith relates to the Church. In a peculiar
sense of the word Möhler is a theological "materialist," for the Incarnation tells him
that the material *Gestalt* of Jesus Christ provides an analogy for the material *Gestalt*
of the church which means that the visible dimensions of the church not only have
a human-institutional impact, but also have a theological and anthropological impact. Ultimately this leads him to phrase the relation between the invisible and
visible dimensions of the church in terms of the Chalcedonian formula. (cf. Sy I, 143,
152, 401).[8]

This mystical and at the same time "materialist" solution brings us to the
second problem, with which Möhler still has to deal, i.e., the fact of different confessions. Already in *Einheit* this problem definitely plays a background role. That is
not surprising because the work was written to understand the way the individual
is related to the mystery of the unity of the church. But the view of the relation
between Catholicism and other religious communites is not entirely clear in all
aspects. When, for example, Möhler discusses the question of the function of
heresy (E., 461), he sometimes seems to suggest that heresy, although it has no
positive being in itself, nevertheless has a necessary function, as "negative dialectics," analogous to the way in which the consciousness of evil is a necessary
condition for the coming into existence of the consciousness of what is ultimately
good (E., 104). At other points, however, he seems to correct this view, stating that
heresy does not fulfill a necessary function at all, and that everything depends on
the freedom of the church to contrast true faith with the complete negativity of

heresy (E., 157). This latter conviction will govern the central views in *Symbolik*. But apart from this evident necessity of clarifying one's own position over against Protestantism (its function for Catholicism), it is obvious that if a theologian like Möhler addresses the mystery of the unity of the Catholic Church, precisely in order to penetrate the deeper meanings of the external dimensions of the church, he must take account of the existence and the meaning of Protestantism as comprising the most significant religious parties outside the actually existing Catholic Church. The "logic" of his thinking pushes him to the confessional problematic.[9] And it is important to realize that from the beginning, i.e., from *Einheit,* the underlying, but nevertheless decisive question, is what meaning one should give to Protestantism in its function for Catholicism. The question is in what way the existence of Protestantism can be used to give Catholics a more intensive understanding of the essence of the Catholic Church. Thus, in *Symbolik* Möhler was not interested in Protestantism in itself but in its function for Catholicism.

Context

Even a superficial knowledge of the social and church-political context of the 1830's in the southwestern part of the German *Länder* makes understandable why Möhler's views on the problem of the confessions evoked so much interest among the educated Catholics of his time, and why *Symbolik* fitted so neatly into the religious climate of those days. It is not unusual for theologians to look upon the nineteenth century as "the century of the church." Indeed, never in the history of Christianity did the church declare with greater emphasis that its essence, its mission, its form, and its discipline were of utmost importance. One could even imagine that one best served God and Christ by representing the greatness and the authority of the church. Such an interpretation was given by Emanuel Hirsch on Protestant theology in the nineteenth century.[10] But it also fits well the Catholic way of thinking, and in particular Möhler's theology.

It is very important to realize that this rather over-strained theological concentration on the church has to be interpreted from a macro-sociological view as a reactive attempt to deal with the overall trend toward the diminishing relevance of religion for social, cultural and moral life. According to many sociologists of religion, in particular F.-X. Kaufmann, the self-generation of "christendom" as church, which involved the development of doctrinal ecclesiology and the institutional extension of the organization, is the distinctive answer of the main branches of the Christian confessions to the differentiation of society.[11] Such an assertion calls for some clarification.[12]

Already in the eighteenth century there existed a trend toward distinguishing religion and church on the one side from the state and public life, including public morality, on the other. After the wars of religion the princely rulers and their civil bureaucracies were determined to curtail the secular power of the religions. Secular power wished to employ religion and the churches only in so far as they were subservient to the absolutist state. Parallel to this politically instigated move toward differentiation was a form of moral secularization. The idea of tolerance in the

Aufklärung, for instance, not only functioned as a public call for self-restriction of the formerly agressive claims of the mainline religions, but also promoted the distancing of the claim that religious truth should determine life in all aspects. The temporary climax of this trend was the political and constitutional secularization in the first decade of the century, symbolically represented by the *Reichdeputationshauptschluß* of 1803, which ensured that the churches now definitely were a minor factor in the shaping of society, not only with respect to political society and to legal power but also with respect to civil society. Particularly in the first three decades of the century the church was almost completely deprived of institutional instruments for shaping political and public life.

Still more significant for our understanding of the context was that the churches were now situated on one sociocultural field. Deprived of their political power and, as far as the Catholic Church was concerned, seriously stripped of financial support and economic wealth, the churches no longer held a monopoly on the public arena; they simply became competitive institutions in the private field. Although each of the religious parties continued to claim that only by means of its own church was religious truth accessible, the Christian churches found themselves confronted with a common task. For they all now had a common relationship to state and to society and its individual members. This structural state of affairs potentially created a situation in which the churches felt themselves pushed to display and expand their ideology (=theology) and their institutional apparatus precisely over against one another. In other words, the confessions became "antagonistic partners." In this climate, Möhler's *Symbolik* fits very well.

As far as the specific situation of the Catholic Church is concerned, another factor must be added. Although the churches were granted equal rights in the strictly legal sense of the word, the Catholic part of the population did not feel equal and emancipated at all. Particularly in Württemberg there was the oft-mentioned *Überfremdungsangst* of the Catholic population, in part due to the actual social-economic and political hegemony of Protestants. And of course, there was the *Staatskirchentum*, the system of mechanisms by which the semi-absolutist bureaucracies were trying to mold the Catholic population into a disciplined religion, loyal to the local state. And we also have to consider here that the state-apparatuses in almost all of the German *Länder* actually were controlled by Protestants of a liberal mind-set.

In this situation *Symbolik* could function not only as a theological work, but also as a church-political work. It functioned as a church-political work because in the debate on whether the church should be free from the repression of the state or free from Rome, the position of the Catholic *Aufklärung*, it overtly took the side of the first position.[13] It functioned also as a political work because the book answered the need of the Catholic population for public cultural self-confidence. The book reassured its readers in many ways that Catholicism is the real basis for humanity and civilization, whereas Protestantism, being basically subjective, had inflated itself into the lust for human power, even into self-deification or, more probably, into self-destruction (cf. Sy I, 26f.). We may interpret these convictions as a church-political message. And we are entitled to assume that although Möhler himself did not have explicit church-political intentions, he nevertheless must have been aware of the latent functions of his work. If we read, for example, his letters to Döllinger from April, 1830, just before he started his lectures on *Symbolik*, the sentence that "our episcopate is a crippled institution" would stand out. He is pointing to Bishop von Keller who, according to Möhler and many other austere ultramontanists of that time, did not resist sufficiently the pressure of the *Landesherrliche Verordnung* of the Protestant bureaucracy. "We can do no more than to equip our young theologians with a properly ecclesiastical mind ...."[14] Möhler in his intellectual journey was not seeking a deeper understanding of Protestantism, but rather aimed at strengthening Catholicism.

We must add a few more comments regarding Möhler's *Symbolik* in its context. Differentiation characterizes modernity. Already in Möhler's day, however, it took shape in more radical forms than that between state and church or between political and clerical interests. There also were signs of differentiation between ecclesiastical and nonecclesiastical forms of religiosity. Within the complex and divided world of the Catholic *Aufklärung* there was a trend toward a strong relativization of dogma, doctrine, and ecclesiastical institutions in view of an assumed universal religiosity. Often the nexus of religious sentiments centered around an inner experience of Jesus Christ or around the moral following of Jesus' way of life. Often closely connected with this kind of religiosity were interconfessional theory and praxis.[15] By contrast, it is quite clear that Möhler's sharp-edged formulation of doctrinal differences allows neither a dialectical mediation of the confessions into a higher unity nor a reduction of the confessions to some kind of universal or natural religion. (R. Rieger has elaborated this view impressively; and we will notice some manifestations of it below).[16] *Symbolik* may be regarded as an austere rebuttal of both views.

Even more revealing for our understanding of the function of *Symbolik* in its context is the fact that the "Secularization" of 1803 also signalled the trend that religious truth would have less and less impact on moral life and ethical reflection within the national community. In other words, differentation also had consequences for the relation between religion and morality. At the same time this form of differentiation was felt as a major problem. And if *Symbolik* is read with this concern about the basis of individual and collective morality in mind, we will be struck by the fierceness with which Möhler combats this form of differentiation.

The structure of the central dogmatic theological argument, which he develops against Protestantism can reveal his concern and anxiety. I shall reconstruct his argument on the level of substantial dogmatics. Möhler is convinced that the all-pervading difference (*Urdifferenz*) between Catholicism and Protestantism is located on the level of theological anthropology. Although he is well aware of the fact that Lutheranism theologically focuses on the doctrine of justification, he argues that the false view of the Reformers is due to the false representation of the state of humanity before the fall. So Möhler himself founds his rebuttal of Protestantism and his own presentation of anthropology on what we may call his view of the original condition. If a theologian advances claims about a primitive condition even if he considers it as an historical event, as Möhler explicitly does, we may be fairly sure that these claims function as the underpinning and legitimizing of a pressing need.[17]

The structure of Möhler's argument here is that in all three doctrines concerning primitive revelation (original justice, fall and original sin, justification) Protestantism does not grasp the right relationship between God and humanity. In particular, with regard to original righteousness Protestantism does not realize that Adam's complete justification before God is absolutely impossible for unaided human nature. This relationship must be based on a divine gift, while Protestantism, according to Möhler, considers original righteousness to be an element of human nature (Sy I, 64f.). The Protestant view brings forward consequences that are in the final analysis theologically impossible. For Protestants either presuppose the full human rightousness before God, which is impossible because this view actually would deny human freedom of choice, and so the possibility of the fall. Ultimately such a view would lead to the conviction that God himself is the original creator of evil. Or they see only the complete sinfulness of humanity, which is why they are always on the verge of the abyss of all-pervading pessimism (cf. Sy I, 75, 107, 110, 113, 282f., 287, 292, 296ff.; Sy II, 461, 514f.). Another consequence is that justification, which for Möhler means the restoration of original righteousness through Jesus Christ (Sy I, 57, 167) cannot ever really come into contact with the inner life of the human person. So justification ends up always being an external mechanism (Sy I, 175ff.). But the human being, according to Möhler, is a fully isolated creature in the Protestant view and cannot endure this ultimate lack of inner connection with God's grace and with his church (Sy I, 470; Sy II, 154f.), which can seduce humans either into usurping the place of Christ (Sy I, 26f.) or into indulging an unwarranted glorification of humanity's own potential (Sy I, 468f.). This danger is observed by Möhler in modern Protestantism represented by Friedrich Schleiermacher and above all by Möhler's harshest opponent, F.C. Baur (cf. Sy I, 60f., 297ff., N.U. 121ff.).

The point at stake in this kind of argument appears when we realize that Möhler reproaches Protestantism, because it promotes even unintentionally moral antinomism and undermines the sacred moral order (Sy I, 279–288; cf. 131f., 178ff, N.U. 218ff.). Ultimately Protestantism separates moral life from religion, and ethical thinking from God's actual grace. A closer analysis of *Symbolik* reveals that Möhler, in order to clarify his own position, uses two series of theological propositions, which cannot actually be united by logic. The first series of propositions aims at the conclusion that the human person is a deficient creature, a morally crippled being, who from the beginning relies on structures which mediate God's supernatural grace (i.e., the church). In the second series of propositions Möhler emphasizes that humanity nevertheless bears responsibility and culpability for its deeds; the human being is basically a creature who deserves a verdict of "guilty" (cf. N.U. 68f., 131f., 175ff.).

Obviously Möhler is addressing a classical theological problem. However, it is useful to realize that seen from the church-political context, Möhler also serves the interests of the Catholic Church of his day. For as a matter of fact, he is constantly suggesting that participation in this church is absolutely necessary for genuine moral praxis and ethical reflection. In this respect we may interpret *Symbolik* as a kind of preparation for the political Catholicism that came to the fore after 1848. The implicit message of *Symbolik* is that human beings should feel themselves driven to the moral discipline of the church. Only by subordination to its guidance for example can people learn real humility (Sy I, 226, 240). *Symbolik* is not to be read as an attempt to deal with Protestantism itself, but as a deeper understanding of Catholicism, i.e., as a major force in criticism of the moral situation of Möhler's time.

Theology

A short elaboration of the main features of *Symbolik* will confirm this intention. The subtitle of the book is "Exposition of the Doctrinal Differences between Catholics and Protestants, as Evidenced by their Symbolic Writings." This exposition is not carried out from a position external to both confessions. Rather according to Möhler, it is essential that the Catholic "symbolist" be personally involved in Catholicism, i.e., intellectually, practically, and religiously. This living, personal outlook is precisely what enables him to unify the bare facts into a whole.[18] We may even say that Möhler, as far as his view on religious truth is concerned, anticipates the concept of *Leben*, which means in this respect that truth is only accessible for those who live within the circle of the church.[19] The outline of this circle is measured and determined by the doctrinal authority of the church. This authority functions as a guidance for the way in which the individual believer should try to ascertain the doctrinal content of his faith. The consequence of this concept of religious truth for Möhler is that the individual believer alone cannot search for truth. The individual does not possess normative autonomy and independence. The believer is already living out God's grace mediated by the church, which means that at best he only can penetrate deeper into the given truth. This man of faith finds himself confronted with the ecclesiastical demand to purify the church from the erring spirit and to exclude false doctrine.

Now we can understand why Möhler approaches Protestantism from a heresiological perspective. Being more radical here than in *Einheit*, he actually considers Protestantism not as an oppositional phenomenon, that is to say not as a *Gegensatz*, an antithesis, but exclusively as a shrill dissonant, a reckless and chaotic contradiction directed at denying Catholicism itself, a *Widerspruch*, although Möhler does not use the word *Widerspruch* in his *Symbolik*. With *Gegensätze* there is some common ground between the opponents; that is simply not the case when there is a *Widerspruch*. There are no opponents then, only enemies.

The religious ground for the plain contradiction which, according to Möhler, Protestantism plainly is, would be the incapacity to acknowledge the principle of the Incarnation. If we look closely at Möhler's designations on this point, we will notice that he does not in the first place address the way in which Protestantism supposedly misunderstands the theological content of this dogma. That is to say, he does not point explicitly at false Protestant concepts in the field of substantial christology. Instead, Möhler is above all interested in the relevance of the Incarnation to understand how real faith comes into existence and endures. He constantly urges the necessity of the ultimate condition for a faith in which one's inner life is really transformed: the subordination of the believer to the external authority of the church. Faith can only be real when it is based on an authority which comes from outside and which itself is founded on the divine (Sy I, 395–403).

Möhler acknowledges that Protestantism arose in the struggle against undeniable wrongs and errors in the church and admits that individual Protestants were deeply devout, although muddled. Simultaneously, he wants to understand Protestants better than they understand themselves, i.e., as ensnared in actual self-destruction.[20] This impacts on how *Symbolik* is to be understood. Möhler had little interest in the confessions in their own rights. As a romantic-idealist thinker, he was quite convinced of the impossibility of absolute, static countertheses. But a comparison with something that is basically nothing, a mere negation, is impossible, for life cannot be compared with death. The conclusion can only be that Möhler was not really concerned with Protestantism but with Catholic self-assertion.

Readers of *Symbolik* will not fail to notice that what is at stake is the principle of the movement to isolation, *Vereinzelung*. According to Möhler, this is the principle of modernity—a judgment which was and still is not unusual. In his *Grundlinien der Philosophie des Rechts,* Hegel characterized the modern period by saying that it generally recognizes freedom, the property of the mind that it is in-itself-for-itself. For this relation of the individual to self, Hegel mentions some implications: individualism i.e., the endlessly specific singularity; the right to criticism, whereby that which is recognized by all should appear warranted to the individual as well; and also the autonomy of subjective moral behavior.[21]

It seems safe to say that Möhler feared this modern configuration of subjectivity. He never tired of insisting that freedom does not mean that the human, hence finite, mind is in-itself-for-itself. In his view, a person in isolated singularity is not in a position to discover his own normative base. The isolated Christian, seeking to determine this foundation, would be lost either in an increasingly alienating past or in the emptiness of a subjectivity ultimately oriented to itself, which would seem to indicate the ultimate reason why Protestantism simply is "an individuality exalted into generality" and why it basically does not know a real church (Sy I, 26f.). Möhler regards this as "heathenish doubt," and its consequences fill him with fear, uncertainty and "indefiniteness of the mind, *Unbestimmtheit des Geistes* (Sy I, 397, cf. 399, 354, 487ff., 495).

Möhler's constant attention to finding the all-pervading difference between the denominations, together with his attempt to understand Protestants better than they do in their own self-understanding, also leads him automatically to look upon actually existing Protestantism as nothing more than a contingent historical *Gestalt* of the heretical principle of isolation. He notes that Protestantism moves toward either the dualist worldview of the gnostics or the worldview of pantheistic idealism (Sy I, 292ff.). As he sees it, the modern idealistic philosophical and theological systems, too, are but a consistent continuation of Reformation principles (Sy I, 302). But if we consider that *Symbolik* as a kind of Catholic self-assertion, a shield and fence against the negative principle, we may suspect that Catholicism *itself* is touched by the principle of isolation. After all, one shuts out precisely what internally threatens one's own existence. To be sure, the text of *Symbolik* does not directly address internal Catholic heretical phenomena. But, I think that its readers would naturally assume that Möhler also had in mind the Catholic *Aufklärung*, the opposition within Catholicism as well as other theological projects moving in the direction of modern philosophy. The context renders this expectation plausible, as does Möhler's work as active adversary of the Catholic *Aufklärung*. In 1828 he had published an extensive polemic, *Elucidation of the Memorandum regarding Abolition of the Celibacy for the Catholic Clergy*, in which the rebuttal of subjectivist isolation is a cornerstone of his argument.[22]

In addition to the theological significance of the church, i.e., the status of ecclesiology, Möhler was primarily concerned with the problem of modern subjectivity. Already the *Pragmatische Blicke*, a text dating from 1824 and edited by Reinhold Rieger, but not published by Möhler himself, would show that Möhler in his actual polemic against Protestants primarily addresses such themes as the status of the Bible, historical biblical research, and the immediacy of the individual Christian to God. In short, these are the themes that touch the core of the access of the isolated believer to divine truth.[23] When we recall that in *Symbolik* Möhler puts extraordinary emphasis on the requirement that the individual should first of all conform to the external authority of the church because this first step in the way of faith is indispensable to inner vital religiosity (Sy I, 482 ff.),[24] then we can say, that not only in *Symbolik*, too, the question of the access of the individual believer to Christian truth is the hidden core, but also that ecclesiology provides the perspective for Möhler's Christian anthropology, i.e., for his answer to the question as to whether the individual shaped by modernity can approach Jesus Christ at all. Unfortunately, this is not without a complication, for it seems that in his *Symbolik* Möhler goes out of his way to present the visible and authoritative *Gestalt* of the Catholic Church as the theological-transcendental condition, the inner human necessity, for the access of the believer to Christ. And that means that Möhler cuts off the problem of modern subjectivity, precisely because he keeps pointing to the church. This makes the church both presupposition and crown of Möhler's Christian anthropology.

Aporias of modern subjectivity

Möhler criticized modern subjectivism. Traditional "old" Catholic theology has also rejected modernity. This Catholic criticism harbors a sensitivity for the aporias of modernity, which should be explicated. The problem of modern subjectivity leads to aporias for the isolated individual. Möhler is particularly sensitive to this, when he finds in Protestantism the propensity to lose itself either in the historical past or in the inner self in its quest for the ultimate certainty of faith. The state of affairs reminds me of Michael Foucault and Reinhart Koselleck. I shall give a sketch of some of their insights.

Foucault has asserted that modernity does not refer only to such processes as rationalization, urbanization, industrialization, etc., but must be associated primarily with the way in which we on the preconscious and prelinguistic level relate to reality and to that which is true, good, and reliable. Stated simply, the idea is that prior to the so-called anthropological revolution the correlation between thought and language on the one hand and the world on the other was theologically and metaphysically secured. The will of God was the divine guarantee that "representation" was the ontological center where simultaneously thought and language and the world are in essential agreement. But with the advent of transcendental thought, i.e., with the prior differentiation between the experiencing, representing, thinking subject and objectivity, almost all thinking fixed its attention on the capacity and greatness of subjectivity, whereby to the degree that the subject came to be seen as a pure and self-related entity, the so-called objective world became more chaotic and was optimistically viewed at first as the domain for human intervention.

According to Foucault and to many modern philosophers, something quite remarkable in fact occurred.[25] On the one hand the human subject takes on divine traits because he or she is considered capable of determining not only that which is individually good and true, but also objectivity. The subject is the master of chaos, especially in matters social, since according to many thinkers reality is socially constructed. On the other hand, the word "chaos" hints at an indeterminate but nonetheless real anxiety. For, Foucault says, the subject becomes caught in aporias because the individual is aware of the never-ending task of controlling chaos to construe objectivity and is also aware of the below-the-surface links with chaos. The subject is a transcendental master, and can impose order on reality. Indeed, as soon as one part of the subject reflects cognitively on another part and so attains self-knowledge, the experience of entrapment in the world protrudes. Our body, language, and labor are intertwined with the world, which is not yet the domain of consciously reflexive subjectivity. Thus, the modern individual is confronted with an unbearable aporia. The subject is sovereign lord, though enchained. Moreover, this subject is dangerous, inclined to exploit his sovereignty to the extreme, or else in resentment to submit to anything other and unknown. With Foucault, we can distinguish three aspects to the aporias of modern subjectivity. Möhler confronts these aporias with an appeal to the authority of the Church.

a) The first aporetic aspect was mentioned earlier. According to Foucault, this is the aporia between the transcendental and the empirical or historical, the situation in which the subject constructs an environment according to human criteria and at the same time continues to depend on that in the empirical and historical field that somehow transcends the human. Many have been the attempts to invent a space where the subject is both transcendental and empirical-historical.

In *Symbolik* Möhler is on the way to thinking of the empirical-visible church as a transcendental configuration for the individual believer. Möhler does not use the term "transcendental." But many statements point to it or at least to the closely connected notion that being part of the church, as he wrote in a letter to Otto von Lassaulx (May, 1834), agrees with a true and profound human need.[26] In *Symbolik* he points out, for example, that the idea of opposing the church evokes resistance deep by within the believer and also that the idea of a church community is identical to the innate religious-ethical task of each individual; Möhler emphasizes the word "ethical" (Sy I, 392). Möhler is not precise here. For example, he refers to the relationship between the individual and the church as "a miraculous, mysterious, never completely unraveled interwovenness" of the singular person with humanity (Sy I, 403).[27] But, this is sufficient to permit us to assume that, according to Möhler, every individual already has, as it were ontologically founded, an essential relationship with the church, so that conversely the ecclesial community unlocks the true inner core of the person.[28] And precisely because the church as a transcendental reality always resides in the subject, joining the visible church and sharing the life of the church can only be an act of freedom, for the individual acts in harmony with the human essence. In this way Möhler neutralizes the first aporia through the church, because the subject can both legitimately as well as freely desire a context made to human measure and submit to the external authority of the church.

b) The second aporia concerns the contradiction between the mastery sought by objective thought and that which cannot be thought at all: the cogito and the unthinkable. Psychologically speaking, the aporia appears, for example, in the virtually universal human experience that when we go in search of the conditions and the sources of our own existence, we run into aspects and factors which keep escaping our cognitive grasp. In other words, we are dealing with the aporia between that which can be experienced and the "other," on which we have no hold, although we are aware that this "other" is uncommonly important for truth.

Once again, the authority of the church offers the believer an opportunity to cope with this difficulty. It does this already in a general sense, since for Möhler the church is a fully human, visible, and hence knowable institution; it is completely open to research in the form of modern empirical theology. The authority of the church also assures us that in this recognizable form "our other" can be mediated, the "other," which ultimately carries and envelops us.

More specifically, Möhler informs the readers of *Symbolik* that a merely worldly knowledge of a human being's self and his common world is impossible: "For it is part of the fate of the person estranged from God that he becomes a stranger to himself, neither knowing what he was nor what he will be" (Sy I, 57; cf. Sy II, 364).[29] In other words, only a vague, piecemeal awareness of "the other of us" is left. And it is precisely the message proclaimed through the authority of the Church, which genuinely throws a person back upon self. In the church the individual human being and "the other which is part of him" come together, and this is how the modern aporetic dilemma finds an equilibrium.

Presumably this also indicates the basic reason why the church resolves the modern restlessness which, according to many thinkers, including Hegel arises from this aporetic aspect. This restlessness is usually traced back to the two-sided image of the modern human person: the image of the self-assured, one who knows that the self is the center of all determination, and the image of doubt, often intensified to despair, when a person encounters that which is extremely important but beyond reach. The "normal" consequence of this two-sidedness would be a restless pursuit, an ongoing striving to overcome doubt. For Möhler the authority of the church intervenes. For example, he demands that with respect to scientific exegesis the believer should simply acknowledge that the essence of the church's doctrine of faith and morality is authentically biblical. Möhler worries that if this were not the case, the believer would become caught up in a frenzied and endless search (cf. Sy I, 439 ff).

c) The third and last aporia of modern subjectivity concerns the experience of time, the relation of the isolated subject to the past and to the future. The modern aporia in this context is, according to Reinhart Koselleck, that on the one hand our common experience is that history is made and will be made by people, while on the other hand history has its own power, so that we increasingly experience that history is beyond experience.[30] The claim made is that in premodern times, the past constituted a framework of potential experience, filled with exemplary models, transmitted through stories of marvellous achievements and great figures which, one might say, prestructured all experience. The further claim is that premodern anxieties regarding the future were put to rest by the church, since religion kept alive the expectation of the coming end of the world, together with the experience of the present world as evidently a time of grace. But when experience became temporal, i.e., with the rise of an awareness of the continuous dynamism of relationships, and most importantly, with the historical consciousness that everything, every animal, every human being, every age has its own unique rhythm of rise and fall, the premodern vision came to its end. In modern times two basic affective attitudes to time developed one full of hope because the modern, liberated history opens a perspective on the unknown and humanity accepts the task of planning the future, the other pessimistic because insight into the unique historicity of experience leads to greater distance from the past and disruption of hopeful planning.

However that may be, Möhler's *Symbolik* seems to present the church as the encompassing space where this aporia, too, is neutralized. For example, Möhler's view of ecclesiastical tradition in the subjective sense of the word (Sy I, 415–418) was developed within the framework of his ecclesiology, where his intention was to show how the authority of Holy Writ as the "mediation" of the authority of Jesus Christ can have validity for us in the ongoing dynamic of history. For Möhler this is a very important question because it is the incarnation of the *Logos,* which confers meaning and order on history. At stake in Möhler's brief exposition of the tradition in the subjective sense is the transmission of a Christian consensus which not only surrounds the individual, but also permeates him entirely. The point is that in submission to the authority of Christ, mediated through this ecclesiastical consensus, the historical past of Jesus never becomes foreign to the individual. The tradition of the church turns the past into an eternal present ("eine ewig dauernde Gegenwart", cf. Sy I, 353ff.). In this way the church copes even with this aporia.

Conclusion

Möhler summarizes his position in this striking refutation of his opponents' objection: "I hear the words spoken with contempt: Nothing but church, church, church; and I reply: this is how it is and it can not be otherwise, because without church there is no Christ for us, no Holy Writ."[31]

If we consider the church-political context in which Möhler was writing, we can understand this statement and sympathize with it. If, however, we ask in what way this statement is significant for the present situation, we must realize that Möhler's majestic vision of the church can be seen as just one moment in a social process, a process which reached from the 1830's to the 1960's. It was a process in which the various Christian confessions were trying to cope with differentiation and secularization. The lesson theology can learn from the sociology of religion is that this social process showed up a form of *Verkirchlichung*, the confinement of religion to the institutional church, which for many European Catholics eventually led to the sacralisation of the institutional structures of the Catholic Church.[32] Such an image of the Catholic Church is no longer viable. Moreover, *Symbolik* is not a general and total unmasking of Protestant theology.[33] Möhler's significance does not depend on his answers regarding the church and other Christian confessions. His continuing significance has to do with the underlying, not clearly expressed questions he wished to answer to help clarify Catholicism and oppose Protestantism. These questions point to the lacerating aporias of our modern and postmodern subjectivity. Möhler's significance lies in his intuitive apprehension of those always real aporias.

NOTES

1. Möhler (1796–1838) prepared five editions of his *Symbolik*. The first one was published in 1832, the last one appeared shortly after his death. I shall use the most recent critical edition: Johann Adam Möhler, *Symbolik, oder Darstellung der dogmatischen Gegensätze der Katholiken und Protestanten nach ihren öffentlichen Bekenntnisschriften*, 2 vols., ed. Josef Rupert Geiselman (Cologne and Olten: Hegner 1960). Vol. I will be designated in the text as Sy I, vol. II as Sy II. Möhler defended his *Symbolik* against F.C. Baur: *Neue Untersuchungen der Lehrgegensätze zwischen den Katholiken und Protestanten: Eine Vertheidigung meiner Symbolik gegen die Kritik des Herrn Professors Dr. Baur in Tübingen* (Mainz, 1835). This work will be designated as N.U.

2. E. Borgman, "Veranderingen in een spiegel: Het beeld van de katholieke Tübingers in de recente theologiegeschiedenis," in *Tussen openheid en isolement: Het voorbeeld van de katholieke theologie in de negentiende eeuw*, ed. E. Borgman and A. v. Harskamp (Kampen: Kok, 1992), pp. 135–151, at 142.

3. For an impression with regard to the judgments on Möhler as a precursor in the theological history of ideas in ecumenical thinking: R. Rieger, "Johann Adam Möhler— Wegbereiter der Ökumene," *Zeitschrift für Kirchengeschichte* 101 (1990): 267–286, at 267– 270.

4. W. Kasper, "Johann Adam Möhler—Wegbereiter des modernen Katholizismus," *Internationale Katholische Zeitschrift Communio* 17 (1988): 433–443, at 439.

5. *Die Einheit in der Kirche, oder das Prinzip des Katholizismus*, ed. J.R. Geiselmann (Cologne: Hegner, 1956); designated in the text as: E.

6. F. Vigener, *Drei Gestalten aus dem modernen Katholizismus: Möhler - Diepenbrock - Döllinger* (Munich and Berlin: Oldenbourg, 1926), p. 17.

7. R.J.F. Cornelissen, *Offenbarung und Geschichte: Die Frage der Vermittlung im Überlieferungsverständnis bei J.A. Möhler in seiner Frühzeit* (Essen: Luderus, 1972), pp. 61f., 166.

8. J.R. Geiselmann, "Der Wandel des Kirchenbewußtseins und der Kirchlichkeit in der Theologie Johann Adam Möhlers," in *Sentire Ecclesiam: Das Bewußtsein von der Kirche als gestaltende Kraft der Frömmigkeit*, ed. J. Daniélou and H. Vorgrimler (Freiburg i. Br.: Herder, 1961), pp. 531–675 at 627.

9. Addressing the significance of the concept 'Symbolik' and the influences of other theologians on Möhler on the level of the history of theological ideas, H. Wagner gives a penetrating insight into this 'logic'; H. Wagner, *Die eine Kirche und die vielen Kirchen: Ekklesiologie und Symbolik beim jungen Möhler* (München: Schöningh, 1977), pp. 248–252; idem, "Möhler auf dem Weg zur 'Symbolik'," *Catholica* 36 (1982): 15–30.

10. *Geschichte der evangelischen Theologie* (Gütersloh: Bertelsmann, 1954), 5:145.

11. F.-X. Kaufmann, *Kirche begreifen: Analysen und Thesen zur gesellschaftlichen Verfassung des Christentums* (Freiburg i. Br.: Herder, 1979), pp. 48ff. and 60ff.

12. For the subsequent observations, see Anton van Harskamp, *Theologie: Tekst in context* (Nijmegen: Diss. KUN, 1986; forthcoming at Tübingen and Basel: Francke, 1997) chapters 4 and 5, as well as Anton van Harskamp "Katholicisme en protestantisme als antagonistische medestanders," in *Tussen openheid en isolement: Het voorbeeld van de katholieke theologie in de negentiende eeuw*, ed. E Borgman and A. v. Harskamp, (Kampen: Kok, 1992), pp. 41–71.

13. Kasper, pp. 434f.

14. "Es bleibt nichts mehr übrig, als die jungen Theologen mit einem recht kirchlichen Sinne auszurüsten ...." *Gesammelte Aktenstücke und Briefe*, ed. St. Lösch (Munich Kösel & Pustet, 1928), 1: 227.

15. G. May, *Interkonfessionalismus in der ersten Hälfte des 19. Jahrhunderts* (Paderborn: Schöningh, 1969).

16. R. Rieger, "Johann Adam Möhler—Wegbereiter der Ökumene? Ein Topos im Licht neuer Texte," *Zeitschrift für Kirchengeschichte* 101 (1990): 2–3, 268–286. See also, H.F. Geisser, "Die methodischen Prinzipien des Symbolikers Johann Adam Möhler: Ihre Brauchbarkeit im ökumenischen Dialog," *Theologische Quartalschrift* 168 (1988): 83–97.

17. Cf. W. Pannenberg, "Christentum und Mythos," in *Grundfragen systematischer Theologie 2* (Göttingen: Vandenhoeck & Ruprecht, 1980), pp. 13–65.

18. J. Fitzer, *Moehler and Baur in Controversy, 1832–38: Romantic-Idealist Assessment of the Reformation and Counter-Reformation* (Tallahassee: AAR, 1974), p. 22.

19. The following lines are based on Rieger, p. 274.

20. As is also explicitly stated by Möhler himself in a letter to his friend Gengler; see, St. Lösch, *Prof. Dr. Adam Gengler (1788–1866): Die Beziehungen des Bamberger Theologen zu J.I.I. Döllinger und J.A. Möhler* (Würzburg: Schöningh, 1963), p. 64.

21. Cf. G.W.F. Hegel, *Grundlinien der Philosophie des Rechts* (Frankfurt/M: Suhrkamp, 1976) sec. 124 (p. 233), sec. 134 (pp. 259f.), sec. 139 (pp. 260ff.), sec. 140 (pp. 265f.).

22. W. Leinweber, *Der Streit um den Zölibat im 19. Jahrhundert* (Münster: Aschendorff, 1978), p. 231. It is not surprising at all that Möhlers *Symbolik* was attacked by representatives of the Catholic *Aufklärung*. They argued that confessional peace was endangered by Möhler. See, K. Geiger, "Katholische Urteile über Möhlers Symbolik: Ein Beitrag zur Geschichte der katholischen *Aufklärung*," *Deutsch-evangelische Blätter* 16 (1891): 369–400, at 376 and passim.

23. Cf. Rieger, p. 275.

24. Cf. H.F. Geisser, "Glück und Unglück eines Theologen mit seiner Kirche—am Beispiel der beiden Tübinger Johann Adam Möhler und David Friedrich Strauß," *Zeitschrift für Theologie und Kirche* 83 (1986): 85–110, at 101.

25. For the following lines I shall use M. Foucault, *Les mots et les choses: Une archéologie des sciences humaine* (Paris: Gallimard, 1966), pp. 77–81, 323–339; cf. H.L. Dreyfus and P. Rabinow, *Michel Foucault: Beyond Structuralism and Hermeneutics* (Chicago: University of Chicago Press, 1982), pp. 26–41.

26. *Möhler Gesammelte Aktenstücke und Briefe,* p. 285.

27. "... eine wundervolle, geheimnisreiche, nie genug zu enträtselnde Verschlungenheit ..."

28. Geiselmann, p. 621.

29. "... denn auch das ist ein Teil des Schicksals des von Gott entfernten Menschen, daß er zugleich sich selbst entfremdet wird, und weder wahrhaft weiß, was er anfangs gewesen, noch was er geworden ist."

30. For the following I mainly make use of R. Koselleck, *Vergangene Zukunft: Zur Semantik geschichtlicher Zeiten* (Frankfurt/M: Suhrkamp, 1979).

31. "Ich höre die Verachtung aussprechenden Worte: Nichts als Kirche, Kirche, Kirche; und ich antwortete: es ist nicht anders und kann nicht anders sein; denn ohne Kirche haben wir keinen Christus und keine Heilige Schrift" (N.U. 482).

32. K. Gabriel, *Christentum zwischen Tradition und Postmoderne* (Freiburg: Herder, 1992) pp. 90ff.

33. Does this mean that we have to deny that Möhler was a precursor of ecumenical thinking? I did not elaborate my views on this question. Yet I suspect my position has become clear. It is based on the simple assumption that the answer depends on the disciplinary perspective one wishes to use. If one wishes to treat Möhler as a systematic theologian and contemporary partner in theological debate, it is obvious that Möhler is an ardently antiecumenical figure. His designation of "the negative principle" which makes individual Protestants incline to self-deifying mechanisms and which will lead the Protestant communities further on the path to self-destruction, does not leave space for any doubts. Even if one chooses the perspective of a theological history of ideas, Möhler cannot be considered as a precursor of ecumenical thinking. For if one does so, one overlooks as a matter of fact the Catholic *Aufklärung* before and during Möhler's lifetime, a religious movement which was, seen from our present situation, a far more ecumenical phenomenon than Möhlers *Symbolik*. And yet, I think it is not quite inaccurate to consider Möhler as a precursor of Catholic ecumenism, but only in a very paradoxical way and from a sociological perspective. Why? One may say that Möhler lived in a world in which the confessions on the level of almost all their faithful adherents were not really and consciously aware of the existence of the other party's religious claims. One knew of course of the existence of the other religious party, but because one lived—save a relatively small and learned elite—in separate socio-cultural spaces, one could not really know or even imagine that the claims of the other were presented as claims for one's own party too. So speaking sociologically, *Symbolik* made the claims of Protestants visible as claims of real religious enemies who have either to surrender to Catholicism or who must be kept away as far as possible from Catholicism. The paradox is that Möhler made Protestants visible as those who are so (self)destructive and so inimical that they should be kept at a distance. But making visible a group of people who once were not perceived at all from a sociological view is a step forward, viz. the situation where enemies are transformed into real adversaries, i.e., into those people with whom it can be useful to quarrel because one may hope for a real reconciliation. So the whole argument is based on the assumption that after the "Secularization" of 1803-1810, after the definite removal of the confessions from political power, the plausible way for a "meeting" of the two confessions runs through the following stages: first ignorance and indifference with respect to each other; second, religious antagonism, even hostility; third, the situation in which the confessions can become adversaries. Only if seen in this historical-sociological sequence can one conclude that Möhler was a precursor of ecumenism.

12

History and Grace

The Tübingen School Encounters Postmodernism

— ELMAR KLINGER—

The title of this essay refers to a breakthrough in the tradition of the theology of grace; it deals with the central themes of Nature and Supernature. The Tübingen School places these themes within history itself, so that the Supernatural becomes a principle of human self-discovery in thought and deed. Because of this, the School has sometimes been accused of semirationalism. In the case of the principle advocate of this position, Johannes Evangelist Kuhn, this accusation led to a fierce controversy with representatives of the Roman School.

In this essay this position of the Tübingen School and the development leading to it will be situated within the horizon of postmodernism. The postmodern is the "horizon of dialogue" of the present moment. It emphasizes breakthrough and discontinuity with the tradition of modernity itself. Its key themes are not reason, self-consciousness and development, but particularity, relatedness, language, and power. The principle subjects within postmodernism are nature, women, and the poor. The discussion of the historical character of discontinuity, difference and newness are of particular importance. These aspects point to the future of history. Bridge-moments do not demolish, but they do bring about radical change and real transformation. They do not disregard and reject the past, but they do lead to a new assessment of it. The postmodern does not see the past historiographically but archeologically. In this context, the Tübingen School is of fundamental importance. It allows the others of our history to become bearers of history and thereby subjects of theology. The Tübingen School remained within the context of the Enlightenment and so broke with the Tradition; but it also defended the Tradition against the Enlightenment and so broke with rationalism. This essay is in three sections: 1. Kant and Lessing; the Enlightenment—a breakthrough in history and theology; 2. The Supernatural in the Tübingen School—dealing with the subjectivity of the other: Drey, Staudenmaier and Kuhn; and 3. The Tübingen School in America: The others as a challenge to postmodernity.

I

"Enlightenment" is a word with a variety of meanings. It signifies both a historical fact and a systematic perspective. It embraces a program of life and of thought. Historically, the word designated an epoch-making event. The Enlightenment designates a period of European history extending politically from the Westphalian Peace Treaty in 1648 until the French Revolution beginning in 1789; in the history of philosophy, it marks the epoch between Descartes (1596–1650) and Kant (1724–1804); and in terms of church history, it refers to the time between the rise of denominationalism at the close of the 16th century reformation until the end of the pre-secularized church, usually referred to as *Reichskirche* at the beginning of the 19th century. The Enlightenment is, however, not only an epochal term but a problematic idea. It stands for a program of life and thought, which took shape in the above mentioned period but which is in no way restricted to that period. It embraces new dimensions of life which continue even today. Hegel spoke of "the unfulfilled [*unbefriedigte*] Enlightenment." Horkheimer and Adorno speak of a "dialectic of Enlightenment," and Marcuse of a "second Enlightenment." Always the term includes a demand for the independent use of reason and encourages autonomous thinking.

In his essay in the "Berliner Monatsschrift" in 1783 Kant formulated programatically the answer to the question: "What is Enlightenment?":

> Enlightenment is man's emergence from his self-incurred immaturity. Immaturity is the inability to use one's own understanding without the guidance of another. This immaturity is self-incurred if its cause is not a lack of understanding, but lack of resolution and courage to use it without the guidance of another. The motto of Enlightenment is therefore: *Sapere aude!* Have courage to use your own understanding! Laziness and cowardice are the reasons why such a large proportion of men, even when nature has long emancipated them from alien guidance, nevertheless gladly remain immature for life. For this reason, it is all too easy for others to set themselves up as their guardians. It is so convenient to be immature![1]

Enlightenment breaks away from all traditions and institutions that foster or justify tutelage. Reason enables the present to judge the past, the subordinate the superior, and society the state. It gives them the courage to evaluate the other, and it empowers them to defend themselves against a thirdparty. This means that it is an historical action. Enlightenment proclaims the right of human beings to make use of understanding in a self-responsible way and the duty of the rest of humankind to recognize and secure that right. It rebels against absolutism and authoritarianism. The breakthrough embodied in the Enlightenment has a wide significance. Such a breakthrough is not limited to science and to society; it has a special effect on church and theology.

The writer who gave a clear and precise focus to this issue was Gotthold Ephraim Lessing when he wrote that every judgment on history is a breakthrough within history. The judgment of history and one's personal judgment are never identical.

> Fulfilled prophecies, which I myself experience are one thing; fulfilled prophecies, of which I know only from history that others say they have experienced are another. Miracles, which I see with my own eyes and which I have the

opportunity to verify for myself, are one thing; miracles, of which I know only
from history that others say they have seen them and verified are another.[2]

The report of events differs from the events themselves. Recognition of miracles
and prophecies which one has seen for one's self is reasonable. They are credible
and worthy of assent facilitated through the judgment of one's own reason. Historical miracles and prophecies reported by others are never credible as Lessing
explained:

> If no historical truth can be demonstrated, then nothing can be demonstrated
> by means of historical truth. That is: *accidental* truths of history can never
> become the proof of necessary truths of reason. [...] That, then, is the ugly,
> broad ditch which I cannot get across, however often and however earnestly I
> have tried to make the leap. If anyone can help me over it, let him do it, I beg
> him, I adjure him. He will deserve a divine reward from me.[3]

By editing the *Wolffenbüttel Fragments*, he widened and deepened the ugly,
broad ditch still further in Christology. Lessing argued that the religion of Christ
and the Christian religion are not the same. His theses in the *Fragments* on "The
Religion of Christ" are:

> I. It is a question whether Christ was more than a mere man. That he was a real
> man if he was a man at all and that he never ceased to be a man, is not in dispute.
> II. It follows that the religion of Christ and the Christian religion are two
> different things. [...] V. How these two religions, the religion of Christ and the
> Christian religion, can exist in Christ in one and the same person, is inconceiv-
> able. [...] VII. The religion of Christ is therein contained in the clearest and
> most lucid language. VIII. On the other hand, the Christian religion is so
> uncertain and ambiguous that there is scarcely a single passage which, in all the
> history of the world, has been interpreted in the same way by two men.[4]

The Tübingen School as a whole and its founder Johann Sebastian Drey in
particular acknowledged this breakthrough. They acknowledged the truth of the
Enlightenment. The question of the relation of reason and history is a basic problem of theology. They attempted to pose the question anew and answer it afresh.
    Drey makes it an important subject of discussion. In his view, theology is both
phenomenal and noumenal. Statements about God are historical phenomena. As
historical developments, they bear the stamp of history. Such statements of positive religious phenomena, however, are not merely historical facts. In talking about
God, they make a judgment on history and its phenomena. In any such judgment,
there is a normative claim which makes reason with all its demands a criterion of
positive religion. Thus, there is a religion of reason. These two poles of religion,
breakthrough and discontinuity, history and rationality, constitute theology. Theology is talk about God and about our striving toward God in the phenomenal
world. Drey describes theology as a science based in these phenomena. Grounding himself on these basic normative data, Drey develops a holistic concept of

theology in his work, *Brief Introduction to the Study of Theology with Reference to the Scientific Standpoint and the Catholic System.*[5] In this he outlined all the areas of theology and levels of its phenomena and discussed them thematically.

But theology is not only talk about God and God's manifestations in the world; it is also talk about these manifestations and their relationship to God. It discusses both God and how one deals with reflecting on God. It complies with the claims of reflection and so creates history. It demonstrates the autonomy of the person talking about God. In such talk, both God and one's self are revealed in this historical act.

So theology has both a rational and an empirical focus. It is a positive science. Drey emphasizes this focus in his second work, *Apologetics.* He describes theology as the science of "the divinity of Christianity in its manifestations" [*der Göttlichkeit des Christentums in seiner Erscheinung*]. It lays the foundation for his doctrines of Grace and Revelation. The supernatural is the "supra"/"beyond" of the natural; the natural is the locus of the manifestations of the supernatural. The human person finds self in that which transcends the human. The otherness of one's self—and especially the totally Other, God—belongs to the human as human.

Theology, which bases its ability to talk about God in this talk about the other, is thus necessary for human beings. It is itself a breakthrough in history. Drey writes:

> Theology, as a purely intellectual engagement with religion, arises necessarily within humanity, i.e., it arises in accord with the necessary laws of the total nature of the human person, specifically those according to which he seeks to clarify his experiences although they are in themselves obscure and to give them permanence, although they are in themselves fleeting, so that he renders permanent in *concepts* what has affected his heart pleasantly or painfully and can by conceptual means deliberately recall and renew whenever he wants what first affected him as external and alien factors.[6]

Theology treats history from the perspective of reason. But it also treats reason historically. One's image of the divine and one's image of the human are historically connected. The way one thinks of God affects one's perception also of self. The way one thinks about human beings affects how one perceives God. So Drey argues:

> Thus theology is in the religious area what in every other area of human concern is termed apprehension, conceptualization, or knowledge. It is the expression and results of those mental laws by which our minds resolve all data, external and internal, all experiencing, feeling, and willing, into concepts. [...] One's theology depends on one's religion, one's stance toward God; this is our first axiom. One's theology depends on one's level of spiritual culture; this is our second.[7]

Both axioms are significant. The first breaks with traditional supernaturalism; it is the Enlightenment. The second breaks with Enlightenment naturalism; it is tradition.

The Tübingen School has both a normative and an empirico-historical focus. It declares reason to be the highest norm, because nothing in history replaces its judgment on history. Autonomy is constitutive for theology. But theology is also constitutive for autonomy. In judging history, reason encounters not only history but itself. Discovering the other is the way one discovers one's self. Autonomy means both responsibility for others and the responsibility for one's self. This is why the Other is constitutive for theology in this process of self-discovery. But the process is itself the history of this self-discovery. It is the history of one's dealings with others—and the Other.

The empirico-historical focus is constitutive of theology. It embodies the positive character of theology. The Other, who confronts theology externally, is also intrinsic to theology. In engaging the Other, theology is challenged; only then is theology able to distinguish itself and develop itself. In speaking about the Other theology discovers its own true self.

Thus, the Enlightenment contains an important historical significance. It opens the way to the other. The Tübingen School has taken this way. It makes the other of history the principle of its own identity. There is no history of dogma without heresies, no Bible without both Jews and gentiles, and no Christianity without Christ and Christians. The Enlightenment's breakthrough into history makes history come alive and leads to a reorganization of its study. Drey demanded this reorganization, i.e., a "revision of the church and of theology."

II

Theology has its ground in Scripture and Tradition, its essential sources. The Enlightenment posed questions concerning the historical and objective value of these sources. How are they situated in time? Can they be reliably passed on to future generations? Do they meet the demands of autonomous reason?

A theology that allows for these questions and asks them itself acknowledges the breakthrough in history that occurred with Enlightenment rationalism. Such a theology operated within the context of this breakthrough and makes it the principle of its own self-determination. Such a theology does not talk at random but will be well informed; it will not only pass on information to posterity but will take responsibility for it; it will not only talk about God but about human beings and their capacity for talking about God. A theology of this kind both makes statements and recognizes their implications. Such recognition does not destroy the statements of theology but makes them transparent. The rational and the suprarational, the natural and the supernatural, the intelligible and the mysterious meet and penetrate one another within this knowledge. This type of theology does not dissolve the suprarational, the supernatural and the mysterious, but accounts for them.

Thus, knowledge of oneself and knowledge of the other mutually condition one another in knowledge itself. The known other forces knowledge to reflect upon itself. The other demands my knowledge's self-contemplation and self-determination. The other does not restrict my autonomy but stands in its own right. It can communicate only with one who is autonomous. It says: "Be autonomous or I cannot communicate with you. Accept me for what I am, or I cannot meet you. In order to give myself to you, I must awaken your attention. To meet me you must be yourself."

The biblical foundation and model for all theologizing within the context of rationality is Jesus' category of the Kingdom of God. In it we find the exemplary basis for secular language about God. This is so because the Kingdom of God is the historical Jesus' idea of history in its totality. It is also a truly rational idea, for it designates generally God's relation to human beings and their relation to God. Kant placed it as the central idea of the religion of reason [*Vernunftreligion*] and made it the measure of positive religion and the church. The person who fulfills the categorical imperative draws a step closer to the Kingdom of God. Within it is contained the central idea of all human life, i.e., the Golden Rule: "Do unto your neighbor as you would have him do unto you. For this is the law and the prophets," said Jesus in the Sermon on the Mount (Mt. 7:12).

While the Kingdom of God is a basic idea of natural religion, it is simultaneously the epitome of the supernatural. God as God saves human beings. Theology, which is by its nature supernatural, can thus constitute itself within the context of reason. It is natural for human beings to talk about God. It is a principle of the historical self-determination of human reason.

Drey described the Kingdom of God as the highest idea of Christianity from which all its other ideas issue. It contains within it "Christ, who brings about this universal recognition." He is "the *visible head of the Kingdom,* just as its visible expression and tangible realization is the *church.*" Drey writes that this "true idea of reason" [*wahre Vernunftidee*], like all other ideas, "was first energized thanks to the stimulating light of educative revelation so that it emerged independently in reason."[8]

All theology in Germany in the first half of the nineteenth century is dominated by this approach. That is why it is often referred to as "Kingdom-of-God-theology." Thus, Drey introduced an important new concept into theology in his encyclopedic *Brief Introduction*. The same idea also shaped his unpublished outlines of the history of dogma.

In our encounter with the other we discover ourselves. History is the process of this self-discovery. It develops out of such encounters. Hence, the other and especially the totally Other are its principle. Interiority and exteriority, the natural and the supernatural, belong to the very essence of history. There is no history without both dimensions. The natural within the supernatural is that which develops itself and must discover itself and so passes beyond itself. The supernatural is the "beyond" of the natural; it is the principle of nature's growth in self-discovery and of transcendental self-determination. However, because the natural has no claim upon the supernatural, the history of nature is itself a grace for nature. Grace in its supernaturality belongs to nature *qua* nature, and therefore grace manifests itself within nature. Grace both makes and embraces history. History and grace are the two dimensions of the progress of the natural and are manifestations of its principle factors.[9]

Drey understands revelation too within this same interior-exterior relationship of the natural and the supernatural. Revelation gives us the meaning of God's utterances and deeds in the world. Revelation is both a principle and an embodiment of history. Drey writes: "God's revelation is the expression of God's being in another which is not God and so to that extent outside God's self. Outside God's self is the universe and that alone. All God's revelation can thus occur only in the universe and the universe is nothing other than that revelation."[10]

The utterances and deeds of God in the world belong to the world. They go beyond the world, but they also embody it. They are its "advance determinations." They do not decree but disclose the possibilities and opportunities which they open up. They provide both the power and the project of the (self-)determined future of the world.

This view of the supernatural is very different from the general scholastic view. It envisions the supernatural not as nature beyond the natural, but as the determining ground of the natural itself. It is the natural relating to itself in its dealing with all that is the other. Grace is history. Grace cultivates the self-consciousness of human beings from within; it energizes their lives and establishes human dignity through their own decisions. Through dealing with themselves, their fellow human beings, and God, humans become persons.

From its inception with the work of Johann Sebastian Drey until that of Johann Evangelist Kuhn, the Tübingen School advocated this thesis on the nature of the supernatural, continued to develop it, and vigorously defended it against numerous attacks. The ongoing debates on this thesis have given the Tübingen School its identity and have broadened our horizon in a manner similar to that of other religions and denominations, as well as historical, lifestyles and thought-patterns. Such phenomena serve to amend our habitual behavior and renew our self-consciousness; they are new opportunities. History always leads us on by creating new relationships, by altering long-standing behavior and by stimulating individuals and the whole human race to seek out new paths. Such grace leads us to transcend the narrowness of our own worlds.

So, within the Tübingen School, the other is of fundamental importance. Under the rubric of the other, the School dealt with the themes of revelation, nature, God, consciousness, spirit, and even human personhood. By establishing the direction, Drey situated theology within the external-internal context of positivity and ideality, historicity and rationality, naturality and supernaturality. He treated all the fundamental ideas of theology in this way. According to Drey, revelation is one's presentation of one's inner being to the other. This revelation meant that God can become present in the other which was not God's self. He constantly brings into being within the other his own Otherness, and so what comes into being in the world is the phenomenon of God.

Grace is, therefore, a (bi-)polar event. Grace is external and internal. *External grace* consists of space-time events, which involve and so affect human beings. It forces their self-determination and leads to decision and action (praxis). It offers itself as an opportunity seeking realization. *Internal grace* illumines and inspires human beings. It is both a capacity and an opportunity for perception so that one can become accustomed to determining one's own actions.

The position on nature and supernature, which Drey outlines in his *Apologetics*, makes his view on grace a comprehensive theme. He developed this further in his proposals for dogmatics. There is no interior growth without exterior encounter. That which is manifested externally can affect us internally. This is the principle of human self-determination in history. Franz Anton Staudenmaier, Drey's student, continued this basic theological framework in his theory of consciousness and theory of history. In his critique of Hegel, he takes as his starting point the claim that the unfolding of consciousness is always the knowledge of the other. Staudenmaier writes: "Thus, both true cognition and the knowledge that we cognize must be joined in one consciousness in such a way that, in our consciousness of ourselves, our awareness of the other which is external to us is not excluded so that it may continue to excite and engage us."[11] In the process of the self-discovery of the spirit, the complete Otherness of God and the world are not preliminary steps or progressive stages, but a permanent foundation. The reality of the Other moves the spirit and leads it further. Staudenmaier calls history "the revealed kingdom of God" [*das offenbar gewordene Reich Gottes*]. He writes: "In this sense, the history of Christianity is a history within history, or in other words, the truth of all history."[12] Staudenmaier does not distinguish between a natural and a supernatural providence in the manner of scholasticism. He considers providence the general prerequisite for both the natural and the supernatural.

Johann Evangelist Kuhn was our last member of the Tübingen School in the 19th century. On the eve of the first Vatican Council, he was heavily engaged in debate with the advocates of Neoscholasticism on the supernatural destiny of the natural. The core of the conflict concerned the status of human reason. Does the human person possess the capacity to deal with self and the other according to temporal knowledge and conscious? Or does reason play no significant role in the relationship between the person and the other, so that naiveté is the highest virtue? Kuhn accuses the neoscholastic Roman school of misunderstanding

> the concept of the human being as presupposed by the whole of Christian anthropology. This concept is simply the one which we usually attach to the word "human," a rational being with free will which is differentiated from animals. It distinguishes the physical and the moral and then unites these two elements. Without clarifying this condition and this fundamental distinction, as we have repeatedly noted, one will not arrive at an understanding of grace and the supernatural in accord with Catholic dogma and at the true understanding of Christian supernaturalism.[13]

Being related to the other is intrinsic to human willing and reasoning. Such a relationship develops and perfects human beings. So grace affects will and reason. Grace is the principle of growth and of the perfection of human beings, not of complementing their nature and elevating it. It has a personal rather than a natural character. It makes self-determination possible and resists external determination.

Grace is the work of the Holy Spirit who invigorates and strengthens human beings in the process of their becoming human. Thus, Kuhn writes that theologically everything depends on appreciating that "the essentially supernatural quality of the grace which sanctifies and interiorly unites us with God allows us both to recognize that we are spiritually conformed to God, made like him in attitude and will, and helps us to avoid any notion of physical change in the essence of our souls or of physical participation in the divine nature."[14] This grace is a relationship with the totally Other, and opens the possibility for new ways of acting. It links faith in God with love for the world. It is a power to form and transform the world.

III

The Enlightenment required the courage to think for oneself. It distinguished those with courage from those that lack it and so remain resigned, those who suppress the call for Enlightenment and so deny it, or those who think it unnecessary and so remain uneducated and underdeveloped. This does not abolish the problem of human domination over one's fellow human beings but itself represents the problem of power.

The Tübingen School placed theology within this context. This School embodied the courage necessary to think for oneself in theology. But such theology must also speak for those who are without this courage and power, those who suppress it, and those who despair of it. Thus, the question of political and intellectual capabilities is a question of the struggle for power. Postmodernity is concerned with this problem. It centers on the "losers" in modernity, those whom modernity not only leaves undeveloped, but also robbed of courage and the capacity to think for themselves, those who are enslaved even to the extent of having their right of existence called into dispute. The Enlightenment meant liberation for the European middle class, but for the third world it meant only deterioration.

When the French conquered Algeria in the nineteenth century, for example, virtually all its inhabitants could read and write. But today, because of the importation of a foreign language, there is extensive illiteracy in Algeria. Much the same scenario can be found among the Indians in Paraguay after the 19th century revolution. Postmodernity highlights the problem that freedom restricts and autonomy silences. The courage to think for oneself destroys the ability of others to think. It alienates thinking from its roots. The underprivileged remain outside the new order. They are not represented within it. Unfamiliar thinking remains silenced within the limits set up by the dominant groups. Postmodernity parts company with modernity, for it identifies those who have been left alienated by modernity, its others, displaced settlers, the silenced, and women, as its central concerns. Thus, plurality is required by postmodernity. As Wolfgang Welsch has said: "The postmodern departs from all forms of monism, of unification and totalization, from all encompassing utopias and many hidden forms of despotism, and turns its attention instead to multiplicity and diversity, variety and competition, paradigms and the coexistence of the heterogeneous."[15] In essence, "The postmodern is here understood as constituted by radical pluralism and postmodernism as an intellectual framework for its defense."[16] The question arises, therefore, whether a theology which was shaped by modernity can survive in postmodernity? Does the postmodern grant any future to such a theology?

The Tübingen School has been a paradigmatic instance of theology within the context of modernity. It justified the use of reason and celebrated the breakthrough into history as the principle of progress. These initiatives were great achievements for the Tübingen School, and their importance for theology has not been fully recognized even today. But where there are winners, there also losers. Progress can also bring regress as seen in the existence in those alienated within modernity, its others, the displaced settlers, the silenced ones. Thus, these others are a challenge to the Tübingen School in postmodernity. Can the school survive? Is the school confined to the 19th century or has it a future in the 21st century?

If it is to meet this challenge, the Tübingen theology has to confront the question: Who are the others? In the Tübingen School, the others are a religious instance. They are the representatives of a religious faith. They were also the philosophers and poets of German idealism. Above all, they were other teachers of the Christian tradition in doctrine and life. The others who were marginalized by modernity are not even mentioned. This omission stands out most clearly in the theology of the Kingdom of God. Such a theology necessarily has a political dimension: the Kingdom of God belongs to the poor. The rich cannot enter it. It is revealed to the little ones; it remains hidden from the clever and the wise. Either one does full justice to the revolution of the Gospel in its integrity, or else one will dilute this revolution and transform it into a simple moral exhortation.[17]

This critique of the Tübingen School may sound anachronistic. After all, how can the themes of the end of the 20th and beginning of the 21st centuries be the concerns of the 19th century? But postmodernity does insistently draw attention to the other. Autonomy and its opposite, intellectual bondage, are not merely problems of education; they are also political and social challenges. They are part of the problem of power. Within the Tübingen School of the 19th century, neither those deprived of rights, nor the displaced, nor women were subjects of theology. The Tübingen School's view of history and revelation is a meta-explanation that does not account for the non-conceptual in the lives of particular individuals. But the Tübingen School's capacity for future relevance is based on its strong insistence on the other. In fact, the other constitutes and allows to emerge one's own historical existence, according to the school. The Other determines the to-be and the not-to-be of everything. It is the grace one experiences.

So the Tübingen School does introduce a basic framework for a theology of the other. Theology is not limited to recording the historiographical past. It seeks the origin of history in an archeology of the future. This attitude is exemplary for every theology that deals with the otherness of modernity compared to the postmodern. It recognizes that those who break with history thereby make history, that history comes into being in dealing with the others, and that all historical identity, social meaning, and true power is based only on this foundation of process. Modernity was not the end of history but its new beginning. Thus postmodernity is unavoidable. Postmodernity deals with the others of modernity and so affects theology. Many groups in our societies belong under the rubric of the other: the poor, women, nonwestern religions and traditions, the whole of humanity and creation itself, and even the second Vatican Council within the church.

And so there are many theologies which are elaborated in terms of the other and remain indebted to the other. The question is posed anew to history which is grace and to grace which both has and makes history. Thus, remembering the Tübingen School and attending to its members can be illuminating and beneficial. What does grace mean within the history of a society? Is it not liberation for the poor? Is it not the destruction of patriarchy and a recognition of the wisdom of women? What does grace mean for overexploited nature within a mechanized world? May we not say that grace means mercy and compassion for all nature, the redeeming of the subject, and a memory of the future about to begin?

Too often, the neoscholastic understanding of the doctrine of grace stresses possession. Is the supernatural an historical/personal event of encounter with the totally Other, or is it an uncreated substance which overwhelms created substances? Ultimately, all contemporary forms of theology must face this question since the riddle remains unsolved. The inability to answer this question effectively leads at best, to a disregard of theology and, at worst, to its condemnation. The entire church is suffering because of a failure to answer this key question. The Second Vatican Council declared that Christ is the key to the understanding of world history which opens up to all humanity the deep mystery of its own existence. Does it not follow that social revolution is, therefore, a grace of the Gospel?

How one evaluates the breakthrough from modernity to postmodernity remains a highly disputed question, not least in Germany. I think it noteworthy that the stereotypes often employed in this discussion are reminiscent of the Enlightenment problematic at the beginning of the 19th century. Habermas defends modernity and all its achievements. Sloterdijk breaks with modernity and speaks of a cynicism of reason. Foucault seeks to give voice to the mentally disordered. Welsch tries to link modernity and postmodernity with his idea of a "transversal reason" and speaks of a "modern postmodernity."

The Tübingen School has emphasized the breakthrough of reason within history as a central theme. It is a model for future theology in the 21st century. It may yet provide a basic framework for theologies of liberation and revolution and feminist theology in America. Who are the others in this world? They are Native Americans, African-Americans, Latin Americans, women, the inhabitants of the rain forest and dwellers on radiation-contaminated Pacific islands. How do we regard them: As a problem? Or as a grace for the Americas and for all human beings?

NOTES

1. Hans Reiss (ed.), *Kant, Political Writings* (Cambridge: Cambridge University Press, 1971), p. 54.

2. Henry Chadwick, *Lessing's Theological Writings* (London: Black, 1956), p. 51. Cf. the German original: "Ein andres sind erfüllte Weissagungen, die ich selbst erlebt habe, ein andres, erfüllte Weissagungen, von denen ich nur historisch weiß, daß sie andere wollen erlebt

haben. Ein andres sind Wunder, die ich mit meinen Augen sehe, und selbst zu prüfen Gelegenheit habe: ein anderes sind Wunder, von denen ich nur historisch weiß, daß sie andere wollen gesehen und geprüft haben."(G. E. Lessing, "Beweis des Geistes und der Kraft," in *Werke*, VIII (München: Hanser, 1979), pp. 9–14.

3. Chadwick, pp. 53–55. Cf. the German original: "Wenn keine historische Wahrheit demonstrieret werden kann: so kann auch nichts *durch* historische Wahrheit demonstrieret werden. Das ist: *zufällige Geschichtswahrheiten können der Beweis von notwendigen Vernunftwahrheiten nie werden.* [...] Das, das ist der garstig breite Graben, über den ich nicht kommen kann, so oft und ernstlich ich auch den Sprung versucht habe. Kann mir jemand hinüber helfen, der tu es; ich bitte ihn, ich beschwöre ihn. Er verdient ein Gotteslohn an mir."(Lessing, *Werke*, VIII, pp. 11–13)

4. Chadwick, p. 106. Cf. the German original: "§1 Ob Christus mehr als Mensch gewesen, das ist ein Problem. Daß er wahrer Mensch gewesen, wenn er es überhaupt gewesen; daß er nie aufgehört hat, Mensch zu sein: das ist ausgemacht. §2 Folglich sind die Religion Christi und die christliche Religion zwei ganz verschiedene Dinge. [...] §5 Wie beide diese Religionen, die Religion Christi sowohl als die christliche, in Christo als in einer und eben derselben Person bestehen können, ist unbegreiflich. [...] §7 Die Religion Christi ist mit den klarsten und deutlichsten Worten darin enthalten. §8 Die christliche hingegen so ungewiß und vieldeutig, daß es schwerlich eine einzige Stelle gibt, mit welcher zwei Menschen, so lange als die Welt steht, den nämlichen Gedanken verbunden haben." (Lessing, *Werke*, VII [München: Hanser, 1979], pp. 711–712).

5. Translated with an introduction and annotation by Michael Himes (Notre Dame/ London: University of Notre Dame Press, 1994); referred to in the text as *Brief Introduction*. The German title reads: *Kurze Einleitung in das Studium der Theologie mit Rücksicht auf den wissenschaftlichen Standpunkt und das katholische System.* (Tübingen, 1819).

6. *Brief Introduction*, p. 16. Cf. the German original: "Die Theologie als bloß intellektuelle Beschäftigung mit der Religion, entsteht notwendig im Menschen; d.h., sie entsteht nach notwendigen Gesetzen der gesamten Natur des Menschen, namentlich nach denjenigen, zufolge derer er seine Empfindungen als etwas an sich Dunkles klarer zu machen, als etwas an sich Vorübergehendes festzuhalten sucht, auf daß er im Begriffe bleibend mache, was ihm als vorübergehende Lust oder Unlust das Herz bewegt hat, auf daß er mittels des Begriffs freitätig erwecken, und so oft er will erneuern könne, was ursprünglich als äußere oder fremde Anregung auf ihn gewirkt hat."(*Kurze Einleitung*, § 38, p. 23).

7. *Brief Introduction*, pp. 16f. Cf. the German original: "Die Theologie ist also in Ansetzung der Religion dasselbe, was in Ansetzung aller übrigen Dinge, die den Menschen berühren, alles Erkennen, Begreifen und Wissen ist; [...] Wie des Menschen Religion, wie seine Stellung gegen Gott, so ist auch seine Theologie, dies ist der erste Grundsatz; wie des Menschen geistige Bildung, so ist auch seine Theologie; dies ist der andere."(*Kurze Einleitung*, § 39/40, p. 24).

8. *Brief Introduction*, p. 27. Cf. the German original: "erst durch den von außen anregenden Strahl der erziehenden Offenbarung zu freiem Hervortreten in der Vernunft geweckt wurde."(*Kurze Einleitung*, §65, p. 41).

9. Cf. Elmar Klinger, *Offenbarung im Horizont der Heilsgeschichte* (Zürich: Benziger, 1969) and Elmar Klinger, "Die Bedeutung Dreys für die Theologie der Aufklärung. Offenbarung, Natur, Geschichte," in Abraham Kustermann, ed., *Revision der Theologie— Reform der Kirche: Die Bedeutung des Tübinger Theologen Johann Sebastian Drey (1977– 1853) in Geschichte und Gegenwart* (Würzburg: Echter, 1994), pp. 246–256.

10. *Brief Introduction*, p. 7. Cf. the German original: "Offenbarung Gottes ist Darstellung

seines Wesens in einem anderen, was nicht Gott ist, und insofern außer ihm. Außer Gott ist das Universum, und dieses allein; alle Offenbarung Gottes also kann nur geschehen im Universum, und dieses selbst ist jene, nichts anderes." (*Kurze Einleitung*, §16, p. 10).

11. Cf. the German original: "Beides also, wirkliches Erkennen, und das Wissen, daß *wir* erkennen, muß zu *einem Bewußtsein* verbunden werden, und zwar so, daß Bewußtsein unserer selbst dem Bewußtsein von einem Anderen vorhergeht, wobei nicht ausgeschlossen ist, daß unser Bewußtsein von einem Anderen außer uns zuerst erregt und in Tätigkeit gesetzt werden könne oder müsse."("Rezension Enzyklopädie Hagenbach," 56, 11, in Klinger, *Offenbarung*, p. 62).

12. Cf. the German original: "In diesem Sinn ist die Geschichte des Christentums eine Geschichte in der Geschichte oder mit anderen Worten die Wahrheit aller Geschichte."(*Der Geist des Christentums* § 620/621, in: Klinger 1969, p. 119).

13. Cf. the German original: "Begriff vom Menschen, wie er in der gesamten christlichen Anthropologie vorausgesetzt ist. Dieser Begriff ist kein anderer als der gewöhnliche, den wir mit dem Worte Mensch verbinden, wenn wir ihn als Vernunftwesen mit freien Willen vom Tiere unterscheiden. Er basiert auf der Unterscheidung des Physischen und Moralischen, und setzt sich aus diesen beiden Elementen zusammen. Ohne diese Unterscheidung vorauszusetzen und zu Grunde zu legen, kommt man, wie wir wiederholt bemerken, nicht zu dem Begriffe der Gnade und des Übernatürlichen im Sinne der katholischen Kirchenlehre, nicht zum rechten Verständnis des christlichen Supernaturalismus."(Johannes Kuhn, *Die christliche Lehre von der göttlichen Gnade* [Tübingen, 1868], § 18, p. 166) .

14. Cf. the German original: "Das Wesen der heilligmachenden und uns mit Gott aufs innigste vereinigenden Gnade als eine übernatürliche Qualität, vermöge der wir geistig, in Gesinnung und Willen, Gott gleichförmig, ihm ähnlich sind, zur Geltung zu bringen, und den Gedanken einer physischen Veränderung des Wesens unserer Seele und einer physischen Partizipation an der göttlichen Natur abzuweisen."(Kuhn, *Die christliche Lehre*, § 28, p. 422).

15. "Die Postmoderne entfernt sich von allen Formen des Monismus, der Unifizierung und Totalisierung, von der einen verbindlichen Utopie und den vielen versteckten Despotismen und geht statt dessen zu einem Dispositiv der Multiplizität und Diversität, der Vielfalt und Konkurrenz der Paradigmen und der Koexistenz des Heterogenen über." (Peter Kemper, ed., *'Postmoderne' oder Der Kampf um die Zukunft. Die Kontroverse in Wissenschaft, Kunst und Gesellschaft* [Frankfurt: Fischer, 1988], p. 33).

16. "Postmoderne wird hier als Verfassung radikaler Pluralität verstanden, Postmodernismus als deren Konzeption verteidigt." Wolfgang Welsch, *Unsere postmoderne Moderne* (Weilheim: Akademie Verlag, 1987), p. 4.

17. To the importance of this question, cf. Elmar Klinger, 1978: *Ekklesiologie der Neuzeit* (Freiburg: Herder, 1978); and Elmar Klinger, *Armut eine Herausforderung Gottes. Der Glaube des Konzils und die Befreiung des Menschen* (Zürich: Beuzige, 1990).

List of Contributors

Donald J. Dietrich

Professor of Theology
Boston College

Stephen Fields, S.J.

Assistant Professor of Theology
Georgetown University

Anton van Harskamp

Doctor of Theology
Vrije Universiteit Amsterdam

Zachary Hayes, OFM

Professor of Systematic Theology
Catholic Theological Union

Michael J. Himes

Professor of Theology
Boston College

Bradford E. Hinze

Associate Professor of Theology
Marquette University

Peter Hünermann

Professor of Fundamental Theology
University of Tübingen

Elmar Klinger

Professor of Fundamental Theology
University of Würzburg

Abraham Peter Kustermann

Doctor of Theology
Akademie der Diözese Rottenburg - Stuttgart

Thomas O'Meara, OP

William K. Warren Professor of Theology
University of Notre Dame

Hermann J. Pottmeyer

Professor of Fundamental Theology
Ruhr - Universität Bochum

John E. Thiel

Professor of Religious Studies
Fairfield University

Reinhold Rieger

Doctor of Philosophy